THE AA GUIDE TO
Scotland

About the authors

Robin Gauldie studied history at Edinburgh University, and then worked in a museum in Stirling. After a stint as a reporter on local newspapers in and around his native Dundee, he moved to London to become a travel journalist. He returned to Edinburgh in 2003, and contributes to newspapers and magazines including *The Scotsman*, *The Scots Magazine* and *Historic Scotland*, as well as writing about Scotland for newspapers, magazines and websites around the world.

Sally Roy grew up in the Scottish Highlands, was educated at St Andrew's University, and lived for many years in a remote glen in Perthshire. She knows and loves Scotland, having explored from Muckle Flugga to Galloway, and everywhere in between. She has written and contributed to numerous books on Scotland, ranging from city guides and gazetteers to handbooks of walks and drives.

Published by AA Publishing (a trading name of AA Media Limited, whose registered office is Fanum House, Basing View, Basingstoke, Hampshire RG21 4EA; registered number 06112600)

© AA Media Limited 2016
Reprinted 2017
Second edition 2018

Maps contain data from openstreetmap.org
© OpenStreetMap contributors
Ordnance Survey data © Crown copyright and database right 2018.

A CIP catalogue record for this book is available from the British Library.

ISBN: 978-0-7495-7946-3

A05591

Cartography provided by the Mapping Services Department of AA Publishing.
Printed and bound in Italy by Printer Trento Srl.

Every effort has been made to trace the copyright holders, and we apologise in advance for any accidental errors. We would be happy to apply the corrections in the following edition of this publication.

The contents of this book are believed correct at the time of printing. Nevertheless, the publishers cannot be held responsible for any errors or omissions or for changes in the details given in this book or for the consequences of any reliance on the information it provides. This does not affect your statutory rights. We have tried to ensure accuracy in this book, but things do change and we would be grateful if readers would advise us of any inaccuracies they may encounter by emailing travelguides@theaa.com.

THE AA GUIDE TO

Scotland

CONTENTS

USING THIS GUIDE

Introduction – has plenty of fascinating background reading, including articles on the landscape and local mythology.

Top attractions – pick out the very best places to visit in the area. You'll spot these later in the A–Z by the flashes of yellow.

Before you go – tells you the things to read, watch, know and pack to get the most from your trip.

Campsites – recommends a number of caravan sites and campsites, which carry the AA's Pennant rating, with the very best receiving the coveted gold Pennant award. Visit theAA.com/self-catering-and-campsites, theAA.com/hotels and theAA.com/bed-and-breakfasts for more places to stay.

A–Z – lists the best of Scotland, with recommended attractions, activities and places to eat or drink. Places Nearby lists more to see and do.

Eat and drink – contains restaurants that carry an AA Rosette rating, which acknowledges the very best in cooking. Pubs have been selected for their great atmosphere and good food. Visit theAA.com/restaurants and theAA.com/pubs for more food and drink suggestions.

Index – gives you the option to search by theme, grouping the same type of place together, or alphabetically.

Atlas – will help you find your way around, as every main location has a map reference, as will the town plans throughout the book.

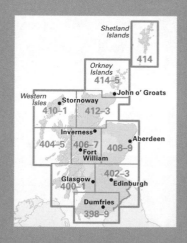

INTRODUCTION

Spectacular landscapes, buzzing cities and a lively cultural scene that embraces low comedy as well as high art are key ingredients in the recipe that makes Scotland special. Then there's history and heritage that span not just centuries but millennia, from the mysterious brochs and stone circles of the far north and the islands to the traces of Roman fortifications, the romantic ruins of scores of medieval castles like Eilean Donan, Urquhart Castle or Dunnottar – each, it seems with its own ghost story or tragic tale to tell – and the stately homes of monarchs and aristocrats.

Scotland is of course a country in its own right, and in recent years it has regained a massive amount of cultural and economic self-confidence, not to mention a lot of political clout. And from the visitor's point of view, few countries pack so much into such a relatively small area.

If you're a lover of wide open spaces, you'll probably be tempted to head straight for the bens, glens and lochs of regions such as Torridon or Caithness, the high moorland of the Cairngorms, the rolling hills of the Borders or the

dramatic shores of Loch Lomond and Loch Ness. If you're a beachcomber at heart, you'll find long swaths of sandy beach and rocky shoreline on sweeping bays and narrow sea lochs. Island hoppers can explore the harbours of the Western Isles and the Orkney and Shetland archipelagos.

All of these wild and lovely regions are home to a plethora of wildlife, from red deer, reindeer, otters and beavers to the iconic golden eagle. You can see dolphins, seals and whales close to the shores of the Moray Firth, the Sound of Mull and Aberdeenshire.

But let's not forget Scotland's cities, each with its own identity. For millions of visitors each year, Edinburgh, with its castle, multiple festivals, and the medieval and Georgian architectural heritage of Old Town and New Town, is the big attraction. Scotland's capital has been given a new vibrancy since devolution and the advent of a new Scottish Parliament (although many grumble about the cost). Edinburgh's arch-rival Glasgow makes up for what it lacks in medieval glories with grand collections of art and design like the Kelvingrove Art

Gallery and Museum and the Burrell Collection, and unique spots such as its grandiose hilltop Necropolis. Scotland's biggest city also offers some of the best food and drink you'll find in the country. Aberdeen combines the buzz of being at the centre of the world's energy industry with historic attractions like medieval King's College and St Machar's Cathedral. Dundee is in the process of reinventing itself as a 21st-century cultural hub, with rejuvenation of its scenic waterfront proceeding apace. Stirling Castle, made famous by its links with the stories of William Wallace, Robert the Bruce and the Battle of Bannockburn, is the key attraction of Scotland's fifth city, Stirling. Inverness, the so-called capital of the Highlands, is the gateway to Scotland's far north – and, of course, to Loch Ness, home of the legendary monster.

Scotland has been through a culinary revolution in recent years. You'll find acclaimed chefs using locally sourced produce such as beef, lamb and game from Scottish moors, and seafood from the North Sea and the Atlantic in gourmet restaurants and gastropubs – but you can still enjoy the best fish and chips in the world in unassuming village chippers. No trip to Scotland is complete without visiting at least one distillery to see how the national drink is made and sample a dram or two of single malt.

And for active holidaymakers, the choice is as seemingly endless as Scotland's beaches and mountain vistas. Long-distance walking trails like the West Highland Way and John Muir Way traverse rugged and breathtaking scenery, but there are gentler walks that skirt beautiful coastline too, like the Fife Coastal Path. Water activities range from canoeing and rafting on lochs and rivers to sea kayaking, sailing and windsurfing. And, of course, there's golf. For keen golfers, playing a round at the Royal and Ancient Golf Club in St Andrews, home of the sport, is an experience to savour, but there are other iconic courses like Troon, Turnberry, Gleneagles and Carnoustie, plus hundreds more links and greens scattered all over Scotland's glens and coasts.

◀ Previous page: Old Man of Storr, Trotternish Peninsula, Isle of Skye
▶ Highland cow

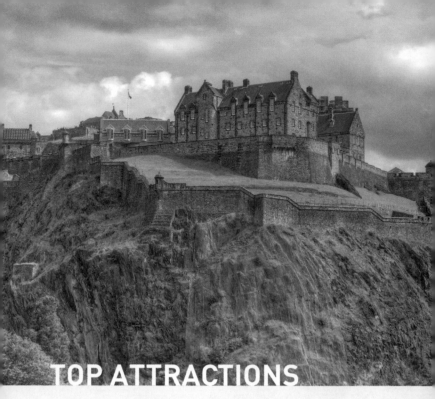

TOP ATTRACTIONS

▲ Explore Edinburgh Castle

High above the city, impressive Edinburgh Castle (see page 167) is the best place to get your bearings when you arrive in Scotland's capital. From its formidable ramparts there are stunning views from all points of the compass. Inside the castle walls, there is much to admire in the Royal Palace and the National War Museum, which pays tribute to the part Scots soldiers have played in Britain's wars, from Culloden to Helmand.

▼ Climb Arthur's Seat

Edinburgh's own mini-mountain offers you a sense of wilderness in the heart of Edinburgh. Arthur's Seat (see page 178) rises 823 feet (251m) above the city centre. The splendid panoramic views from the top are plenty reward for the hour-long climb to the summit.

◀ Admire treasures at the Palace of Holyroodhouse

Magnificent Holyroodhouse (see page 169) and its adjacent ruined abbey, which dates from the 12th century, has been home to Scottish (and later British) monarchs for hundreds of years. It's still the Queen's official residence in Scotland. Within are splendid state rooms, and the Great Gallery houses a fine art collection.

▶ Unravel the mysteries of Rosslyn Chapel

Lovers of mystery are drawn to this 15th-century church (see page 342) by the many theories linking it to the Holy Grail, the Ark of the Covenant or the Knights Templar. But even sceptics are impressed by the numerous pagan, biblical and esoteric images carved into its walls. The most stunning carving is the ornate Apprentice Pillar.

◀ Visit the People's Palace and Winter Gardens

To get under the skin of the city of Glasgow, visit the People's Palace and Winter Gardens (see page 219). Re-created scenes invite you to experience everyday Glaswegian life in times gone by – step into a single-room 1930s house and a public bath house, or try out your moves in the dance hall.

◀ See art and more at Kelvingrove Art Gallery and Museum

It doesn't take long to see why the Kelvingrove Art Gallery and Museum (see page 216) is one of Scotland's most-visited attractions. Inside this cavernous Edwardian palace there are wide-ranging collections of art and culture, packed display halls with costumes from overseas continents, exhibits hung from the ceiling and more.

▶ Take the high road to Loch Lomond

Walk, sail, cruise and waterski on the waters of Scotland's best-loved loch. The largest lake in Britain, Loch Lomond (see page 286), is dotted with islands and surrounded by lush woodland. Two long-distance walks, the West Highland Way (see **page 291**) and John Muir Way (see **page 134**), meet near its southern edge.

◀ Discover Scotland's industrial heritage at New Lanark

Those who think Scotland is all about lochs and glens will find New Lanark (see page 303) an eye-opener. This United Nations Educational, Scientific and Cultural Organization (UNESCO) World Heritage Site surrounds a revolutionary 19th-century industrial community. There is also a trail to the Falls of Clyde.

▲ Walk through a city of the dead at Glasgow Necropolis

Ornate tombs clutter a hillside graveyard (see page 212) above Glasgow. The wealthy merchants and industrialists of the city's 19th-century heyday commissioned grand mausoleums and monuments so that their fame would live on after their death. The most elaborate are surmounted by effigies of the deceased.

▼ Go monster hunting on Loch Ness

Monster hunters come to deep, dark Loch Ness (see page 294) in search of the legendary 'Nessie'. Whether or not you are a 'Nessie' believer, a cruise on the 24-mile loch can be enchanting, with forested slopes on either side and a view of the ruined Castle Urquhart on the northern shore. Loch Ness is linked to the other lochs of Scotland's Great Glen by the Caledonian Canal, stretching between Inverness and the west coast.

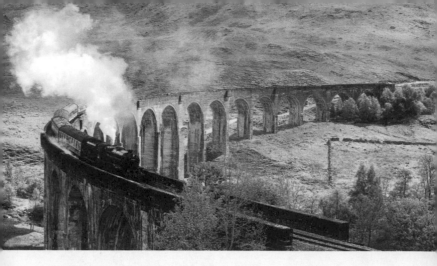

▲ Watch the Hogwarts Express crossing Glenfinnan Viaduct

You've seen the iconic Glenfinnan Viaduct (see page 237) in more than a few movies (and on the Bank of Scotland's £10 note). Yes, this is the picturesque railway bridge that appears in the *Harry Potter* films. In summer, time your visit to watch the steam train used as the Hogwarts Express in the movies crossing the viaduct.

◀ Walk round a grim battlefield at Culloden

Visit the barren moorland where the last pitched battle on Scottish soil was fought between the Jacobite army of Bonnie Prince Charlie and the Duke of Cumberland's redcoats (see page 117).

▶ Unlock the history of Stirling Castle

Once called the key to the kingdom, Stirling Castle (see page 370) looms on its crag above the city of Stirling, overlooking the River Forth. Inside, you can visit the magnificent Renaissance Great Hall, built for James IV, a regimental museum and re-created medieval kitchens.

▲ Go back to the Stone Age at Skara Brae

Lost for millennia, Orkney's Skara Brae (see page 316) was rediscovered in 1850, when a storm swept away the sand that hid this amazing Neolithic village built of stone slabs. One of the houses has been reconstructed, showing how the original dwellers made their homes comfortable. Fragments of pottery and bone tools and ornaments show that they were skilled artisans.

▶ Visit a frontier fortress

Caerlaverock Castle (see page 102), with its triangular plan and water-filled moat, was once one of Scotland's most impressive strongholds. Now a splendid ruin, it has a maze of stairs and corridors connecting its echoing halls.

◀ Tour Aberdeenshire's historic castles

There are more castles to the acre in Aberdeenshire than anywhere else in Britain. They range from evocative ruins to lonely tower houses and well-kept baronial strongholds to royal palaces. Visit four of them at Dunnottar, Fyvie (both page 66), Huntly (see page 67) and Tolquhon (see page 68).

HISTORY OF SCOTLAND

Standing on the high moorland plateau of the Cairngorms, you can almost visualise the first small parties of early hunter-gatherers trickling into what is now Scotland.

There's evidence of human presence in Scotland as long ago as 12,000 BC, but it wasn't until about 7,000 years ago that Mesolithic people began to arrive in numbers. They came to a land covered with thick woodland and peat bog, which was rich in game such as wild cattle and boar. Their tiny settlements are marked today by flakes of chipped stone and middens of bone and shell fragments.

Settled communities began to emerge from about 3000 BC. Neolithic people learned agricultural skills and built structures of stone, earth and wood. Houses made of stone slabs at Skara Brae (see page 316) in Orkney show that they were skilled builders.

In the region of 2000 BC, the art of smelting bronze from copper and tin spelt the end of the Stone Age and ushered in a new, warlike era, as seen in the bronze swords and spearheads found in ancient burial sites and on show in the National Museum of Scotland (see page 174).

Picts, Romans, Britons and Scots
When legions of the Roman Empire reached the land they called Caledonia in AD 70, they encountered a Celtic warlord culture, the Picti, whose tribal warriors fiercely resisted occupation. In AD 130 the Romans began work on the coast-to-coast rampart that's still named after the emperor who ordered it to be built – Hadrian.

◀ Hadrian's Wall

Hadrian's Wall proved an ineffective defence against northern marauders. The tribes overran it and invaded Roman Britain again and again. By AD 383, a weakened Empire could no longer defend the Wall. In about AD 410, the last Roman legions left Britain.

We first hear of the Scots in the fourth century AD, when they came from across the Irish Sea to join the Picts to overrun Roman Britain between AD 367 and 369. Over the next two centuries, the trickle of Scots settlers from what is now Northern Ireland became a flood. By the mid-sixth century the Scottish kingdom of Argyll, north of the Clyde, was a force to be reckoned with, and over the next three centuries the Scots expanded their realm into Pictish lands to the northeast, by dynastic marriages and by conquest.

Monks and missionaries

A Scotto-Irish prince is credited with bringing Christianity to his fellow Scots and the heathen Picts. A British missionary, St Ninian, founded the first Christian settlement at Whithorn in Galloway in the fourth century AD, but it was St Columba (AD 521–597) who spread the word further, from his monastery on Iona, in the inner Hebrides. Others followed, including St Mungo (or Kentigern), who founded a religious community at Glasgow. By the eighth century, Picts as well as Scots had mostly converted to the new religion.

Vikings and Angles

The Anglo-Saxons of Northumbria invaded Pictland next, in AD 685, but were decisively trounced at the Battle of Necthansmere, near Forfar. A new threat emerged in the late eighth century, with the first of the Viking raids that terrorised the British Isles for the next 300 years or more. In 839 a Viking host invaded Fortriu, in the heart of Pictish territory. Both sons of the Pictish king Oengus II were killed in battle – which opened the way for Kenneth MacAlpin (Cinaed mac Alpin), King of Scots, to take over the Pictish throne too. Over the next century or so, his successors consolidated the nation that became known as Alba. For a while, it was the largest and most powerful nation-state in Britain.

Wars of conquest

After the Saxon kingdom of Wessex fell to William of Normandy in 1066, William and the Anglo-Norman rulers who followed him were bent on further conquests. Over the centuries that followed, Scotland would struggle to maintain its independence. In the late 13th century, the untimely death of Alexander III, followed by that of his only heir, left the Scottish throne vacant, and Edward I of England mounted the invasions that earned him his nickname,

Hammer of the Scots. And hammer them he did, eventually appointing his own governors to rule Scotland.

Not all Scots opposed Edward's rule, but those who did not swear allegiance to the English king were outlawed. One of them was William Wallace. His first act of defiance was the killing of William de Heselrig, High Sheriff of Lanark, in 1297, and not long after Scotland was in the grip of a full-blown rising against English rule. The Scots led by Wallace were at first successful, beating a much greater English force at Stirling Bridge, but when Edward led a second invasion the following year they were routed at Falkirk. Wallace went on the run, but in 1305 he was captured and taken to London, where he was hung, drawn and quartered.

Soon another leader emerged. Unlike Wallace – who was content to title himself one of the Guardians of Scotland – Robert Bruce, Earl of Carrick, wanted the throne for himself, and had himself crowned in 1306. His reign got off to a bad start when his army was routed at Methven only three months after his coronation and for a while he became a fugitive. Over the next eight years, he fought a guerrilla campaign that gradually eroded English control. By 1314 he felt strong enough to face the English in pitched battle, and on 23 June he inflicted a crushing defeat on Edward II, son of the Hammer of the Scots, at Bannockburn near Stirling (see page 373). The tide had turned, but the war dragged on until 1328, when Bruce's forces drove the invaders out once and for all.

The new dynasty

When the last of the Bruces died without an heir in 1371 the nobles of Scotland elected Robert the Steward to take the throne. He was the first of a dynasty that would rule Scotland – and, eventually, England too – for the next 343 years.

In 1503, Robert's great-great-great grandson, James IV, sought peace with England by marrying Margaret Tudor, daughter of Henry VII. But he fell out with his brother-in-law, Henry VIII, and formed an alliance with England's old enemy, France. After invading England, James IV was killed in 1513 at the Battle of Flodden, along with 10,000 of his men. His son and heir was only two years old, and once again aristocratic factions fought to control the country. The young James V was a prisoner of one side or the other until the age of 16, when he escaped from Edinburgh Castle, raised an army, seized power, and ruthlessly reimposed royal control. He died young, aged 31, leaving no male heir.

Reformation Scotland

James's baby daughter was less than a week old when she became Mary, Queen of Scots. She, like her father, became a pawn in a game of thrones that had become even more complicated.

Inspired by the Reformation in England and northern Europe, Scots reformers sought to bring Protestantism to Scotland. Some of the Scots lords supported them. Others sided with the established Catholic bishops. Each faction sought support from abroad – the reformers from Protestant England, the conservatives from Catholic France. Mary was married off to the heir to the French throne. But the young Francois II died in 1560, and she returned to Scotland. She then married a Catholic noble, Henry Lord Darnley, and then dallied with David Rizzio, her Italian secretary, who was soon murdered in front of her by Darnley's cronies. Less than a year later, Darnley was killed when his Edinburgh house was blown up by gunpowder. Chief suspect: James Hepburn, Earl of Bothwell, who married Mary only three months later.

Catholic Mary was disliked by the reformers. In 1567, they forced the queen to quit the throne and imprisoned her in the island castle of Loch Leven. She escaped and fled to England, only to be imprisoned again by her cousin, Elizabeth I. In 1587, after being held in relatively comfortable captivity, she was executed on suspicion of plotting against Elizabeth.

Union of crowns

Meanwhile, Mary's infant son was proclaimed king in 1567. James VI was more cunning than his ancestors. He could be ruthless, but he also knew how to compromise and manipulate. By the time he was in his thirties he had neutralised the aristocracy and made peace with the Protestant Kirk. But his greatest triumph came with the death of Elizabeth I. The professed virgin queen of England died childless. James, son of her cousin, was first in line for the English throne. In 1603, he became James I of England, uniting the two kingdoms under one – Scottish – ruler.

King James was succeeded to the throne by his son Charles in 1625. Charles I inherited none of his father's political nous. His attempt to impose Anglican forms of worship on Scotland led to the proclamation of the National Covenant – a declaration of independence in all but name. Meanwhile, his autocratic rule south of the border provoked civil war in England. After Charles I's defeat by the Roundhead army, Oliver Cromwell's Parliamentarian forces led an occupation of Scotland that lasted until the restoration of Charles II in 1660.

Charles II paid little attention to Scotland. Continued attempts to curb the Presbyterian faith led to a low-key civil war in the 1680s, known as the Killing Time. This grew more intense after Charles's brother, the openly Catholic James II, succeeded him in 1685. James was soon ousted by his Protestant son-in-law, William of Orange, a move that met little resistance in England. In Scotland, many of the Highland clan chiefs supported what became known as the Jacobite cause. Led by Robert Graham of Claverhouse – commonly named Bonnie Dundee – they crushed a Williamite force at the Pass of Killiecrankie, in Perthshire, but lost their leader to a musket ball. Soon after the Jacobite host was stopped in its tracks by the staunch Covenanter defence of Dunkeld and the survivors limped back to their glens.

A united kingdom?

Although their crowns were united, Scotland and England remained separate nations. However, that was soon to change. English politicians were keen to expand their powers by uniting Scots and English parliaments. It wasn't a popular scheme in Scotland, but the country was bankrupt and the offer of a massive cash subsidy and free trade between Scotland and the expanding English empire was too good an offer to turn down. In 1707, Scottish politicians acceded to a Treaty of Union that dissolved the Edinburgh Parliament. From now on, Scottish politicians would take their seats at Westminster.

But the Jacobite cause wasn't quite finished. In 1715, supporters of the exiled James Stuart, son of James II and VII, staged a rebellion that fizzled out after just one indecisive battle. Thirty years later, James's son Charles Edward, also known as Bonnie Prince Charlie, stirred up another, more threatening rising. This time, his Highlanders got as far as Derby before they turned tail and retreated home. They made a last stand at Culloden, near Inverness, where they were wiped out by the Duke of Cumberland's cannon and muskets.

Coal, steel and steam

The modern world came to Scotland with a vengeance in the decades following Culloden. Roads, canals and steamships drew the country closer together. The Forth and Clyde Canal opened in 1790, followed by the Union Canal and the Caledonian Canal in 1822. The world's first passenger steamship service began puffing its way up and down the Clyde in 1812. The first railways arrived in the 1840s and by the late 19th century trains ran from London to Aberdeen, crossing the great Forth and Tay bridges on the way.

Famine (caused by potato blight) struck the Scottish Highlands in 1847. At about the same time, Highland landlords drove many of their tenants from their crofts to make way for more profitable sheep-grazing. Tens of thousands of Highlanders were forced to emigrate to Canada and other British colonies, while many more drifted to places like Glasgow, Dundee and Falkirk to work in new mills, foundries, mines and shipyards. Clydeside became the greatest shipbuilding centre in history, turning out passenger liners, cargo vessels and warships by the thousand.

▲ Forth Bridge

War and peace

The bosses of Scotland's new heavy industries prospered. Their workers did less well and lived in some of the Empire's worst slums. This poverty fostered the growth of socialism and the trade union movement in Scotland in the later 19th century.

The end of World War II brought social change, with notorious urban slums being demolished and their people rehoused in new high-rise estates and so-called new towns. However, the industries that Scotland's economy depended on were in decline. The last of the Clydeside shipyards closed despite fierce resistance from its workers in the early 1970s, as did the last of the Dundee jute mills.

A nation once again?

The discovery of oil beneath the North Sea transformed Scotland's economy – and its politics. Aberdeen became the base of the North Sea oil industry and changed from a fishing port into a boom town, its population growing to make it Scotland's third-largest city.

The Scottish National Party's slogan 'It's Scotland's Oil' helped to start the SNP on its long march to power. Meanwhile, UK Prime Minister Margaret Thatcher's radical Conservatism was rejected by the Scots and the Tories lost seat after seat in elections between 1979 and 1997. In a referendum in 1997, Scots voted convincingly for devolution of power from London to the Scottish Government in Edinburgh, but devolution has not satisfied many nationalists. A second referendum in 2014 should have settled the issue, with a majority of Scots voting to stay within the United Kingdom. Instead, it seemed to energise the independence-seekers still further. Who knows what may follow the UK's next general election, in 2022.

BACK TO NATURE

Scotland's landscapes range from the grassy hills of
the Southern Uplands to the high peaks and rolling
moorland of the Cairngorms, the ancient forests of
Perthshire, the tundra-like Flow Country of Caithness
and the tidy, fertile farmland of lowland regions such as
Tayside, Lothian and Aberdeenshire.

Long, sandy beaches are features of the North Sea and Atlantic
coasts. Bays and tidal estuaries are features of the Moray and
Solway Firths, and the Firths of Forth, Clyde and Tay. Off Scotland's
shores lie dozens of islands. Some, like Skye, are so close to the
mainland that they can be reached in a matter of minutes by ferry
or even by road bridge. Getting to others, such as the Outer
Hebrides and Shetland, can involve flying or taking an overnight
ferry. The remote islands of the uninhabited St Kilda archipelago
lie some 100 miles from the mainland.

All Scotland's landscapes have been shaped by the movement of
glaciers during the Ice Ages that ended about 14,500 years ago. In
many places, you'll see great boulders, known as 'erratics',
abandoned by the retreating ice on moors and hillsides. Deep sea
lochs carve their way into the west coast, and the Great Glen – a
chain of lochs that includes Scotland's longest and deepest bodies

▲ Clockwise from left: Pine trees, red deer stag, puffin, red squirrel

of water, Loch Ness and Loch Morar – cuts diagonally from Inverness, at the head of the Moray Firth, to Fort William and Loch Linnhe on the west coast.

Much of Highland Scotland looks like pristine wilderness. You may be surprised to hear that the land has been shaped as much by people as by nature. When the first humans arrived, and for many thousands of years afterwards, most of Scotland was covered by thick forest. Gradually, forests were felled to clear space for farming and to supply firewood and building materials. By the mid-18th century, much of the country was treeless. Huge demand for timber during World War I contributed to further deforestation. In 1919, the Forestry Commission was set up to create new reserves of woodland. New forests were planted all over Scotland. Today, you'll still see huge swaths of conifers such as Sitka spruce, Scots pine, larch and Douglas fir, but in recent years there has been a drive to create more environmentally sensitive mixed forests of broad-leaved trees such as oak, beech, birch and sycamore as well as conifers. You can find some of Scotland's most impressive forests in Perthshire – nicknamed Scotland's 'Big Tree Country' – and around Loch Lomond, less than an hour from Glasgow. Here, too, you'll find colourful expanses of rhododendron that blaze scarlet and purple in summer. This Himalayan shrub, introduced by Victorian gardeners, thrives all too well here, choking out native vegetation, and efforts are being made to eradicate it except in parks and gardens. Another invader introduced as a decorative plant during the 19th century is giant hogweed, which flourishes along urban streams and rivers in and around Edinburgh, Glasgow and Dundee and elsewhere. Be very careful not to touch the leaves of this triffid-like plant. Its sap causes agonising blisters that may require hospital treatment and take ages to heal.

Scotland's varied landscapes and seascapes shelter a rich diversity of wildlife. On land, herds of red deer roam the moors. Smaller roe deer prefer woodland and forest habitats. Wild boar, hunted to extinction by the 16th century, have made a comeback in the 21st century. There are at least three breeding populations, all descendants of boar that have escaped from farms, and their numbers are estimated to be into the hundreds. Other long-extinct animals that have returned to the wild in Scotland include beavers, which were experimentally reintroduced in southwest Scotland in 2009 and that also appear to be thriving on Tayside. Reindeer, extinct for about 800 years, were reintroduced in 1952 and Britain's only free-ranging reindeer herd now roams a 10,000-acre expanse of Cairngorms moorland. Wolves, brown bears and lynx all once lived in Scotland (the last Scottish wolf was shot in 1680) and there have been controversial proposals to reintroduce these predators too. Unsurprisingly, some farmers fear for their flocks if wolves and lynx once again roam Scotland, but some environmentalists suggest that reintroducing them would help to control wild deer, which are now so numerous that they have become a pest in parts of Scotland, decimating crops, damaging forests and becoming a hazard on roads.

Otters have made a happy comeback in recent decades, helped by the cleaning up of streams and rivers. They're plentiful on rivers such as the Tay, but you have a better chance of seeing them hunting and playing in rock pools at low tide along the shores of sea lochs like Loch Morar or Loch Linnhe, on the west coast or along the Moray Firth.

Two emblematic Scottish mammals are sadly faring less well. Scotland is one of the last British redoubts of the red squirrel, whose future is threatened by a virus carried by the non-native grey squirrel. Greys are less widespread in Scotland than in England, and culling them may be the only way to save the reds. Meanwhile, the Scottish wildcat – nicknamed the Highland tiger – is endangered by interbreeding with domestic cats, so that soon there may be no pure-bred wildcats outside zoos.

When walking in the Highlands, keep an eye open for the unmistakable and emblematic golden eagle soaring in the sky above. Scotland has more than 400 breeding pairs.

Other raptors that you will almost certainly spot in the Scottish countryside include kestrels, sparrowhawks and buzzards (listen for their mewing cry). Red kites, which were reintroduced in the 1980s, are increasingly common, and if you're very lucky you may see another spectacular raptor that has recently been reintroduced, the white-tailed eagle, over the shores of Fife and on the northwest coast.

Puffins, gannets and other seabirds nest in large numbers on islands in the Firth of Forth and on less accessible coasts. Vast numbers of migrant waterfowl – including greylag and pink-footed geese – flock to the tidal estuaries of the Solway Firth and the Firth of Tay in autumn and spring, and the Hebridean islands, such as Jura, host huge flocks of barnacle and white-fronted geese.

Climate change may account for the appearance in parts of Scotland of birds more often associated with warmer climates like the collared dove, which arrived in force in the 1970s, and the little egret, which has been spotted in eastern Scotland.

Scotland's waters shelter some breathtaking sea mammals. Bottlenose dolphins are an everyday sight in the Moray Firth and off the Aberdeenshire coast. You may sight migratory humpback and minke whales in Hebridean waters. Grey and common seals are easy to see as they bask on the shores of western sea lochs. Take a stroll along the beach at Tentsmuir, between Dundee and St Andrews, to see dozens of them sunbathing on sandbanks at the mouth of the Tay and the River Eden. They're amazingly vocal – a seal-covered sandbank sounds like a very lively party in full swing.

Scottish summers are brightened by colourful butterflies including the gorgeous peacock with its distinctive eye-spots, red admiral, small tortoiseshell and several blues and fritillaries. Look out for day-flying moths such as the cinnabar moth, with its glossy black and scarlet wings. Its orange-and-black striped caterpillars feed on ragwort and have been described as worms in football jerseys.

▼ Golden eagle

Finally, everyone's least favourite Scottish creature is one of the tiniest – the hated midge. These wee bloodsuckers appear in swarms in summer and are a real pest, especially in boggy areas. They are resistant to insect repellent but a layer of baby oil on the skin offers some protection.

LORE OF THE LAND

In proud Scotland's best known legend, Robert the Bruce, hiding from his English pursuers in the early 1300s, was inspired to struggle on to liberate his kingdom by seeing a spider make seven attempts to anchor a web.

Those who enter the country's lowlands are still warned against spirits known as redcaps, which reputedly attack and kill anyone entering their ruined castle residences. Said to dye their hats with their victims' blood, they are believed to be so speedy that despite wearing iron boots and carrying heavy pikes they can never be outrun. In the Pentland hills walkers must beware the Pentland Imp that snatches food, jewellery – and even picnics – from the unsuspecting, although redheads, which strike the impertinent imp with terror, are allegedly immune.

Capital and castles

A quite different creature is believed to inhabit Edinburgh's docks at Leith. Here the shell-clad Shellycoat inhabits a barnacle-encrusted boulder, the Penny Bap, around which children once dared one another to circle three times, chanting a rhyme to induce him to appear. At night he is said to issue a loud, menacing laugh that is audible for miles.

◀ Stirling Castle

On the capital's streets the tap-tapping of a stick in West Bow is the dreadful reminder of Major Weir, who was burned to death in 1670 holding his 'magic' staff – a Devil's gift. Ghostly happenings also occur in Edinburgh Castle, where the Lone Piper can be heard as he walks the dark tunnels beneath this fortification, having been lost from view centuries ago. At the castle entrance a phantom dog appears, surrounded by a misty glow, while the Palace of Holyroodhouse was legendarily founded on the site where a fiery cross appeared between the antlers of a white stag; it was chased by King David I in the 12th century and has never been seen since.

Outside the capital, castles with ghostly associations abound. At Borthwick in Lothian an apparition of Mary, Queen of Scots has been sighted, while at Stirling Castle she renders her presence as a Pink Lady. A Green Lady, dressed in the colour unlucky to the Celts, appears there too, as a bringer of bad news. Braemar Castle is stalked by a blonde ghost, and by the spirit of John Farquharson of Inverey, the so-called Black Colonel, a violent murderer.

Legends of the lochs

There are few British legends as famous as Nessie, the Loch Ness Monster. Its first recorded human encounter may have been with St Columba who, when the beast attacked one of his monks, cried out, 'Go no further, nor touch the man.' Monster hysteria stepped up in the 20th century with the building of a road along the north shore of the loch in 1933. Hundreds of people claim to have seen something in the loch since then, and monster hunters have spent small fortunes in pursuit of the elusive Nessie.

Other inhabitants of Scotland's lochs are the enticing kelpies, supernatural water horses that also live in lonely rivers. They appear to their victims as ponies but anyone unfortunate enough to mount one is taken at once to a watery grave. Not far distant from Loch Ness is Loch Morar where the appearance of its resident monster spells doom. It is even possible that the two lochs are joined deep below ground. In Argyll's lochs reside Boobries, malevolent shape-shifting creatures like gigantic cormorants or, occasionally, water bulls. Their favourite victims are livestock transported aboard ships.

Glen, ben and moor

It is said that before God sent Earth spinning through space he patted it and thus his fingers created the five beautiful Glens of Angus. In contrast, Glencoe is known as the valley of death. Here the Campbells massacred their deadly rivals the MacDonalds, whose ghosts haunt the hills. The notes of the fairy pipers who led returning Campbell troops off course are said to resound even today. A quite different phantom stalks Ben Macdhui in Aberdeen; the horrific Grey Man of Macdui, some 10 feet tall, will pursue walkers miles to their deaths. On Ben Nevis, whose name means venomous, climbers are warned to beware of a sleeping giant.

Helpful and welcome fairies feature throughout Scottish folklore, telling of how they assist in homes with spinning, washing and weaving, but no one would wish to encounter a Joint Eater, an invisible fairy who sits beside a diner, scoffing his food. In the Highlands, Black Donald is a Devil who casts malevolent spells, while the Cailleach Bheur is a blue-faced hag who guards animals.

Stones of Destiny

If sat on by anyone other than the Scottish monarch, the famous Stone of Scone or Stone of Destiny was said to issue a thunderous groan. Tales of its origins vary widely. This block of red sandstone could have been brought to Scotland by Joseph of Arimathea – or by St Columba, who rested his head on it as he died on the island of Iona. Or it may have first been used by Irish kings. Captured by Edward I in 1296, it was not returned to its rightful home until 1996.

Standing stones and cairns grace highland and island landscapes, many dating to Neolithic times. At Cailleach in Glen Lyon stand stones forming a remote shrine to the Celtic goddess Cailleach, while on Orkney the Standing Stones of Stenness are associated with Norse rituals. The Odin Stone, to the north of the henge, said to have magical powers, is pierced with a circular hole through which couples would plight their troth. Many stones mark burial sites and have astronomical significance. By tradition

▼ Glencoe

the prehistoric Calanais (Callanish) Standing Stones on the island of Lewis were both a lunar observatory and the petrified forms of giants who refused to convert to Christianity. On each midsummer morning a cuckoo call is said to herald the arrival of the Shining One, a powerful mysterious entity with a body as bright as the moon, before he walks the imposing stone avenue.

Around the coast

Mermaids abound in stories from Scotland's coast, as at Colonsay, where the laird was captured by a sea nymph and confined to a cave. Even after his release she continued to sing to him from the depths. At Yell on Shetland a creature said to be a mermaid was caught in 1823, although it may have been a marine mammal – maybe a manatee. Mermen, as well as merwomen, beautiful creatures with fish-like tails, were recorded as coming on land at Ve Skerries in Shetland. In the same region live the Selkies, mythical creatures able to transform themselves from seals to humans and back again. In one story a man finds a Selkie sunbathing on the beach, steals her skin and forces her to become his wife. Years later she finds the skin and returns to the sea.

Said to look like an island surrounded by weeds with the back of a monster the Kraken's territory lies off Burra in Shetland. By Scandinavian tradition just two of these creatures were created and are destined to survive to Earth's end, although in reality they may be giant squids. Between the Shaint Islands and Long Island in the Highlands live the Blue Men of the Minch. Exerting their evil from underwater caves, they are routinely blamed for shipwrecks.

▼ Calanais Standing Stones, Lewis

TARTAN, KILTS AND BAGPIPES

There's nothing that says 'Scotland' quite as loudly as a tartan kilt – unless it's the skirl of bagpipes. These days, the kilt is more fashionable than ever. Wherever you come from, kiltmakers on Edinburgh's Royal Mile will dig deep to find your Scottish roots and come up with a tartan you can wear with pride. There's even a Singh tartan, created for Scotland's first Sikh peer, Baron Sirdar Iqbal Singh.

You can create your own tartan and make it official by registering it with the Scottish Register of Tartans. Or you can abandon tartan for a polka-dot kilt, or perhaps a sporty little black leather number with a fluffy pink sporran. Is this flying in the face of tradition? Not a bit of it. The clan and regimental tartans worn today are quite recent inventions.

Highlanders traditionally wore the plaid, a garment like a huge blanket worn over a saffron-dyed linen shirt and strapped about by sword belt and bandolier. It was woven from wool dyed with pigments made from lichens, roots, berries and tree bark that yielded muted shades of green, blue, grey and tan. This traditional garb, like other symbols of Gaelic culture such as pipe music and the right to bear arms, was banned following the defeat of the Jacobite rising of 1745–46. The ban was lifted in 1781, and the British army's elite Highland regiments, raised by chieftains, who were now loyal subjects of the British crown, each adopted a distinctive tartan. Sir Walter Scott, orchestrating King George IV's visit to Scotland in 1822, urged Highlanders to turn out in traditional dress to hail their monarch. George himself ordered a full-on outfit in a new so-called Royal Tartan and had his portrait painted by the fashionable Edinburgh artist David Wilkie. Suddenly, tartan was fashionable, and a whole new industry grew up, inventing and codifying new patterns for each clan and sept or sub-clan. Lowlanders who had never before worn the plaid wanted to get in on the act too, keeping weavers and kiltmakers busy.

George IV's tartan is now known as Royal Stewart, and it's probably the most famous of them all. It's the personal tartan of Queen Elizabeth II, who wears it when she attends the Royal Braemar Gathering (see page 51), but it's also the tartan of rockers like the Bay City Rollers and Rod Stewart, the punks of the 1970s and Scotland's notorious so-called Tartan Army of football fans.

If you want a proper Highland outfit for formal occasions, with kilt, silver-buttoned jacket, sporran, hose and dress shoes, expect to spend a lot more than you'd pay for an off-the-peg tux. But if you're just looking for a party kilt you can pick one up for the price of a pair of jeans. Just remember to go regimental, as they say in the Army's Highland battalions. Nothing is worn under the kilt.

You'll see (and hear) massed bands of kilted pipers from the Royal Regiment of Scotland at events such as the Royal Edinburgh Military Tattoo (see page 50), playing the battle anthems that drove the regiments forward at every battle from Malplaquet and Waterloo to El Alamein and D-Day. Most people think of this as the archetype of pipe music. But visit other events like the Highland gatherings held all over Scotland in summer and you'll hear gentler sounds from the bagpipe. The *piobaireachd* (pibroch) or lament, played by a solo piper, is melancholy and always moving.

▼ A selection of tartans

INDUSTRIAL HERITAGE

Romantic, semi-legendary figures such as William Wallace, Robert the Bruce and Bonnie Prince Charlie cast long shadows over Scotland's turbulent history. As a result, Scotland's industrial heritage is sometimes overlooked. Of the six designated UNESCO World Heritage Sites in Scotland, only two celebrate industry and technology. Yet 19th-century Scotland was one of the great workshops of the world.

The Industrial Revolution transformed the nation's economy. Cities like Glasgow and Dundee became centres of shipbuilding and the textile industry. Coal mining changed the very geography of some parts of Scotland, leaving scars on the landscape that still linger in places like Fife and Lothian, where former slagheaps have been transformed into country parks and venues for activities like trail biking and quad-riding. There's no better place to start a tour of Scotland than New Lanark (see page 303), the factory village founded by David Dale and developed by his son-in-law Robert Owen into a model community for mill workers and their children. New Lanark was founded on the cusp of the Industrial Revolution, when water power was the essential force behind Scottish industry.

Its weaving machinery was driven by the River Clyde, and continued to use water power as late as the 1870s.

As well as driving machinery, water became an essential transport resource during the 18th and 19th centuries. Canals were built to connect Scotland's east and west coasts. The Forth and Clyde Canal (see page 22), built in 1790, and the Union Canal, which opened in 1822, linked the two cities of Glasgow and Edinburgh. The Caledonian Canal (see page 240), also completed in 1822 (12 years late and £436,000 over budget) joined the waters of the Great Glen in a 60-mile chain of lochs, locks and aqueducts. No longer in commercial use, Scotland's canals have become heritage attractions in their own right. The Falkirk Wheel (see page 373), a hi-tech boat lift built in 2002 to carry boats between the Forth and Clyde and Union canals, has become quite a tourism icon.

Ironically, the Scottish canals quite soon became victims of the Industrial Revolution they had helped to bring about. By the 1820s, small railways were carrying coal from mining areas to Scotland's cities. The second half of the 19th century was the era of the commonly named railway wars between rival railway companies to complete routes between London and Scotland's major cities. The most impressive monument to the great age of rail in Scotland is the Forth Bridge (see page 364). Straddling the Firth of Forth, this colossal crossing was the world's first great steel structure.

Declared a UNESCO World Heritage Site in 2015, it still carries rail traffic, which says something for the engineering skills of the men who built it and its engineers, John Fowler and Benjamin Baker. On 4 March 1890 Edward, Prince of Wales, ceremonially tapped in the last of the 6.5 million rivets that hold its girders together.

If you look down from a train crossing the Firth of Tay between Fife and Dundee, you can just make out relics of a less successful experiment in railway engineering. The stumps of stone pillars that are exposed a few feet above the water are all that remains of the first railway bridge across the Tay. Completed in a hurry, it collapsed in a high gale in 1879, taking a train and more than 70 passengers with it. Work began on a replacement bridge in 1883. It opened four years later, and, like the Forth Rail Bridge, it still carries trains running on the main Scottish east coastline. Altogether, perhaps as many as 80 workers died in accidents during the building of the Forth and Tay rail bridges.

Steam power industrialised Dundee's weaving trade in the 19th century. Within living memory, the city's skyline bristled with the stacks (chimneys) of weaving mills that employed most of the city's workers. The jute-weaving industry perished in the second half of the 20th century, but you can find out how it shaped Dundee's modern history at Verdant Works (see page 141), one of the last working jute mills and now an industrial heritage visitor centre. Cox's Stack, a mill chimney cunningly disguised as an Italianate bell tower by a design-conscious 19th-century jute magnate, is still a city landmark.

Over on the west coast, Clydeside became the shipbuilding centre of the world in the second half of the 19th century, and remained so well into the 20th. The iconic relic of this part of Scotland's past is the Titan Crane, which looms above the former John Brown & Company dockyard at Clydebank. Completed in 1907, this was a revolutionary piece of machinery in its day, using massively powerful electric hoists to lift gun turrets, boilers and engines into the hulls of warships like HMS *Duke of York* and liners such as *Queen Mary* and *Queen Elizabeth*.

When it comes to city transport, Glasgow's horse-drawn trams were introduced in 1872, revolutionising local transport for ordinary people. The city said goodbye to its trams, by now electric, in 1962. Both the horse-drawn and electric models were built in the city at Coplawhill Tramcar Works. If you'd like to find out more about the city's transport history, you'll find everything you need to know at Glasgow's Riverside Museum (see page 221), with its collection of cars, buses, ships and locomotives built during Scotland's industrial golden age.

▶ Sandwick Bay, Shetland

ISLAND LIFE

Scotland has almost 800 islands, although fewer than 100 are permanently inhabited. Some lie far out in western and northern waters. Others are so close that you can walk to them at low tide, while Skye is linked to the mainland by a road bridge that opened in 1995. They range in size from the largest, Lewis and Harris, to dots on the map like Eigg, Muck and Canna.

Skye is firmly on the beaten tourist track, while the white-sand beaches of Tiree attract those looking for privacy. Other, smaller isles like tiny Berneray in the Outer Hebrides, Papa Westray in the Orkneys, lonely Fair Isle, or Unst, Britain's northernmost inhabited island, don't see many visitors. Scotland's remotest island, Rockall, lies 260 miles out into the Atlantic and has never been inhabited except by a flock of seabirds.

Life on Scotland's islands proceeds at its own pace. Fishing and farming remain important parts of the way of life in the Western Isles and in Orkney and Shetland, although fishing has dwindled along with Atlantic and North Sea fish stocks. You'll see stacks of peat, the traditional fuel of Hebridean crofters, drying by the roadside, and the toasty reek of peat fires is one of the distinctive aromas of the isles. Whisky distilling is important on islands including Jura, Islay and Skye in the Hebrides, and in Orkney. Tourism is a big summer earner on the best-known islands, but the season is short and few can make a year-round living from the holiday business.

The cultural gap between each island group – and sometimes even between neighbouring islands – can be as wide as the gulf between islands and mainland. Most of Scotland's 60,000 or so Gaelic speakers live in the Hebrides, but Gaelic has never been spoken in Orkney or Shetland, where a dialect known as Norn – descended from the Norse spoken by early Viking settlers – was the common tongue until the late 18th century. Since then, Norn has been ousted by a dialect of Scots that's similar to the Doric of the northeast mainland, although a scattering of old Norn words are still in use. There are distinct musical traditions too – some of Scotland's most legendary pipers have come from the Hebrides, but in the Northern Isles it's the fiddle that reigns supreme.

Since the late 1970s, the North Sea oil industry has transformed the economies of Orkney and Shetland and has become a major employer. The isles have their political differences, too. The Western Isles are a Nationalist stronghold, but Orkney and Shetland have long been a Liberal Democrat outpost, and in 2017 re-elected Scotland's only Lib Dem MP.

Many people in Lewis and Harris adhere to hardline Presbyterian churches that insist on strict observance of the Sabbath – Sunday ferry services between Stornoway and the mainland only began in 2009. Meanwhile, just a short island-hop away, tiny Barra is a Roman Catholic enclave in a Protestant sea. Barra retained the old religion through the Reformation and the intolerant centuries that followed partly because it's so remote, but

▼ Glenuig Bay and Lochailort looking out to the isles of Rùm and Eigg

also because the local MacNeil chiefs themselves remained Catholic when many others converted. Clan loyalties and rivalries have shaped the history of all the Hebridean islands. Lewis is the island heartland of Clan Donald and of the northern branch of the MacLeods. The chiefs of Clan Maclean make their home in Duart Castle on Mull. Dunvegan Castle, long the home of Clan MacLeod of Skye, is Skye's biggest man-made tourist attraction.

The logistics of getting from one island to another also reinforce local identities. Travelling between islands, even if they are within sight of one another, can entail taking a ferry to the mainland, travelling by road to a different port, and then taking a second ferry to your destination. And if you want to travel, say, from Islay in the southern Hebrides to Stornoway on Lewis, the quickest and easiest way is probably to fly via Glasgow.

A number of islands are privately owned. Some, like Eigg, are owned by community trusts, sometimes in partnership with local government or the National Trust for Scotland. NTS is the owner of several islands, including deserted St Kilda, whose islanders gave up their primitive way of life in 1940 and resettled on the mainland.

Iona, off Mull, is the birthplace of Scottish Christianity and is home to the Iona Community, founded in 1938 as a place of spiritual pilgrimage and contemplation.

The recent history of tiny Gruinard is less pleasant. During World War II it was used as a germ warfare test area, and it was quarantined until 1990, when it was decontaminated, pronounced safe and returned to its original owners. There's still a military presence in the Western Isles, with areas maintained by the Ministry of Defence. A more peaceful use for missiles was proposed by German inventor Gerhard Zucker, who in 1934 unsuccessfully sent mail by rocket between Harris and Scarp.

LOCAL SPECIALITIES

Scottish cuisine is legendary – although many south of the border will regard it with horror. It's not all porridge, entrails and deep-fried food, however; fresh fish is also high on the menu. And if that's not to your liking, there's always the famous Scotch whisky to wash it down.

A CULINARY TRADITION

Think of Scottish specialities and two dishes spring immediately to mind. The first is **porridge**. Traditionally the staple food of rural folk, in its most spartan form this is just oatmeal boiled in water, but the more luxurious version offered in most Scottish hotels and guest houses is made with milk. Purists insist porridge should be flavoured with salt, but you can add cream, honey or syrup if you like.

The second iconic Scottish dish is **haggis**, celebrated by Scotland's national bard, Robert Burns, in his *Address to a Haggis* and traditionally consumed in his honour on Burns Night, when it is accompanied on the plate with **bashit neeps** (mashed turnip).

But the haggis isn't Scotland's only pudding (a word borrowed from the French *boudin*). Scots also consume **black pudding**, made from offal, blood and fat. The best, it's claimed, come from Stornoway, on the Isle of Lewis. Fried, sliced black pudding is a keystone of any full Scottish breakfast. It's also battered, deep-fried and served with chips in every fish and chip shop in the land. So is its cousin, **white pudding** or **mealie pudding**, made with oatmeal, herbs and fat. Another chip shop delicacy is the infamous **deep-fried Mars Bar**, said to have been invented in

Stonehaven in 1992. Desserts less likely to clog your arteries include **cranachan**, made from oatmeal, sweetened cream and fresh berries. You'll find it on the menu at many restaurants and gastropubs.

With thousands of miles of North Sea and Atlantic coastline, Scotland naturally offers a rich seafood menu. Loch Fyne, on the west coast, is famous for its **oysters**. The fishing village of Findon, in Aberdeenshire, is the birthplace of **finnan haddie** (cold-smoked haddock fillet). Arbroath is the home of the **smokie** (haddock smoked in its skin and on the bone). Either or both of these can go into **Cullen skink**, a hearty, chowder-like soup. Another soup that is almost a meal in itself is **Scotch broth**, made with chicken stock, barley, dried split peas, lentils, onions and carrots.

Scots love pies and savoury pastries like the **Forfar bridie**, a semicircular pastry filled with minced beef and onions that can be eaten hot or cold.

BOTTOMS UP

Whisky, of course, is the national drink, but beer and ale have been brewed in Scotland for more than 2,000 years.

There has been a brewing renaissance in Scotland in recent years, with renewed interest in creating heritage ales flavoured with old-style ingredients such as heather buds, spruce and pine shoots, gooseberry and even seaweed. You'll find distinctive ales from craft breweries such as **Williams Brothers**, makers of **Fraoch** heather ale, and **Harviestoun**, brewers of **Ola Dubh**, a beer that is matured in malt whisky casks. From Scotland's oldest independent brewery, Traquair, come potent brews such as Traquair 50, which has an alcohol content of seven per cent.

Whisky and freedom go together, claimed Robert Burns. Many Scots would agree. Spirit distilled from malted barley is the key ingredient in **Scotch whisky**. Blended Scotch is made by combining this malt spirit with neutral grain alcohol. Better blends use higher proportions of malt, while cheaper whiskies, made on an industrial scale and mass produced for export, use more of the cheaper neutral spirit. But for connoisseurs, blended Scotch doesn't compare with elite single malt whiskies made entirely with malt spirit. The Scotch Whisky Association insists that both blends and single malts must be aged for at least three years. Quality whiskies may be aged for up to 12 years or even more, but it's unlikely that allowing the spirit to age for more than 20 years adds any extra depth or flavour.

Traditionally, oak sherry casks were used in this ageing process, but many distillers now also use casks that have held bourbon, port, madeira or other wines and spirits to create single malts that have different background tones.

Each whisky-making region has its own style of single malt, influenced by factors like local water and the fuel used to fire the stills. Whiskies from **Islay** and **Jura** have a distinctive peaty, even seaweedy tang. Malts from **Speyside** are lighter in colour and flavour, with heathery, even flowery notes. If you want to take more than one bottle of a stand-out malt home but have little room in your luggage, you can buy **cask strength** malt to take home. This is the stuff that comes out of the barrel to be diluted with water before bottling. With an alcohol content of almost 100 per cent, one bottle of cask strength malt is equivalent to more than two standard bottles. Dilute with water to taste, but please use a good quality table water – to use tap water would be sacrilege.

A distillery tour followed by a whisky sampling can be one of the high points of your Scottish holiday. There are almost 100 distilleries scattered around Scotland's mainland and islands – too many to visit in one holiday, or even a lifetime. But more than 40 of them cluster on Speyside, where you can visit the places where world-famous malt whiskies like **Glenlivet** and **Glenfiddich** are made, and discover smaller, less well-known distilleries like **Dallas Dhu**.

Finally, a word about Scotland's other national drink: **Irn-Bru**. This caffeine-loaded, fizzy, rusty orange beverage is one of the world's original energy drinks. It has been produced by Scottish drinks company A G Barr since 1901 and is now exported right across the world. It's renowned as a good hangover remedy, but many also find it goes very well with vodka – this may account for its huge popularity in places like Russia.

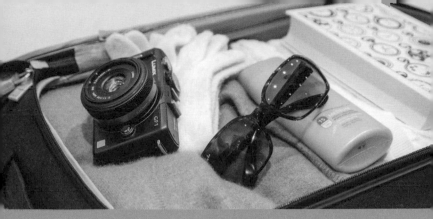

BEFORE YOU GO

THINGS TO READ

Christopher Winn's *I Never Knew That About Scotland* (2007) and *I Never Knew That About The Scottish* (2009) are quirky collections of Caledonian trivia and are perfect travelling companions wherever you go in Scotland. John Prebble's *Glencoe* and *Culloden* (both 1961) and *The Highland Clearances* (1963) are informative and readable broad-brush accounts of three tragic events in Scottish history. Prebble's *The Lion in The North* is another reliable survey of the history of Scotland from the dawn of the kingdom of Alba to the creation of the United Kingdom. *Battle for the North*, by Charles McKean (2006), tells the dramatic story of the race between rival companies to open railways to Scotland in the 19th century.

Robert Louis Stevenson's *Kidnapped*, first published in 1886 and still in print, is an enjoyable historical romp set in Scotland after the 1745 Jacobite rising. Lewis Grassic Gibbon's *A Scots Quair* trilogy (1934), set in Aberdeenshire in the early 20th century, is recognised as one of the landmarks of modern Scottish literature.

Iain Banks achieved immediate acclaim for his first novel, *The Wasp Factory* (1984), set on a remote, unnamed Scottish island. Banks went on to establish himself as one of Scotland's foremost literary voices with books such as *The Crow Road* (1992), set in rural Argyll and Glasgow, *Stonemouth* (2012) and *The Quarry* (2013), published shortly after Banks's untimely death aged 59. Banks's sole non-fiction work, *Raw Spirit* (2003), is a celebration of Scotch whisky and an essential companion for anyone planning a tour of Scotland's distilleries. *The Smiling School for Calvinists*, by Bill Duncan (2001), is a compendium of wry, perceptive and sometimes surreal short stories set in Dundee and Broughty Ferry.

Walk down the mean streets of Scotland's cities in the company of fictional crime-fighters created by a cohort of Scottish crime writers whose genre has been dubbed tartan noir. Detective Inspector John Rebus, created by Fife-born author Ian Rankin, is a dour, old-school copper whose cases take him into Edinburgh's darkest corners. You can meet Rebus for the first time in *Knots and Crosses* (1987) and follow his career through 18 more books. The Rebus books are great reads, and they also make good guides to some truly excellent Edinburgh pubs.

Another fictional sleuth, Jack Parlabane, maverick investigative journalist, is the creation of Glaswegian author Christopher Brookmyre. Jack first appears in the darkly funny *Quite Ugly One Morning* (1996), set in Edinburgh, and most recently *Dead Girl Walking* (2015), set mainly in Scotland.

Poetry has been at the heart of Scottish culture since the birth of the Scottish nation. *100 Favourite Scottish Poems* (2006) is a good introduction to the works of Scots bards from Robert Burns and Sir Walter Scott to 20th-century poets such as Edwin Morgan, Hugh McDiarmid, Liz Lochhead and Jackie Kay, Scotland's makar (national poet). Finally, there must be mention of William Topaz McGonagall (1825–1902). He is widely regarded as the worst poet ever to write in English. This opening verse of 'The Tay Bridge Disaster', penned in 1880, gives some idea of his inimitable style:

Beautiful railway bridge of the silvr'ry Tay
Alas! I am very sorry to say
That ninety lives have been taken away
On the Last sabbath day of 1879
Which will be remember'd for a very long time.

THINGS TO WATCH

Scotland's glens and city streets, and its ruined castles, have been the backdrop for dozens of movies. For heavily romanticised versions of real historical events, it's hard to beat *Braveheart* (1995), starring Mel Gibson as medieval freedom fighter William Wallace, or *Rob Roy* (1995), based on Sir Walter Scott's historical romance, with Liam Neeson as the outlaw Rob Roy MacGregor. For pure daftness, though, neither of these beats *Highlander* (1986), with French actor Christopher Lambert as a 16th-century clansman who is fated to become an immortal warrior. Lambert's accent is all over the place, and the only Scot cast in a starring role, Sean Connery, plays a Spaniard. In all three, the Highland scenery is the real star. The location has a big part to play too in *Local Hero* (1983), still one of the best-loved films set in Scotland. Burt Lancaster is the Texan oil billionaire who wants to buy up and demolish a picturesque fishing village to make way for an oil refinery, a scheme that divides the community. Village scenes were shot in Pennan,

Aberdeenshire, but the beaches that appear in the film are in Morar and Arisaig on the west coast. Watch out also for Twelfth Doctor Peter Capaldi, in only his second screen role.

Another picturesque village, Lusk, on the shores of Loch Lomond, stood in for the fictional Glendarroch in the long-running soap *Take the High Road* (STV, 1980–2003). And parts of *The Wicker Man* (1973) were filmed around Isle of Whithorn, notably its terrifying climax at Burrow Head.

Several of Scotland's fictional crimebusters have had their own TV series. Ken Stott is perfectly cast as the shambolic Edinburgh detective in *Rebus* (ITV, 2006–7). Jason Isaacs plays Jackson Brodie, the private eye created by author Kate Atkinson, in the TV series *Case Histories*, also set in Edinburgh.

THINGS TO KNOW
▶ Approximately 1.6 million of Scotland's estimated 5.2 million people live in the country's six largest cities.

▶ Some Scots are keen to see a revival of the Gaelic language, and you'll see road signs and station signage in both Gaelic and English in some places. However, only about 60,000 Scots speak Gaelic as their mother tongue. Most of Scotland's Gaelic speakers live in the Highlands and on the Islands, especially on the Western Isles.

▶ Scots from Highlands and Lowlands fought on both sides during the Jacobite risings of 1715 and 1745 – as did Englishmen. Several hundred men of the Manchester Regiment fought for Bonnie Prince Charlie, and many of them were executed after being captured by the Duke of Cumberland's Hanoverian forces. Meanwhile, five of the 19 battalions fielded by Cumberland at Waterloo were made up of Scots.

▶ It's Scots or Scottish not Scotch – unless you're talking about Scotch whisky, Scotch pies (beloved by football supporters), Scotch eggs, Scotch Mist (a whisky-based cocktail) or Scotch bonnet peppers, so called because they reminded settlers in the Caribbean of traditional Highland headgear.

▶ Tomintoul in Banffshire claims the title of Scotland's highest village at 1,160 feet above sea level. Aultnaharra in Sutherland, and Braemar on Deeside vie for the title of the coldest place in Scotland – both locations have recorded winter lows of 27.2°C.

▶ The highest temperature in Scotland was recorded at Greycrook, in the Borders, where in August 2003 the mercury rose to 32.9°C. If you're looking for sunshine, your best bet could be Dunbar, on the east coast, where more than 1,500 hours of sunshine per year have been recorded several times.

▶ Pack an umbrella and wellies if you're planning to visit Glen Etive, in Argyll, which has an average annual rainfall of 130 feet, making it the wettest place in Britain.

▶ Scots consume the equivalent of 50.5 million litres of pure alcohol every year – 25 per cent more than people in England and Wales. Scotland also exports more than £4 billion worth of whisky every year. France is the biggest overseas market, followed by the USA and – surprisingly – Singapore.

▶ Scots have emigrated all over the world, and it's estimated that there are now more than 50 million people of Scottish descent in countries ranging from the USA and Canada to South Africa, Australia and New Zealand. Some 25 million Americans claim Scots ancestry, and 23 US presidents, from James Monroe to Barack Obama (who according to one genealogist is a remote descendant of a 12th-century King of Scots, William the Lion), have some Scots blood. So does Donald Trump, President of the USA, whose mother came from the Isle of Lewis.

▶ Elvis Presley's ancestors came from Lonmay in Aberdeenshire, and the King himself briefly set foot on Scottish soil at Prestwick Airport in 1960 – his only visit to the UK.

▶ Scottish surnames such as Campbell, Stewart and Monroe are common in Caribbean countries like Jamaica and Barbados, where some Scots were plantation overseers and slave owners, while others were exiles convicted of rebellion in the 17th and 18th centuries.

▶ Halls of Scotland holds (as of 2017) the record for the world's largest haggis. In June 2014, the North Berwick haggis-maker created a 2,226lb 10oz, 9-foot 2-inch monster, truly, in Burns' words, a 'great chieftain o' the pudding-race'.

▶ The first sighting of the Loch Ness monster is recorded in the *Life of St Columba*, by the seventh-century chronicler Adamnan, who credited the saint with saving a swimmer from the monster by the power of prayer. Since the story of Nessie began, no one has yet managed to film or photograph the beast. The so-called surgeon's photograph, the most famous image, was revealed as a hoax in 1993, some 60 years after it was taken. Explanations of the phenomenon range from the prosaic to the fanciful. It's been suggested that some sightings have been of floating logs or giant bubbles of natural gas rising from the depths. Giant catfish, conger eels and

sturgeon are other candidates. It's even been suggested that some sightings were of swimming elephants taking a break from a travelling circus.

THINGS TO PACK

▶ To get the most out of your visit to Scotland, you'll need warm and waterproof footwear, a fleece or sweater, a hat or umbrella, and a windproof, waterproof coat or jacket.

▶ Even in summer, it's important to be properly prepared when venturing into the Cairngorms National Park or other rugged terrain. Weather can change quickly and dramatically, so you need to be prepared for all weathers – blizzard conditions have been experienced in May on high ground.

▶ If you plan to venture into the hills – even if within sight of Edinburgh or Glasgow – you'll need stout walking boots, not just trainers.

▶ Swarms of tiny midges infest the boggy countryside of the Highlands and the Western Isles in summer. They seem immune to chemical mosquito repellents, but a slather of baby oil helps to keep them off.

▶ Wetsuits for kids (and grown-ups) are definitely a good idea if you plan to spend any time in the sea.

▶ Even this far north, sunburn is a risk in summer, so if you burn easily you should pack sunscreen and lip block.

BASIC INFORMATION

If you want to get to Scotland by road from southern and central England, by far the fastest and easiest route is via the M6 and M74. It's motorway all the way to Glasgow and, via the M8, to Edinburgh. Motorways also connect Edinburgh with Stirling and Perth. North of Perth and Dundee, you're on a mixture of dual carriageway and two-lane roads on key routes. It makes sense to use caution on these roads and not succumb to risky overtaking. Heading deeper into rural Scotland, most roads are two-lane but in summer can be busy with convoys of caravans and motor homes. In parts of the Highlands, there are long stretches of single-lane roads with signposted passing places. If you see another vehicle approaching, or if a driver behind you wants to pass, pull into the nearest passing place on your left or pause before the nearest on your right.

Travel in Scotland has hazards that may take drivers from more temperate climes by surprise. Long after winter is over down south, roads – even major roads like the Perth to Inverness A9 – may be affected by heavy snow. If you're visiting in winter, bear in mind that it gets dark by about 4pm. On the other hand, visiting in summer, it hardly gets dark at all in the far north.

Scottish weather is notoriously changeable, but there's plenty to do indoors if it turns nasty. In Edinburgh, you can while away a wet afternoon at The Real Mary King's Close (see page 172), a spooky maze of tunnels beneath the Royal Mile; visit Our Dynamic Earth (see page 179), a science centre filled with interactive exhibits; and explore the treasures of the National Museum of Scotland (see page 174). In Glasgow, the collection of vintage vehicles and the tall ship Glenlee in the

Riverside Museum keep children entertained (see page 214). Intu Braehead, a leisure and retail centre at Renfrew on the outskirts of Glasgow, has indoor rock climbing, skiing, snowboarding and laser combat games. In Aberdeen you'll find ten-pin bowling and other indoor activities at Codona's Amusement Park (see page 62), and in Stonehaven you can swim at the heated Stonehaven Open Air Pool (see page 65).

Walkers, cyclists and campers have right of access to almost all of Scotland's land, lochs and shores. There are some exceptions – you're not allowed to tramp through people's gardens or across fields of crops. There's no automatic right of access to farmyards, although few farmers will object to you following paths that traverse their patch. Land owned by the Ministry of Defence, such as Royal Air Force (RAF) airfields and Army firing ranges, is also usually off-limits. You can camp freely on most beaches and areas of unenclosed land, but you should obey certain simple rules when wild camping: leave no traces of your campfire (or even better, use a camping stove); never cut wood from trees; and bury your poo and don't pee in the stream. For more information, see the Scottish Outdoor Access Code (outdooraccess-scotland.com/outdoors-responsibly/access-code-and-advice/soac).

FESTIVALS & EVENTS

▶ JANUARY

Celtic Connections
celticconnections.com
Second fortnight in January
Britain's biggest festival of Celtic music brightens up Glasgow in January. Celtic Connections celebrates folk and world music, not just Scots and Irish traditions.

Up Helly Aa
uphellyaa.org
Last Tuesday in January
Dressed as Norse warriors, the Guizer Jarl and his Viking crew march in torchlit procession through the streets of Lerwick in Shetland. The grand finale is the spectacular burning of a replica longship.

▶ FEBRUARY

Glasgow Film Festival
glasgowfilm.org/glasgow-film-festival
Second fortnight in February
Glasgow Film Festival is really three events in one, embracing the Glasgow Youth Film Festival and Glasgow Short Film Festival as well as the main event. You can watch screenings of classics, art-house movies and new cinema in unique venues and listen to directors, writers and actors talking about their craft.

▶ MARCH

Glasgow International Comedy Festival
glasgowcomedyfestival.com
Glasgow has spawned comedy legends like Stanley Baxter, Billy Connolly, Frankie Boyle and Susan Calman. Established and up-and-coming comedy talents flock to the city in March, daring to perform in front of some of the toughest-heckling audiences in the world.

▶ APRIL

Beltane Fire Festival
beltane.org
30 April
Drummers and torch-bearers lead the way in procession to the summit of Edinburgh's Calton Hill, where a huge bonfire is lit to celebrate the beginning of summer in an imaginative and fun recreation of an ancient Celtic festival.

▶ MAY

Spirit of Stirling Whisky Festival
spiritofstirlingwhiskyfestival.co.uk
First weekend in May
If you're already a malt whisky connoisseur, a visit to this annual celebration of Scotland's national drink will take you to seventh heaven. If you've never taken whisky seriously, the Spirit of Stirling Whisky Festival may convert you into a fan. There are scores of whiskies to sample, from the light, flowery malts of Speyside to the punchy products of Hebridean distilleries, with masterclasses in tasting to help you in the nigh-impossible task of deciding your favourite dram.

▶ JUNE

Border Rideouts

returntotheridings.co.uk

June–August

Hundreds of horse-riders follow their standards and banners around the Border towns of Duns, Selkirk, Hawick, Jedburgh, Galashiels, West Linton, Melrose, Coldstream and Kelso, in an annual event that echoes the days of the ferocious Border reivers.

▶ JULY

Hebridean Celtic Festival

hebceltfest.com

Third week in July

Head to the Outer Isles for this vibrant festival of international Celtic music, held in different venues around Stornoway on Lewes, with community shows elsewhere on both Lewes and Harris. Headline acts have included the Waterboys, Runrig, Imelda May and Van Morrison.

Skye Festival

seall.co.uk

Jul–Aug

Taking place mainly in venues around the Sleat peninsula at the southern end of the island of Skye, the ever expanding Skye Festival or Fèis an Eilein is a celebration of island culture and performing arts with a strong focus on Scottish traditional music. Fringe events include ceilidhs.

▶ AUGUST

Belladrum Tartan Heart Festival

tartanheartfestival.co.uk

First weekend in August

Top acts at the Tartan Heart Festival at Belladrum, near Inverness, have included The Manic Street Preachers and Kaiser Chiefs, with a supporting cast of rock, pop and world music bands, DJs and comedians.

Cowal Highland Gathering

cowalgathering.com

Last weekend in August

It's wall-to-wall tartan in Dunoon, where competitors meet at the biggest Highland games event in the world to take part in contests of dancing, piping, traditional wrestling and other heavy sports. You can also tap your foot to music from ceilidh bands.

Edinburgh International Festival

edinburghfestivalcity.com

August

Opera, ballet, Classical music, drama and contemporary dance are celebrated at the Edinburgh International, while spin-off events throughout August include the Edinburgh Film Festival, Book Festival, Art Festival, the multicultural Edinburgh Mela, and the ever-popular comedy, cabaret and experimental theatre of the Edinburgh Festival Fringe.

Royal Edinburgh Military Tattoo

edinburghfestivalcity.com/
festivals/royal-edinburgh-
military-tattoo

August

Massed pipe bands are the focus of one of the world's greatest military-themed events, along with Scottish dancers, performances by military teams from around the world and nightly fireworks on Edinburgh's Castle Esplanade.

Strathaven Balloon Festival

strathavenballoonfestival.co.uk

Last weekend in August

Expect a lot of hot air at this event as brightly coloured balloons fill the sky above Strathaven, near East Kilbride. The first flight is soon after dawn, but perhaps the most spectacular display is at dusk, when the huge aerial globes light up. Enthusiasts of veteran vehicles will also find a display of classic models.

▶ SEPTEMBER

Braemar Gathering
braemargathering.org
First weekend in September
Members of the Royal Family always attend the most famous of Scotland's many Highland events at Braemar, not far from Balmoral. Listen to pipers, watch Highland dancers, and wince as kilted musclemen vie at heavy sports like tossing the caber, putting the stone and throwing the hammer. For children, there are less challenging and more fun events like sack races.

Loopallu
loopallu.co.uk
Last weekend in September
This friendly festival held every year near Ullapool (yes, Loopallu is Ullapool spelt backwards) has established itself as the place to wind up the summer open-air music festival season. Cross your fingers and hope it doesn't rain, but bring warm, waterproof gear just in case.

Wigtown Book Festival
wigtownbookfestival.com
Last week in September–first week in October
Wigtown, commonly called Scotland's book town, hosts novelists, biographers, comedians, poets and authors of all kinds for this ten-day celebration of the printed word. Authors and critics discuss what makes a great read, and there are signings, talks and readings, and events for kids and young adults.

▶ OCTOBER

Dundee Literary Festival
literarydundee.co.uk
Third weekend in October
Dundee's annual literary event celebrates everything from poetry and comics to novels, thrillers and children's books. Authors and poets such as Jeanette Winterson, Jackie Kay and Janice Galloway talk about the process of writing, and the £10,000 Dundee International Book Prize has become Britain's top prize for new literary talent.

▶ NOVEMBER

Dundee Mountain Film Festival
dundeemountainfilm.org.uk
Last weekend in November
Speakers, exhibitions, award-winning film screenings and live drama at this unusual film festival investigate the past, present and future of the world's mountains and the people who are driven to climb them.

▶ DECEMBER

Edinburgh's Hogmanay
edinburghshogmanay.com
31 December
Hogmanay (New Year's Eve) is celebrated in every Scottish community with music, dancing, singing, fireworks and drinking. Take your pick from big city celebrations or village ceilidhs where everyone's welcome. Edinburgh's Hogmanay is the biggest of Scotland's New Year's Eve festivities, with a massive street party, live rock, folk and Classical music, and spectacular pyrotechnics over the castle at midnight.

Stonehaven Fireball Festival
stonehavenfireballs.co.uk
31 December
Daring men and women whirl great balls of fire as they march through the streets of Stonehaven in the most famous of several New Year fire festivals across Scotland. These events probably go all the way back to the days of the Norsemen.

CAMPSITES

For more information on these and other campsites, visit theAA.com/self-catering-and-campsites.

Blair Castle Caravan Park ►►►►►

blair-castle.co.uk/caravan-estate
Blair Atholl, PH18 5SR
01796 481263 | Open Mar–Nov
An attractive site set in impressive seclusion within the Atholl Estate, surrounded by mature woodland and the River Tilt. There is a choice of grass pitches, hardstandings and fully serviced pitches.

Broomfield Holiday Park ►►►

broomfieldhp.com
West Shore Street, Ullapool, IV26 2UT | 01854 612020 | Open Easter or Apr–Sep
Set right on the water's edge of Loch Broom and the open sea, with lovely views of the Summer Isles. This clean, well-maintained park is close to the harbour and town centre. The Ullapool ferry allows easy access to the Hebridean islands.

Carradale Bay Caravan Park ►►►

carradalebay.com
Carradale, PA28 6QG
01583 431665 | Open Apr–Sep
A beautiful, natural site on the sea's edge with superb views over Kilbrannan Sound to the Isle of Arran. Pitches are landscaped into small bays broken up by shrubs and bushes, and backed by dunes close to the long sandy beach. Lodges and static caravans are available for holiday hire. The surrounding area is a haven for birds and wildlife.

Craigtoun Meadows Holiday Park ►►►►►

craigtounmeadows.co.uk
Mount Melville, St Andrews, KY16 8PQ | 01334 475959
Open mid-Mar to Oct
This attractive site is set unobtrusively in mature woodlands, with large pitches in spacious hedged paddocks. All pitches are fully serviced, and there are also some patio pitches. The licensed restaurant and coffee shop are popular, and there is a takeaway, indoor and outdoor games areas and a launderette. It's located a mile and a half from St Andrews town centre.

Drumroamin Farm Camping and Touring Site ►►►
drumroamin.co.uk
1 South Balfern, Kirkinner, DG8 9DB
01988 840613 | Open all year
An open, spacious site overlooking Wigtown Bay and the Galloway Hills. Located near Wigtown and Newton Stewart, this is an easily accessible site for those wishing to stay in a rural location. There is a good bus service at the top of the road.

Glen Nevis Caravan and Camping Park ►►►►
glen-nevis.co.uk
Glen Nevis, Fort William, PH33 6SX | 01397 702191
Open mid-Mar to Oct
A tasteful site with well-screened enclosures, at the foot of Ben Nevis in the midst of some of the most spectacular Highland scenery; an ideal area for walking and touring. The park boasts a restaurant that provides good value for money.

Huntly Castle Caravan Park ►►►►►
huntlycastle.co.uk
The Meadow, Huntly, AB54 4UJ
01466 794999 | Open Apr–Oct
A quality parkland site within striking distance of the Speyside Malt Whisky Trail, the beautiful Moray coast and the Cairngorm Mountains. There are some fully serviced pitches. The town of Huntly is only a five-minute walk away, with its ruined castle plus a wide variety of restaurants and shops.

Skye Camping and Caravanning Club Site ►►►►
campingandcaravanningclub.co.uk/skye
Loch Greshornish, Borve, Arnisort, Edinbane, Isle of Skye, IV51 9PS
01470 582230 | Open Apr–Oct
Situated on the beautiful Isle of Skye, this campsite stands out for its stunning waterside location and glorious views. There is an on-site shop, two camping pods to let and car hire is available on the site.

Thurston Manor Leisure Park ►►►►►
thistleparks.co.uk/touring
Innerwick, Dunbar, EH42 1SA
01368 840643 | Open mid-Feb to Jan
A pleasant park set in 250 acres of unspoilt countryside. The touring and static areas of this large park are in separate areas. The park boasts a well-stocked fishing loch, a heated indoor swimming pool, steam room, sauna, jacuzzi, mini-gym and fitness room, plus seasonal entertainment.

Witches Craig Caravan and Camping Park ►►►►
witchescraig.co.uk
Blairlogie, Stirling, FK9 5PX | 01786 474947 | Open Apr–Oct
In an attractive setting with direct access to the lower slopes of the dramatic Ochil Hills, this is a well-maintained family-run park. It is in the centre of 'Braveheart' country, with easy access to historical sites and many popular attractions.

A–Z of Scotland

VISIT THE MUSEUMS | GET OUTDOORS | EXPLORE BY BIKE | GO BACK IN TIME | TAKE A TRAIN RIDE | MEET THE WILDLIFE | TAKE IN SOME HISTORY | HIT THE BEACH | EAT AND DRINK | GET INDUSTRIAL | VISIT THE GALLERIES | GO CANOEING | TRY HORSE-RIDING | PLACES NEARBY | CATCH A PERFORMANCE | GO ROUND THE GARDENS | TAKE A BOAT TRIP

▶ Abbotsford MAP REF 403 D4

scottsabbotsford.com

Melrose, TD6 9BQ | 01896 752043 | House and Gardens open Mar and Nov
daily 10–4 and Apr–Oct daily 10–5; Visitor Centre open Apr–Oct daily 10–5;
Nov and Mar daily 10–4; Jan–Feb Wed–Sun 10–4

This overblown, turreted and crenellated grey mansion is
a must for an insight into the eclectic mind of the writer
Sir Walter Scott (1771–1832), best known for epic romantic
poems such as *The Lady of the Lake*, and novels including
Ivanhoe, *Kenilworth* and *Redgauntlet*.

Abbotsford was the home he built for himself in 1812 on the
banks of the River Tweed, two miles west of Melrose (see page
297). The house was designed by William Atkinson, whose
plans had to incorporate the somewhat whimsical ideas of
Scott and his friends. The result is a house of great character,
mixing Gothic, Tudor and traditional Scottish styles, and its
contents powerfully reflect their creator, for it is the treasure-
house of a magpie with a gift for romantic history. It's filled with
historical curiosities, some of which – like the condemned
criminals' door from the old Tolbooth in Edinburgh – are built
into the fabric of the house. You can view Scott's library, the
gracious dining room with windows looking down to the river,
and a bristling armoury, its walls covered with guns (including
Rob Roy's) and other paraphernalia. There's even a collection
of knick-knacks of the famous, including Rob Roy's purse,
James IV's hunting bottle, a pocket book worked by Flora
MacDonald and a cup belonging to Bonnie Prince Charlie.

The overall effect is one of mock antiquity—a distillation of
his novels. The Visitors' Centre tells the story of Scott's life and
displays documents about the building of the house, paintings,
manuscripts, books, letters and engravings.

▼ Abbotsford House

▶ **Aberdeen** MAP REF 409 F3

It's easy to see why Aberdeen is nicknamed the Silver City. In contrast to Glasgow's signature red sandstone and the creamy Craigleith stone that's characteristic of much of Edinburgh's architecture, Aberdeen's iconic buildings are built of hard-edged grey granite that's flecked with mica and gleams in sunshine. And yes, the sun does actually shine on Aberdeen. Scotland's third city was once a popular seaside resort, and the long sweep of golden sand that stretches between the mouths of the River Dee in the south and the River Don, on the northern edge of the city, are still popular places to paddle, walk the dog, surf and windsurf. Admittedly, wearing a wetsuit lets you stay in the water longer – summer air temperatures can sometimes hit 25°C, but the North Sea isn't one of the world's warmest stretches of water.

Aberdeen's roots drill deep into Scotland's past. Its foundations as a royal burgh go back to the early 12th century, and venerable Aberdeen University, founded in 1495, is Britain's fifth-oldest. During the Middle Ages, Aberdeen was one of

▼ Marischal College

Scotland's most important seaports, trading with northern European entrepôts such as Hamburg, Bergen, Lubeck and Riga. Wool, and dried and salted cod and haddock were among its main exports, while imports included Baltic timber, textiles and steel tools and weapons. Aberdeen merchants also shipped claret from French ports like Bordeaux. There was a two-way trade in scholars between Aberdeen's colleges and universities in mainland Europe, and there was also a steady trickle of Scots soldiers of fortune who travelled east to serve as mercenaries in European armies.

Until the second half of the 20th century, Aberdeen was home to Scotland's biggest fishing fleet. The decline of the fishing industry coincided with the discovery of huge reserves of oil beneath the North Sea in the mid-1970s – a subsea discovery that changed the city beyond all recognition. Trawlers still use Aberdeen Harbour, but they share it now with the many support vessels that ferry supplies back and forth to the oil rigs that lie beyond the horizon. Thousands of people migrated to Aberdeen to work in the oil sector and its service industries, swelling the city's population so that it outstripped rival Dundee to become Scotland's third biggest city. The oil business also broadened Aberdeen's cultural horizons. It's a much more diverse community than it was even a generation ago, with people from all over the European Union, and as far away as Thailand and Nepal, now calling it home.

The bustling harbour is still the heart of the city, but Aberdeen has grown far beyond the rivers Dee and Don that once bounded it to the north and south. Union Street, lined with imposing granite buildings, is the city centre's main artery. Shopping centres, museums and galleries cluster at its eastern end, where the striking Marischal College is one of the city's major landmarks. Completed in 1895, this granite building is now the home of Aberdeen's city council.

King Street links the city centre with Old Aberdeen, the city's medieval nucleus, situated about 1 mile north of Aberdeen Harbour. This part of town is dominated by the distinctive twin towers of St Machar's Cathedral and the buildings of King's College, at the heart of the University of Aberdeen campus. Aberdeen's long seafront Esplanade follows the beach from Footdee (pronounced 'Fitty'), the attractive old fishing settlement at the harbour mouth, to the mouth of the River Don. Between the Esplanade and Old Aberdeen, you'll find the King's Links golf course, while across the river in the northern suburb of Bridge of Don is the Royal Aberdeen Golf Club, a classic links course that claims to be the sixth-oldest golf course in the world.

TAKE IN SOME HISTORY

St Machar's Cathedral

stmachar.com

The Chanonry, AB24 1RQ

01224 435988 | Open Apr–Oct daily
9.30–4.30; Nov–Mar daily 10–4

You can't miss this remarkable
building, with its twin towers
soaring above the cobbled
streets of Old Aberdeen. Inside,
you can admire two luminous
stained-glass windows which
portray St Machar, the
cathedral's sixth-century patron
saint, and the three bishops
who made it a great centre of
Christian piety and learning in
medieval times. William
Wallace's arm is said to be
buried in the cathedral wall.

King's College

abdn.ac.uk

King's College, AB24 3FX | 01224
272000 | Open daily 10–3.30

The Crown Tower is the iconic
landmark of the quadrangle of
buildings at the heart of the
medieval King's College
campus at the University of
Aberdeen. Below the tower,
King's College Chapel has a
superbly preserved medieval
interior, noted for painted
canvases that date from the
16th and 17th centuries.
The tombs of Bishop William
Elphinstone, who founded
King's College, and Hector
Boyce, the college's first
principal, are within the chapel.

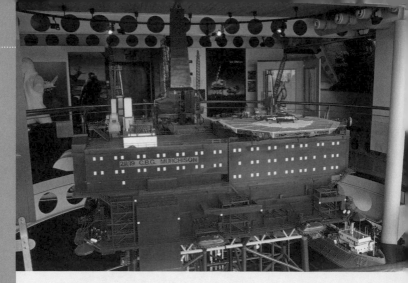

▲ Aberdeen Maritime Museum

VISIT THE MUSEUMS AND GALLERIES

King's Museum
abdn.ac.uk/museums
Old Aberdeen Town House, High Street, AB24 3EN | 01224 274330
Open Tue–Fri 1–4.30
This museum, housed in Aberdeen's Georgian Old Town House, is a showcase for exhibits from the University of Aberdeen's ethnographic collections. These include masks, weapons and costumes from Africa and the Pacific. Among the most impressive are the Nunalleq collection of wooden carvings from a 14th-century Yup'ik (Eskimo) village in Alaska.

Aberdeen Art Gallery
aagm.co.uk
School Hill, AB10 1FQ | 01224 523700 | Closed until mid-2018; some works on display at Aberdeen Maritime Museum (see right)
Aberdeen Art Gallery's collection includes works by 19th- and 20th-century painters such as James McBey (1883–1959) and by contemporary artists. It also includes prehistoric finds from archaeological sites in northeast Scotland, as well as Greece and Egypt.

Aberdeen Maritime Museum
aagm.co.uk
Shiprow, AB11 5BY | 01224 337700
Open Mon–Sat 10–5, Sun 12–3
Oil may have ousted fishing as Aberdeen's biggest earner, but you can still have a good look at the city's seafaring past at this interesting museum, where a modern glass-and-steel building adjoins Provost Ross's House, home of a 16th-century local dignitary. Inside, you'll find ship models, paintings and charts. There's also a collection devoted to the North Sea oil industry. Until Aberdeen Art Gallery reopens in 2018, the Maritime Museum will display some of the gallery's collection

of paintings by 19th- and 20th-century artists.

Tolbooth Museum

aagm.co.uk

Castle Street, AB10 1EX | 01224 621167 | Mon–Sat 10–5, Sun 12–3

The Maiden, a 17th-century guillotine used for public executions, is the gruesome centrepiece of this museum's collection of instruments of punishment and torture, along with displays on local history.

You can visit the grim jail cells dating from the 17th and 18th centuries, when the Tolbooth was the city's prison as well as its council meeting place and counting-house. The museum is in the Tolbooth's Wardhose tower, built between 1616 and 1629. Since then, it's been much altered, partly demolished and rebuilt several times.

Provost Skene's House

aagm.co.uk

45 Flourmill Lane, AB10 1AS

01224 641086

This grand medieval mansion is central Aberdeen's don't-miss visitor attraction. Its splendid painted ceilings and gracious rooms and galleries were commissioned by a wealthy 17th-century merchant, Matthew Lumsden. Later, it was the home of George Skene, the city's Lord Provost. Amazingly, it came close to being demolished in the 1930s, but was instead preserved and painstakingly restored. It's a real architectural gem.

CATCH A PERFORMANCE

His Majesty's Theatre Aberdeen

aberdeenperformingarts.com

Rosemount Viaduct, AB25 1GL

01224 641122

The opulent His Majesty's Theatre has been Aberdeen's main venue for shows, plays, musicals, dance, opera and pantomimes. Over the years it has hosted stars ranging from Noel Coward and Sir Alec Guinness to Sean Connery and Billy Connelly. Scottish Opera and Scottish Ballet often perform here.

The Lemon Tree

aberdeenperformingarts.com

5 West North Street, AB24 5AT

01224 641122

The Lemon Tree is Aberdeen's theatre for new, adventurous drama and for music, dance and comedy. It's also home to one of Scotland's biggest youth theatre companies.

Music Hall

aberdeenperformingarts.com

Union Street, AB10 1QS

01224 641122 | Closed until November 2017

Aberdeen's landmark Music Hall first opened its doors in 1822. In 2016, it closed for a £7 million renovation, and it is expected to reopen in November 2018, when you will once again be able to hear performances of Classical music by the Royal Scottish Orchestra and Scottish Chamber Orchestra in its grand auditorium. The reborn Music

Hall will also continue to host jazz, big band and rock and pop concerts.

WATCH A FILM
Belmont Filmhouse
belmontfilmhouse.com
49 Belmont Street, AB10 1JS
01224 343500
You can take in independent, foreign and classic films at this popular cinema in a historic building where movies have been shown for more than a century. Since 2014, it has been managed by the Centre for the Moving Image, which organises the Edinburgh International Film Festival and also manages Belmont's sibling, Edinburgh Filmhouse, in the capital.

Vue Aberdeen
myvue.com
10 Shiprow, AB11 5BW | 0345 308 4620 (calls cost 13p per minute plus your phone company's access charge)
This big cinema complex with seven huge screens and more than 1,500 seats shows all the latest blockbusters and films for all the family. There are discounts for teenagers and children and if you buy a cut-price family ticket all family members pay the child rate.

ENTERTAIN THE FAMILY
Aberdeen Science Centre
aberdeensciencecentre.org
The Tramsheds, 179 Constitution Street, AB24 5TU | 01224 640340
Open Mon–Fri 10–4, Sat–Sun 10–5
This hands-on science centre has more than 50 interactive exhibits that will keep kids entertained (and even educated) on a rainy day. Its newest attraction, added in 2015, is a full-dome planetarium.

Codona's Amusement Park
codonas.com
Beach Boulevard, AB24 5ED
01224 595910 | See website for opening times
Aberdeen's much-loved seaside funfair offers all sorts of thrills and spills, from slides to dodgems and roller-coaster rides. It's an all-weather attraction, with indoor activities including ten-pin bowling and video games.

GO FOR A SWIM
Beach Leisure Centre
sportaberdeen.co.uk
Sea Beach, AB24 5NR | 01224 507739 | Open daily
Aberdeen has a splendid beach, but the North Sea isn't exactly welcoming all year round. Fortunately, there are warmer alternatives for families. Beach Leisure Centre, overlooking the sea, has four flumes, rapids and wave pools, so it's far from tame. There's also a creche for younger family members.

LOOK FOR DOLPHINS
Clyde Cruises
clydecruises.com
Eurolink Pontoon, Commercial Quay, AB11 5NT | 01475 721281
Scheduled cruises. Call for departure times
The waters off Aberdeen are home to one of the largest schools of bottlenose dolphins in Britain. They often come

close inshore and you can even see them in the harbour or playing at the mouth of the River Dee. The best place to spot them from the shore is the Torry Battery, a one-time gun emplacement on the south bank of the Dee. It's a short drive from the city centre, and car parking is available. To get even closer to dolphins – as well as seals, other sea mammals, and seabirds such as gannets, guillemots and puffins – Clyde Cruises runs dolphin adventure cruises from Aberdeen Harbour.

WALK IN THE PARK
Duthie Park and David Welch Winter Gardens
aberdeencity.gov.uk
Duthie Park, Polmuir Road, AB11 7TH | 01224 585310 | Open May–Aug daily 8–7; Apr and Sep–Oct daily 8–5.30; Nov–Mar daily 8–4.30
Duthie Park is a pleasant place for a stroll most of the year, with play areas, sculptures, fountains and a boating pond.

Its all-weather attraction is the David Welch Winter Gardens, one of Europe's largest indoor gardens, where you can walk among cacti, tropical ferns and bamboos.

PLAY A ROUND
Auchmill Golf Course
auchmillgolfclub.co.uk
Bonnyview Road, West Heatheryfold, AB16 7FQ | 01224 714577 | Open daily all year
A young parkland course with fine views of Aberdeen and the surrounding area. Tree-lined fairways, open drainage ditches and tightly cut greens.

Deeside Golf Club
deesidegolfclub.com
Golf Road, Bieldside, AB15 9DL 01224 869457
Contact club for opening times
An interesting riverside course with several tree-lined fairways. A stream comes into play at nine of the 18 holes on the main course.

▼ Aberdeen Harbour

5 top wildlife cruises

Hazlehead Golf Course

aberdeencity.gov.uk
Hazlehead Avenue, AB15 8BD
01224 321830 | Open daily all year
Three picturesque courses for a true test of golfing skills, with gorse and woodlands being a hazard for any wayward shots.

Murcar Links Golf Club

murcarlinks.com
Bridge of Don, AB23 8BD | 01224 704354 | Open daily all year
Seaside links course with a prevailing southwest wind. Its main attraction is the challenge of playing round and between gorse, heather and sand dunes.

Royal Aberdeen Golf Club

royalaberdeengolf.com
Links Road, Balgownie, Bridge of Don, AB23 8AT | 01224 702571
Mon–Fri times vary, after 3.30pm weekends
A championship links course with undulating dunes. Windy, but with easy walking.

EAT AND DRINK

Fusion ◉

fusionbarbistro.com
10 North Silver Street, AB10 1RL
01224 652959
Blurring the line between bar and restaurant, Fusion's upstairs Gallery restaurant is a chic spot to see and be seen in with its lime green seats, wooden floors and stencilled white walls. The creative modern British menu suits the upbeat vibe.

Moonfish Cafe ◉

moonfishcafe.co.uk
9 Correction Wynd, AB10 1HP
01224 644166
Moonfish Cafe has been on the local foodie radar since 2004. It's a relaxed set-up, its pared-back looks enlivened by changing artworks and fish motifs on the large windows. There's plenty of sharp technique in the cooking. The gin list is worth a visit, too.

Old Blackfriars

oldblackfriars-aberdeen.co.uk
52 Castle Street, AB11 5BB
01224 581992
In Aberdeen's historic Castlegate, this traditional city-centre pub stands where a friary of Dominican monks, known as the Black Friars for the colour of their habits, once stood. Inside you'll find stunning stained glass, a good selection of real ales, and a large choice of malt whiskies. The pub is also renowned for good food, serving all the pub grub favourites plus more modern treats.

The Silver Darling ◉◉

thesilverdarling.co.uk
North Pier House, Pocra Quay,
AB11 5DQ | 01224 576229
The Silver Darling, which is
named after the Scottish
nickname for the herring, has
enjoyed a reputation as
Aberdeen's top restaurant since
1986. There's more competition
these days, but it continues to
stand out with superbly
imaginative seafood dishes.

▸ PLACES NEARBY

Aberdeenshire's Castles
see highlight panel overleaf

Stonehaven Open Air Pool

stonehavenopenairpool.co.uk
Queen Elizabeth Park, The Links,
AB39 2RD | 01569 763162 | Open
30 May–3 Jul and 18 Aug–9 Sep
Mon–Fri 1–7.30, Sat, Sun 10–6; 4
Jul–17 Aug Mon, Wed, Thu 10–7.30,
Tue, Fri 6.30am–7.30pm. Midnight
swim each Wed 10.30pm–midnight
You can swim outdoors in
subtropical warmth at the
Stonehaven Open Air Pool,
Britain's northernmost lido. The
Olympic-sized pool, 15 miles
south of central Aberdeen, is
heated to 29°C from the end
of May to September. On
Wednesday evenings you can
even go for a late-night dip, as
the pool opens until midnight.

The Creel Inn

thecreelinn.co.uk
Catterline, Stonehaven, AB39 2UL
01569 750254
It would be worth making the
short pilgrimage to Catterline,
south of Stonehaven, just for
the scenery. This tiny fishing
village, wedged into a rocky
cove among cliffs where puffins
and kittiwakes nest, is one of
the most picturesque spots and
has inspired well-known local
painters such as Joan Eardley.
The menu at the Creel Inn pub
and restaurant concentrates
on seafood, with offerings
including a different mussel
dish every day.

▾ David Welch Winter Gardens, Duthie Park

▶ Aberdeenshire's Castles

▶ Dunnottar Castle MAP REF 409 E4

dunnottarcastle.co.uk

Stonehaven, AB39 2TL | 01569 762173 | Open Apr–Sep daily 9–6; Oct–Mar daily 10–5 (or sunset if earlier). If bad weather, call to check castle is open

On the rugged coastline south of Aberdeen a great stack of rock projects into the stormy North Sea, topped by a jumble of buildings spanning several centuries. Joined to the land by a narrow, crumbling neck of rock, great cliffs protect this natural fortress on all sides, while a thick wall and a gatehouse defend its entrance.

Dunnottar is one of Scotland's most spectacular ruins, and has been chosen as a location for films including Franco Zeffirelli's *Hamlet* (1990), starring Mel Gibson, and most recently *Victor Frankenstein* (2015), starring James McAvoy and Daniel Radcliffe.

There's almost nothing left of the original 12th-century castle. The L-shaped tower house built in the 14th century dominates the rest of the castle, its 50-foot walls still in good repair, although it is roofless. More buildings were raised in the 16th century, forming a handsome quadrangular courtyard.

The Honours of Scotland (Scotland's crown jewels) were spirited out of Dunnottar by Royalist sympathisers before the castle fell to the Roundheads, and hidden in nearby Kinneff Church – where they remained until Charles II was restored to the throne in 1660. In 1685, Charles's successor, James VII and II, had 167 Presbyterian Covenanters imprisoned in the cramped, cold chamber still known as the Whigs' Vault, where many of them died of cold and hunger.

▶ Fyvie Castle MAP REF 409 E2

nts.org.uk

Near Turriff, AB53 8JS | 01651 891266 | Castle open Apr–May and Sep Sat–Wed 11–5.15; Jun–Aug daily 11–5.15; Oct Wed–Sat 11–5. Grounds open daily 9–dusk

This magnificent mansion, set in a landscaped park in the valley of the River Ythan, has a cream frontage 150 feet long, dominated by the massive gatehouse. It is said that five of Scotland's great families – the Prestons, Meldrums, Setons, Gordons and Leiths – each contributed a tower as they owned the castle in turn. The oldest part dates from the 13th century and incorporates the architectural highlight: a spiral staircase of broad, shallow stone steps known as a wheel-stair, a 16th-century addition. The opulent 20th-century interiors include portraits by Raeburn, Romney, Gainsborough and Hoppner.

▲ Dunnottar Castle

▶ **Huntly Castle** MAP REF 409 D2

historic-scotland.gov.uk

Huntly, AB54 4SH | 01466 793191 | Open Oct daily 10–4; Nov–Mar Sat–Wed 10–4

This once-magnificent castle is now decayed and crumbling, but it has nonetheless been described as one of the noblest baronial ruins in Scotland. Approaching the castle along an avenue of trees, you are faced with the vast five-storeyed facade, with its inscriptions, fine oriel windows and handsome carvings. A former Catholic stronghold, Huntly Castle remains an elegant and imposing ruin.

There have been three castles at Huntly. In the 12th century a wooden structure was raised by the Normans – Robert the Bruce stayed here in 1307 – but this building was burned down. In the early 15th century, the Gordons built a second castle, of which only the foundations remain. However, in the 1450s the 4th Earl of Huntly began what he called his new werk and this was the basis of the palatial castle that can be seen today. Although it was intended to be an elegant residence, defence was not totally abandoned in favour of comfort. The walls are thick, and there are gun ports and iron gates for added protection.

In 1594 the 5th Earl revolted against King James VI, who then attacked Huntly with gunpowder. Royal favour was lost and won quickly, however; three years later the castle was restored to the Earl, and building work resumed. In 1640 Huntly was occupied by the Covenanters, a religious and political group.

▶ Tolquhon Castle MAP REF 409 E2

historic-scotland.gov.uk

Tarves, AB41 7LP | 01651 851286 | Open daily Apr–Sep

It doesn't take much to imagine how splendid this now-ruined castle, 15 miles north of Aberdeen, must have looked in its heyday. The auld tour, or Preston's Tower, was raised in the early 15th century, probably by John Preston. It was built of granite, with thick walls, and had small rooms, which would probably have been ill-lit and cramped for the people living in them.

When the seventh Lord of Tolquhon, the cultured William Forbes, inherited the castle in the late 16th century, he set about turning it into the fine palatial building that can be visited today. Forbes used Preston's Tower as one of the corners of his new castle, and extended the building to make a four-sided structure around a large courtyard. It was entered through a gatehouse which, although it appears formidable with its gun loops and round towers, had thin walls and would not have withstood a serious attack.

An impressive array of buildings lines all four sides of the fine cobbled courtyard. To the east are the kitchens and an unpleasant pit prison, while the main house is to the south. This building contained the hall and the laird's personal chambers, along with additional bed chambers and a gallery.

Forbes' renovations did not stop with his fine new house. The hall and his private chamber looked out over a formal garden, and though this has long since disappeared, the remains of a dovecote and recesses for bees have been discovered in the walls.

▶ **Aberfeldy** MAP REF 407 E5

The quaint stone-built town of Aberfeldy, on the banks of the River Tay in Perthshire, has two claims to fame. In 1733, the multi-skilled William Adam, known as Scotland's Universal Architect, designed the town's handsome hump-backed bridge. It was part of a network of almost 250 miles of military roads and bridges planned by General George Wade. Wade was commander-in-chief of the army in Scotland from 1724 to 1740, and his roads probably played a bigger part than muskets, bayonets and cannon in pacifying the Highlands. Most of the region's main roads follow the routes he laid out, and most of his bridges – including this one, with its four obelisks and five graceful spans – still stand. Next to it, there's a monument to the soldiers of the Black Watch, so-called because of its dark green tartan. Officially the 43rd Regiment of Foot, this Perthshire regiment held its first muster here in 1740. Now part of the Royal Regiment of Scotland, you can find out more about its history at the Black Watch Regimental Museum in Perth (see page 328), not far from Aberfeldy.

While Wade put Aberfeldy on his military road map, Robert Burns helped to make it a popular Perthshire tourism destination when he penned *The Birks o' Aberfeldie* in 1787. Burns was inspired by the beauty of the birch ('birk' in Scots) woods nearby. Signs in Aberfeldy point the way to walking trails that lead to the birchwoods and waterfalls celebrated by Burns. You may even see native red squirrels. To the west, at Weem, is the 16th-century stronghold of Castle Menzies, a restored Z-plan tower house.

Loch Tay lies 5 miles to the west of Aberfeldy, with the picturesque village of Kenmore at its eastern end. The town has a great water sports centre where you can hire motor cruisers and sailing boats. At the Kenmore Hotel, which claims to be the oldest inn in Scotland, you can see a poem graffitied beside the fireplace by Burns when he visited in the 1780s – now carefully covered by glass. The River Tay rises on the slopes of Ben Lawers, Perthshire's highest summit. It flows into the west end of Loch Tay before flowing out at Kenmore. Just below the village, it's joined by its main tributary, the River Lyon. Near the mouth of the glen is the trim and tidy village of Fortingall, where you'll find one of Perthshire's more unusual sights. The huge yew tree that spreads gnarled limbs over Fortingall's churchyard may be 3,000 years old – which would make it the oldest living thing in Europe. Archaeologists have found traces of a Roman legionary camp just outside Fortingall, lending some faint credence to an old local tale that the village was the birthplace of Pontius Pilate.

GO BACK IN TIME
Scottish Crannog Centre
crannog.co.uk

Kenmore, PH15 2HY | 01887 830583 | Open daily Apr–Oct 10–5.30

Just outside Kenmore, on the south shore of Loch Tay, you'll see a round wooden building with a thatched roof, perched on timber pilings above the waters of the loch. This is the Scottish Crannog Centre, a re-creation of an Iron Age lake dwelling, based on the remains of 18 similar crannogs that have been found on the bottom of the loch. The cold, peaty waters have preserved wood, plant and food remains and even scraps of cloth, revealing much about the way of life of the people who built these houses. You can watch demonstrations of Iron Age skills, and try your hand at weaving and other crafts, or, weather permitting, hire a replica dugout canoe.

GET ON THE WATER
Loch Tay Boating Centre
loch-tay.co.uk

Pier Road, Kenmore, PH15 2HG 01887 830279 | Open mid-Mar to mid-Oct

The usually calm waters of Loch Tay beckon anyone who loves messing about in boats. The Loch Tay Boating Centre hires out motorboats, sleep-aboard cabin cruisers, kayaks and canoes, as well as mountain bikes for those who want to explore the shores onland.

◀ The Wade Bridge over the River Tay

Riverside, Aberfeldy, PH15 2EB
01887 829202 | Advance reservations essential. Call beforehand to meet at an agreed location

You can take to the Perthshire hills to learn all about winter survival skills and experience a range of other outdoor activities such as orienteering, gorge walking, climbing and abseiling in and around Aberfeldy with specialist mountain company Beyond Adventure.

WATCH FOR WILDLIFE
Highland Safaris
highlandsafaris.net
Aberfeldy, PH15 2JQ | 01887 820071 | Reservations essential. Call in advance

Explore Aberfeldy's high mountain hinterland on a four-wheel-drive tour. You can expect to spot wildlife including grouse, mountain hares and red deer. On a good day you may even see golden eagles. Binoculars and telescopes are provided.

PLAY A ROUND
Aberfeldy Golf Club
aberfeldy-golfclub.co.uk
Taybridge Road, PH15 2BH | 01887 820535 | Open daily all year

Founded in 1895, this flat, parkland course is situated by the River Tay near the famous Wade Bridge and Black Watch Monument, and enjoys some splendid scenery. The layout will test the keen golfer.

Splash
rafting.co.uk
Dunkeld Road, PH15 2AQ | 01887 829706 | Advance reservations essential. Minimum age 8 for rafting, older for other activities

There are more turbulent stretches of water on the River Tay, downstream from Aberfeldy. Splash offers a range of white-water rafting and kayaking adventures, including lots of activities for families such as trips on duckies, a cross between a raft and a kayak. On land, you can try canyoning, abseiling and high-ropes courses.

GET ACTIVE
Beyond Adventure
beyondadventure.co.uk

EAT AND DRINK

The Watermill

aberfeldywatermill.com
Mill Street, Aberfeldy, PH15 2BG
01887 822896

This converted watermill includes a bookshop, music shop and art gallery, all infused with the aroma of fresh coffee. Enjoy a fruit smoothie on the terrace, or a speciality coffee with your cake – all the products are locally sourced or organic where possible. The old waterwheel is still used to power the lighting.

Kenmore Hotel

kenmorehotel.com
The Square, PH15 2NU
01887 830205

You can feed the ducks while enjoying an alfresco lunch beside the Tay at this charming hotel, restaurant and bar, which claims to be the oldest inn in Scotland. Or you can dine in the hotel's Grill Room, which has an old-school, classic menu that accentuates big steaks, gourmet burgers and dishes like Isle of Mull scallops and slow-cooked shoulder of lamb.

▶ Applecross MAP REF 405 E2

It's hard to believe that tiny Applecross, set on its lovely curve of pink sand, was once the hub of a community of 3,000 people who raised their black cattle in the green, fertile valley around this quiet village. They were cleared from their land when the Mackenzie lairds sold it off for a sporting estate. Only the faint outlines of their deserted cottages remain.

Until the last century this peninsula was almost as isolated as Knoydart (see page 279). Rough tracks linked the old settlements along the coast down to Toscaig, and access up from the south was via the breathtakingly spectacular Bealach-na-Ba pass, or Pass of the Cattle, which rises to some 2,050 feet (625m).

▼ Applecross

The settlements on this remote west-coast peninsula only became fully accessible by road in the 1970s. This winding single-track road is the slow, scenic route between Shieldaig (see page 361) and Kishorn, via the Bealach-na-Ba pass to the south, and the southern shore of Loch Torridon to the north. (Bealach-na-Ba is not suitable for vehicles towing caravans/trailers.) In between, acid moors and hummocks stretch to mountains inland, while the remains of deserted villages along the coast overlook Raasay and Skye (see page 254).

EAT AND DRINK
Applecross Inn
applecross.uk.com/inn
Applecross, IV54 8LR
01520 744262
This village inn serves great seafood straight from Applecross Bay. Crabs, king scallops, oysters, lobsters and prawns (langoustines) are prominent. To add variety, you'll find local games, curries and a decent selection of vegetarian dishes.

▶ Arbroath MAP REF 409 D6

Arbroath is a pleasant harbour town that's famous for two things. Here, in 1320, most of Scotland's earls and barons put their names to the Declaration of Arbroath, a defining act of defiance that still resonates in Scotland today. It was drafted by the Abbot of Arbroath, a man who had a way with words:

'It is not for glory, nor riches, nor honours that we are fighting, but for freedom – for that alone, which no honest man gives up but with life itself.'

It's also the home of the Arbroath Smokie – a haddock smoked on the bone over slow-burning beech wood. The reek from harbourside smokehouses wafts over the city centre.

▼ Arbroath Harbour

TAKE IN SOME HISTORY
Arbroath Abbey
historic-scotland.gov.uk
Abbey Street, DD11 1EG | 01241
878756 | Open Apr–Sep daily
9.30–5.30; Oct–Mar daily 10–4
The red sandstone ruins of
Arbroath Abbey, founded by
King William the Lion in 1178,
are still evocative of its former
grandeur. Until the Reformation
of the 16th century, this was
one of the wealthiest religious
foundations in Scotland. A new
exhibition tells the story of the
Stone of Destiny, the slab on
which Scottish kings were
crowned at Scone until it was
carried off to Westminster by
Edward I of England, the
commonly called Hammer of
the Scots, in the 13th century. In
1951, a group of Scottish
nationalists stole the Stone
from its place in Westminster
Abbey and smuggled it back to
Scotland, where, as a symbolic
gesture, they left it at Arbroath
Abbey. It was taken back to
Westminster, but returned to
Scotland in 1996, in response to
rising nationalist sentiment. You
can now see it at Edinburgh
Castle (see page 167), alongside
the Honours of Scotland.

VISIT THE MUSEUM
Arbroath Signal Tower Museum
angus.gov.uk
Ladyloan, DD11 1PU | 01241
435329 | Open Mon–Sat 10–5
You can see for miles out to sea
from the Arbroath Signal Tower
Museum. On the horizon is the
pencil-thin silhouette of the
world's oldest offshore
lighthouse, 11 miles from
land. The picturesque signal
tower, built in 1811, was the
shore base for the Bell Rock
Lighthouse. Although no longer
manned, the lighthouse was
an engineering marvel in its
day. It perches on a reef that
is under 16 feet or more of
water at high tide. Inside the
signal tower, the museum
tells the story of the
lighthouse's construction.

TAKE A TRAIN RIDE
Kerr's Miniature Railway
kerrsminiaturerailway.co.uk
West Links Park, Queen's Drive, D11
1QD | 01241 879249 | Open 28
Mar–27 Sep Sat, Sun 11–4 (also local
school holidays daily 11–4)
The first steam trains ran on
the small-gauge track at Kerr's
Miniature Railway on the
outskirts of Arbroath in 1935.
Despite ups and downs, it's still
going strong during summer
holidays. It's one of Arbroath's
best-loved family attractions,
and claims to be Scotland's
oldest miniature railway.

PLAY A ROUND
Arbroath Golf Course
arbroathgolfcourse.co.uk
Elliot, DD11 2PE | 01241 875837
Open daily all year
A typical links layout,
predominately flat, with the
prevailing southwesterly wind
facing for the first seven holes,
making a big difference to how
certain holes play. When the
wind is in a northerly direction
the back nine is very tough.

Letham Grange Golf Club
lethamgrangegolfclub.co.uk
Colliston, DD11 4RL | 01241
890373 | Open daily all year
Often referred to as the Augusta
of Scotland, the Old Course
provides championship standards in spectacular
surroundings with attractive
lochs and burns. The Glens
Course is less arduous and
shorter, although it's still
challenging, using many natural
features of the estate.

▶ Ardnamurchan Peninsula MAP REF 405 D5

Make your way to Ardnamurchan Point to stand on the
westernmost point on the British mainland. The Ardnamurchan
Peninsula is a narrow finger of land. At its very tip, there's a
lighthouse from which you can look out towards Mull, Coll and
Tiree (see page 382).

The whole peninsula, with its rocky hills and desolate
moorland, gale-blown trees and pretty heather-capped
promontories, has an end-of-the-world feeling. The main road
mostly hugs the northern shore of Loch Sunart, rich in birdlife,
and you can take a minor road to Ardnamurchan's north coast
as the main road passes round Beinn nan Losgann, or continue
to the little crofting village of Kilchoan, where a ferry goes to
Tobermory on Mull. The 13th-century Mingary Castle, built on
its sheer rock to guard the entrance to Loch Sunart, is the
place where King James IV finally accepted the submission of
the Lord of the Isles in 1495; Hanoverian troops built barracks
inside it 350 years later.

▼ Portuairk Beach, Ardnamurchan Peninsula

Morvern, across Loch Sunart, is a rugged land with gentler green glens. Lochaline, a popular yachting haven, is reached either by road along Glen Gleann, or by ferry from the Isle of Mull. Visit the remains of Ardtornish Castle, east of the village. Fiunary, along the Sound of Mull, was the birthplace of George MacLeod, founder of the Iona Community. It is also the source of a haunting lament, the song 'Farewell to Fiunary'. Caisteal nan Con is a small fortress guarding the Sound of Mull. The road ends some 4 miles beyond, near Drimnin, with views towards Tobermory.

The rocky coastline of remote northern Ardnamurchan has successive bays reaching east from Sanna Bay past Port Ban to the enclosed sandy reaches of Kentra Bay. Former fishing villages, such as Portuairk, Sanna, Fascadale, Kilmory and Ockle, punctuate the shoreline, backed by bare rocky hills such as Meall nan Con at 1,434 feet (437m) and Beinn Bhreac at 1,171 feet (357m). Ardnamurchan's rocks are of volcanic origin, and headlands like Rubha Carrach, Ockle Point and Rubha Aird Druimnich impart a stern ruggedness to the scene.

GO TO THE VISITOR CENTRES

Ardnamurchan Lighthouse Visitor Centre

ardnamurchanlighthouse.com
Ardnamurchan Point, Kilchoan, PH36 4LN | 01972 510210
Open daily Apr–Oct 10–5

You can climb to the top of a historic lighthouse tower here, at the farthest tip of the Ardnamurchan Peninsula. There are displays that explain the history of Scotland's lighthouses and their importance to navigation in the 19th century. It's also a good place for spotting seals, otters and even minke whales and basking sharks, if you're lucky.

Ardnamurchan Natural History Centre

ardnamurchannaturalhistorycentre.co.uk
Glenmore, Acharacle, PH36 4JG
0197 250 0209

Open Apr–Oct Sun–Fri 8.30–5

To explore the natural history and geology of this wild and remote part of Scotland, visit the Ardnamurchan Natural History Centre. This privately run visitor centre offers you an introduction to the landscapes and wildlife of Ardnamurchan. Its biggest asset, especially for families, is its 'Living Building' – a rough structure designed to attract birds and mammals that are content to live side by side with humans, such as bats, swallows and house martins.

MAKE A PHOTO STOP

Castle Tioram

Eilean Tioram | Castle not accessible to visitors

You can walk to the tiny, rocky island of Eilean Tioram at low tide for a look at one of the most picturesque and romantic ruins in western Scotland. Castle

Tioram (pronounced Cheerum) is very dilapidated, and going inside is inadvisable because of the risk of falling masonry. It was built in the 13th century by the Clanranald family, who lived here until about 1685. When they moved to a more comfortable home in South Uist, they left the castle to crumble.

During the 1745 Jacobite rising, rebel clansmen stored guns, swords and pistols at Castle Tioram, but by the mid-18th century it was a complete ruin.

After the final defeat of the Jacobite cause at Culloden (see page 117) in 1746, Bonnie Prince Charlie (Charles Edward Stuart) escaped to France aboard the French frigate *L'Heureux*. At nearby Borrodale, a small cairn on the shore of Loch nan Uam marks the spot where he embarked.

Plans to restore Castle Tioram as a private home are being considered by Historic Environment Scotland, following proposals by the current, private, owner.

▶ Ardvreck Castle MAP REF 412 B3

26 miles northeast of Ullapool | Open daily 24 hours

There's not much left of this small 16th-century tower house. Perched on a rocky peninsula that juts out into Loch Assynt, it was once a stronghold of the MacLeod lairds of Assynt. The Royalist commander James Graham, Marquess of Montrose, was imprisoned here in 1650 before being handed over to Cromwell's Parliamentarians and summarily executed.

This was a simple structure – rectangular, with a staircase turret on the southeast corner. The basement had three chambers with vaulted roofs. One of the chambers is little more than a passage, but the gun loops pierced in its outer wall suggest that it could have been used to defend the castle. Although it is now a total ruin, it stands amid some of northwest Scotland's most dramatic loch and mountain scenery.

▼ Ardvreck Castle

▸ Arran & Bute

▸ Isle of Arran MAP REF 401 D4

Often described as Scotland in miniature, this scenically attractive island, caught between the Ayrshire coast and the Kintyre Peninsula, has been a popular holiday resort for generations of Clydesiders, with opportunities for outdoor activities such as walking, golf and horse-riding around the island. Brodick is the biggest town, and home to the island's most popular attraction, the red sandstone Brodick Castle. Scattered round the 56-mile coastline are villages catering for visitors, including Lamlash. Ferries to Arran make the hour-long crossing from Ardrossan (year-round) to Brodick, and Claonaig, in Kintyre, to Lochranza (summer).

The Highland Boundary Fault runs through the island, and while the mountain of Goatfell (2,867 feet/874m) dominates the skyline to the north, the south is much more level. It was in the hills of Glen Cloy that Robert the Bruce mustered his troops before heading to the Scottish mainland to try once more to oust the English and claim the throne. According to legend, he was roused from despair and inspired to fight once more – and succeed this time – by watching a spider, spinning its web and succeeding only on the seventh attempt to attach its thread.

These granite northern peaks are home to red deer, unique vegetation and raptors, while the narrow coastal plain has typically Hebridean raised beaches, on which tiny clachan (hamlet) settlements have developed, many now in ruins after the infamous Highland Clearances of the 19th century.

▾ Drumadoon Sill at Drumadoon Point, Isle of Arran

TOUR THE TOWN
Brodick

Brodick is set on a wide bay, a resort in a truly stunning setting. It is Arran's main hub, with shops and places to stay.

TAKE IN SOME HISTORY
Brodick Castle

nts.org.uk
KA27 8HY | 01770 302202 | Castle open Apr, Oct daily 11–3; May–Sep daily 11–4; Walled garden open daily 10–4.30; Country park open daily 9.30am–sunset

The red sandstone Brodick Castle, once the seat of the Dukes of Hamilton, is Arran's biggest attraction. Most of the present buildings date from the 19th century, when the castle was hugely expanded, but it has a history going back more than 1,600 years and its grounds form the only island country park in Britain. The present-day, largely Victorian castle, with its extensive collection of porcelain and silver, 19th-century sporting pictures and trophies, was started by the 11th Duke in 1844.

The gardens contain three national collections of rhododendrons, some of which are in flower almost all year round. There are almost 10 miles of marked trails to explore in the park.

The walled garden, which dates from 1710, has been restored in the Victorian style, while the woodland garden, with its world-famous display of rhododendrons, was first planted in 1923.

▲ Brodick Castle

Arran Heritage Museum

arranmuseum.co.uk
Rosaburn, KA27 8DP | 01770 302636 | Open Apr–Oct daily 10.30–4.30

It's the social history that will catch your imagination here, with restored 19th-century interiors, complete with furniture, bedding and knick-knacks. You can also learn about the Clearances, and Arran's role in World War II.

GO BACK IN TIME
Machrie Moor

Arran has a multitude of prehistoric sites but the most famous impressive are found on Machrie Moor. The monuments are part of a complex ritual landscape dating from the Neolithic era and into the early Bronze Age (in the region of 3500–1500 BC). There are six stone circles, all remarkably close together and all different, and you'll find standing stones, cairns and cists as well. There is also evidence of hut circles.

Circle 2 is the most dramatic, its remaining three stones stretching impressively high (the tallest is 18 feet). The setting, surrounded by mountains, is very beautiful.

GO WALKING
Isle of Arran Coastal Way
coastalway.co.uk

This long-distance, waymarked path runs for 65 miles all the way round the island, and you can walk as much or as little of it as you choose, enjoying some wonderful views.

TAKE A DRINK
Isle of Arran Brewery Company
arranbrewery.com
Cladach, Brodick, KA27 8DE | 01770 302353 | Open Apr–mid-Sep Mon–Sat 10–5, Sun 12.30–4.30; mid-Sep–Mar Mon–Sat 10.30–4.30

If beer is your tipple, come and see it being brewed at Cladach, near Brodick. The entry fee includes a taste of the beer.

Isle of Arran Distillers
arranwhisky.com
Distillery and Visitor Centre, Lochranza, KA27 8HJ | 01770 830264 | Open Mar–Oct daily 10–5.30; Nov–Feb daily 10–4

The distillery in the north of the island produces Arran's own single malt whisky. Take the fascinating guided tour, enjoy the exhibition and don't forget to buy a gift or bottle of Arran whisky in the shop. Tours include a taste of the whisky.

GO RIDING
Cairnhouse Riding Centre
cairnhousestables.com
Blackwaterfoot, KA27 8EU
01770 860466 | Open all year

There are horses and treks for all ages and abilities at this friendly stables – a two-hour

ride may include a woodland or moorland trek on tracks and private road, followed by a canter along a sandy beach.

PLAY A ROUND
Machrie Bay Golf Course
machriebay.com
Machrie Bay, KA27 8DZ
01770 840329 | Open daily all year

This Edwardian nine-hole seaside course, with its beautiful setting on the west coast of the island, was designed at the start of the 20th century by William Fernie. Its mix of links and moorland, level fairways and the length of the holes make it an ideal golfing destination for families.

▸ Isle of Bute MAP REF 401 D3

Bute, standing at the end of the Firth of Clyde, has been the holiday playground for generations of Glaswegians, most of whom arrive at Rothesay on the ferry from Wemyss Bay. The island largely consists of green and fertile hills, with superb views across the narrow Kyles of Bute to the mainland and to mountainous Arran.

Bute's main town is Rothesay, whose palm-tree-lined promenade curves round a wide bay, backed by some fine examples of Victorian buildings. Just off the east-coast road is one of Bute's hidden gems, the extraordinary Victorian Gothic Mount Stuart House, surrounded by extensive gardens that lead down to the shore. To escape the crowds, head for the sparsely populated west coast, which has the island's best beaches.

▾ Port Bannatyne, Isle of Bute

TAKE IN SOME HISTORY
Rothesay Castle
historic-scotland.gov.uk
PA20 0DA | 01700 502691 | Open
Apr–Sep daily 9.30–5.30; Oct–Mar
Mon–Wed, Sat, Sun 10–4
This uniquely circular castle
dates back to the 13th century,
when it was built to defend the
island against the Norwegians.
Its hereditary owners were the
royal dynasty of the Stuarts,
from whom the current Duke of
Rothesay, Prince Charles (the
Duke of Rothesay is the Scottish
royal title for the heir apparent),
is descended. The four towers
and massive gatehouse were
added later, and the castle was
restored in the 19th century.

Mount Stuart
mountstuart.com
PA20 9LR | 01700 503877 | Open
May–Sep Mon, Tue, Thu guided tours
hourly 11.30–3.30, Wed, Fri–Sun
12–4 open access
Five miles south of Rothesay,
the Gothic mansion of Mount
Stuart, seat of the Marquess of
Bute, overlooks the Firth of
Clyde. Built in the 1870s, it's a
monument to both Victorian
taste and craftsmanship. The
showpiece is the Marble Hall,
with its stained-glass windows
and vaulted ceiling, but be sure
to take in the decorative details
everywhere – animals and
plants, books, manuscripts and
heraldic symbols. Apart from
the building itself, Mount Stuart
houses the Bute Collection,
one of the foremost private
collections of art and artwork
in Britain. Paintings include
Italian, Dutch and Flemish
old masters and portraits,
furniture, silver work, porcelain
and a huge library and archive.

GO ROUND THE GARDENS
Ardencraig Garden
gardens-of-argyll.co.uk
Ardencraig Lane, PA20 9EZ | 01700
504644 | Open May–Sep Mon–Fri
9–4, Sat, Sun 1–4
These riotously planted
gardens were originally laid
out as a private garden for
Ardencraig House. They are
now run as a learning and show
garden by the local council and
feature extensive municipal
bedding – a rare sight today
– and a series of Victorian
hothouses. Don't miss the
exotic birds in the aviaries.

PLAY A ROUND
Port Bannatyne Golf Club
portbannatynegolf.co.uk
Port Bannatyne, PA20 0PH
01700 504544 | Open daily all year
This seaside hill course is
almost unique in having 13
holes, with the first five being
played again before a separate
18th. Difficult fourth (par three).

Rothesay Golf Club
rothesaygolfclub.co.uk
Canada Hill, PA20 9HN
01700 503554 | Open daily all year
This scenic island course was
designed by James Braid and
Ben Sayers. The 18 holes are
fairly hilly, with views of the
Firth of Clyde, Rothesay Bay
or the Kyles of Bute. Winds
make the two par five holes
extremely challenging.

▶ **Assynt Coigach** MAP REF 412 A3

The Assynt and Coigach National Scenic Area (NSA), embracing the peaks of Suilven, Stac Pollaidh and Quinag, sprawls across 348 sq miles of wild and rocky terrain, from Eddrachillis Bay in the north to two-pronged Loch Broom in the south, on the remote northwest coast of Scotland. This is a landscape of ancient, metamorphic rock that has been worn by ice, scattered with chains of serpentine lochs and hundreds of smaller, jewel-like *lochans*, and punctuated by the dramatic sandstone-cored mountains.

Strangely shaped Suilven, at 2,398 feet (731m), seems to soar above this almost otherworldly landscape. It has a long summit ridge with three separate tops: the spire-like Meall Bheag (so-called Little Hill, 2,001 feet/610m) and Meall Mheadhonach (Middle Hill, 2,372 feet/723m) at the eastern end, and at the western end, the rounded tower of Caisteal Liath

▼ Suilven

(Grey Castle, 2,365 feet/721m), all surrounded by beetling cliffs. Even at its highest point, Suilven doesn't even qualify as a Munro – but, as anyone who has made it to the top will tell you, it's one of the toughest non-technical ascents in Scotland, with a near-vertical scramble up a rock-strewn gully, and then a hair-raising walk on a knife-edge ridge to the highest point, where you're rewarded by one of Scotland's greatest views.

Other peaks in the NSA, which contains some of the wildest and most rugged scenery in Scotland, include Ben More Coigach at 2,139 feet (652m), Ben More Assynt at 3,274 feet (998m), Cul Mor at 2,785 feet (849m) and Quinag at 2,654 feet (809m). Reached by a restored pathway leading from its foot is Stac Pollaidh – often anglicised to Stack Polly – one of the most popular peaks for walkers. Its bristling, shattered sandstone crest rises to 2,008 feet (612m) above Loch Lurgainn.

Ben More Assynt's vast bulk dominates the Inchnadamph Forest on the eastern boundary of the NSA. Rising to the east of the Moine Thrust, an earth movement that took place in the region of 400 million years ago and that shaped so much of this part of the Highlands, it looks quite different to the mountains to its west.

The deeply indented coastline of the region is no less dramatic than the interior. Eddrachillis Bay has a scattering of islands, which catch the constantly changing western light, while the long narrow sea loch of Loch a' Chairn Bhain and its tributaries of Loch Glendhu and Loch Glencoul are surrounded by towering peaks and bare, rugged hills. In the south, off Achiltibuie, the delightfully named Summer Isles – the largest of which are Tanera Beg and Tanera Mor – form a broken seaboard in sharp contrast to the solid mass of Ben More Coigach to the east. The small fishing community of Lochinver is the most popular base for exploring the wild, rocky coast of Assynt. From here, you can take boat trips to the many islands that dot Enard Bay, make an assault on peaks like Suilven and Stac Pollaidh, go fishing, and look for the white-tailed eagles that have recently been reintroduced.

6 top gardens

- ▶ Attadale Gardens
  page 85
- ▶ Crarae Garden
  page 247
- ▶ David Welch Winter Gardens
  page 63
- ▶ Drumlanrig Castle Gardens
  and Country Park
  page 127
- ▶ Inverewe Garden
  page 248
- ▶ Royal Botanic Garden
  Edinburgh
  page 176

▶ Attadale Gardens MAP REF 406 B2

attadalegardens.com

Strathcarron, IV54 8YX | 01520 722603 | Open Apr–Oct Mon–Sat 10–5.30

You can walk for miles through magnificent coastal scenery without ever leaving this splendid estate in northwest Scotland. The Attadale estate stretches from the south shore of Loch Carron inland to Loch Monar, 15 miles to the east. Attadale Gardens gradually evolved around a Highland mansion, built in 1755 in a spot sheltered by the hill from the prevailing northwest wind. The gardens' architect was Captain William Schroder, son of a German baron and banker, who acquired the estate in 1910. He laid out the gardens, creating hill paths through his trees and rhododendrons and an elaborate rose garden with pergolas, topiary birds and numerous small beds.

When Ian Macpherson bought the estate in 1952, the trees had taken over the garden. The flowerbeds were overgrown with grass and bracken and the woodland criss-crossed with rabbit wire. Devastating storms in 1984 and again in 1989 destroyed thousands of trees, but revealed old paths and steps that had been hidden for years. Ewen and Nicky Macpherson, who inherited the estate in 1984, seized the opportunity to remodel the gardens on lines that reflected their own passions.

The result is gardens that have been likened to a painting by Monet. The old mill stream has been widened into a series of ponds and small waterfalls linked by elegant bridges. Its banks have been planted in almost subtropical profusion with large-leaved plants, bamboos and grasses. Steps and paths lead to the old Rhododendron Walk, at the end of which a viewing platform has been built with splendid views of the house and down Loch Carron to the Cuillins of Skye. The Macphersons' sculpture collection can be seen throughout the gardens.

The Sunken Garden, surrounded by dry-stone walls and hedges, planned to give colour all through the year, has been planted to resemble a Persian carpet, each quadrant repeating in reverse the pattern of its neighbour. An avenue of Japanese birch trees leads to a gateway into the Japanese Garden where lichened rocks and raked gravel imitate the Mystic Islands of the West and the River of Life.

Old quarries behind the house provide ideal shady, damp conditions for the Old Rhododendron Dell and the Fern Garden, where tender ferns are housed in a geodesic dome made of triangular panels like a miniature Eden Project dome.

After the controlled chaos of the woodland, the Kitchen Garden is a neat-freak's delight, with its immaculately kept raised beds, box and yew hedges and paved herb garden.

▶ Ayr MAP REF 398 B3

Ayr's top attractions are its seaside, its golf courses and its associations with Scotland's national bard. The town has a long and eventful history. It began as the settlement serving a Norman castle erected in what was then border country – Galloway, to the south, was disputed territory until becoming part of Scotland in the 13th century. In 1315 Robert the Bruce held a parliament in the Church of St John here: a later tower from the church is still standing, as is the Auld Brig, a stone bridge built in 1432. The town was once Scotland's leading west-coast harbour, until it was overtaken by Glasgow (see page 206) during the Industrial Revolution.

Cromwell made Ayr his centre of government for much of Scotland and replaced the Norman castle with a vast fortress, of which only the outer walls now survive. By the 18th century Ayr was trading across the Atlantic, and in the 19th century it became a major industrial port. At the same time, as sea bathing became fashionable, it blossomed as a smart resort for the local gentry, whose town residences have been transformed into hotels and boarding houses.

Many visitors to Ayr are pilgrims on the trail of Robert Burns, heading for the Robert Burns Birthplace Museum in Alloway, a couple of miles south of town. The museum's grounds connect places in the actual landscape where he grew up – the cottage where he was born in 1759, the ruin of the 17th-century Auld Kirk where he was baptised and the Brig o' Doon he commemorated in poetry – with a modern museum presenting the poet's life and times.

Just as many visitors, however, are drawn to Ayr by two iconic golf courses. Troon and Turnberry are on the bucket list of any really keen golfer, and are within easy reach of the town.

**VISIT THE MUSEUMS
AND GALLERIES**

**Robert Burns
Birthplace Museum**

burnsmuseum.org.uk
Murdoch's Lone, KA7 4PQ | 01292
443700 | Museum open daily 10–5;
Birthplace Cottage open daily 11–5

Robert 'Rabbie' Burns (1759–96) is Scotland's most famous poet and songwriter. You can walk in his footsteps at the Robert Burns Birthplace Museum in Alloway. Opened in 2010, celebration of the Scots language is built into its very fabric, with words and phrases carved into the stonework. Light and airy inside, the museum houses a collection of some 5,000 artefacts and manuscripts, including the original drafts of 'Scots Wha Hae' and 'Tam O'Shanter'. The main display is in four sections, reflecting on the bard's identity, sources of inspiration, his fame both in his lifetime and beyond, and interpreting and accessing his poetry today. In the last section you can hear Scots' voices bringing Burns' work to life in performance.

Burns' birthday (25 January) is celebrated worldwide as Burns Day. The humble Alloway cottage where he was born in 1759 was built by his father, William Burnes, in 1757. It was a simple building of clay and thatch, with whitewashed walls. Robert was the first of seven children, and as the two-room cottage was also where the family's livestock lived, it was a very crowded place. Burns lived here for the first 18 years of his life.

Burns wasn't the best behaved of poets. His loves and illegitimate children were the stuff of legend – he married Jean Armour in 1788, but only after many other romantic liaisons. Yet his love of life, and celebration of humanity with all its foibles, was extraordinary, and is why his poetry is still enjoyed all over the world today.

Alloway's village centre now forms the focus of the Burns National Heritage Park, where the Statue House brings to life Burn's famous comic ballad *Tam O'Shanter*, whose drunken ride home leads him to spy on a party of witches. The Burns cult sprang up quickly after he died, with public subscription funding the first stones of the Burns Monument at the far end of the park, in 1820, styled as a Greek temple. A venue for events, it offers views over Burns' beloved Alloway from its roof.

Rozelle House and Maclaurin Art Gallery

themaclaurin.org.uk

181 Monument Road, KA7 4NQ

01292 443708 | Open Mon–Sat 10 5, Sun 12–5

There's more Burnsiana at Rozelle House and Maclaurin Art Gallery, where you can admire a collection of more than 50 paintings by artist Alexander Goudie that tell in pictures the story of Burns's tipsy protagonist Tam O'Shanter and his narrow escape from a coven of witches. The 19th-century building also houses the Ayrshire Yeomanry Museum, which tells the exciting story of the local regiment. Formed in 1793 as the Earl of Carrick's Own, the regiment served in the Boer War and during World War I and II. It's now part of the Queen's Own Yeomanry.

▸ Burns Monument

ENTERTAIN THE FAMILY
Heads of Ayr Farm Park
headsofayrfarmpark.co.uk
Dunure Road, KA7 4LD | 01292
441210 | Open Mar–Oct daily 10–5
You can take the family to
Heads of Ayr Farm Park to meet
farm animals and more exotic
creatures, go quad riding, play
on bumper boats and enjoy a
giant indoor soft play area with
slides. The farm also has a
shop and snack bar.

Pirate Pete's
piratepetes.co.uk
The Esplanade, KA7 1EQ | 01292
265300 | Open daily 9.30–6
Toddlers and under-12s can
play in an outdoor fun park,
enjoy laser games and play a
round of mini-golf at Pirate
Pete's, a fun family attraction in
Ayr's charming old seafront
pavilion building.

GO TO THE THEATRE
Gaiety Theatre
thegaiety.co.uk
Carrick Street, KA7 1NU | 01292
288235 | Contact theatre for times
of performances
For an evening of comedy, jazz,
drama, pop or ballet you can
head for the busy Gaiety
Theatre in the heart of Ayr. This
lively venue, which was
renovated in 2010, hosts a wide
variety of touring productions
throughout the year.

PLAY A ROUND
Two of Scotland's great golf
courses, the Trump Turnberry
and Royal Troon, lie within easy
reach of Ayr.

Royal Troon Golf Club
royaltroon.co.uk
Craigend Road, KA10 6EP | 01292
311555 | Open Mon, Tue, Thu all year

Troon was founded in 1878 with just five holes on links land. It became Royal Troon in 1978 on its 100th anniversary. Royal Troon's reputation is based on its combination of rough and sandy hills, bunkers and a severity of finish that has diminished the championship hopes of many. The British Open Championship has been played at Troon nine times; in 2016 it was won for the first time by a Swede, Henrik Stenson. It has the shortest hole of any course hosting the Open.

It is recommended that you apply to the course in advance for full visitor information.

Trump Turnberry
trumpturnberry.com
Maidens Road, Turnberry, KA26 9LT
01655 331000 | Open daily all year
Turnberry is one of the finest golf destinations, where some of the most remarkable moments in Open history have taken place. The legendary Ailsa Course is complemented by the King Robert the Bruce Course, while the nine-hole Arran Course, created by Colin Montgomerie and Donald Steel, has similar challenges such as tight tee shots, pot bunkers and thick Scottish rough. There are few vistas to match the first tee here.

Belleisle Golf Course
ayrbelleislegolfclub.com
Belleisle Park, KA7 4DU | 01292 441258 | Open daily all year

This parkland course has beautiful sea views and offers first-class conditions.

EAT AND DRINK
Enterkine Country House ◉◉
enterkine.com
Annbank, KA6 5AL | 01292 520580
Menus at Enterkine Country House emphasise Ayrshire produce, but you'll also find items such as fillet of Orkney beef with foie gras, parsnips, chanterelles and spinach. The kitchen adds a contemporary spin, and well-conceived main courses manage to balance traditional ideas with the more modern.

Fairfield House Hotel ◉
fairfieldhotel.co.uk
12 Fairfield Road, KA7 2AS
01292 267461
Confident modern Scottish cooking is the kitchen's forte here, with pedigree Scottish produce used as the bedrock of an appealing menu of big flavours.

Lochgreen House Hotel ◉◉◉
lochgreenhouse.com
Monktonhill Road, Southwood, KA10 7EN | 01292 313343
You don't need to have any interest in the action on the venerable links at Royal Troon to eat here, as the main draw is what is going on in the Kintyre Restaurant, where head chefs Andrew and Bill Costley like to wave the flag for Scottish produce, which they put to good

use in their thoroughly accomplished modern cooking, delivering punchy flavours and clever texture contrasts.

MacCallums of Troon ⦿

maccallumsoftroon.co.uk
The Harbour, KA10 6DH
01293 319339

This is a seafood restaurant in a glorious harbourside setting within a converted pump house. They even have a fish and chip joint next door called the Wee Hurrie. It is simple stuff, cooked with care.

The Marine Hotel

themarinetroon.co.uk
Crosbie Road, KA10 6HE
01293 314444

This imposing coastal hotel is home to the Truin restaurant, which is part of a Glasgow-based group with three restaurants in the city. The dining room occupies a couple of spaces including a conservatory area, with views over Royal Troon golf course, and the atmosphere is on the refined side without being stuffy. There's a fishy theme at play in the decor, and while the menu does deal in the fruits of the sea, there are plenty of meaty options up for grabs.

Trump Turnberry ⦿⦿

trumpturnberry.com
Maidens Road, KA26 9LT
01655 331000

The 1906 Restaurant of this luxurious golf-centric hotel is named after the year it opened. There's a lot more than just food to take in: the Turnberry sits on the glorious Ayrshire coast, with sweeping views across greens and fairways to the hump of Ailsa Craig. For those not bitten by the golfing bug, there's pampering in a top-notch spa, and the Grand Tea Lounge is resurrected for genteel afternoon teas. For the full-on dining experience, however, it's back to 1906, where the setting resembles a giant wedding cake, and the kitchen puts a luxury modern spin on Escoffier's classics.

▷ **PLACES NEARBY**

Electric Brae

A719, between Ayr and Dunure
You'll find a famous optical illusion at Electric Brae, where the lie of the land either side of the road makes stationary cars appear to be travelling slowly uphill. Until you get your head around it, it's an unsettling phenomenon.

Culzean Castle and Country Park (see page 120) is just to the south.

▼ Beach at Ayr

▶ Banffshire Coast MAP REF 409 D1

Fertile farmland gives way to wild and rugged coastline along the Banffshire coast, on the south shore of the Moray Firth. You may spot dolphins, otters and minke whales from these windswept headlands.

Small fishing ports, rocky coves and sandy bays are scattered along this stretch of coastline. There are picturesque villages – Portsoy, which hosts an annual festival of traditional boats every June, Findochty (say Finechty) and Portknockie. There are also workaday fishing ports, but even these have plus points. Unlovely Macduff, for example, has an interesting marine aquarium, while Fraserburgh, where the Firth opens into the North Sea, has a brilliant museum dedicated to Scotland's lighthouses. On the outskirts of Banff itself, you can visit the northernmost cultural outpost of the Scottish National Gallery at Duff House.

Although it's so far north, the Banffshire coast has a surprisingly mellow microclimate. The North Atlantic Drift, a warm current mostly known by its more familiar name, the Gulf Stream, takes the chilly edge off the waters of the Firth, and the coast is sheltered from prevailing southwesterly winds by the massif of the Grampian Highlands. As a result, this is one of the driest spots in Britain, and much of the year strolling along sandy strands is a pleasure.

You'll find one of the region's best beaches at Cullen, a fishing village where prettily painted houses stand around a charming 19th-century harbour designed by Thomas Telford. Cullen lends its name to the region's iconic seafood soup, which is celebrated every year in November at the Cullen Skink World Championships, where cooks compete to be acclaimed for the best traditional Cullen Skink made from fresh, local produce.

TAKE IN SOME HISTORY

Duff House
historicenvironment.scot
Banff, AB45 3SX | 01261 818181
Open Apr–Oct daily 11–5; Nov–Mar Thu–Sun 11–4

Tucked away in an apparently quiet corner of Banff, Duff House provides the perfect, glittering backdrop to a wealth of paintings including portraits by the Scottish painters Raeburn and Ramsay, and paintings of the Italian, Dutch and German schools of art. The house itself is a grand mansion designed by architect William Adam for the First Earl of Fife. It was started in 1735, but unfortunately the Earl's pride in his new house was seriously dented when a crack appeared in the structure, and he never lived there. Look for El Greco's *St Jerome in Penitence*.

▲ Macduff Marine Aquarium

VISIT THE MUSEUM
The Museum of Scottish Lighthouses
lighthousemuseum.org.uk
Kinnaird Head, Stevenson Rd, AB43 9DU | 01346 511022 | Open daily 10–5. Tours at 11, then hourly 1–4
The highlight of a visit here is a 45-minute guided tour to Kinnaird Head Lighthouse, the first lighthouse built on mainland Scotland. There is also a purpose-built museum, housing an amazing collection of glass lenses, lighting technology and social history artefacts covering the lives of the men (and their families) who guarded Scotland's coastline for more than 200 years. There are audio-visual displays and interactive exhibits.

MEET THE SEALIFE
Macduff Marine Aquarium
macduff-aquarium.org.uk
11 High Shore, Macduff, AB44 1SL
01261 833369 | Open daily 10–5
You don't have to put on a wetsuit and plunge into the North Sea to discover the sealife of the Moray Firth. Instead, you can visit the spectacular Macduff Marine Aquarium. The centrepiece here is a deep-sea tank, open to the heavens and complete with wave machine, offering realistic conditions for the inhabitants of a living kelp reef. Clear sides enable you to see plants and creatures inhabiting the different levels in this naturalistic setting, from sea anemones and conger eels to

commercial species of fish such as cod and whiting. Three times a week you can watch dive shows through the giant window in the theatre, when divers feed the fish. There are about 100 species of fish and invertebrate to see here.

EXPLORE BY BIKE
You can set off from Cullen to explore the Banffshire coast on foot or by bike along stretches of the Moray Coast Trail and the Moray Coast Cycle Route, looking out for local landmarks like Bow Fiddle Rock at Portknockie, a natural rock arch shaped by thousands of years of wave action.

Moray Coast Trail
morayways.org.uk
The waymarked Moray Coast Trail stretches about 50 miles between Cullen and Forres (see page 197).

Moray Coastal Cycle Route
morayways.org.uk
This well-signposted cycle trail from Burghead to Cullen leads you along rugged, unspoiled coastline and past sheltered coves on well-surfaced and waymarked paths. For those exploring by car, there's free parking in all coastal villages.

5 top golf resorts

▶ **Gleneagles**, page 115
▶ **Royal Aberdeen**, page 64
▶ **St Andrews**, page 347
▶ **Troon**, page 88
▶ **Turnberry**, page 89

PLAY A ROUND
Duff House Royal Golf Club
duffhouseroyal.com
The Barnyards, AB45 3SX | 01261 812062 | Contact club for details
A flat parkland course, bounded by woodlands and the River Deveron. Well bunkered and renowned for its large, two-tier greens.

Buckpool Golf Club
buckpoolgolf.com
Barhill Road, Buckpool, AB56 1DU
01542 832236 | Open daily all year
Links course with a superlative view over the Moray Firth.

Strathlene Buckie Golf Club
strathlenegolfclub.co.uk
Portessie, AB56 2DJ | 01542 831798
Open daily all year
Raised seaside links course with magnificent views. A special feature of the course is approach shots to raised greens (holes four, five, six and thirteen).

▶ Barra
see **Western Isles**, page 394

▶ Benbecula
see **Western Isles**, page 392

▶ Ben Nevis MAP REF 406 C5

It's a tough slog to the top of Britain's highest summit. The easiest route to the top of Ben Nevis is the Pony Track, constructed in 1883 in order to get building materials to the summit for the construction of the Scottish Meteorological Society's observatory. Teams of weather-watchers lived for weeks at a time in the tiny building, making observations of rainfall, temperature, wind speed and hours of sunshine. Before the observatory closed in 1904, climatologists recorded averages of 756 sunny hours a year – just two hours a day – and average mean temperatures of just 0.33°C. The summit was under more than 6.5 feet of snow for up to eight months a year; the deepest snow (nearly 12 feet) was recorded in April 1883.

You can expect the 4,400-foot (1,341m) ascent to the top to take about four hours from the Glen Nevis Visitor Centre, near Achintee in Glen Nevis. The trail ascends gradually to the broad saddle that contains Lochan Meall an t-Suidhe (the Halfway Lochan). A steep series of zig-zags then takes you up the broad west face of the Ben, where you eventually reach the relatively flat summit and the remains of the observatory. The northern side of Ben Nevis is dominated by Coire Leis. Described by the distinguished mountaineer W H Murray as 'the most splendid of all Scottish corries', Coire Leis is flanked by Carn Mor Dearg,

▲ Ben Nevis

Aonach Beag and the tremendous northern buttresses of Ben Nevis. Here stands the Charles Inglis Clark (CIC) hut, a refuge for generations of climbers on the Ben, built in 1929 as a memorial to the mountaineer who died during World War I. It is now maintained by the Scottish Mountaineering Council.

▶ **PLACES NEARBY**

Glen Nevis, which runs south and then east beneath the massive southern shoulder of Ben Nevis, climbs from pastoral lower reaches, through glorious oak, alder, pine and birch woodlands that rise above the fast-flowing Water of Nevis. It was used as a location for two tartan blockbusters – *Rob Roy*, with Liam Neeson in the title role, and *Braveheart*, starring Mel Gibson as William Wallace. The upper glen is a place of peaceful, almost alpine, meadows, enhanced by the backdrop of the tremendous 350-foot leap of the Steall Waterfall as it crashes down the lower cliffs of Sgurr a' Mhaim. To reach the waterfall, you must cross a vertiginous, three-stranded wire bridge over the rushing stream. The glen is bounded to the south by the smooth-sided ridge of the Mamore Range, which includes 14 peaks above 3,000 feet. South of that is the fjord-like trench of Loch Leven, with the former industrial village of Kinlochleven at its head. Kinlochleven was one of the first towns in Britain to have street lighting, via hydroelectric power from the Blackwater Dam.

Glen Nevis Visitor Centre

ben-nevis.com
Glen Nevis, PH33 6PF | 01397 705922 | Open daily summer 8.30–6, spring and autumn 9–5, winter 9–3

Before setting off to ascend Ben Nevis, visit the Glen Nevis Visitor Centre, where friendly, experienced staff – most of whom have made the ascent many times – will advise you on weather conditions, clothing and equipment. You will also find information on walking and the history and geology of the local area.

Nevis Range

nevisrange.co.uk
Torlundy, PH33 6SQ | 01397 705825

You can see the summit of Ben Nevis and enjoy a panoramic view of surrounding peaks and lochs the easy way by taking a Nevis Range cable-car gondola from Torlundy to the upper slopes of Aonach Mòr, lowest of the two mountains next to Ben Nevis. On the way, there are great views of the Ben and of its closest neighbour, Carn Mor Dearg. From the cable-car terminus, you can walk on easy trails to scenic viewpoints. There's a restaurant and bar where you can enjoy a meal or a drink while waiting for your gondola ride home. Visit in ski season to enjoy winter sports on Scotland's highest ski slopes, which include green, blue and red pistes.

▶ **Biggar** MAP REF 402 B4

Equidistant from Glasgow and Edinburgh, the bustling Borders town of Biggar has retained its character, with a broad main street and wide central square surrounded by shops and tea rooms. The town's heritage is preserved in an interesting museum, well signed from the centre.

VISIT THE MUSEUM
Biggar and Upper Clydesdale Museum

biggarmuseumtrust.co.uk
156 High Street, ML12 6DH | 01899 221050 | Open Mar–Oct Tue–Sat 10–5, Sun 1–5; Nov–mid-Feb Tue–Sat 10–4, Sun 1–4; mid-Dec–Feb Sat 10–4

Visit the new Biggar and Upper Clydesdale Museum, which opened in 2015, to see a collection that includes flint blades and arrowheads, Celtic and medieval brooches, and other exhibits spanning more than 10,000 years of local history, from the Stone Age to the early 20th century. There's a separate collection devoted to the persecution of the devoutly Presbyterian Covenanters, who refused to accept the 1680s established church.

ENTERTAIN THE FAMILY
Biggar Puppet Theatre
purvespuppets.com
Puppet Tree House, Broughton Road,
ML12 6HA | 01899 220631 | Box
office open Tue–Sat 10–8. Check
website or call for dates and times
of performances
Families shouldn't miss a visit
to Biggar Puppet Theatre,
home of a world-renowned marionette troupe. Purves
Puppets has been going for
more than 40 years, and tours
the world. Catch them at the
puppet theatre in Biggar
(clearly signposted from the
main road), which has weekly
shows for all the family and
backstage tours. The whole
attraction is designed to
delight children.

▶ Black Isle MAP REF 412 C5

Neither black nor an island, the Black Isle is the broad and
fertile peninsula that lies opposite Inverness on the north
shore of the Moray Firth and is bounded by the waters of
the Cromarty and Beauly firths. At its northeast point is the
attractive harbour town of Cromarty, which was largely rebuilt
in the late 18th century. The land rises to the wooded ridge of
Ardmeanach in the centre of the Black Isle, while wild sea cliffs
tip down to low-lying ground in the west. From the Kessock
Bridge, 3,465 feet long, which connects Inverness and the
Black Isle, car passengers have great views of the Moray and
Beauly firths. Drivers, however, are best advised to keep their
eyes on the road. The bridge is sometimes closed to vehicles
due to high winds, a fact that you should keep in mind when
touring by car in this part of Scotland.

TAKE IN SOME HISTORY
Fortrose Cathedral
Fortrose looks out across the
Moray Firth. The cathedral was
completed in the 15th century,
but was then unroofed in the
16th century, before Oliver
Cromwell plundered its great
sandstone blocks to build the
fortifications in Inverness. On
the other side of the spit (once a
popular spot for witch-burning,
but now dedicated to golf) lies
Rosemarkie, notable for the
magnificent Pictish carvings
displayed at the Groam House
Museum, on High Street.

▼ Kessock Bridge

VISIT THE MUSEUMS
Courthouse Museum
cromarty-courthouse.org.uk
Church Street, IV11 8XA | 01381
600418 | Open daily Easter to
mid-Oct 12–4
Computer-controlled, animated
figures tell the story of
Cromarty and the Black Isle at
the Courthouse Museum.

Hugh Miller's Birthplace Cottage and Museum
nts.org.uk
Church Street, IV11 8XA | 01381
600245 | Open mid-Apr–Sep daily
12–5; first 2 weeks Oct Tue, Thu,
Fri 12–5
The renowned 19th-century
geologist, author and social
reformer Hugh Miller (1802–56)
was born in Cromarty. You will
find a statue of him in the town,
and his birthplace is now a
museum dedicated to his life
and works.

GET OUTDOORS
The shores of the Black Isle are
a heaven for birders and wildlife
watchers. The tidal mudflats of
the Beauly Firth attract large
flocks of waterfowl, including
greylag and pink-footed geese
that can be seen grazing in
nearby fields, and a variety of
sea ducks, including goldeneye
and scoter. Red kites, first
reintroduced into Scotland in
1989 at the nearby Royal
Society for the Protection of
Birds (RSPB) Tollie Red Kites
(see page 374), are now a
common sight. Rare visitors,
like the American wideon, can
sometimes be spotted.

MEET THE SEALIFE
Moray Dolphins
moraydolphins.co.uk
The Moray Firth has become
Britain's foremost dolphin-
watching destination. Up to 100
bottle-nose dolphins make their
home here and this useful
website is full of practical
information about how and
where to see them – all without
leaving land. Both Chanonry
Point and the village of North
Kessock are excellent spots;
head for either as the tide rises
and the dolphins come in to
feed. You'll also have a good
chance of spotting the whiskery
heads of local seals.

EcoVentures
EcoVentures.co.uk
Victoria Place, Cromarty, IV11 8YE
01381 600323 | Call or see website
for scheduled departures
For an even more exciting sea
mammal adventure, head
further out into the Moray
Firth with specialist cetacean
spotters like Cromarty-based
EcoVentures. In the wider,
deeper stretches of the firth,
you may see not just dolphins
and harbour porpoises but
rarer visitors such as pilot
whales and basking sharks.

MAKE A WISH
Munlochy Clootie Well
scotland.forestry.gov.uk
Munlochy, IV8 8PE | Open daily
24 hours
At the Clootie Well at Munlochy,
trees around a deep natural
spring are festooned with
ragged strips of cloth or plastic.

Local tradition claims that if you tie a rag to a handy branch, make the sign of the cross and take a sip from the well, your wish will be granted.

Before the Reformation, the well's patron saint was apparently St Boniface – although why a seventh-century Anglo-Saxon monk should be associated with this weird pre-Christian superstition is anybody's guess.

EAT AND DRINK
The Factor's House 🌸
thefactorshouse.com
Denny Road, Cromarty, IV11 8YT
01381 600394
This attractive red sandstone house with just three guest rooms stands in alluring grounds on a coastal inlet. A daily changing four-course dinner menu, including Scottish cheeses, is the offering; there is real personality to the dishes.

▶ **PLACES NEARBY**
Bonar Bridge
The River Oykel flows southeast through the Kyle of Sutherland to the Dornoch Firth, widening into a broad estuary as it reaches the North Sea. Where the loch narrows, you'll find the village of Bonar.

The first bridge was built in cast iron by Thomas Telford to replace the old ferry after a disaster in 1809, which killed more than 100 people. It was swept away in a flood in 1892 and replaced by a steel-and-granite bridge, which in its turn was superseded by an elegant steel construction in 1973. This was the only crossing of the Dornoch Firth until a suspension bridge was opened downstream in 1991, saving a distance of more than 20 miles on the east-coast route to Scotland's far north.

An iron foundry was established at Bonar in the 14th century, using ore from the west coast and fuelled by wood from the nearby forests. When James IV of Scotland passed through on a pilgrimage in about 1500 it is said that he noticed the deforestation of the area and ordered it to be planted with oak trees; oak woods remain to the village's east.

▶ **Blair Castle** MAP REF 407 E5
blair-castle.co.uk
Blair Atholl, PH18 5TL | 01796 481207 | Open Easter–Oct daily 9.30–5.30
This white-harled and turreted mansion, set against forest 8 miles north of Pitlochry (see page 333), seems the archetypal romantic Scottish castle. It's been the ancestral home of the Murray and Stewart Dukes and Earls of Atholl for more than 700 years, and boasts its own private army, the Atholl Highlanders, thanks to a favour granted by Queen Victoria in 1845. They're the only private army in Britain and are recruited largely from the estate, acting as a private bodyguard.

▲ Blair Castle

The medieval castle occupied a strategic position on the main route to Inverness, so it's no surprise that in 1652 Cromwell's army seized it. The castle also played an important role in the Jacobite uprisings of 1715 and 1745, when the Murray family's loyalties were tragically divided. In more peaceful times, the castle was recast as a Georgian mansion by the second Duke. The railway arrived in 1863, and the seventh Duke inherited in 1864, taking the name Stewart-Murray. He at once embarked on a grand building scheme, turning the Georgian mansion back into a romantic castle in the best Scottish tradition. Crow-stepped gables and blue-slate-roofed pepperpot towers were fully restored and Cumming's Tower was rebuilt to its original height. The entrance hall was added along with the magnificent ballroom, which is still popular for Highland balls and grand dinners.

There's lots to see in the castle, from portraits and rich furnishings to an original copy of the National Covenant and the small tartan-clad tower room where Bonnie Prince Charlie slept in 1745. Look for Raeburn's portrait of the legendary fiddler Neil Gow (1727–1807), and Gow's own fiddle, in the ballroom. The Treasure Room at the end is stuffed with Jacobite relics, jewellery and intriguing personal items. Leave time to explore the mature gardens and grounds, including Diana's Grove, with conifers up to 188 feet tall.

The nearest village to Blair Castle is Blair Atholl, named for the dukes whose castle dominates it.

▶ Boat of Garten MAP REF 408 B3

Boat of Garten is an attractive little Victorian village on the west bank of the River Spey, between Aviemore and Grantown, set in the north of the Cairngorms National Park (see page 105). It gets its rather unusual name from the ferry that once operated here, which was replaced by a more convenient bridge in 1898. It is a key stop on the now preserved and restored Strathspey Steam Railway. The town also has a challenging golf course, described by some in the golf fraternity as a miniature version of Gleneagles.

GET OUTDOORS
**RSPB Loch Garten
Osprey Centre**
rspb.org.uk
Open daily Apr–Aug 10–5
Two miles to the east of Boat of Garten lie the still waters of Loch Garten, set within the Abernethy Forest, where ospreys have nested since 1959. At the Loch Garten Osprey Centre, overlooking the nesting site, you can watch the activities of the birds in intriguing close up via a video-link. There are walking trails all through the woods around the loch. Abernethy Forest, a National Nature Reserve, is the biggest Scots pine forest remaining in Britain and home to other birds found only in Scotland's northern woodlands, such as crested tits, crossbills and capercaillies, as well as a range of other wildlife.

TAKE A TRAIN RIDE
Hop on a Strathspey Steam Railway train at Boat of Garten to steam between Aviemore (see page 110) and the little country station at Broomhill.

PLAY A ROUND
Boat of Garten Golf Club
boatgolf.com
Boat of Garten, PH24 3BQ
01479 831282 | Open daily all year
Designed by James Braid (1870–1950), this is a challenging course. It is set amid stunning scenery, cutting through beautiful moorland and birch forest, maximising the natural landscape.

ENTERTAIN THE FAMILY
Landmark Forest Adventures
landmarkpark.co.uk
Carrbridge, PH23 3AG0
0800 731 3446 | Open daily 10–5,
Jul, Aug 10–7
To the north of Aviemore, at Carrbridge, the Landmark Forest Adventure Park has displays on local history and wildlife. There's a treetop walk with the chance to feed red squirrels, as well as adventure playgrounds, a maze and water slides.

▶ Bute
see **Arran & Bute,** page 81

▶ Caerlaverock Castle MAP REF 399 E5

historicenvironment.scot

Glencaple, DG1 4RU | 01387 770244 | Open Easter–Sep daily 9.30–5.30;
Oct–Mar daily 10–4

The spectacular wreck of Caerlaverock Castle, nine miles south of
Dumfries, is one of Scotland's most impressive and unusual castle
ruins. Its name means 'rock of the skylark', and indeed you may
hear larks singing in the sky high above if you visit in summer. The
castle was the seat of the Maxwell family, wardens of the Scottish
West March and Earls of Nithsdale.

Unlike most Scottish castles, Caerlaverock still has a water-
filled moat, which makes it all the more picturesque. It was once
close to the shores of the Firth, but the coastline has shifted over
the centuries, and it's now well inland. The remains of three huge
round towers mark out the corners of this ruined, triangular castle
of pink sandstone. The castle dates from the 13th century, and saw
plenty of action before extensive rebuilding in the 15th century.

Caerlaverock changed hands several times when Edward I
invaded Scotland. He laid siege to it in 1300, and the story of the
siege is told in *The Song of Caerlaverock*, composed by Edward's
herald. It's one of the most complete surviving documents of its
time, and name-checks all 87 of the knights who accompanied the
so-called Hammer of the Scots on this campaign. You can read a
translation in the small visitor centre next to the castle. The ballad
makes much of Caerlaverock's formidable defences, but the
garrison numbered just 60 men, who surrendered to Edward after a

siege of only two days. Edward hanged a few of their leaders from the castle walls and freed the rest, who promptly joined the English.

Caerlaverock was besieged four more times during its eventful history. Often, if the Scots took a castle but were unable to hold it, they would destroy it so that the English could not use it. This was Caerlaverock's fate in 1312.

It was rebuilt in the 15th century, following the previous design, although gun ports were added, and the gatehouse strengthened to withstand cannon fire. In the centre of the castle courtyard stands the attractive Nithsdale Lodging – a 17th-century residence built by Robert Maxwell, the First Earl of Nithsdale. The facade is embellished with ornate Renaissance stone carvings.

In 1640, during the Civil War, Caerlaverock was besieged yet again, taken and partly destroyed by Protestant Covenanters. It was never re-occupied.

▶ PLACES NEARBY

Caerlaverock Wildfowl and Wetlands Trust Centre

wwt.org.uk

East Park Farm, DG1 4RS | 01387 770200 | Open daily 10–5

This vast expanse of reedbeds, channels and tidal mudflats is arguably at its best if you visit in autumn or spring, when vast flocks of migrant waterfowl darken its skies their way to and from their summer breeding grounds in the Arctic. Tens of thousands of barnacle geese descend on the Solway Firth in winter, along with whooper swans and dozens of other species. For keen birders, there are hides and towers scattered all over the reserve. You can also watch swans, ducks and geese up close through the windows of the new Sir Peter Scott Observatory, or use web cams to watch nesting barn owls and ospreys. In summer, you can wander along miles of nature trails or join a free, guided wildlife safari.

Nith Estuary

The estuary of the River Nith is dominated by the granite cone of Criffel. This 1,867-foot (569m) hill is a prominent feature on the horizon. The neat little village of New Abbey lies at its foot and grew as a service town for Sweetheart Abbey.

Sweetheart Abbey

historicenvironment.scot

DG2 8BU | 01387 850397 | Open Oct daily 10–4; Nov–Mar Sat–Wed 10–4

Sweetheart Abbey is a romantic name, and the picturesque ruins tell a sad tale of devotion. The Cistercian abbey was founded in 1273 by Devorgilla, Lady of Galloway and wife of John Balliol, an Anglo-Norman baron. He was 18 and she only 13 when they married, but it may have been a love match in the end. After he died in 1268 she carried his heart in a casket with her for the next 20 years.

In 1290, Devorgilla and her husband's heart were buried in

front of the high altar of the abbey church. You can still see her stone sarcophagus, bearing her headless effigy. It was defaced during the iconoclastic years of the Protestant Reformation, when the abbey was partly destroyed. Left to crumble – and occasionally used by local landowners as a handy source of building stone – the abbey was rescued from total demolition in 1779.

New Abbey Corn Mill

historicenvironment.scot
Open Oct daily 10–4; Nov–Mar Sat–Wed 10–4

Some of the stones pillaged from Sweetheart Abbey may have gone into the foundations of New Abbey Corn Mill.

It's amazing to realise that this 18th-century watermill was in use within living memory – the last miller retired in 1947. It's a superbly well-preserved piece of agro-industrial architecture, with its complex array of wooden machinery, driven by wooden belts that lead power from a massive waterwheel to its weighty grindstones. Built in 1792 for the local Stewart lairds of Shambellie House, it was cutting-edge technology in its day, and a prime example of rural free-market capitalism in action – advances in techniques meant local farmers were producing far more grain than the older mill on the site could grind.

A video shows how the mill worked, and you can buy a variety of oatmeal products in the mill shop.

▶ Cairngorms National Park

MAP REF 408 C3

The Cairngorms National Park is Britain's quintessential pocket wilderness. It contains the largest area of sub-Arctic landscape in the UK, and it's home to rare alpine flora and mammal and bird species, including golden eagles, red deer, osprey, capercaillie, ptarmigan and even free-roaming reindeer. Yet it's easily accessible. The Angus Glens (see page 278), on its southern fringe, are less than an hour's drive from Dundee (see page 135), while on its eastern edge the park is similarly close to Aberdeen (see page 57).

Britain's biggest national park covers 1,467 sq miles and embraces the UK's highest mountain massif. The landscape of heather moorland, rocky uplands and gentler glens has been shaped by Ice Age glaciation. Its horizons are dominated by the peaks of Ben Macdhui (4,295 feet/1,309m), Braeriach (4,249 feet/1,295m), Cairn Toul (4,242 feet/1,293m) and Cairn Gorm (4,085 feet/1,245m).

Between them runs the ancient north–south pass of the Lairig Ghru, and around the northwest edge the settlements of Speyside and the resort of Aviemore. The centre of the national park is made up of the high granite plateaus of the Cairngorm mountains, riven by steep-sided glens and deep corries, creating, above the 1,970 feet (600m) contour line, an environment that is unique in Britain. The lofty central plateau represents the closest we come to arctic conditions in Britain. Patches of snow linger almost year round in some north-facing corries.

▼ Ben Macdhui from Glen Lui

About half the area of the park has been cleared of trees over the centuries, and is now open heather moorland, managed for grouse shooting. Around the margins, ancient areas of native woodland survive; the original forests have been felled and replanted for their timber many times. The park takes in two great river valleys, the Spey and the Dee, and it is along these that most of its small population of about 16,000 people live and work. Their numbers are swelled by up to 500,000 visitors every year.

There's an extensive network of paths in the glens and forests around the Cairngorms, from starting points such as Nethy Bridge, Rothiemurchus, Aviemore – the premier town of the Cairngorms – Glenmore, Grantown-on-Spey, Tomintoul, Ballater, Braemar and glens Tanar, Doll and Feshie. More experience is needed to tackle the heights such as Ben Macdhui (4,295 feet/1,309m), Cairn Gorm (4,085 feet/1,245m) and Cairn Toul (4,242 feet/1,293m). There are plenty of great opportunities for cycling, fishing and golf, and water sports are focused on Loch Insh and Loch Morlich. There are ski centres at Cairngorm, the Lecht and Glenshee, and a funicular railway runs to the summit of Cairn Gorm.

Many of the higher valleys contain icy lochs or lochans, including Britain's highest lake, Loch Etchachan, at 3,025 feet (922m). This lies in the shadow of Ben Macdhui, the highest mountain in the range and the second-highest mountain in Britain after Ben Nevis. Five of Scotland's nine 4,000 feet (1,219m) summits dominate the range: Ben Macdhui, Braeriach, Cairn Gorm, Cairn Toul and Sgor an Lochain Uaine.

▼ Braeriach and Loch Einich

A vast, horseshoe-shaped plateau sweeps round from Ben Macdhui to Cairn Gorm, the principal summit in view from Aviemore and the Spey Valley, and the mountain (meaning blue hill) that has given its name to the whole range. Ben Macdhui's encircling ridges shelter two of Britain's most spectacular and remote mountain lakes, Loch Etchachan and Loch Avon.

Ringed by lovely beaches of fine white and golden sands, Loch Avon (or A'an) is 1.5 miles long and up to 1,000 feet wide. It is watched over by the famous Shelter Stone, a house-sized fallen boulder. The Sticil, or Shelter Stone Crag, at the head of the loch has been used by generations of hillwalkers as a refuge from the biting Cairngorm wind, rain and snow.

The other 4,000 feet (1,219m) tops of the Cairngorms lie to the west of the Lairig Ghru. Braeriach, the third-highest mountain in Britain, is the northernmost, while a glorious ridge sweeps south to the beautiful cones of Sgor an Lochain Uaine, also known as the Angel's Peak, and Cairn Toul. Cairn Toul's shapely southern outlier, the wickedly named Devil's Point, has the simple shelter of the Corrour bothy at its foot. The literal meaning of the mountain's Gaelic name, Bod an Deamhain, is the Devil's penis.

The Braeriach plateau ends abruptly in the west by the deep, glacial chasm of Glen Einich, containing beautiful Loch Einich at its head. To the south of Glen Einich is a remote plateau known as the Moine Mhor (or great moss). The third group of Cairngorm summits lies to the east of the Derry Burn and is dominated by tor-topped Beinn a'Bhuird at 3,927 feet (1,197m) and Ben Avon at 3,842 feet (1,171m).

▼ Cairn Toul and Braeriach

North and east of the main mountain mass, the braes lead gently down to the River Spey and the whisky capital of Glenlivet. The remains of the once-mighty Caledonian Forest soften the scene, perpetuated in the ancient pine forests of Glen Feshie, the Glenmore Forest Park, and the Abernethy Forest, which surrounds the osprey-haunted Loch Garten (see page 101).

To the south, across the National Trust for Scotland's Mar Lodge estate, near Braemar and the mighty eastward-flowing River Dee, lies the lofty White Mounth or Lochnagar plateau. It reaches its highest point at Lochnagar itself, a forbidding 3,789 feet (1,155m) north-facing amphitheatre of crags and deep gullies much beloved of ice climbers in winter. The range gradually relents as it spreads eastwards down the broad reaches of Glen Muick towards the town of Ballater. The Glenshee skiing area lies to the west of the White Mounth, where the A93 slices through the range via the Devil's Elbow.

The harsh, tundra-like climate and the vegetation of the Cairngorms mean that many British rarities grow here, some of which are only found elsewhere beyond the Arctic Circle or in the Alps. A quarter of the 400 rare and endangered British plant species are found within the national park. Examples of these include the three-pointed rush, dwarf willow and dwarf cudweed. Crowberry and blaeberry occupy the more sheltered spots, while heather is more common in the surrounding foothills, often colonising the surface of glacial moraines.

The mountains of the central Cairngorms, when seen from a distance, are gently rounded. Crags are only found in the steep, glaciated sides of the glens, where the effects of the Ice Age glaciers, which retreated about 10,000 years ago, can still be seen. Several summits, like those of Ben Avon, the Barns of Bynack and Beinn a'Bhuird, have rounded summit tors. They can reach up to 80 feet high in places, but more usually reach no higher than about 30 feet.

The going can be tough on the rough boulder fields of the Cairngorm high tops. Accidents are not uncommon,

◀ Ticket office, Boat of Garten

especially, ironically, in summer when some walkers underestimate their ability to manage weather and terrain.

In October 2010, the area known as Highland Perthshire and Glenshee was included in a southward extension of the park, increasing its size by one fifth. It now covers about six per cent of the total area of Scotland. The southern extension takes the park boundary down to Glen Garry, taking in the town of Blair Atholl, with its Scottish baronial Blair Castle (see page 99), and home of the Duke of Atholl's private army of highlanders. The southern Cairngorm bastions of Beinn A'Ghlo (hill of mist) and Beinn Dearg are also included, along with the southward-running valleys of Glen Shee, Glen Tilt and Glen Bruar.

The natural gateway to the Cairngorms National Park is Aviemore, created from scratch in the 1960s as Scotland's first purpose-built winter sports destination. From Aviemore, you can take a steam train the length of Strathspey, or ride a funicular to Britain's highest ski slopes.

TAKE IN SOME HISTORY
Balmoral Castle Grounds & Exhibition
balmoralcastle.com
AB35 5TB | 01339 742534 | Open Apr Jul daily 10–5 (last admission 4.30)
Queen Victoria and Prince Albert first leased the original Balmoral Castle in 1848, and bought the property four years later. The family found the building too small, and so a new castle was commissioned. It was completed in 1856, and is still the Royal Family's Highland residence. Queen Victoria spent a lot of time here after Albert died, last visiting in late 1900, a few months before her death.

The gardens were first opened to the public in 1931, and now you can explore the exhibitions, grounds, gardens and trails as well as the magnificent Castle Ballroom. Guided tours and landrover safari tours are available.

MEET THE WOLVES...
Highland Wildlife Park
see page 272

...AND THE REINDEER
Cairngorm Reindeer Centre
cairngormreindeer.co.uk
Glenmore, PH22 1QU | 01479 861228 | Hill trips Jul, Aug daily at 11 and 2.30 (also 3.30 tour Mon–Fri); May, Sep daily at 11 and 2.30; Oct–Apr daily at 11 only
You can meet the only free-roaming herd of reindeer in Britain, introduced to the Cairngorms from Scandinavia in the 1950s, on the hills above Glenmore, at the Cairngorm Reindeer Centre.

GET OUTDOORS
Rothiemurchus Estate
rothiemurchus.net
Rothiemurchus, PH22 1QH | 01479 812345 | Open daily 9.30–5.30
At the Rothiemurchus Estate, 1.5 miles south of Aviemore, you'll find outdoor pursuits,

▲ Summit Cairn, Cairngorm Mountain; red squirrel

beautiful mountains, lochs and Caledonian pine forest. This is the remains of the Old Wood of Caledon that once covered much of the country, when it harboured wolves and bears. Try your hand at anything from clay-pigeon shooting to off-road driving, or activities such as birding, cycling, fishing and horse trekking. Don't miss the local cheeses and estate venison in the farm shop.

TAKE A TRAIN RIDE
Strathspey Steam Railway
strathspeyrailway.co.uk
Aviemore Station, Dalfaber Road, PH22 1PY | 01479 810725
For timetables, see website
From Aviemore, you can take a heritage train ride on the Strathspey Steam Railway across moorland, and then along the serpentine Spey Valley as far as Grantown-on-Spey (see page 368), by way of Boat of Garten (see page 101) and Broomhill. The pride of the Strathspey Railway

Association's fleet of old locomotives and carriages is the former Caledonian Railway engine No. 828, in its gleaming blue livery.

Cairngorm Mountain Railway
cairngormmountain.org
PH22 1RB | 01479 861262
For seasonal timetables, see website
Cairngorm Mountain Railway, the fastest, highest funicular railway in Britain, takes you from Aviemore to the Cairn Gorm ski area, near the top of the sixth-highest mountain in the UK. You'll find some of Britain's best pistes and toboggan runs here in winter. The best time for winter sports is generally from January to March, although good snow is not uncommon as late as April. Outside of winter sports season, it's still worth taking the ride for the amazing panoramic views – on a clear day in summer, it sometimes feels like the whole of Scotland is laid out beneath you.

▶ Canna
see **Small Isles**, page 363

▶ Coatbridge   MAP REF 402 A3
Like so many places on the outskirts of Glasgow (see page
206), Coatbridge was once a thriving industrial community,
home to some of the biggest iron and steel foundries in
Scotland. An excellent attraction here, the Summerlee
Museum of Scottish Industrial Life – billed as Scotland's
noisiest museum – takes you back to Coatbridge's industrial
heyday. A 19th-century visitor compared it to Hell, writing: 'the
blast furnaces on all sides might be imagined to be blazing
volcanoes at which smelting is continued day and night.'

GET INDUSTRIAL
**Summerlee Museum of
Scottish Industrial Life**
culturenl.co.uk/summerlee
Heritage Way, ML5 1QD | 01236
638460 | Open Apr–Oct daily 10–5;
Nov–Mar daily 10–4
Ride a historic tram to visit a
reconstructed mine and miners'
cottages for a glimpse of how
tough life was for working folk
here in the 19th century.

ENTERTAIN THE FAMILY
The Time Capsule
nlleisure.co.uk/time-capsule
100 Buchanan Street, ML5 1DL
01236 449572 | Open Mon–Fri 3–8,
Sat and Sun 10–8
This water park is a great place
for families, with a tsunami-
style wave pool, exciting flumes,
a gentler lazy river ride, a play
island for younger children and
a three-level soft play area.

▶ Coll
see **Western Isles**, page 386

▶ Colonsay
see **Western Isles**, page 386

▶ Craigievar Castle   MAP REF 409 D3
nts.org.uk
Alford, AB33 8JF | 01339 883635 | Castle open Jul–Aug daily 10.30–5; Mar–
Jun and Sep–Oct Fri–Tue 10.30–5. Grounds open all year sunrise to sunset
The quintessential Scottish baronial tower house, Craigievar
has a fairytale quality that makes it stand out from its fellows.
The castle was built by merchant trader William Forbes
between 1600 and 1626, and – unusually – remained unaltered
in the following centuries of occupation. The result is a

▲ Craigievar Castle

six-storey pinkish-harled fantasy of turrets on a central Great Tower, a delight to the eye in the leafy setting of the Don Valley.

Standing amid attractive woodland, and built of a pink-harled granite, Craigievar is one of the most romantic of the 17th-century Scottish tower houses. It was also one of the last of its kind to be built. Within two decades of its completion the Civil War broke out in England, and many castles and fortified houses came under devastating bombardment from cannons. It was no longer possible to build a house that could withstand such firepower indefinitely; fortresses became obsolete, and in their place came the elegant Classical-style mansions and town houses that categorise the 18th century.

No expense was spared by the wealthy Forbes. He ordered the decorative turrets that adorn each corner and the elegant carvings high up on the walls.

Inside the castle many rooms have retained their impressive Renaissance plaster ceilings, and the elegant hall has arcaded panelling with a royal coat of arms over the granite fireplace. This magical L-plan castle is now owned by the National Trust for Scotland. Artificial lighting has never been installed at the castle, in accordance with the Forbes-Sempill family's wishes, so it's best to visit on a bright day.

▶ Cramond MAP REF 402 C3

Whitewashed houses with red pantiled roofs stand on the east side of the River Almond, where yachts bob at anchor at Cramond. Cramond was a hive of water-powered industry in the 18th century, with ironworks and a paper mill. Today, it's a sought-after residential address.

In the kirkyard, you can see the foundations of a Roman legionary fortress built in the mid-second century, when the Roman Empire under Septimius Severus made its last attempt to subjugate the territory north of Hadrian's Wall. A mile-long causeway connects uninhabited Cramond Island with the shore, and it's an easy (but slippery) walk at low tide. It's a great place to play Robinson Crusoe, but be aware that there's a risk of being marooned for real when the tide comes in. More than 100 people get stranded here every year and are rescued by lifeboat. Before setting out for the island, text CRAMOND to 81400 for times of high and low tides, supplied by the Royal National Lifeboat Institution (RNLI).

TAKE IN SOME HISTORY

Lauriston Castle

edinburghmuseums.org.uk
2A Cramond Road South, EH4 5QD
0131 336 2060 | Castle open (guided tours only) Apr–Oct Sat–Thu 2pm; Nov–Mar Sat, Sun 2pm. Grounds open all year

This gabled and turreted mansion, overlooking the Firth of Forth, offers up a slice of neatly preserved Edwardian comfort and style. Once a simple tower house, Lauriston was remodelled and extended several times, most notably in 1827 by architect William Burn (1789–1870), before it came to William Robert Reid. He was the wealthy head of a firm of cabinetmakers, and an avid collector of fine furniture and precious objects – his collection of pieces made from the

▼ Causeway to Cramond Island

fluorspar mineral Blue John is particularly unusual. He left the castle to the city in 1926.

Dalmeny House
dalmeny.co.uk
Dalmeny, EH30 9TQ | 0131 331 1888 | Open (guided tours only) Jun, Jul Sun–Wed 2.15

The original building on this site, Barnbougle, was a 13th-century castle, built on the seashore by the Mowbray family. In 1662 Sir Archibald Primrose bought the Dalmeny Estate and lived in Barnbougle Castle, but by the end of the 18th century the castle was in a bad state of repair. The Earl refused to make improvements, but his son, the Fourth Earl, did not agree, and decided to build another dwelling: Dalmeny House.

In 1814 two architects – William Wilkins and Jeffrey Wyatt – were commissioned to submit plans for the house. The Fourth Earl preferred Wyatt's Tudor Gothic design to Wilkins' neoclassical Greek style, but because he and Wilkins had been at Cambridge together, he asked Wilkins to submit another design in the Tudor Gothic style, accepted it, and Dalmeny House was born. Wilkins also designed some of the furniture, including sofas, stools and chairs. It is thought that Dalmeny House became the inspiration for many 19th-century Scottish houses, by architects such as William Burn and David Bruce.

The entrance hall has a stunning hammer-beam ceiling and a rare set of tapestries designed by Goya to be hung in Spanish royal palaces: only two sets exist outside Spain, and the Queen has the other.

TAKE A WALK
You can walk all the way from Cramond to South Queensferry (see page 364), along sandy beaches and through fields and the wooded grounds of the Dalmeny Estate. There are plans to open a mini-ferry, replacing the rowing ferry that carried walkers across the mouth of the River Almond until the service was suspended in 2001. Until it reopens, walkers must detour inland to cross the Almond at Cramond Bridge. This adds a couple of miles to the walk.

▶ Crieff MAP REF 402 A1

Crieff is a hub for activities including mountain biking, water sports and angling on nearby Loch Earn, and walking in the surrounding hills – Knock Hill offers the best views. It grew up as a centre for Highland cattle drovers, who passed through here on their way south. The Drummonds had their castle 3 miles south of the town, and while the castle itself is still private, the fabulous formal 17th-century garden has been restored to its former state and is open on summer afternoons. The burial chapel of the Drummonds stands beside the

Innerpeffray Library, founded in 1691 and remarkable as the oldest lending library in Scotland.

To the north of Crieff a narrow road leads up the remote Glen Turret to Loch Turret, passing the scenic beauty spot at the waterfalls of the same name.

▶ **PLACES NEARBY**

Drummond Castle
drummondcastlegardens.co.uk
Muthill, PH7 4HN | 01764 681433
Easter weekend, May and Sep–Oct
daily 1–6; Jun–Aug daily 11–6
Drummond Castle has an extensive formal garden, laid out in the 17th century, and restored in the 1950s.

Gleneagles
gleneagles.com
Auchterarder, PH3 1NF | 0800 389 3737 | Open daily all year
The Professional Golfers' Association (PGA) Centenary Course, created by Jack Nicklaus, has an American–Scottish layout with raised contoured greens. It was host to the Ryder Cup in 2014.

Glenturret Distillery
experience.thefamousgrouse.com
The Hosh, PH7 4HA | 01764 656565
Open Mar–Dec daily 9–6; Jan–Feb
daily 10.30–4.30 | Call for tour times
The Glenturret Distillery, on the banks of the River Turret, dates from 1775, and claims to be Scotland's oldest. It offers The Famous Grouse Experience.

Royal Hotel 🏵
royalhotel.co.uk
Melville Square, Comrie, PH6 2DN
01764 679200
The 18th-century stone building on the main street is now a plush small-scale luxury hotel, with a peaceful library and lounge for pre-dinner drinks, and a restaurant split into two areas linked by double doors.

▶ **Crinan Canal** MAP REF 400 C2

Winding for 9 miles between Ardrishaig on Loch Fyne and Crinan harbour on the Sound of Jura, the Crinan Canal is a narrow waterway through an attractive region of woodland and open marsh. It was built in 1793–1809 by the engineer John Rennie (1761–1821), when fishing craft and the so-called puffers, the small steam-driven boats that transported vital supplies to all parts of the Scottish coast, used it to avoid the 130-mile trip around the Kintyre peninsula. Today it is still well used by yachts and small fishing boats, which must negotiate 15 locks along its course.

From the basin at Ardrishaig, where it leaves Loch Fyne, the canal hugs the wooded hillsides as it climbs up to its highest point of 64 feet. On the hills above Cairnbaan are reservoirs that constantly replenish the water down in the canal as it descends underneath the unusual hand-wound rolling bridge at Dunardry. Beyond this the landscape then opens out into flat marshland. The canal ends at picturesque Crinan Harbour.

EAT AND DRINK
Crinan Hotel
Crinan, PA31 8SR | 01546 830261
This romantic retreat enjoys fabulous views across the Sound of Jura. For more than 200 years this hostelry has been welcoming travellers to this tiny fishing village. The cuisine is firmly based on the freshest seafood – landed daily just 50 yards from the hotel.

▶ Culloden
see highlight panel opposite

▶ Culross MAP REF 402 B2

With its winding cobbled streets and old buildings with crow-stepped gables, quaint little Culross looks like the paintings of very old Scottish burghs. It was one of Scotland's early industrial communities, and as early as the 16th century was involved in coal mining and salt panning. As the local coal was gradually worked out, the emphasis on industrial activity swung to other parts of the Forth Valley and Culross became a backwater. Many of the merchants' and workers' houses dating from the 17th and 18th centuries were never replaced by later buildings; paradoxically, it was Culross's poverty that created the picturesque groupings so admired today.

In the centre of Culross you'll also find a statue of the town's most famous son, Admiral Thomas Cochrane, the Tenth Earl of Dundonald. He is one of the country's more colourful naval heroes, convicted for fraud as well as being one of the Royal Navy's most heroic naval captains during the Napoleonic Wars.

TAKE IN SOME HISTORY
Culross Palace, Town House and Study
nts.org.uk
Culross, KY12 83H | 01383 880359
Open Easter week daily 10–5; mid-Apr–May and Sep Sat–Mon 11–5; Jun–Aug daily 11–5. Town House (guided tours only) 1.30, 2.30 and 3.30, depart from palace Culross Palace, built between 1597 and 1611 for the wealthy coal and salt merchant Sir George Bruce, is the most remarkable of Culross's well preserved collection of historic buildings. The ochre-painted mansion has a striking painted interior and is filled with 16th- and 17th-century antiques. It's surrounded by a re-created medieval garden.

Suspected witches were locked up in the nearby Town House's attic awaiting trial during the 17th century.

▶ Culloden MAP REF 407 E2

A boggy moor on a windy ridge 5 miles east of Inverness is the emotive scene of the final battle fought on Scottish soil, where Bonnie Prince Charlie made his last stand before abandoning his loyal followers and fleeing back to France. The Jacobite defeat at the Battle of Culloden, fought on 16 April 1746, was the dismal outcome of a civil war that had split families in England as well as Scotland and hastened the end of the already disintegrating clan system in Scotland.

Culloden marked the end of Stuart ambitions to reclaim the British throne from the Hanoverians. On this bleak and desolate moorland, 5,000 Highlanders under the command of the Young Pretender – Bonnie Prince Charlie – faced 9,000 troops led by the Duke of Cumberland, youngest son of George II. It was bitterly cold, with snow flurries. The Highlanders, used to short skirmishes, were no match for the disciplined and well-armed soldiers, and despite courageous fighting were swiftly defeated. Cumberland ordered that no prisoners should be taken.

Prince Charles Edward Stuart (1720–88), later known as Bonnie Prince Charlie, was raised in European exile. He was heir to the

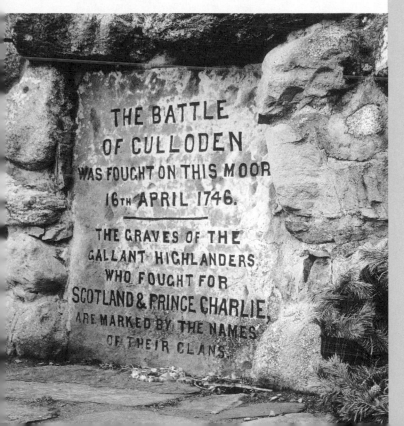

Scottish throne that the Catholic Stuarts still claimed through Charles Edward's father, son of the deposed James II and also named James, known to his enemies as the Old Pretender (Jacobus in Latin, hence Jacobite as the name for the political movement). The French were keen on stirring up political matters with the Protestant Hanoverian government in Britain, and encouraged the Prince's madcap expedition to claim the throne in 1745. Charles landed at Glenfinnan and raised a mixed bag of Highland fighters, some of them coerced by their chiefs. Initially the Prince's army was successful, and reached Derby in central England before running out of steam. The Highlanders retreated northwards, but by the spring of 1746 the Hanoverian forces were closing in.

When the two armies met at Culloden, the Prince's outnumbered and exhausted forces faced an army of disciplined, professional infantry, cavalry and artillery. A tactical blunder placed his Highlanders within range of the government artillery, and the Jacobites were blown away in under an hour. More than 1,500 Jacobites and 50 Hanoverians died. Stones and flags mark the battlefield today, to show where the clans fell.

In the aftermath, the Duke of Cumberland earned the nickname The Butcher when he sanctioned one of the worst atrocities ever carried out by the British Army. Military looting was legalised throughout the Highlands, irrespective of loyalties, and the Highland way of life changed for ever. Jacobite propaganda retreated into sentimentality, and the romantic figure of the Prince hiding, never betrayed as he fled to exile, became legendary.

Recently upgraded footpaths make the battlefield accessible to wheelchair users and families with buggies, and a portable

audio-visual guide, available from the Visitor Centre, helps you find your way around landmarks such as the Cumberland Stone, the giant boulder that marks the spot from which the Hanoverian commander directed his troops.

CHECK OUT THE VISITOR CENTRE

Culloden Battlefield Visitor Centre

nts.org.uk

Culloden, IV2 5EU | 01463 796090

Open Jun–Aug daily 9–6; Apr, May daily 9–5.30; Feb, Mar, Nov, Dec daily 10–4

Inside the visitor centre you can listen to first-hand accounts of the battle by those who were there, voiced by actors, and watch a four-minute panoramic video show that immerses you in the centre of the action and gives you some idea what it was like to be a Hanoverian redcoat facing a Highland charge – or, indeed, a clansman charging the bayonets of Cumberland's infantry. An animated so-called battle table uses digital technology to bring the battlefield to life in miniature, allowing you to understand the tactics used by each side. From the roof, you have a bird's-eye view of the moorland where the battle was fought.

▶ **PLACES NEARBY**

Clava Cairns

historicenvironment.scot

Signposted from B9091, 300 yards

▲ Passage grave at Clava Cairns

east of Culloden Battlefield

Open daily 24 hours

The fascinating Clava Cairns near Culloden open a window on our remote ancestors. A site of major archaeological importance, and beautifully set among beech trees, it has three large stone burial mounds, each surrounded by a circle of standing stones. They were probably built between about 2000 and 1500 BC. The two outer cairns, still partly covered in small boulders, have stone-lined passages to the centre. The northeast cairn has an interesting series of cup marks on one of the larger boulders. The middle one is hollow, although with no passage. Instead, it has rough cobbled pavements leading away from it. Clava Cairns is part of a whole series of such monuments found only in the region of the Moray Firth.

◀ Old Leanach Cottage

▶ Culzean Castle & Country Park MAP REF 398 B3

culzeanexperience.org

Maybole, KA19 8LE | 01655 884455 | Castle open daily Apr–Oct 10.30–5.
Country park open all year

Culzean (pronounced Cullane) is the National Trust for
Scotland's most popular property. That's partly thanks to the
surrounding country park, 563 lush green acres of wild gardens
and leafy woodland threaded with trails. You can discover a
walled garden, a herb garden, a deer park and lots of follies
dotted around. In summer, there are daily guided ranger walks
around the grounds. There are also regular forays along the
coast and even into the estate's little-known caves, as well as
music and theatre events.

The golden stone castle, set right at the edge of the cliffs, is
handsome rather than beautiful, with its baronial towers and
castellated roofline. It is reached via a bridge, and rises high
above a terraced garden. Inside, it's an 18th-century show
home, the masterpiece of Scottish architect Robert Adam, who
worked on it from 1777 to 1792 for the powerful Kennedy
family, who had dominated this part of Ayrshire since the 12th
century and could trace their ancestry to Robert the Bruce.

Highlights include the graceful oval staircase and the
circular Saloon, with lofty sea views to the craggy island of
Ailsa Craig. The top floor was granted to General Eisenhower in
1945, for his lifetime, as a thanks from the people of Scotland
for American help during World War II; there are photographs
and mementoes of his visits, and for an exclusive thrill, you can
even stay in the Eisenhower apartment. You can also see the
original castle kitchens.

From the castle courtyard there are views across to the Isle of Arran (see page 78), and the park has several miles of coastline with some remarkable and steep cliffs. Among the highlights in the grounds are the walled gardens, designed both to provide food for the kitchens and to be an attractive place for guests and visitors to wander around. There are exotic birds in the aviary, an orangery, follies and fountains. You'll also find the vinery, in one of the greenhouses, which was built close to a heated wall in order to allow exotic plants to grow.

The original castle was a stone tower house dating from the late 14th century. Over the next two centuries the Kennedy family occupied it only occasionally; there were phases of improvements, but it was not until David Kennedy, the Tenth Earl of Cassilis, inherited it in 1775 that plans began to transform the castle into the magnificent structure we see today. Neither Kennedy nor Robert Adam saw the work finished: both died in 1792, Kennedy with huge debts from rebuilding costs.

▶ PLACES NEARBY
Souter Johnnie's Cottage
nts.org.uk
Main Road, Kirkoswald, KA19 8HY
Open Apr Sep Fri–Tue 11.30–5
This charming thatched cottage was the home of John Davidson, immortalised by Robert Burns as Souter Johnnie, Tam O'Shanter's 'drouthie' (thirsty) friend. A souter was a cobbler, and inside the cottage you can see Johnnie's lasts and other shoemaker's tools. Beaming effigies of Tam and Johnnie sit inside, tankards in hand.

▶ Cupar MAP REF 402 C1
The small town of Cupar stands by the River Eden, in central Fife. It has kept some of the character of a 17th-century market town, with a Mercat (Market) Cross dating from 1683 and a handful of historic buildings, including its Old Parish Church and Corn Exchange.

PLAY A ROUND
Cupar Golf Club
cupargolfclub.co.uk
Hilltarvit, KY15 5JT | 01334 653549
Open Sun–Fri
This hilly parkland course has fine views over northeast Fife. The fifth hole is most difficult It's said to be the oldest nine-hole club in the UK.

EAT AND DRINK
Ostlers Close Restaurant ◉◉
ostlersclose.co.uk
Bonnygate, KY15 4BU
01334 655574

Down a narrow alley just off the main street, this one-time scullery of a 17th-century Temperance hotel has been a favoured foodie bolthole since 1981. Seasonal Scottish produce takes centre stage, and you may spot an occasional Spanish influence amid the well-crafted modern repertoire.

▶ **PLACES NEARBY**

Hill of Tarvit Mansion

nts.org.uk

Hill of Tarvit, KY15 5PB | 01334 653127 | Open Apr–Jun Thu–Mon 11–4.30; Jul–Aug daily 11–4.30; Sep–Oct Thu–Mon 11–4

Two miles south of Cupar, Hill of Tarvit is an Edwardian mansion containing a collection of fine Dutch paintings, works by Scottish artists including Sir Henry Raeburn, Chippendale furniture and delicate Chinese porcelain. You can play a round of old-fashioned hickory golf or a game of croquet on the lawn, or play billiards in the spacious billiard room, while the restored Edwardian laundry is an interesting curiosity.

Scottish Deer Centre

tsdc.co.uk

Bow of Fife, KY15 4NQ | 01337 810391 | Open Jul, Aug daily 10–5.30; Sep–Jun daily10–4.30

See website for times of falconry displays and scheduled feeding times

More than a dozen kinds of native British and exotic deer roam the enclosures at this wildlife park, where you can also see wolves, wildcats, lynx and bears and watch displays of falconry. You can get close to the animals at feeding times (several times daily). There's also a pedal cart track, a picnic spot and an adventure play area.

Wemyss Ware

wemyss-ware.co.uk

Kirkbrae, Ceres, KY15 5ND | 01334 828373 | Open Mon–Sat 2–4.30

This family pottery has revived the famous hand-painted Wemyss Ware style of curious cats and floral pigs, popular in the 19th century. To find it, follow signs with a grinning, pop-eyed yellow cat.

Cairnie Fruit Farm and Mega Maze

cairniefruitfarm.co.uk

Cairnie, KY15 4QG

01334 655610 | Mega Maze open mid-Jul–Oct 10–4

The Mega Maze is the big attraction here in the summer months, but Cairnie also offers trampolines and motorised mini-tractors.

▶ ## Dalkeith & Gorebridge MAP REF 402 C3

South of Edinburgh's city bypass lies a swathe of former coal-mining country. The pits were closed in the 1980s, and former mining communities like Dalkeith, Newtongrange, Bonnyrigg and Gorebridge have become dormitory suburbs of the city. However, you'll find a scattering of fascinating visitor attractions for families and interesting things to see and do that make the short trip from the city worthwhile.

Getting here became much easier with the 2015 re-opening of the Borders Railway; closed in 1969, it now runs from Edinburgh Waverley to Tweedbank, 30 miles south of the city, with stops at Newtongrange and Gorebridge.

Gorebridge is a rather sleepy residential suburb these days. In the 19th century it produced gunpowder for Wellington's armies and Nelson's warships, and its peace was occasionally shattered by accidental explosions. You can see the scanty remains of the gunpowder mills nearby, but Gorebridge's real attraction is a grand Georgian mansion built for a dynasty of Scottish magnates: Arniston House.

TAKE IN SOME HISTORY

Arniston House
arniston-house.co.uk
Gorebridge, EH23 4RY | 01875 830515 | Open for tours only May–Jun Tue–Wed 2 and 3.30; Jul to mid-Sep Tue–Wed, Sun 2 and 3.30

In the 18th century Robert Dundas presided over the Court of Session, Scotland's supreme civil law court. It was he who commissioned William Adam to design a Palladian family seat worthy of his status. The house contains works by Ramsay and Raeburn.

The splendid mansion, completed by William's eldest son John, incorporates some of the original house, notably the panelled Oak Room, but fireplaces and decorative features were added. Other rooms, including the drawing room, dining room and library, have notable plasterwork and intricate friezes characteristic of William Adam's work. The kitchen still has its Victorian food lift.

▶ Arniston House

The grounds have developed over centuries from formal layouts to more natural landscapes in the style of 'Capability' Brown.

Dalhousie Castle
dalhousiecastle.co.uk
Bonnyrigg, EH19 3JB | 01875 820153 | Call for falconry and archery bookings

Standing in wooded grounds outside Bonnyrigg, Dalhousie Castle claims to be the oldest inhabited castle in Scotland. Built in 1450, it's now a luxury hotel and spa, but guided tours are available by arrangement. For families, the big attraction here is the falconry centre, where you can see different

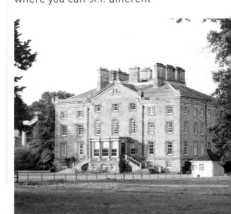

species of owls, hawks and eagles in flight. You can also try your hand at archery.

VISIT THE MUSEUM
National Mining Museum Scotland
nationalminingmuseum.com
Lady Victoria Colliery, Newtongrange, EH22 4QN | 0131 663 7519 | Open Apr–Oct daily 10–5; Nov–Mar daily 10–4
Housed in one of the best-preserved 19th-century collieries in Europe, the National Mining Museum Scotland pays tribute to the men and women who worked in Scotland's mines with photos, displays of equipment and recordings of their life experiences in their own words and voices. There's a mini-miners soft play area for kids.

ENTERTAIN THE FAMILY
Edinburgh Butterfly World
edinburgh-butterfly-world.co.uk
Melville Nursery, Lasswade, EH18 1AZ | 0131 663 4932 | Open May–Sep daily 9.30–5.30; Oct–Apr daily 10–5
Children can handle snakes and tarantulas, marvel at scorpions that glow in the dark and admire hundreds of colourful butterflies in the tropical gardens at Edinburgh Butterfly World. You can also watch fish, quails and snakes being fed.

EAT AND DRINK
The Sun Inn ◉
thesuninnedinburgh.co.uk
Lothian Bridge, EH22 4TR
0131 663 2456
This gastropub combines a good dose of rustic-chic style with the original oak beams, exposed stone and panelling. An eclectic menu delivers pub classics as well as inventive contemporary dishes.

▶ PLACES NEARBY
Glenkinchie Distillery
discovering-distilleries.com
Pencaitland, EH34 5ET | 01875 342012 | Open Mar–Oct daily 10–5; Nov–Feb daily 10–4
Glenkinchie is the closest distillery to Scotland's capital. You can visit the exhibition, take a tour of the distillery and taste the whisky. Children under eight are not allowed in the production area. Booking is recommended.

▶ Dornoch MAP REF 413 D4
Despite its northerly location, Dornoch claims to be one of Scotland's sunniest spots, and its miles of sands are popular with windsurfers in summer. Founded in the 11th century, Dornoch was the seat of the Bishops of Caithness and has a well-preserved 13th-century cathedral. The so-called Witch's Stone on Dornoch's central square marks the spot where, in 1727, Janet Horne was tarred, feathered and burned. Accused of changing her daughter into a pony, she was the last person in Scotland to be executed for witchcraft.

TAKE IN SOME HISTORY
Dornoch Cathedral
dornoch-cathedral.com
The Square, IV25 3SJ | 01862
810296 | Open daily
Gilbert de Moravia, Bishop of
Caithness, built the cathedral at
his own expense between 1222
and 1239, for which he was
rewarded after his death in
1245 by being made Saint
Gilbert of Dornoch. Among his
other exploits, he is credited
with ridding Sutherland of a
fearsome dragon that
terrorised the region.

Gilbert's cathedral was
devastated by fire in 1570, and
what you see today is a
restoration dating from 1924,
which returned it to its original
medieval appearance. Its
splendid stained-glass windows
were endowed by the Scots-
American philanthropist
Andrew Carnegie.

VISIT THE MUSEUM
Historylinks Museum
historylinks.org.uk
The Meadows, IV25 3SF | 01862
811275 | Open Jun–Sep daily 10–4;
Apr, May, Oct Fri–Mon 10–4
Historylinks traces the
Dornoch area's past from
the era of Picts and Vikings
through the 15th and 16th
centuries to the town's
transformation into a seaside
resort and golfing destination
with the coming of the railway
in the 19th century.

PLAY A ROUND
Royal Dornoch Golf Club
royaldornoch.com
Golf Road, IV25 3LW | 01862
810219 | Open daily all year
The championship course is
rated among the world's top
courses. It is wild and isolated
with a pure-white sandy beach
dividing it from the Dornoch

▼ Dornoch Cathedral

Firth and has hosted golfers since 1616. It was granted a Royal Charter by King Edward VII in 1906.

EAT AND DRINK
Dornoch Castle Hotel
dornochcastlehotel.com
Castle Street, IV25 3SD
01862 810216
This 15th-century castle has a conservatory-style restaurant with a charming atmosphere. The kitchen works a modern vein without losing sight of regional traditions.

▸ PLACES NEARBY
Brora Heritage Centre
visitscotland.com
Coal Pit Road, KW9 6LE | 01408 622024 | Open May–Oct daily 10.30–4.30
You can find out all about Brora's history as a centre of the whisky, coal-mining and wool-weaving industries at this community visitor attraction in the centre of Brora village.

Dunrobin Castle
dunrobincastle.co.uk
Golspie, KW10 6SF | 01408 633177
Open Jun–Sep daily 10–5; Apr–May and Oct daily 10.30–4.30; Falconry displays Jun–Aug daily 11.30 and 2, Apr, May, Sep, Oct Mon–Sat 11.30 and 2

Looming above its gardens like a French chateau, Dunrobin Castle boasts 189 rooms, making it the largest mansion in northern Scotland. It dates back to about 1275, but its outward appearance is overwhelmingly Victorian, thanks to extensions added between 1845 and 1850 by Sir Charles Barry (better known as the architect of London's Houses of Parliament).

Like most ancient Scottish castles, Dunrobin started out as a keep, or tower, and is probably named after Robert, the sixth Earl of Sutherland, who built the first castle here in 1401. Enlargements in the 17th, 18th and 19th centuries created the splendid, gleaming, turreted castle that today's visitors see.

Peregrine falcons and golden eagles are the stars of the falconry displays that take place in the formal and ornate French-style gardens, modelled on those at Versailles.

Beyond the castle walls, in a converted summerhouse, a museum has been set out to display various collections that reflect the wide-ranging interests of the family over the

◂ Dunrobin Castle

centuries. These range from ornithology to Egyptology. There's a lot of taxidermy, including an elephant's head and a giraffe, among other curiosities, so those of a sensitive disposition may wish to skip that part.

▶ Drumlanrig Castle, Gardens & Country Park
MAP REF 399 D3

drumlanrigcastle.co.uk

Thornhill, DG3 4AQ | 01848 331555 | Castle open Easter–Aug daily 11–4. Gardens and country park open Easter–Sep daily 12–5

'Bonnie Prince Charlie slept here' is the proud claim of more than a few of Scotland's castles, inns and country houses. It's fair to say that Charles Edward Stuart got around a bit during his brief and ultimately unsuccessful UK tour of 1745–46. But Drumlanrig Castle does him proud. The bedroom that he occupied on his retreat northwards on 22 December 1745 has been dedicated to his memory. A pastel of the Prince and an oil painting of his father hang either side of one window, and several personal items are on display.

This imposing 17th-century mansion, 18 miles north of Dumfries, is one of several homes that are part of the 280,000-acre, £320 million portfolio of the Duke of Buccleuch, Scotland's largest private landowner. Four square towers

▼ Drumlanrig Castle and Gardens

guard the corners, each topped by little turrets that give this castle its unmistakable skyline; the famous view is the one up the straight avenue as you approach. Inside, the art collection is internationally famous. Outside you can wander through the formal gardens, visit the plant centre and forge, and even hire a bicycle to explore the grounds.

Drumlanrig was a Douglas stronghold as far back as the 14th century and Sir James Douglas was the right-hand man of Robert the Bruce, King of Scotland. Indeed, the family crest of a winged heart surmounted by Bruce's crown, which appears throughout the house, stems from that alliance.

The present palatial structure was built around the original castle by William Douglas, First Duke of Queensberry. An impressive horseshoe staircase and colonnaded archway lead up to the castle entrance. Masterpieces such as Leonardo da Vinci's *Madonna with the Yarnwinder*, Hans Holbein the Younger's *Sir Nicholas Carew* and Rembrandt's *Old Woman Reading* adorn the Staircase Hall.

A tour of the castle reveals room after room of priceless works of art, from the exquisite Grinling Gibbons carvings and Meissen Monkey Band in the drawing room to the Dutch and Flemish paintings in the Boudoir.

▲ Dumbarton Rock and Castle

▶ PLACES NEARBY
Museum of Lead Mining

leadminingmuseum.co.uk
Wanlockhead, ML12 6UT | 01659
74387 | Open Apr–Sep daily
11–4.30

Drive up to Wanlockhead, Scotland's highest village (1,535 feet), set amid the windswept Lowther Hills, and you arrive in a different world. A heritage trail from the visitor centre around the settlement shows you a community where generations of miners toiled to extract lead. You can wander into Straitsteps Cottages for a taste of family life here in 1740 and 1890, and discover the little lending library, founded in 1756 and thought to be the second-oldest in Europe. Best of all, you can follow a miner into the hillside, down the workings of an old lead mine, to see how the men really worked.

▶ Drumnadrochit
see **Loch Ness & Drumnadrochit**, page 294

▶ **Dumbarton** MAP REF 401 E3

You may find it hard to believe, but this unassuming suburb of Glasgow (see page 206) was among the most important places in Scotland during two widely separated eras in the nation's history. Between the fifth and ninth centuries, it was the seat of Alt Clud, a powerful Brythonic (British) kingdom that dominated much of southern Scotland until it was absorbed into the new Scottish kingdom in about AD 870. It then became the seat of Scots kings until 1018, when Dunfermline became capital. In the 19th century, it was one of the world's greatest shipbuilding centres, giving birth to iconic vessels including the clipper *Cutty Sark* and the steamer *Sir Walter Scott,* which still carries passengers on Loch Lomond (see page 286). Dumbarton's unmissable landmark is Dumbarton Rock, a superb natural stronghold.

TAKE IN SOME HISTORY
Dumbarton Castle
historicenvironment.scot
Castle Road, G82 1JJ | 01389 732167
Open Apr–Sep daily 9.30–5.30; Oct
daily 10–4; Nov–Mar Sat–Wed 10–4
Standing on Dumbarton Rock, it's easy to see why Britons and Scots valued this castle highly. This 250-foot volcanic plug is a magnificent defensive site, visible from miles away. Long after it ceased to be a royal seat, it continued to be an important stronghold. Its battlements, overlooking the Clyde, were modernised during the 18th and 19th centuries.

VISIT THE MUSEUM
Scottish Maritime Museum
scottishmaritimemuseum.org
Castle Street, G82 1QS | 01389 763444 | Open Mon–Sat 10–4
Highlights of the Scottish Maritime Museum's Dumbarton outpost include the world's first ship model experiment tank. First used by naval architects at the William Denny shipyard, it was a forerunner of present-day computer modelling and revolutionised ship design in the 19th century. There's a chance to see Denny's drawing office and tours of the building are available.

▶ **Dumfries** MAP REF 399 D4
Straddling the River Nith (where you may see red-breasted mergansers playing on the weir in summer), Dumfries has strong associations with Robert Burns, who farmed nearby and returned to Dumfries towards the end of his life. He died here in 1796, aged 37. You'll find Burns-related visitor attractions in and around town, plus a portfolio of other sights ranging from ruined castles and abbeys to quirky museums.

VISIT THE MUSEUMS AND GALLERIES
Burns House
burnsscotland.com
Burns Street, DG21 2PS | 01387 255297 | Open Apr–Sep daily 10–5

This modest town house where Robert Burns spent his declining years is a place of pilgrimage for the poet's fans. Its collection includes original letters, manuscripts and early editions of his works, including the famous Kilmarnock and Edinburgh editions.

Dumfries Museum and Camera Obscura

dumfriesmuseum.demon.co.uk
The Observatory, DG2 7SW | 01387 253374 | Open Apr–Sep Mon–Sat 10–5; Oct–Mar Tue–Sat 10–1, 2–5
You can see for miles from the Camera Obscura, which occupies the top floor of the 18th-century windmill on a hill overlooking the River Nith and the centre of Dumfries. Next door, the museum has a collection of early Christian carvings, costumes, tools, weapons and farm implements.

Gracefield Arts Centre

exploreart.co.uk
28 Edinburgh Road, DG1 1NW
01387 262084 | Open Tue–Fri 10–5, Sat 10–12, 2–5
You'll find one of Scotland's important collections of modern art at the Gracefield Arts Centre, a 10–minute walk from the centre of Dumfries. The centre houses a collection of more than 600 paintings and other works of art by painters and sculptors ranging from the Scottish Colourists to 20th- and 21st–century figures such as Joan Eardley, Peter Howson and Eduardo Paolozzi. In the gardens, you'll find works by artists such as Andy Goldsworthy and Charlie Poulsen.

▲ Robert Burns statue, Dumfries

▶ PLACES NEARBY

Ellisland Farm

ellislandfarm.co.uk
Holywood Road, Auldgirth, DG2 0RP | 01387 740426 | Open Apr–Sep Mon–Sat 10–5, Sun 2–5; Oct–Mar Tue–Sat 10–1, 2–5
Robert Burns took up farming at this whitewashed farmhouse in 1789. It wasn't a great success. Burns admitted that he chose the farm for its inspiring landscapes rather than for practical reasons, and after only two years trying to wring a living out of its infertile, badly drained soil he gave up farming and moved to Dumfries to follow a career as an exciseman (tax collector) – a less romantic but more practical way of making a living.

**Dumfries and Galloway
Aviation Museum**
dumfriesaviationmuseum.com
Heathhall Industrial Estate, DG1 3PH
01387 251623 | Open Jul, Aug
Wed–Fri 11–4, Sat, Sun 10–5;
Easter–Jun, Sep, Oct Wed 11–4,
Sat, Sun 10–5
A collection of historic
warplanes surrounds the original control tower of a
former Royal Air Force airfield.
You can clamber over an
assortment of vintage fighter
aircraft and helicopters here,
while inside the former control
tower there are rooms full of
wartime RAF memorabilia,
ranging from ejector seats and
uniforms to maps and photos.

▶ Dunbar MAP REF 403 E3

Dunbar's old high street is lined with quaint red sandstone
buildings that include a small museum, housed in the former
Town House, and the town is the birthplace of John Muir, the
father of the environmentalist movement. The town's prosperity
was built on fishing and whaling, and its three historic
harbours are still home to a busy fleet of small fishing boats.
The oldest of the three, Cromwell Harbour, was begun in 1655
by Oliver Cromwell, five years after his Roundheads smashed a
Scots Royalist army at Doon Hill, just outside the town. This
Cromwell Harbour wasn't finished until 1730, by which time
what's now called the Old Harbour was already in business. It's
overlooked by the ruins of
Dunbar Castle. Demolished in
the mid-16th century, the
castle's ruins now provide a
home to a vast colony of 600
pairs of kittiwakes.

The 18th-century fort and
battery, built to defend the
harbour from US privateers
who were active during
the American War of
Independence, are in better
shape. Dunbar's third haven,
the Victoria Harbour, was
built in 1842. There are
breathtaking stretches of
coastal scenery either side of
Dunbar. You'll see gannets
plummeting into the sea close
to shore, and inquisitive seals
sometimes swim right into
the Old Harbour.

▼ Dunbar Harbour

▲ West Barns beach, on the John Muir Way

VISIT THE MUSEUM
Dunbar Town House
Museum and Gallery
eastlothianmuseums.org
High Street, EH4 1ER | 01620
820699 | Open daily Apr–Sep 1–5
The 16th-century Town House
has had a recent facelift and
contains a collection of historic
photographs and documents,
as well as housing a changing
schedule of exhibitions.

TRY THE BEER
Belhaven Brewery
belhaven.co.uk
Brewery Lane, EH42 1PE | 01368
869200 | Call or book online for
tours
This part of Scotland is famed
for its brewing and here at
Belhaven's plant on the
outskirts of Dunbar you can
tour one of Scotland's longest
established breweries, founded
in the 18th century.

GO BIRDING
John Muir Country Park
eastlothian.gov.uk
01620 827459 | Open daily
24 hours
In summer, you'll hear larks
singing high above the four-
mile sweep of dunes, sandy
shoreline and saltmarsh that
forms the John Muir Country
Park, named after the Dunbar-
born explorer, naturalist and
father of conservation. Muir
emigrated to the US in 1838 at
the age of 11, and spent much
of his life campaigning to
protect America's wilderness
from the ravages of logging,
mining and other industries.

Eider and shelduck nest in
the dunes, and you'll see
gannets skimming the waves on
their way to and from their
fishing grounds and roosts on
the nearby Bass Rock. Look out
too for common blue butterflies

and vivid crimson and black cinnabar moths, whose black-and-yellow striped caterpillars feed on the ragwort that grows among the dunes.

WALK THE JOHN MUIR WAY

johnmuirway.org

Allow about ten days if you plan to walk the full length of the John Muir Way, Scotland's newest long-distance walking trail, which stretches for 134 miles between Dunbar and Helensburgh, on the Firth of Clyde. It skirts the Forth coast for about half its length.

GO SURFING

Coast Surf School

c2csurfschool.com

to book call 0791 990 361

Learn to surf or body-board and catch some waves on Belhaven Bay with this surf school

10 top Scottish writers

▶ Iain Banks, 1954–2013

▶ J M Barrie, 1860–1937

▶ Robert Burns, 1759–96

▶ Sir Arthur Conan Doyle, 1859–1930

▶ Carol Ann Duffy, b. 1955

▶ Alexander McCall Smith, b. 1948

▶ Val McDermid, b. 1955

▶ Sir Walter Scott, 1771–1832

▶ Ali Smith, b. 1962

▶ Robert Louis Stevenson, 1850–94

PLAY A ROUND

Dunbar Golf Club

dunbargolfclub.com

East Links, EH42 1LL | 01368 862317 | Open Mon–Wed, Fri–Sun

It is said that members of this natural links course were the first to take the game of golf to the north of England. With a wall bordering one side and the seashore on the other side, this is quite a challenging course for all levels. The wind, if blowing from the sea, is a problem.

EAT AND DRINK

The Creel

creelrestaurant.co.uk

25 Lamer Street, EH42 1HJ

01368 863279

This casual bistro near the harbour serves super local seafood from Dunbar itself and from nearby Eyemouth. Look out for mussels, crab and other shellfish, as well as locally sourced meat dishes.

▶ PLACES NEARBY

A short drive away is East Linton, where you'll find the area's last working watermill.

Preston Mill and Phantassie Doocot

nts.org.uk

East Linton, EH40 3DS | 01620 860426 | Open May–Sep Thu–Mon 12.30–5. Tours every 45 minutes

Kids can feed the ducks on the pond at this pretty 18th-century watermill. The huge, beehive-shaped dovecote, where hundreds of pigeons were kept for meat and eggs, is eyecatching.

▶ Dundee MAP REF 409 D6

On the north bank of the Firth of Tay, more than a mile wide at this point, Dundee has one of the most spectacular settings of any Scottish city, with the Sidlaw Hills behind, the Fife shore to the south and the North Sea to the east. This is a city that has reinvented itself more than a few times. And as you'll see when you arrive by road or rail via its iconic bridges (two of the longest in Britain), it's busy reinventing itself yet again.

Dundee was an important seaport in medieval times, when it traded with the ports of the Baltic, Scandinavia, France and the Low Countries. It was burned by Edward I's army in 1303, and again in 1547. In 1651 it was comprehensively sacked by the Parliamentarian General George Monck, Oliver Cromwell's right-hand man in Scotland. A generation later, in 1689, the city's burgesses opted for the Williamite cause and closed the city's doors to the Jacobite leader John Graham of Claverhouse, Viscount Dundee.

Thanks to its links with the Baltic, the city was already a major flax-weaving centre by the 17th century. It diversified into cotton weaving, and fortunes were made during Britain's long wars with France in the 18th and 19th centuries as Dundee

▼ The Tay Road Bridge, Firth of Tay

mills turned out vast quantities of canvas sailcloth for the Royal Navy and tent cloth for the Army. Later, the same mills provided the canvas wagon covers that sheltered American pioneers as they headed west. The outbreak of the American Civil War in 1861 cut Dundee off from its main source of raw cotton, and the city's mills shifted to spinning and weaving jute imported from Britain's vast new empire in India. You can still see some of the magnificent homes built by Dundee's 19th-century so-called jute barons along Perth Road, west of the city centre, and in Broughty Ferry, the fishing harbour and ferry port that they transformed into a posh Victorian suburb and resort.

In the absence of heritage attractions to compare with some rival Scottish destinations, Dundee's major selling point is its location. Facing south across the wide, silvery Firth of Tay, it's one of Scotland's sunniest cities. From the summit of Dundee Law, the extinct volcano that dominates its northern skyline, you can look inland to the Cairngorms (see page 105), south over the hills of Fife, far out over the North Sea, or westward up the Tay as far as Perth (see page 327). The long curve of the Tay Bridge, a triumph of 19th-century railway engineering, sweeps across to the Fife shore. Next to it are the stumps of its predecessor, which collapsed in a gale in 1879.

Other Dundee landmarks include Cox's Stack, a jute mill chimney cunningly disguised as an Italianate bell tower. It's one of the few survivors of the chimneys that dominated the city's skyline until the advent of artificial textiles doomed the jute-weaving industry in the second half of the 20th century.

Jute was one of the three Js that supported the city's economy well into the 20th century. The others were jam and journalism. In 1797, James Keiller of Dundee opened the first ever commercial marmalade factory, an enterprise that grew to export its products all over the world. Journalism was, and is, represented by DC Thomson, the Dundee publishing company that brings you newspapers including Dundee's own *Courier and Advertiser*, Aberdeen's *Press and Journal* and the nationwide *Sunday Post*. But for those living outside Scotland, DC Thomson is better known for comics such as *The Beano* and *The Dandy* and characters like Dennis the Menace, Beryl the Peril and Desperate Dan, who you'll find immortalised as bronze statues around the city centre.

Dundee's other big industry was whaling. With an excellent natural harbour conveniently close to Arctic and sub-Arctic waters, it was a home port for a large whaling fleet as early as the 18th century. Whale oil, used to dress yarn and lubricate machinery, was essential to Dundee's weaving industry. As demand for the product grew, Dundee whalers ranged ever

Dundee

0   200 m

further. By the early 19th century – having hunted many Arctic cetaceans close to extinction – they went exploring deep into the uncharted waters of the Southern Ocean.

As the Dundee whalers sailed ever deeper into polar waters, the city's shipbuilders became expert builders of ships that could survive the icy Arctic and Antarctic. It was to Dundee shipwrights that Sir Clement Markham turned to construct the world's first purpose-built scientific research vessel. The Royal Research Ship *Discovery*, which made its first journey to the Antarctic under the command of Captain Robert Falcon Scott, is now Dundee's top attraction and a waterfront landmark.

This entire waterfront area underwent a huge transformation in the second decade of the 21st century, which saw the construction of a new jewel in Dundee's cultural crown, the V & A Museum of Design. Architecturally inspired by Scotland's cliffs, the iconic building juts out over the water, bringing more than a touch of the glamour of London's Victorian and Albert Museum to this new outpost in the north.

Dundee is famous as the childhood home of the man regarded by many as the worst poet ever to write in the English language. William Topaz McGonagall (1825–1902) was a celebrity in his time in Scotland and England, and even toured the United States. Audiences came to hear him recite his *Poetic Gems* while clad head to toe in tartan. His work, with its total lack of any grasp of essentials such as scansion and metre, is inimitable. 'The Tay Bridge Disaster', for example, was penned to commemorate the famous railway catastrophe of 1879:

> *Beautiful Railway Bridge of the Silv'ry Tay!*
> *Alas! I am very sorry to say*
> *That ninety lives have been taken away*
> *On the last Sabbath day of 1879,*
> *Which will be remember'd for a very long time.*

Perhaps it's not so surprising that McGonagall is not honoured with a statue in his adopted home.

The centre of Dundee is compact and best explored on foot. All its main attractions are within a few blocks of St Mary's, one of the city's few remaining medieval edifices. The Steeple Church, its tall, square tower, is a useful landmark, overlooking a large modern shopping centre. A short distance away, the grandiose frontage of the Caird Hall dominates the broad City Square, where you'll find a Christmas market and an open-air ice-skating rink during the festive season. Reform Street leads from the Caird Hall to Albert Square, where you'll find an outstanding museum and art gallery, The McManus, in a grand red sandstone building in Victorian Gothic style.

▼ Dundee at dusk

TAKE IN SOME HISTORY
The Steeple Church
dundeestmarys.co.uk
Nethergate, DD1 4DG | 01382
226271 | Open Jul–Aug Tue, Thu and
Fri 10–12. Services all year Sun at 11

The square tower of Dundee
Parish Church (St Mary's) is the
city's most prominent medieval
landmark. It's one of only a few
buildings in Dundee that survive
from the Middle Ages and it's
regarded as a fine piece of
Scottish Gothic architecture. If it
looks very well preserved, that
is thanks to Sir George Gilbert
Scott, the 19th-century architect
who designed the Albert
Memorial and St Pancras
station as well as The McManus.

Outside the church, a carved
unicorn crowns the stone
column of the city's original
Mercat (Market) Cross, which
has stood here since 1586.

St Mary's was built in about
1440; the steeple was added in
about 1460. Outside, it's ornate,
but within, like most great
Scottish churches, it's a plain
whitewashed, wood-panelled
space with no traces of the
religious artworks that would
have adorned it in the 15th
century. Its original interior was
destroyed when English forces
sacked Dundee in 1547 and the
advent of the Protestant
Reformation in its austere
Scottish form ensured that its
images of the Virgin, saints and
martyrs were never replaced.

...AND SOME
MARITIME HISTORY
Discovery Point
rrsdiscovery.com
Discovery Quay, DD1 4XA | 01382
309060 | Open Apr–Oct Mon–Sat
10–6, Sun 11–6; Nov–Mar Mon–Sat
10–5, Sun 11–5

You can't miss RRS *Discovery*
as you arrive on Dundee's
waterfront. Its triple masts and
single funnel (it was designed
to be powered by both sail and
steam) soar above the dock
where it is moored. Next to the

dock, the glass-domed rotunda of the former ferry terminal now houses a fascinating exhibition and audio-visual display that tell the stories of the Dundee whalers who opened up the polar seas long before more famous explorers ventured there in the late 19th century and early 20th.

After returning from its Arctic mission in 1904, *Discovery* was part of the Hudson Bay Company's merchant fleet until the 1920s, when it made two more research trips to Antarctica. Later moored on the Thames, it became almost derelict. In 1986 it was returned to Dundee and restored. Inside, you can see the cabins, holds, engine room and workspaces, all designed to maximise the cramped spaces available.

Frigate Unicorn
frigateunicorn.org/home
Victoria Dock, DD1 3BP | 01382 200900 | Open Apr–Oct daily 10–5; Nov–Mar Thu–Sun 12–4

A visit to *Unicorn*, the largest wooden Royal Navy warship still afloat, will give you a taste of what life was like aboard a 19th-century warship. There are massive cannons on the gun decks, and you can contrast the crew's spartan living conditions with the accommodation provided for the captain and officers. Built in 1824, *Unicorn* was obsolete even before it was launched, and never went to sea – it was never even fitted with masts. In 1873, it was towed to Dundee docks, where it was used as a training and headquarters vessel until the end of World War II.

VISIT THE MUSEUMS AND GALLERIES

Dundee Museum of Transport
dmoft.co.uk
Unit 10, Market Mews, Market Street, DD1 3LA | 01382 455196
Open Mar–Oct Tue–Sun 10.30–3.30; Nov–Feb Wed, Sat and Sun 10.30–3.30
This museum is a work in progress. One of these days, it

◀ RRS *Discovery* at Discovery Point

will move to a permanent base at the city's Maryfield Tram Depot, which is being restored as an appropriate showcase for this collection of old double-decker buses, steam traction engines, iconic 20th-century sports cars and other historic vehicles. For now, you can just see some of the collection, along with photographs, posters and other memorabilia, at its temporary home in the city centre.

The McManus: Dundee's Art Gallery and Museum

mcmanus.co.uk

Albert Square, DD1 1DA

01382 307200 | Open Mon–Sat 10–5, Sun 12.30–4.30

If it's a rainy day and you have kids with enquiring minds in tow, take them to The McManus and tell them the tragic story of one of the world's most unfortunate sea mammals. No one can even guess why the now legendary Tay Whale – a 41-foot humpback – swam, in 1883, into the Firth of Tay, home of the world's largest whaling fleet. It was, of course, immediately harpooned. The corpse was bought by a Dundee oil merchant and rendered down for its oil, but the skeleton is now a prize exhibit at The McManus. But there's much more here, including an outstanding collection of works by 19th- and 20th-century

Scottish painters. There's also a tremendous and varied assortment of costumes, arts and crafts from virtually every far-flung corner of the former British Empire, many of them brought back by Dundonians who worked or served as soldiers, sailors and colonial civil servants in Asia, Africa, Canada and Australia.

Outside the museum is a modest plaque. It's a memorial to the Dundee men killed while serving with the International Brigades on the Republican side during the Spanish Civil War – and a symbol of Dundee's long history of fierce resistance to... well, just about anything.

Scotland's Jute Museum@ Verdant Works

verdantworks.com

West Henderson's Wynd DD1 5BT | 01382 309060 | Open Apr–Oct Mon–Sat 10–6, Sun 11–6; Nov–Mar Wed–Sat 10.30–4.30, Sun 11–4.30

Verdant Works is a remarkably intact relic of Dundee's once dominant jute industry. It was

▶ Statue of Desperate Dan

one of the last jute mills to close, and its interior has been kept intact. At one time the industry employed 50,000 people in the city. More than half the workforce was female – in many homes, women were the main or sole wage-earners. In the 19th century, this gave working-class Dundee women an unusual degree of control over the family purse-strings.

A visit here is more fun than it sounds, so allow a couple of hours for the full tour. Much of the old weaving and spinning machinery is still in place, and you can listen to recorded stories of everyday life in the mill in the words and voices of the last generation of men and women who worked here.

V & A Museum of Design Dundee

vandadundee.org
1 Riverside Esplanade, DD1 4EZ
See website for opening times and telephone number
The V & A Museum of Design Dundee is not only Scotland's first-ever dedicated design museum, but the only V & A museum outside London. Housed in Kengo Kuma's stunning building, extending from the historic waterfront out over the Tay estuary, its architecture is inspired by the cliffs of Scotland's east coast.

The museum's permanent galleries contain in the region of 300 objects representing a wide range of design – in furniture, textiles, ceramics, fashion, architecture, and print and digital design. The central focus is Charles Rennie Mackintosh's superb Oak Room from Glasgow. Other iconic Scottish designs include objects ranging from a 1745 Jacobite garter and a pair of 18th-century steel Highland pistols to the artwork for a 1960s *Dennis the Menace* comic strip. These help tell the story of Scotland's outstanding design achievements and legacy, bringing together both the V & A collections and loans from all over Scotland.

The museum also offers a changing programme of temporary and internationally important touring exhibitions, presenting the cream of international design.

ENTERTAIN THE FAMILY
Dundee Science Centre

dundeesciencecentre.org.uk
Greenmarket, DD1 4QB | 01382 228800 | Open daily 10–5
This hands-on science centre is a great place to take the family on a rainy day. It's dedicated

◄ Tay Rail Bridge

to understanding the five senses, and kids can search for dinosaur fossils, control robots, watch a live science show and learn about everything from cybernetics to surgery and 3D technology. The climb-through nose – designed to explain what causes snot and what it's for – is a sure-fire hit.

WATCH THE SKIES
Mills Observatory

leisureandculturedundee.com
Balgay Park, Glamis Road, DD2 2UB
01382 435967 | Open Oct–Mar
Mon–Fri 4–10, Sat–Sun 12.30–4;
Apr–Sep open on selected days –
see website

Yet another of Dundee's philanthropists, John Mills, gave the city the observatory that bears his name. Mills was himself a keen amateur astronomer, and the Mills Observatory is rather special. The main building is red sandstone, but the original dome that it supports was made of papier-maché – a light and amazingly strong material that was the ancestor of the cutting-edge composites of the 21st century.

The observatory's massive 16-inch Dobsonian reflector brings the moon, Mars and other planets into close focus, while its fully computerised modern 12-inch Meade Schmidt Cassegrain reflector is capable of locating 30,000 stellar and planetary objects. You'll also find an array of coin-operated viewing devices.

MEET THE WILDLIFE
Camperdown Wildlife Centre

camperdownwildlifecentre.com
Camperdown Country Park, Coupar
Angus Road, DD2 4TF | 01382
431811 | Open Mar–Sep daily
10–4.30; Oct–Feb 10–3.30

This wildlife park, just outside the city, has 85 species of native and other wildlife including lynx, bears, wolves, bats, Arctic foxes, pine martens and horses. New to the centre in 2017 was a troop of 11 endangered macaques. In the summer you can see the animals being fed. Special events year-round include animal handling and feeding days.

TAKE A VIEW
Dundee Law

Walk, drive or cycle to the top of Dundee Law for a view that rivals any panorama in Scotland. Spread out below you from the summit of this extinct volcanic plug are city landmarks like Cox's Stack and the two Tay Bridges. Looking south, you can see all the way across the Firth of Tay to the hills of Fife.

The Law is often called the Law Hill, but as any pedant will tell you, that's a tautology – Law means hill in the old Scots tongue. This was the site of the earliest settlement in the area, but there's nothing left to see of that Iron Age stronghold. On the hill's highest point, the Law Monument remembers the Dundee soldiers who died during World War I and World War II.

GET YOUR SKATES ON
Dundee Ice Arena
dundeeicearena.co.uk
Camperdown Leisure Complex,
Kingsway West, DD2 3SQ
01382 431900
A popular ice rink located just
outside the city, with ice-skating
shows, ice discos, lessons,
public skating, curling and
professional ice hockey games.

CATCH A PERFORMANCE
Caird Hall
cairdhall.co.uk
City Square, DD1 3BB
01382 434940
This venerable venue is home to
Dundee Symphony Orchestra. It
also hosts performances by
visiting classical ensembles,
rock and pop bands, tribute acts
and stand-up comics.

Dundee Rep
dundeerep.co.uk
Tay Square, DD1 1PB
01382 223530
Scotland's leading repertory
theatre is set in Dundee's
up-and-coming cultural
quarter. As well as the summer
repertory season, the theatre
hosts touring productions. The
building is also home to the
excellent contemporary
Scottish Dance Theatre.

Dundee Contemporary Arts (DCA)
dca.org.uk
152 Nethergate, DD1 4DY
01382 909900
The DCA and the Dundee Rep
theatre together form the core
of the arts revival in the city's
cultural quarter. As well as
housing exhibitions of
contemporary art, the DCA is
Dundee's only city-centre
cinema, showing mainstream
and international films.

Whitehall Theatre
whitehalltheatre.com
12 Bellfield Street, DD1 5JA
01382 322684
You'll find old-school
entertainment ranging from
stage hypnotists and magicians
to musicals at this much
loved landmark theatre,
as well as tribute bands and
dance shows.

ENJOY THE NIGHTLIFE
Tropicana, Vogue and Fat Sam's Lounge
tropicanavoguedundee.com
31 South Ward Road, DD1 5JA
01382 228181
You can wallow in an evening of
nostalgia at this 3,500-capacity
club, which has three popular
venues under one roof – retro
dance lounges Tropicana and
Vogue, and the laid-back Fat
Sam's Lounge.

PLAY A ROUND
Carnoustie Golf Links
carnoustiegolflinks.co.uk
20 Links Parade, DD7 7JF | 01241
802270 | Open daily all year
This Championship Course has
been described as Scotland's
'ultimate golfing challenge',
and will host The Open in 2018.
The Open Championship first
came to the course in 1931, and
Carnoustie hosted the Scottish
Open in 1995 and 1996, and was

the venue for the 1999 and 2007 Open Championships.

EAT AND DRINK
Castlehill Restaurant ●●
castlehillrestaurant.co.uk
22 Exchange Street, DD1 3DL
01382 220008

This high-flying restaurant is smart and tasteful and void of cliché. The kitchen, under chef Graham Campbell, makes the most of Scottish ingredients to produce refined and dynamic plates of contemporary food.

DoubleTree by Hilton Dundee
doubletree3.hilton.com
Kingsway West, DD2 5JT
01382 641122

The original stone baronial mansion, bristling with turrets, was built to impress, but the whole place has been brought up to 21st-century spec with a classy conservatory restaurant. The Maze offers an upmarket setting with linen-swathed tables and moody lighting at dinner. The kitchen steers a crowd-pleasing course with appealing menus of tried-and-trusted modern ideas.

Malmaison Dundee ●
malmaison.com
44 Whitehall Crescent, DD1 4AY
01382 339715

The setting for this boutique brasserie is a majestic old hotel, with an intimate candlelit brasserie and darkly atmospheric colour scheme. The menu plays the modern brasserie game too, but isn't scared to step outside the European classics.

Speedwell Bar
speedwell-bar.co.uk
165–167 Perth Road, DD2 1AS
01382 667783

This unspoiled Edwardian art deco bar is worth visiting for its interior alone; all the fitments in the bar and sitting rooms are beautifully crafted mahogany. As well as the cask-conditioned ales, 157 whiskies and imported bottles are offered. The pub is listed so there is no kitchen, but visitors are encouraged to bring their own snacks from nearby bakeries.

▶ **PLACES NEARBY**
Broughty Ferry
Broughty Ferry is a pretty one-time fishing village that has become a suburb of Dundee without losing its distinct character. Streets of small two-storey houses and fisher cottages cluster around a harbour that was once home to a herring fleet, replaced by pleasure boats and a large flock of swans. The medieval castle, rebuilt in the 19th century, commands the harbour and now houses a small museum.

Broughty Castle was an important stronghold in its day. The last time it heard a shot fired in anger was probably during General George Monck's subjugation of Scotland in 1650. In 1651, Monck systematically looted Dundee. Local legend has it that his fleet of more than

▲ Broughty Castle

50 ships laden with gold and silver was sunk by a storm off Broughty Ferry, and that its treasure still lies beneath the sands of the Firth of Tay.

Beyond the castle is a long sweep of golden sand that is popular with windsurfers, kite-flyers and dog-walkers. This is Broughty Beach, and you can walk along it for miles. At its northern end, it merges with the sands of Monifieth, and then stretches all the way to the Barry Buddon peninsula. When the Ministry of Defence firing ranges at Barry Buddon are not in use (keep an ear open for gunfire, and look out for red flags that show firing is taking place) you can walk all the way around this sand-dune-covered peninsula to Carnoustie.

Broughty Castle Museum and Art Gallery
leisureandculturedundee.com
Castle Approach, DD5 2TF | 01382
436916 | Open Apr–Sep Mon–Sat 10–4, Sun 12.30–4; Oct–Mar Tue–Sat 10–4, Sun 12.30–4

Over the four floors of the castle, you can see collections of objects that bring Broughty Ferry's past as a fishing, whaling and sealing community to life. You can also discover the castle's military history as a medieval stronghold, and then as a 19th-century garrison fortress. There are also several paintings from the Orchar Collection, the rest of which can be seen at The McManus in Dundee.

Ne'er Day Dook
If you've over-indulged while on a Hogmanay visit to Dundee, you can join hardy locals who take a 'dook' (dip) in the bitterly cold waters of the River Day at Broughty Ferry on the morning of New Year's Day. It's reputedly an effective, if brutal, hangover cure.

▶ Dunfermline MAP REF 402 B2

The small town of Dunfermline has played a significant part in Scotland's history, and it's dotted with heritage sites spanning some 900 years. Malcolm III made it his capital in the mid-11th century, and several Scots monarchs are buried in its abbey. It remained the royal seat until 1603, when James VI, newly crowned James I of England, moved his court to London.

His son Charles, later Charles I, was born in Dunfermline, as was the great Scots-American industrialist and philanthropist Andrew Carnegie. Famous for fostering self-education for working people by establishing thousands of libraries and reading rooms around the world, he funded the first Carnegie Library in his home town in 1883. In recent years, Dunfermline has made a bigger effort to promote this rich inheritance, referring to its historic heart as the town's 'heritage quarter'.

TAKE IN SOME HISTORY

Dunfermline Abbey and Palace

historicenvironment.scot
KY12 7PE | 01383 739026 | Open Apr–Sep daily 9.30–5.30; Oct daily 10–4; Nov–Mar Sat–Wed 10–4

With its great Romanesque nave, Dunfermline Abbey is one of Scotland's most magnificent medieval places of worship, dating back to the era when Dunfermline was Scotland's capital. Alexander III – whose untimely death in a fall from his horse in 1286 led to Scotland's long wars of independence against England – is buried here, as is Robert the Bruce. David I endowed the abbey in the early 12th century, bringing English stonemasons from Durham to carve its pillars. Next to the abbey are the ruins of the royal palace built by James VI. The abbey fell into disrepair following the Protestant Reformation, and the nave is the only surviving part of the original building.

Abbot House Heritage Centre

abbothouse.co.uk
Maygate, KY12 7NE | 01383 733266
Open Apr–Oct daily 9.30–5; Nov–Mar daily 10–4

Built in the mid-15th century, this is one of Dunfermline's oldest buildings, brilliantly restored in the 1990s by the Dunfermline Heritage Trust. Among the displays are two 14th-century skeletons, discovered during excavations in the mid-1990s. There's also some fine early glasswork. Sadly, Abbot House is temporarily closed, although you can still admire the exterior of this pretty pink-harled medieval building. It is hoped that it will re-open as a cultural and heritage centre with a cafe towards the end of 2018.

Andrew Carnegie Birthplace Museum

carnegiebirthplace.com
Moodie Street, KY12 7PL | 01383 724302 | Open Mar–Nov Mon–Sat 10–5, Sun 2–5

▲ Andrew Carnegie Birthplace Museum

The great philanthropist Andrew Carnegie was born in this weaver's cottage in 1835 and emigrated with his parents to the US in 1848. Aged 13, he started work in a Pittsburgh cotton mill, and began to make his fortune. Mortgaging his family home, he invested $500 in the new railroads, and never looked back.

You could argue that Carnegie was as much an exploiter of the workers in his steel mills as any of his contemporaries, and it's true that he also profited enormously from the American Civil War, which created huge demand for his products. But what sets Carnegie aside was his decision, having amassed one of the greatest fortunes of all time, to give it all away to worthy causes. By the time of his death in 1919, he'd disposed of $350,695,653 – equivalent to $4.75 billion in 2015 terms. Displays and graphics tell the story of his life and legacy.

TAKE A TOUR
Discover Dunfermline Tours
discoverdunfermline.com
07581 572354 | Call or see website to book tours
Discover Dunfermline Tours will take you to spots like St Margaret's Cave, reached by 87 steps, where Malcolm III's saintly queen would pray during the early 11th century, and to other religious sites around Dunfermline and further afield.

PLAY A ROUND
Dunfermline Golf Club
dunfermlinegolfclub.com

Pitfirrane, Crossford, KY12 8QW
01383 723534 | Open daily all year
A gently undulating parkland
course with interesting
contours and no water hazards.
The centre of the course is a
disused walled garden, which
is a haven for wildlife.

EAT AND DRINK
Grill 48
grill48.com
48 East Port, KY12 7JB
01383 720848
This cafe-restaurant in the
centre of Dunfermline serves
snacks, cakes and scones, hot
drinks and light lunches and
evening meals.

▸ **PLACES NEARBY**
Scottish Vintage Bus Museum
svbm.org.uk

Commerce Park, Lathalmond,
KY12 0SJ | 01383 623380 | Open
Apr–Oct Sun 12.30–5
Strictly for lovers of vehicular
nostalgia, this collection of
vintage public transport includes
a restored horse-drawn tram
and dozens of veteran buses.

Knockhill Racing Circuit
knockhill.co.uk
KY12 9TF | 01383 723337
Open Mon–Fri 9–6, Sat–Sun 9–5
You can watch touring car,
superbike and hot hatch racing
at Scotland's National
Motorsport Centre, take the
wheel of a go-kart or off-road
four-wheel-drive vehicle or
drive racing or rally cars.
Children can drive at the
karting centre. Advance
booking is advised.

▸ **Dunkeld** MAP REF 408 B6

Arriving in Dunkeld, it can be hard to believe that this douce
wee town on the east bank of the River Tay was once one of the
most important places in Scotland. Dunkeld is pretty at any
time of year, but the lush woodlands that surround it are
arguably at their best in summer and autumn.

Although the tidy town that you see today dates from the
18th and 19th centuries (and from careful restoration of many
buildings by the National Trust for Scotland in the 1950s),
Dunkeld's history goes far deeper. Kenneth MacAlpin, first King
of Scots, brought relics of St Columba from Iona (see page 382)
to Dunkeld's monastery in AD 849, partly to save them from
Viking raids on that remote island monastery, but also as part
of his drive to cement Picts and Scots into one united kingdom.
Dunkeld was conveniently close to Kenneth's new royal seat at
Scone (see page 350), and became – for a while – one of the
most important religious centres in the country. Sacked by
Protestant reformers in 1560, the cathedral's cavernous nave is
now roofless, but tradition has it that the saintly relics remain
beneath the chancel steps. The cathedral grounds, beside the
River Tay, all neat lawns and rhododendrons, are lovely at any

time of year. The seven-arched bridge that crosses the Tay was built to the design of the great 18th-century architect Thomas Telford.

Dunkeld owes much of its present appearance to the Atholl dukes, who rebuilt the town during the early 18th century after it was almost destroyed in heavy fighting in 1689 between the Jacobite Highland Host and the Cameronians, a regiment from among the hard-line Covenanting sect named after the fiery preacher Richard Cameron. The Highlanders were driven back, but much of Dunkeld was burned. When it was rebuilt, terraced cottages were squeezed into a compact centre of just two main streets – Cathedral Street and High Street – with a neat little square, called The Cross.

TAKE IN SOME HISTORY
Dunkeld Cathedral
dunkeldcathedral.org.uk
Cathedral Street, PH8 0AW | 01350 727249 | Open Apr–Sep daily 10–5.30; Oct–Mar daily 10–4
Dunkeld's ruined cathedral stands in a picturesque, shady setting on the banks of the river, and dates back to the 13th century, although its history as a monastic site goes back to the 6th century. The most substantial part standing today is the choir, which still serves as the parish church. Look out for a sign indicating the Parent Larch behind the cathedral. This particular tree was imported from Austria in 1738, and became the source of many trees in nearby forests.

GET ACTIVE
Dunkeld Park
dunkeldhousehotel.co.uk
Hilton Dunkeld House Hotel
01350 727771
This outdoor centre offers a range of country sports including clay-pigeon shooting, off-road driving, archery, pony trekking, air-rifle shooting and quad biking.

ENTERTAIN THE KIDS
Going Pottie
goingpottie.com
Cathedral Street, PH8 0AW | 01350 728044 | Open Mon–Sat 10–5, Sun 11–4
From daubing a plaster frog to decorating your own dinner service, there's something for all ages at this friendly ceramic painting centre.

◀ Dunkeld Cathedral

▶ **PLACES NEARBY**

Cross Telford's graceful bridge to visit a trio of small visitor attractions in and around Little Dunkeld and Birnam, on the west bank of the Tay. There are good circular signposted walks around here and along the riverbank. Neil Gow (1727–1807), the greatest fiddler of his day, is buried in the Little Dunkeld kirkyard. He was patronised by the Duke and Duchess of Atholl, who paid him £5 a year to play for their guests at Blair Castle (see page 99), where you can see Gow's portrait and his violin.

The Hermitage
nts.org.uk
Off the A9, Dunkeld, PH8 0AN
01350 72864 | Open daily 24 hours
Once part of one of Scotland's most important 18th-century landscapes, The Hermitage has an attractive woodland walk through spectacular Douglas firs (including, at 211 feet, one of the tallest trees in the country), to Ossian's Hall, a folly overlooking the Black Linn falls.
Previous visitors included Wordsworth, Queen Victoria and Turner. Ossian's Hall was refurbished in 2007 with sliding panels and mirrored artwork to recreate its original effect.

Beatrix Potter Garden and Exhibition Centre
birnamarts.com
Station Road, Birnam, Dunkeld
01350 727674 | Open mid-Mar to Nov daily 10–5; Dec to mid-Mar daily 10 4.30

Lovers of Beatrix Potter's tales should head to the Birnam Exhibition and Garden Centre. The author of these much-loved stories for children spent childhood holidays near Dunkeld, and was inspired by the rabbits, red squirrels and landscapes that she saw here. Children can dress up as animal characters like Peter Rabbit and Mrs Tiggywinkle.

Loch of the Lowes Visitor Centre and Wildlife Experience
scottishwildlifetrust.org
Dunkeld, PH8 0HH | 01350 727337
Open Mar–Oct daily 10–5; Nov–Feb Fri–Sun 10.30–4
East of Dunkeld, there is a variety of wildlife at Loch of the Lowes. Ospreys, long extinct in Britain, were reintroduced in 1970 and have bred successfully ever since, migrating to Scotland from Africa every spring. Other migrant birds that visit include thousands of greylag geese, which arrive in autumn to spend the winter here. You can also see red squirrels and – if you're lucky – otter and roe deer.

Nae Limits
naelimits.co.uk
Ballinluig, PH9 0LG | 01796 482600
Open daily 9–9
This adventure sports centre offers water-, land- and snow-based activities. Try sports from white-water rafting to cliff-jumping, according to the season. Age restrictions apply, so check ahead.

▲ Dunoon

▶ **Dunoon** MAP REF 401 D3

Paddle steamers used to bring huge crowds from Gourock to Dunoon, and there are still regular ferry services here. On the grassy headland between the town's two bays are the remains of the 13th-century royal castle, largely destroyed in 1685. Dunoon is busiest each year during late August for the Cowal Highland Gathering, when more than 150 pipe bands from all over the world compete for prestigious trophies.

Morag's Fairy Glen, off the road south from Dunoon, has shaded walks along the Berry Burn, but for more expansive views, continue onward to Toward Point lighthouse (not open), where you can look out across the water to Bute (see page 81) and down to Largs. In the grounds of the stout 19th-century Castle Toward is a ruined 15th-century tower house, somewhat confusingly called Toward Castle. One of the vilest atrocities of the Civil War began here, when Campbell of Ardkinglas besieged the Lamonts, who were Stuart loyalists. Although guaranteed safety, 36 Lamont men were taken to Dunoon and hanged – a monument in Tom-a-Mhoid Road marks the place.

EAT AND DRINK
Perk Up
31 Ferry Brae, Dunoon PA23 7DJ
01369 701516
Locals reckon this friendly cafe to be the best in town, serving up excellent coffee, teas and plenty of home-baked goodies. There's freshly made soup at lunchtime, imaginative sandwiches and filled rolls to take away.

▶ PLACES NEARBY

Near Sandbank, on the shore of Holy Loch, are the huge stones forming Adam's Grave, a Neolithic burial chamber. You can take the Ardnadam Heritage Trail to see the site of a prehistoric enclosure.

To the north is Benmore Botanic Garden, an outpost of Edinburgh's Royal Botanic Garden (see page 176).

Benmore Botanic Garden
rbge.org.uk
A815, near Dunoon, PA23 8QU
01369 706261
Open Mar, Oct daily 10–5; Apr–Sep daily 10–6

This delightful garden has a dramatic mountainside setting on the Cowal Peninsula. The impressive Redwood Avenue through which you enter the garden was planted in 1863 by wealthy American Piers Patrick. The idea of a west-coast botanic garden came from Isaac Bayley Balfour, Regius Keeper of the Royal Botanic Garden in Edinburgh from 1888 to 1922. 'Puck's Hut', tiled in red cedar, and found in the Formal Garden, celebrates him.

There are plantings representing a wide range of world flora, for example, Chile, Tasmania, Japan and Bhutan.

▶ East Kilbride   MAP REF 401 F4

East Kilbride made history in 1947 when it was founded as Scotland's first new town, built to house Glaswegians decanted from the city's notorious slums in more salubrious, newly built homes. Located on the southern outskirts of Glasgow (see page 206), about 8 miles from the centre, its main attraction is the National Museum of Rural Life, an outpost of the National Museums of Scotland.

VISIT THE MUSEUM
National Museum of Rural Life
nms.ac.uk/rural
Wester Kittochside, Phillipshill Road, G76 9HR | 0300 123 6789
Open daily 10–5
Clydesdale horses, Tamworth piglets, blackface sheep, Aberdeen Angus cattle and other heritage breeds of barnyard animal are stars of the show at this family-friendly open-air museum and working farm, set in 170 acres. The museum re-creates farming methods that seem fascinatingly antiquated to today's kids – such as milking cows by hand and ploughing with horses – but that were still used as recently as the 1950s.

GET OUTDOORS
James Hamilton Heritage Park
slleisureandculture.co.uk
Stewartfield Way, G74 5LB | 01355 276611 | Watersports Centre open Jul to mid-Aug Mon–Fri 11–9, Sat, Sun 11–5.30; Apr–Jun Mon–Fri 4–9, Sat, Sun 11–5.30; mid-Aug, Sep Mon–Fri 4–8, Sat, Sun 11–5.30

You can try windsurfing, dinghy sailing and kayaking on the small loch at this country park in East Kilbride. Pedal boats can also be hired.

EAT AND DRINK
Gracie's On the Loch Cafe
slleisureandculture.co.uk
James Hamilton Heritage Park, Stewartfield Way, G74 5LB
01355 244905
This waterside cafe serves up soup, snacks, sandwiches and hot drinks by the loch.

▶ **PLACES NEARBY**
Aside from Glasgow (see page 206), Hamilton (see page 243), another suburb, is to the west, with Coatbridge (see page 111), a little further beyond.

▶ East Neuk MAP REF 403 D2

Fife juts into the North Sea, between the Firths of Forth and Tay that reach deep into Scotland from the North Sea coast. The coast here, along the north shore of the Firth of Forth, is called the East Neuk (neuk means corner in Scots, so this is Fife's east corner).

Small fishing villages are strung along this stretch of coast. They're no longer entirely dependent on fishing, although their small fleets provide fresh-caught seafood to the fishmongers and restaurants of Edinburgh as well as to local fish-and-chip shops – you can eat some of the best fish and chips in Scotland beside the harbours at Anstruther and Pittenweem.

CHECK OUT THE VILLAGES
Crail
The most easterly of the East Neuk fishing villages, Crail has a charter dating back to 1178 and a much-photographed 16th-century harbour. Village houses, with their pantiled roofs and crow-stepped gables, are distinctive examples of Scots vernacular architecture. The square-towered tollbooth has a Dutch bell, cast in 1520. In nearby Marketgate there are some fine 17th- and 18th-century town houses, with a mercat (market) cross, crowned by a rampant unicorn. To the southeast is a good view of the Isle of May, with its lighthouse.

Anstruther
Anstruther is a larger resort town and former herring fishing port. The town also has a history of smuggling, which centred on the Dreel burn (stream) and the 16th-century Smuggler's Inn.

Pittenweem
Pittenweem is the main fisheries port for the East Neuk. The town dates back to the seventh century, when St Fillan based himself in a cave here (in Cove Wynd) while converting the local Picts to Christianity. A priory grew up here in the 13th century, and the harbour dates from the 16th century.

St Monans

The tiny houses of St Monans crowd around its harbour, where shipbuilding as well as fish brought prosperity in the 19th century. The squat Auld Kirk dates from 1362.

Elie

Elie is the most westerly of the East Neuk villages, and its golden sands made it a popular holiday resort in the late 19th century. A causeway leads to a rocky islet, with panoramic views and a watersports centre.

VISIT THE MUSEUM

Scottish Fisheries Museum

scotfishmuseum.org
Harbourhead, Anstruther, KY10 3AB
01333 310628 | Open Apr–Sep
Mon–Sat 10–5, Sun 11–5; Oct–Mar
Mon–Sat 10–4.30, Sun 12–4.30
Visit the Scottish Fisheries Museum for a fascinating glimpse into the life of fishermen and their families in the days when their vessels were propelled by sail or steam. There's a gallery of plans, pictures and models dedicated to the fast sailing boats known as Zulus that were typical of the East Neuk fishing fleets in the 19th century and early 20th. The museum is housed in a complex of historic buildings including the medieval Abbot's House and Merchant House, a cottage that re-creates everyday fisherfolk life, and a boatyard where you can see 19 traditional fishing boats. Several of them, including the 1901 *Reaper*, are still seaworthy, and take part in historic boating events every summer.

GO FOR A WALK

Fife Coastal Path

fifecoastalpath.co.uk
The East Neuk is the most appealing stretch of the Fife

▼ Pittenweem

Coastal Path, which stretches some 117 miles from North Queensferry (see page 365) at its southern end to the Tay Bridge in the north, with an extension along the south shore of the Firth of Tay to Newburgh, near Perth. To walk the full distance will take you up to six days, with plenty of convenient pubs, cafes and places to stay along the way, great views and glimpses of ships, seals and seabirds.

GET ACTIVE
East Neuk Outdoors
eastneukoutdoors.co.uk
Cellardyke Park, KY10 3AW
01333 310370 | Open Apr–Sep daily 10–5, booking recommended
Beside the sea at Cellardyke, just outside Anstruther, East Neuk Outdoors offers activities for the whole family such as archery, abseiling, canoeing and orienteering. You can also hire off-road bicycles and play on a putting green. Minimum age of 8 for activities.

TAKE A BOAT TRIP
Anstruther Pleasure Cruises
isleofmayferry.com
Middle Pier, Anstruther, KY10 3AB
07957 585200 | Sailings daily Apr–Sep. Call or see website for schedules
The *May Princess* sails from Anstruther to the Isle of May. The trip lasts about four and a half to five hours, including two or three hours ashore.

GET ACTIVE
Elie Watersports
eliewatersports.co.uk
Elie Harbour | 01333 330962
Open May–Sep daily 10–6
Sheltered Elie Bay is a great place to learn water sports, and this centre offers windsurfing, sailing and canoeing courses. There are also mountain bikes to hire.

▼ St Monans Windmill, Fife Coastal Path

EAT AND DRINK
Anstruther Fish Bar
anstrutherfishbar.co.uk
42–44 Shore Street, KY10 3AQ
01333 310518
Next to the Fisheries Museum, this fish-and-chip shop also has a small restaurant where you can sample locally caught haddock, mackerel, lobster, crab, organically farmed cod, and venison burgers, as well as Scottish berry and fruit wines from the Cairn o'Mhor winery near Perth.

The Cellar ⊛⊛⊛
thecellaranstruther.co.uk
24 East Green, Anstruther, KY10 3AA
01333 310378
Just off the harbour front is a pretty cobbled courtyard leading to the 17th-century house, once a cooperage and smokery, that is now home to The Cellar. The dining room has lots of period charm with low ceilings and an open fire, with a sophisticated modern British menu.

Tammie Norie Tea Room
scotfishmuseum.org
Scottish Fisheries Museum,
Harbourhead, KY10 3AB
01333 310628
The Fisheries Museum's cosy tea room serves hot and cold drinks, cakes, scones, sandwiches and soups.

▶ PLACES NEARBY
Isle of May
The East Neuk's biggest natural attraction is the Isle of May, home in spring and summer to hundreds of thousands of

5 top walks

▶ **West Highland Way**, Loch Lomond and Fort William, pages 291, 199

▶ **John Muir Way**, Dunbar, page 134

▶ **Fife Coastal Path**, East Neuk, page 155

▶ **Water of Leith**, Edinburgh, page 179

▶ **Isle of Arran Coastal Way**, Isle of Arran, page 80

seabirds. Approximately 120,000 puffins (known in Fife dialect as tammie nories) nest here each year, and there are colonies of terns, eider duck, guillemots, razorbills and kittiwakes. More than 100 grey seals breed here too. Anstruther Pleasure Cruises (see opposite) will take you there every day during summer – allow about five hours, including about two and a half hours on the island.

The island is a rocky outcrop in the Firth of Forth, six miles offshore and clearly visible from the villages of the East Neuk. It has a history of human habitation dating back to the ninth century, when the hermit Adrian lived here until martyred by Vikings in AD 875. He was soon sainted, and by the 12th century there was a monastery dedicated to him. It has been partially excavated, but remains are scanty. Today the most significant buildings here are two lighthouses dating to 1636 and 1816. The seabirds are the big attraction though.

▶ East Stewartry Coast NSA MAP REF 399 D5

This National Scenic Area is centred on Rough Firth, and Orchardton and Auchencairn Bays. The broad tidal flats of the Mersehead Sands, west of Southerness Point, mark the point where the saltings of Preston Merse meet the fossil cliffs and raised beaches of the rocky Sandyhills Coast. Inland, the hills of Dalbeattie Forest rise to more than 984 feet at Maidenpap and Long Fell. To the west, Hestan Island and Rough Island, in the hands of the National Trust for Scotland, provide important sanctuaries for the abundant birdlife of the estuary.

The NSA is enclosed to the west by the ridge of hills running from Balcarry Point to the 1,282-foot (391m) summit of Bengairn Hill, crossing the summits of Screel Hill and Croach Hill to reach the River Urr. Dalbeattie, noted for its granite quarries, is the natural centre for the region but it lies north of the NSA, at the first crossing of the River Urr.

The only settlements within the NSA are Kippford, a yachting centre on Rough Firth, and, to the south, the quiet seaside resort of Rockcliffe. Nearby is the Mote of Mark, the remains of a prehistoric vitrified fort, now cared for by the National Trust for Scotland.

TAKE IN SOME HISTORY
Mote of Mark

nts.org.uk

Rockcliffe | Open access

Overlooking the Urr estuary, this fort was occupied during the sixth century and appears to have been destroyed by fire in the seventh. Archaeologists have determined that the hilltop was enclosed by a huge stone and timber-laced rampart, with a timber hall surrounded by workshops and stables.

This was evidently a wealthy site with trading contacts across Europe, possibly the court or citadel of a powerful Dark Age chieftain. Finds from the site include glass beads and wine jars from central France and glassware from Germany.

Elegant Celtic bronze jewellery has also been discovered. The remains of the ramparts can still be seen and an on-site interpretation panel has a vivid reconstruction of the fort.

▶ PLACES NEARBY
Orchardton Tower

historicenvironment.scot

Castle Douglas, DG7 1QH

Open Apr–Sep daily 9.30–5.30; Oct daily 10–4; Nov–Mar Sat–Wed 10–4

Of all the small tower houses and castles built in 15th-century Scotland, Orchardton is the one that gives the visitor a clear impression of what domestic life must have been like in Scottish medieval feudal society. It's also unusual in being the only round tower house in Scotland.

▶ View from the NSA towards Hestan Island

▶ **Edinburgh** MAP REF 402 C3

Edinburgh is unquestionably one of Britain's most spectacular cities. Its heart, the Old Town, is a treasury of architecture stretching back to medieval times. While the Old Town is an unplanned, higgledy-piggledy labyrinth of narrow lanes (called wynds or closes), Edinburgh's New Town – new only by contrast – is a restrained but splendid district of squares, crescents and gardens surrounded by enviable Georgian town houses. Both Old Town and New Town have UNESCO World Heritage status.

An 18th-century poet, Robert Fergusson, nicknamed Edinburgh Auld Reekie (Old Smoky) because of the smoke from thousands of chimneys that darkened the stonework of its buildings and the spires of its many churches. But Scotland's capital no longer deserves that nickname. Since clean-air legislation enacted in the second half of the 20th century, rain has washed away the soot of centuries. As a result, the copper domes of grand 19th-century public buildings glow a vivid green when the sun shines, as do the statues of the great and good that line the streets of the city centre.

Edinburgh's surroundings are as spectacular as its architecture. The city is dominated by hills and the sea, with the rolling Pentland Hills to the south and the broad expanse of the Firth of Forth to the north. The city's own miniature mountain, Arthur's Seat, looms spectacularly over the Old Town and the Palace of Holyroodhouse, dwarfing even Castle Rock and its crowning, iconic fortress.

Edinburgh Castle is the best place to begin your visit. It's right in the centre of the city, and the panoramic view you get from its ramparts will give you a feel for the city's geography and help you decide where to go next. For many visitors, the logical next step is a stroll down the Royal Mile, the chain of streets (Castle Hill, Lawnmarket, High Street and Canongate) that stretches downhill from Castle Esplanade to the Palace of Holyroodhouse at its foot, with more than a dozen museums and visitor attractions dotted along its length. At the foot of Castle Rock, on its north side, the cobbled Grassmarket is lined with quirky boutiques and old-fashioned pubs. One of these, the Last Drop, stands next to the site of the old gallows, where public hangings took place until 1784, its name a grim play on words. Another, the White Hart Inn, was reputedly a favourite watering hole of Robert Burns (not that Burns ever found a pub he didn't like). The Grassmarket was also a haunt of the

◀ City view from Calton Hill

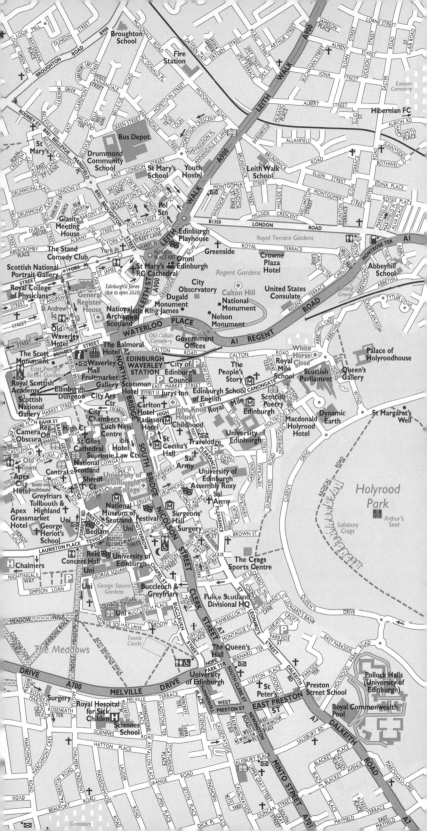

notorious 19th-century so-called body-snatchers Burke and Hare, who murdered their victims to sell on to the anatomists of the city's hospitals.

Below Castle Rock and the spine of the Royal Mile, Princes Street Gardens is a lovely, leafy space that's filled with flowers and greenery in summer. Looming over it is the Gothic spire of the Scott Monument, commemorating 19th-century literary giant Sir Walter Scott.

These gardens – and the New Town that lies south of them – were created in the mid-18th century. The Old Town no longer had room for the city's swelling population and had become unbearably crowded and insanitary. Edinburgh's bourgeoisie wanted a more salubrious environment, and in 1766 a competition was held to decide who should design a new, planned town on open land north of the original city. The winner was an unknown architect, James Craig, who laid out a grid of wide streets and crescents north of what is now Princes Street. Craig's grand plan took shape quickly, and over the next 20 to 30 years the New Town spread downward to the west and north as far as the Water of Leith.

Dividing Old Town and New Town was the Nor' Loch. In 1460, a stream had been dammed to create this shallow body of water and strengthen the defences of the Castle. It quickly became a sewer into which the residents of the Old Town dumped their garbage and emptied their chamber-pots. The stench must have been appalling, and in the modernising spirit of the Age of Enlightenment the loch was drained and a new crossing, North Bridge, was built to connect the Old

▲ Edinburgh at night; John Knox House; Scott Monument

Town with the new, smarter district. Meanwhile, builders digging out the foundations of the New Town created an earthen ramp across the former Nor' Loch by dumping two million cartloads of earth and rubble to create The Mound, where the Scottish National Gallery and the Royal Scottish Academy now stand.

All of this is laid out beneath you as you stand on Calton Hill, at the east end of Princes Street, surrounded by monuments and follies. The grandest of these is the National Monument. Modelled on the Parthenon in Athens, it was conceived as a monument to the Scottish servicemen who died during the Napoleonic Wars, but was left unfinished when funds raised by public subscription ran out in 1829.

From here, views extend north across the Firth of Forth to the hills of Fife, west to the Forth bridges and the hills of central Scotland, south to the Pentlands, and east to the conical mound of Berwick Law and the Lammermuirs, while closer to the city centre are the wooded slopes of the Braid Hills and Corstorphine Hill – very pleasant places for a walk at any time of year, and about 20 minutes by bus from the heart of the city.

Princes Street, Edinburgh's main shopping street, stretches westwards from the foot of Calton Hill to the West End, Edinburgh's theatreland, with George Street and Queen Street running parallel to it. Princes Street is now largely car-free, with access granted only to buses, taxis and Edinburgh's sleek new trams. These finally came into service in 2014, several years late and vastly over budget (originally planned to cost £375 million, the eventual cost to the city is estimated to be about £1 billion). Trams run between York Place (close to the east end of Princes Street) and Edinburgh Airport, taking 20 to 25 minutes.

George Street is lined with smart shops, bars and restaurants. At its western end, the landmark green copper dome of West Register House dominates Charlotte Square. The epitome of New Town style, the square is surrounded by gracious buildings including the beautifully preserved Georgian House and Bute House, official residence of the First Minister.

Edinburgh is – like many cities – a jigsaw of villages, and it's well worth getting beyond the city centre to discover parts of the city that retain their own distinctive character. Down by the Firth of Forth, Leith (see page 280) became part of Edinburgh only in 1920 and Leithers are proud of their separate identity. Leith has recovered from the decline of the docks that were once its living, and its waterfront, The Shore, has some of the city's best pubs and eating places.

A couple of miles east, Portobello is Edinburgh's seaside, with a long stretch of golden sand that attracts droves of city dwellers on sunny summer days. On the northern fringe of the New Town, beside the Water of Leith, Stockbridge takes its name from the river over which cattle were once driven from outlying farms on the way to the city. It's now a charming, stylishly bohemian suburb, with antique and second-hand shops, bars and brasseries.

Heading west, Cramond (see page 113) is a leafy residential suburb that has grown beyond its original settlement of whitewashed cottages where the River Almond meets the Firth of Forth. From here, you can walk along the shore all the way to South Queensferry (see page 364), passing beneath the Forth Bridge on the way.

There's plenty to occupy you in Edinburgh however long you plan to stay, but if you itch to combine Scotland's capital with its other sights it's easy to do. The new Borders Railway, running from Waverley Station in the city centre on a track that closed in the 1960s, makes it easy to get to Galashiels and Tweedbank in the heart of the Scottish Borders. Fast trains and good roads connect you with Scottish cities north of Edinburgh. And with Glasgow (see page 206) less than 40 minutes away by rail, it's easy to combine the attractions of the two cities.

▶ **Edinburgh Castle** MAP REF 162

edinburghcastle.gov.uk
Castle Hill, EH1 2NG | 0131 225 9846 | Open Apr–Sep daily 9.30–6;
Oct–May daily 9.30–5

From its perch high on Castle Rock, with near-vertical cliffs on three sides, Edinburgh Castle dominates the city. There's evidence of Bronze Age settlement on Castle Rock as early at the ninth century BC. It was a stronghold of the Gododdin, who called it Din Eidyn. In AD 638 it fell to Northumbria's Angles, who renamed it Edinburgh. In 1018 it was taken by Malcolm II, and would go on to change hands repeatedly between the Scots and the English over the next several hundred years. In 1296 the castle held out against Edward I, the commonly named Hammer of the Scots, for all of three days, and it only once successfully withstood an English attack, in 1400. In 1573, its walls were reduced to rubble by English gunners. During the turbulent 17th century it was twice taken by the Covenanters, and then by Cromwell's Ironsides, and then in 1689 it fell almost without a fight to the forces of William of Orange. A Jacobite assault in 1715 failed, but prompted the government to strengthen its defences.

The new fortifications helped the castle withstand a second Jacobite attack in 1745, and its new guns fired on Edinburgh itself after the rest of the city surrendered to Bonnie Prince Charlie.

There is still a military presence at Edinburgh Castle, and Castle Esplanade – outside the main gates – is the venue for the Royal Edinburgh Military Tattoo, with nightly performances by the bands of British and Commonwealth armed forces.

The vast sprawl of the castle contains buildings from many centuries. The splendid Great Hall and the Royal Palace were built for James IV in the early 16th century, while the fine half-moon battery and portcullis gate date from the 1570s. The Crown Room, on the first floor of the Royal Palace, contains the castle's greatest treasures: the Honours of Scotland, consisting of crown, sceptre and sword. The Stone of Destiny shares the same display case. Originally at Scone Palace (see page 350), it was the stone on which Scottish kings were crowned until it was pinched by Edward I and taken to Westminster Abbey in London. It was returned by the British Government in 1996 as a sop to rising nationalist sentiment.

The 12th-century St Margaret's Chapel, the castle's oldest structure, is still used for weddings and baptisms. Next to it, you'll see the monumental black hulk of Mons Meg, the huge 15th-century siege gun given to King James II of Scotland by Philip the Good, Duke of Burgundy. This monstrous bombard – cast by the expert iron-founders of Mons – was a truly princely gift. A state-of-the-art weapon, it could hurl a 400-pound cannonball almost two miles. No castle walls could withstand such weapons.

There's more military history at the Scottish National War Museum, in the castle's former artillery store, while on the highest point of Castle Rock, the Scottish National War Memorial honours the 200,000 Scottish dead of World Wars I and II.

▼ Scottish War Memorial and Palace Block, Edinburgh Castle

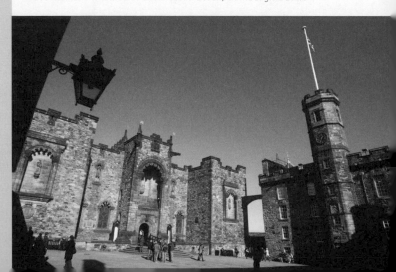

▶ **Palace of Holyroodhouse** MAP REF 163

royalcollection.org.uk
EH8 8DX | 0131 556 5100
Open Apr–Oct daily 9.30–6; Nov–Mar daily 9.30–4.30 (last admission 1 hour
before closing). Liable to close at short notice in May

This pepperpot-towered castle at the foot of the Royal Mile is the
Queen's official home in Scotland, so it may be closed at short
notice. It's thus a living palace, but it's steeped in history and filled
with works of art from the Royal Collection. You'll find fine works
in the Queen's Gallery, which houses a gorgeous collection of
paintings, jewellery and art objects presented to British kings and
queens by loyal subjects and other monarchs.

The palace was probably founded in 1128 as an Augustinian
monastery. In the 15th century it became a guest house for the
neighbouring Holyrood Abbey (now a scenic ruin), and its name is
said to derive from the Holy Rood, a fragment of Christ's cross
belonging to David I (c.1080–1153). Mary, Queen of Scots stayed
and was married here, and a brass plate marks where her
favourite, David Rizzio, was murdered in her private apartments in
the west tower in 1566. Following serious fire damage in 1650
during the Civil War, major rebuilding was required. Bonnie Prince
Charlie held court here in 1745, followed by George IV in 1822, and
later Queen Victoria on her way to Balmoral (see page 109).

The state rooms, designed for Charles II by architect William
Bruce (1630–1710) and hung with Brussels tapestries, are
particularly elaborate and splendid. A number of preposterous
royal portraits painted in a hurry by the Dutch artist Jacob de Wet
between 1684 and 1686 are on display in the Great Gallery.

TAKE IN SOME HISTORY

Canongate Kirk

canongatekirk.org.uk

Canongate, EH8 8BR | 0131 556 3515 | Open Jun–Sep Mon–Sat 10.30–4, Sun 10–12.30; Oct–May Sun 10–12.30

A lively bronze statue of poet Robert Fergusson (1750–74) greets you as you enter the kirkyard of this 17th-century church. Fergusson, who gave Edinburgh its nickname Auld Reekie, is buried here, beneath a headstone paid for by his fellow bard Robert Burns. The church's Dutch gable and plain interior reflect the Canongate's trading links with the Low Countries. At the gable top, note the gilded stag's head, traditionally a gift of the monarch. Zara Phillips and Mike Tindall were married here in 2011.

Craigmillar Castle

historicenvironment.scot

Craigmillar Castle Road, EH16 4SY 0131 661 4445 | Open Apr–Sep daily 9.30–5.30; Oct daily 10–4; Nov–Mar Sat–Wed 10–4

This medieval castle is often overshadowed by its more famous Edinburgh neighbour. But there's enough here to enchant anyone interested in Scotland's history. The core of Craigmillar Castle is a stout 15th-century L-plan tower house with walls up to 9 feet thick, constructed on the site of an older fortification by the Preston family. The main defensive features include massive doors, a spiral turnpike stair, narrow passageways and two outer walls. Mary, Queen of Scots fled here on several occasions when the pressures of life at Holyroodhouse became too great, notably after the murder of her secretary David Rizzio in 1566, and the tiny chamber where she slept bears her name. The castle was abandoned and left to crumble in the 18th century.

Georgian House

nts.org.uk

7 Charlotte Square, EH2 4DR | 0131 225 2160 | Open Apr–Oct daily 10–5; Mar and Nov daily 11–4; Dec 1–17 Thu–Sun 11–4

The north side of Charlotte Square is the epitome of 18th-century New Town elegance, designed by architect Robert Adam. For a glimpse of gracious Edinburgh living in 1800, visit the Georgian House, a preserved residence right in the middle. It is a typically meticulous re-creation by the National Trust for Scotland, reflecting all the fashions of the day. Its symmetrical stonework, ornamented upper levels and rusticated base make it an outstanding example of the style.

Greyfriars Kirkyard

greyfriarskirk.com

Greyfriars Tolbooth and Highland Kirk, Greyfriars Place, EH1 2QQ 0131 225 1900 | Open Apr–Oct Mon–Fri 10.30–4.30, Sat 10.30–2.30; Nov–Mar Thu 1.30–3.30

At the top of Candlemaker Row, opposite the National Museum

▲ Craigmillar Castle

of Scotland, you'll find a favourite Edinburgh landmark: a bronze statue of a little Skye terrier, which has stood here since 1873. The dog's story was memorably told by American Eleanor Atkinson in her sentimental novel of 1912, *Greyfriars Bobby*. The story goes that he was the devoted companion of a local farmer who dined regularly in Greyfriars Place. After Auld Jock died, faithful Bobby slept on his grave in the nearby churchyard for 14 years, while returning to the same pie shop for his dinner.

The Kirk of the Grey Friars was built on the site of a former Franciscan monastery in 1620. Just 18 years later it was the scene of a pivotal event in Scottish history, when Calvinist petitioners gathered to sign the National Covenant, an act of defiance against the king. The church itself was trashed by Cromwell's troops in 1650, and

later accidentally blown up. The kirkyard made a makeshift prison for hundreds of Covenanters captured in the battle of Bothwell Bridge in 1679; they were kept here for five dreadful months. Today it is full of memorials, including the grave of architect William Adam (1689–1748).

John Knox House and Scottish Storytelling Centre

scottishstorytellingcentre.co.uk
43–45 High Street, EH1 1SR | 0131 556 9579 | Open Mon–Sat 10–6; Sun (Jul and Aug only) 12–6

This handsome old house, with its upper storeys overhanging the High Street, is one of the Royal Mile's most picturesque buildings. Built in 1470, it's the only surviving medieval building on the Royal Mile, so you can use your imagination to picture the heart of Edinburgh in the time of James IV and Mary, Queen of Scots. It's beautifully preserved. Inside, you can take a look at the elaborate painted ceiling of the Oak Room (with its hidden demon) and find out about the life of its most famous tenant, the radical reformer John Knox, who is said to have preached from its front window. The house is now part of the Scottish Storytelling Centre.

The Real Mary King's Close

realmarykingsclose.com
2 Warriston's Close, High Street, EH1 1PG | 0131 225 0672
Open Apr–Oct daily 10–9; Nov Mon–Thu 9–5.30, Fri and Sat 9.30–9, Sun 9.30–6.30

Mary King's Close is a narrow alleyway that once led between the tall houses of 17th-century Edinburgh, part of the rabbit warren of the Old Town. It is now preserved under the City Chambers, which were built over the top in 1753.

Guided tours help to create the former atmosphere of the Old Town – you can walk through the houses, see the cramped living conditions and learn about the outbreak of plague in 1644. Tours have limited places and tend to book up quickly; reserve ahead.

VISIT THE MUSEUMS AND GALLERIES

Canongate Tolbooth/The People's Story Museum

edinburghmsueums.org.uk
163 Canongate, EH8 8BN | 0131 529 4057 | Open Wed–Sat 10–5, Sun 12–5

The French-style old Tolbooth dates from 1591 and served as the council chamber for the burgh of Canongate until its incorporation into the city in 1856. It also served as a prison. The building is now the home of The People's Story, a fascinating museum dedicated to everyday life and times in Edinburgh from the 18th century to the present day. Tableaux and objects, sounds and smells evoke life in a prison cell and a draper's shop, and show a servant and a tramcar conductor (a 'clippie',

▼ Gladstone's Land

who clipped the tickets) at work. With a host of other everyday details, the exhibits portray the struggle for better conditions, better health and better ways to enjoy what little leisure the citizens had.

Fruitmarket Gallery

fruitmarket.co.uk
45 Market Street, EH1 1DF | 0131 225 2383 | Open daily 11–6
This contemporary art gallery is built in the city's former fruit market. The wide expanse of glass frontage on this handsome old building reveals lillle to the street, but inside, changing exhibitions showcase the work of new Scottish and international artists.

Gladstone's Land

nts.org.uk
477b Lawnmarket, EH1 2NT
0131 226 5856
Open Jul–Aug daily 10–6.30; Apr–Jun and Sep–Oct daily 10–5; tours only, advance booking (by phone) essential
This fascinating example of 17th-century tenement housing is a highlight of the Old Town. Its narrowness was typical of the cramped Old Town living conditions – the only space for expansion was upwards, and its eventual height of six floors reflects the status of its merchant owner, Thomas Gledstanes, who extended the existing tenement in 1617. The building is unique for its distinctive stone arcading, which was once a common feature along the High Street but has

now vanished elsewhere. Inside, the National Trust for Scotland has reconstructed 17th-century shop booths on the ground floor, and there are original painted ceilings to admire, adorned with flowers and birds.

Museum of Childhood

edinburghmuseums.org.uk
42 High Street, EH1 1TG | 0131 529 4142 | Open Mon and Thu–Sat 10–5, Sun 12–5
Toys and games from the 19th and early-20th century will make older visitors feel a surge of nostalgia and will open the eyes of 21st-century kids who have grown up with virtual games. There is even a re-created 1930s schoolroom.

Museum of Edinburgh

edinburghmuseums.org.uk
Huntly House, 142 Canongate, EH8 8DD | 0131 529 4143 | Open Mon–Sat 10–5 (also Sun 12–5 in Aug)
This museum brings the social history of the city to life with

▼ Canongate Tolbooth

▲ View from the Scott Monument

items such as maps and prints, silver, glass, shop signs and Greyfriars Bobby's collar. You can also see the National Covenant, the document that rejected King Charles I's attempt to impose Anglican forms of worship on Scotland. Signed in 1638 by thousands of Scots, it set the stage for 20 years of complicated civil strife. The museum occupies Huntly House, a 16th-century dwelling much altered through the years, and at one time occupied by a guild, the Incorporation of Hammermen, marked by the three pointed gables.

National Museum of Scotland

nms.ac.uk

Chambers Street, EH1 1JF | 0131 225 7534 | Open daily 10–5

The National Museum of Scotland is really two museums in one. Its modern wing – a striking, multistorey round tower that evokes Scottish baronial architecture – is devoted to Scottish history from the earliest times to the present day. You'll see treasures such as elaborately carved Pictish stones and crosses, hoards of Roman and Viking silver, and exquisite Norse and Celtic brooches, rings and pins. High points include the 12th-century Lewis chess pieces, the first-century Hunterston brooch and the beautiful eighth-century Monymusk Reliquary. One of the most mysterious displays is the group of tiny wooden coffins, each holding a carefully carved body not much longer than an adult finger, discovered on Arthur's Seat in Edinburgh in 1836. Nobody knows who made this spooky collection, or why.

The exhibition Scotland: A Changing Nation tells the story of Scotland's more recent past, from World War I to the present day. It allows Scots to tell their own stories in their own words.

The museum has some fine modern sculptures, most notably *Hearth*, made from wood found when the museum was being built, and *Whale Bones*, an intricate white ball of bones made from the skeleton of a pilot whale.

Linked to the new wing, the museum's original 19th-century building reopened in 2011 after an extensive modernisation that created 16 new galleries dedicated to anthropology, zoology and engineering. You'll find everything here from the skeletons of whales and dolphins to early aircraft and steam engines built in Scotland and much more modern space-age technology.

Scottish National Gallery
nationalgalleries.org
The Mound, EH2 2EL | 0131 624 6200 | Open Thu 10–7, Fri–Wed 10–5

Visit Scotland's National Gallery in the heart of Edinburgh to admire one of the foremost collections of sculpture and paintings in Britain. At its core are paintings by the great masters of Europe, including Vermeer, Hals, Tiepolo, Van Dyck, Raphael, Cezanne, Degas and Titian. Works by Scottish artists are displayed in their own section downstairs.

One of the stars of the show is Sir Henry Raeburn's best-known work – his 1795 portrait, *The Reverend Robert Walker Skating*. Watercolours by J M W Turner (1775–1851) are displayed each January.

You may also see Canova's famous marble sculpture of *The Three Graces* (1815–17), jointly acquired with the V&A in 1994.

The National Gallery is a work of art in its own right. Designed by William Playfair (1789–1857), creator of many of Edinburgh's iconic buildings, it was completed in the year of his death, and it is easily spotted by the huge golden stone pillars of its neoclassical flanks.

Scottish National Gallery of Modern Art and Dean Gallery

nationalgalleries.org

75 Belford Road, EH4 3DR | 0131 624 6200 | Open Thu 10–7, Fri–Wed 10–5

A sweeping, living sculpture of grassy terraces and semi-circular ponds is the first thing you see as you arrive at the main gallery, an installation by artist Charles Jencks. Inside are striking works by the early 20th-century group of painters known as the Scottish Colourists, including canvases by Samuel John Peploe, George Lesley Hunter, Francis Cadell and John Duncan Fergusson. Modern artists such as Andy Warhol, Lucien Freud, Damien Hirst and Tracey Emin are also represented.

Across the road, the Dean Gallery majors on Dada and the Surrealists, and the Scottish sculptor Eduardo Paolozzi (1924–2005). Paolozzi's striding Vulcan statue of welded stainless steel, half-man, half-machine, takes up a two-floor gallery. A room on the ground floor gives an insight into how a sculptor works, with a re-creation of Paolozzi's studio.

Scottish National Portrait Gallery

nationalgalleries.org

1 Queen Street, EH2 1JD | 0131 624 6200 | Open Thu 10–7, Fri–Wed 10–5

The faces of the people who shaped Scotland hang here, forming a fascinating group of the great and the good, the vain and the bad, the beautiful and the long-forgotten. Scottish artists are well represented, including locals Allan Ramsay (1713–84) and Henry Raeburn (1756–1823). This is also where you'll find the original and much copied portrait of poet Robert Burns by Alexander Nasmyth (1758–1840), as well as a host of other familiar faces. The national photography collection is also held here, including work by Edinburgh pioneers David Octavius Hill and Robert Adamson.

Writers' Museum

edinburghmuseums.gov.uk

Lady Stair's Close, Lawnmarket, EH1 2PA | 0131 529 4901 | Open Mon–Sat 10–5 (also Sun 12–5 in Aug)

Robert Burns (1759–96), Sir Walter Scott (1771–1832) and Robert Louis Stevenson (1850–94) are three of Scotland's most famous authors, and this museum, in a 17th-century house, is dedicated to them. Unlike the others, Stevenson has no museum elsewhere dedicated to him, so this collection, including his hand-printing press, is particularly significant. Quotations by famous Scottish writers are set into the paving slabs of Makar's Court.

GO ROUND THE GARDENS

Royal Botanic Garden

rbge.org.uk

20A Inverleith Row, EH3 5LR | 0131 552 7171 | Open Mar, Oct daily 10–6; Apr–Sep daily 10–7; Nov–Feb daily 10–4

▲ Glasshouse, Royal Botanic Garden

The Botanics, as it is known locally, set in more than 70 acres of beautifully landscaped gardens, claims to be one of the largest collections of living plants in the world, with more than 15,500 species on display – 5,000 species in the rock garden alone. On a rainy day, you can shelter among palms, orchids and cacti in ten huge glasshouses that re-create tropical, subtropical and desert biomes. See the giant water lilies in the Tropical Aquatic House, then go downstairs for an underwater view of fish swimming through the roots.

Outdoors, the plants of the Chinese Hillside are part of the largest collection of Chinese plants outside China, and in summer the herbaceous border, backed by a tall beech hedge, is breathtaking. Check out the rhododendron collection and the rock garden.

ENTERTAIN THE FAMILY
Edinburgh Zoo
edinburghzoo.org.uk
134 Corstorphine Road, EH12 6TS
0131 334 9171 | Open Apr–Sep daily 9–6; Oct, Mar daily 9–5; Nov–Feb daily 9–4.30
Edinburgh Zoo remains a great example of its type, allowing close access to many animals while at the same time promoting conservation and education. The site is at Corstorphine, 3 miles west of the city centre, covering an area of some 82 acres. Highlights include the swinging-gibbon enclosure, the Hilltop Safari to the African Plains exhibit, and the ever-popular penguins who stroll outside their enclosure (daily 2.15), weather permitting. The zoo's most famous residents are, of course, the pair of giant pandas, Yang Guan and Tian Tian, on loan from China.

▶ Arthur's Seat MAP REF 402 C3

It takes about an hour (at an easy pace) to climb from Holyrood to the rocky summit of Arthur's Seat, which is worn shiny by the footsteps of millions of visitors over the years. The 823-foot (251m) high extinct volcano is Edinburgh's own mini-mountain and can be seen from all over the city. It's been extinct for about 325 million years, so there's no risk that it will erupt again, but the steep, near-vertical Salisbury Crags on its western side are evidence of the tremendous seismic events that created this landscape.

The cliffs, which often glow an amazing deep red at sunset, inspired Sir Arthur Conan Doyle to write *The Lost World*, his tale of an Amazonian plateau cut off from the outside world by sheer cliffs, where dinosaurs still roam. The slopes of Arthur's Seat are ablaze with the yellow blooms of gorse from spring until autumn, and from the summit you can see for miles out to sea, and inland as far as the Forth Bridges and beyond, or across Fife as far as the distant Cairngorms, while at your feet are all Edinburgh's great landmarks. If you don't have time or energy to assault the summit, you can stroll the gentler slope of Hunter's Glen, a shallow valley that separates the Seat from the Crags, and then loop back to Holyrood by the Radical Road, a footpath that follows the western contour of Salisbury Crags.

Our Dynamic Earth

dynamicearth.co.uk
112 Holyrood Road, EH8 8AS | 0131
550 7800 | Open Jul, Aug daily 10–6:
Apr–Jun, Sep, Oct daily 10–5.30;
Nov–Mar Wed–Sun daily 10–5.30
Our Dynamic Earth offers pop
science and a perfect antidote
to Edinburgh's more staid
attractions. It tells the story of
Earth and its changing nature,
from the so-called Big Bang (as
viewed from the bridge of a
space ship) to the present day
(exactly who lives where in the
rainforest), in slick, bite-sized
chunks of virtual-reality
science. The planet is explored
inside out through 11 galleries,
from the effect of erupting
volcanoes to the icy chill of the
polar regions, and including a
submarine exploration of
strange deep-sea creatures and
coral reefs.

The Time Machine uses
lights and mirrors to create a
star-filled infinity, where a
multitude of stars are created
using lights and mirrors, and a
multi-screen flight over the
mountains and glaciers of
Scotland and Norway in the
Shaping the Surface experience
is a highlight of any visit.

GET OUTDOORS

Arthur's Seat

see highlight panel opposite

Water of Leith Walkway

waterofleith.org.uk
Water of Leith Visitor Centre,
24 Lanark Road, EH14 1TQ | 0131
455 7367 | Visitor Centre open
daily 10–4. Walkway open access

▲ Camera Obscura tower

You can follow the 13-mile
Water of Leith Walkway all the
way from Balerno, on the
outskirts of the city, to Leith
(see page 280), where the little
river meets the Firth of Forth.
For a shorter stroll, the stretch
between Dean Village and
Stockbridge is one of the
prettiest parts of the walk and
takes about 45 minutes.

TAKE A VIEW

Camera Obscura and World of Illusions

camera-obscura.co.uk
Castlehill, EH1 2ND | 0131 226
3709 | Open Jul–Aug daily
9am–10pm; Apr–Jun and Sep–Oct
daily 9.30–7; Nov–Mar daily 10–6
The Camera Obscura, near the
top of the Royal Mile in a
castellated building known as
the Outlook Tower, started life
in 1853 as Short's Popular
Observatory. It grew into the
Victorian equivalent of today's
hands-on science centres.
Using no electricity or digital

tricks, this giant pin-hole camera projects onto a viewing table a live panorama of the city outside, which changes minute by minute. There's also a Magic Gallery of optical illusions, holograms and live viewcams, and from the balcony at the top of the tower there are great views of the city.

Nelson Monument

edinburghmuseums.org.uk
32 Calton Hill, EH7 5AA | 0131 556 2716 | Open Apr–Sep Mon–Sat 10–7, Sun 12–5; Oct–Mar Mon–Sat 10–3
You can climb a steep spiral staircase for a panoramic view of the city from the top of the Nelson Monument, a slender, battlemented tower near the summit of Calton Hill in 1807 to honour the hero of Trafalgar, Horatio, Lord Nelson. Like Edinburgh Castle's so-called One O'Clock Gun, the white ball on top of the tower was a time signal, designed to help ships in the Firth set their chronometers precisely. It drops from its masthead at exactly 1pm every day.

Scott Monument

edinburghmuseums.org.uk
East Princes Street Gardens, EH2 2EJ
0131 529 4068 | Open Apr–Sep Mon–Sat 10–7, Sun 10–6; Oct–Mar Mon–Sat 10–4, Sun 10–3
Slog up 287 steps to the top of the Gothic sandstone pinnacle of the Scott Monument for magnificent views of the Castle, Old Town and New Town. Sir Walter Scott (1771–1832) was arguably the first novelist superstar, and this magnificent memorial reflects his near-mythic status. Completed in 1846, it's encrusted with stone figures of characters from his novels and poems. A larger-than-life marble statue of Scott, with his deerhound Maida, sits at the foot of the monument, draped in a toga.

▼ Debating Chamber, Scottish Parliament

GET POLITICAL
Scottish Parliament
parliament.scot
EH99 1SP | 0131 348 5200 | Tours available; check website for times. Reservations essential

Love it or hate it, you can't ignore the Scottish Parliament building, at the foot of the Royal Mile facing the Palace of Holyroodhouse. Reservations are essential for a guided tour, but if you just want a peep inside, access to the main hall and debating chamber (on non-business days) is free. The building was designed by Catalan architect Enric Miralles, who died before it was completed in 2004 – three years late and more than ten times over budget. It's a striking modern building that somehow fits its much older surroundings. Guided tours take in the Debating Chamber, the Garden Lobby and views of the Members of the Scottish Parliament (MSP) Building.

TAKE A TOUR
City of the Dead Walking Tour
cityofthedeadtours.com
10 Thirlstane Lane, EG9 1AJ | 0131 225 9044 | Tours nightly 8.30, 9.15 and 10pm Easter–Hallowe'en. Advance reservations recommended

Enjoy a night-time guided walk through the dark lanes of the Old Town, ending in a haunted mausoleum in Greyfriars kirkyard. Meet up at St Giles' Cathedral. The night walks are not suitable for younger children, but they may enjoy the history tours that are available.

Edinburgh Bus Tours
edinburghtour.com
Waverley Bridge, EH1 1BQ | 0131 220 0770 | Tours leave daily every 10–15 minutes from 9.30. Last tour 6.30 (Easter–Oct), 3.30 (Nov–Easter)

A guided, open-top bus tour is a great way to see the city. Tickets are valid all day, so you can hop off wherever you like, then hop on the next bus. You can join the tour at Waverley Bridge, Lothian Road, Grassmarket, Royal Mile, Princes Street or George Street. Buy tickets on the bus itself or at the tourist information office. Other tours are also available.

Edinburgh Literary Pub Tour
edinburghliterarypubtour.co.uk
34 North Castle Street, EH2 3BN 0800 169 7410 | Tours start at 7.30pm May–Sep nightly, Apr, Oct, Thu–Sun, Jan–Mar Fri, Sun, Nov, Dec Fri only

A two-hour walking (and drinking) tour of pubs with plenty of literary associations, in the company of some knowledgeable actors. These tours are popular, so advance reservations are recommended. Meet at the Beehive Inn in the Grassmarket. Minimum age 18.

Mansfield Traquair Centre
mansfieldtraquair.org.uk
15 Mansfield Place, EH3 6BB | 0131 555 8475 | Second Sun of each month, extra dates during Festival

One of Edinburgh's most extraordinary hidden treasures is accessed via free guided tours. It's a former church of 1885, remarkable for its decoration from floor to ceiling with murals by the arts and crafts artist Phoebe Anna Traquair (1852–1936). The impact of the freshly restored paintings is stunning.

Mercat Tours

mercattours.com
Mercat House, 29 Blair Sreet. EH1 1QR | 0131 225 5445 | Tours daily, times vary, reservations essential
Take an hour-long guided tour of Edinburgh's haunted underground city, through the vaults at South Bridge, or perhaps a late-night stroll on the Ghosthunter Trail. Meet at the Mercat Cross on the Royal Mile.

The Witchery Tour

witcherytours.com
84 West Bow, EH1 2HH
131 225 6745 | Ghosts and Gore tour nightly May–Aug 7, 7.30pm. Murder and Mystery tour nightly all year 9, 9.30pm, according to demand
For a glimpse of the Old Town's murkier side, including tales of witchcraft, torture and plague, join a guided walking tour. Witchery tours last 1 hour 15 minutes, and meet outside the Witchery restaurant on Castlehill. They're not suitable for the very nervous. Advance reservations are essential.

EXPLORE BY BIKE
BikeTrax

biketrax.co.uk
11 Lochrin Place, EH3 9QX
0131 228 6633 | Open Mon–Fri 9.30–6, Sat 9.30–5.30

Hiring a bike is a great way to explore the city for yourself. Although it's hilly, Edinburgh is quite cyclist-friendly, with some long stretches of car-free cycle lanes in city parks and along the Water of Leith. BikeTrax hires out mountain and hybrid bikes, kids' bicycles, trailers and child seats. It's handily placed for rides along the Union Canal from Edinburgh Quay, in Fountainbridge.

GET ON THE WATER
Epic Ventures

epic-ventures.com
82/13 Harrison Gardens, EH11 1SB 07929 459 613 | Open Mon–Sat 9–5
The Union Canal opened in 1822, connecting the centre of Edinburgh with Falkirk, 35 miles west, where it linked with the Forth and Clyde Canal. It no longer carries freight, but you can take a half-day or full-day guided canoe or kayak trip along the canal with Epic Ventures. If you'd prefer to paddle through less urban surroundings, Epic Ventures also offers days on the River Tweed, about 45 minutes' drive from Edinburgh.

GO TO THE RACES
Musselburgh Racecourse

musselburgh-racecourse.co.uk
Linkfield Road, Musselburgh, EH21 7RG | 0131 665 2859 | See website for fixtures
You can enjoy a day's racing at classy Musselburgh Racecourse, located only 6 miles from the city centre, at any time of year.

CATCH A PERFORMANCE
Edinburgh Playhouse
playhousetheatre.com
18–22 Greenside Place, EH1 3AA
0844 871 3014 (calls cost 7p per minute, plus your phone company's access charge)
The best venue in town for touring productions of big-budget musicals and dance. It's a five-minute walk away from the east end of Princes Street, next door to the huge Vue cinema. The theatre is supposedly haunted by the figure of a man, known as Albert, who wears a grey coat. Competing stories claim him to be either a suicide, or a stagehand killed in an accident.

Festival Theatre
edtheatres.com
13–29 Nicolson Street, EH8 9FT
0131 529 6000
This prestigious venue close to the east end hosts international and top touring productions of dance, theatre, musicals and comedy, from ballet to Scottish Opera. It has a distinctive all-glass facade and the biggest stage in Britain.

King's Theatre
edtheatres.com
2 Leven Street, EH3 9LQ
0131 529 6000
This grand old Edwardian building is one of Edinburgh's oldest theatres, opened in 1906. The King's is great for family entertainment, majoring on shows and musicals, pantomime, comedy and plays, including Shakespeare,

The Queen's Hall
thequeenshall.net
Clerk Street, EH8 9JG
0131 668 3456
If you want a more intimate venue than the Usher Hall, then try the The Queen's Hall, which is located in a converted church, and is a popular spot for jazz, blues, rock and soul, as well as for Classical music and comedy, attracting top names such as Courtney Pine.

Royal Lyceum Theatre
lyceum.org.uk
Grindlay Street, EH3 9AX
0131 248 4848
One of the leading production theatres in Scotland, the magnificent Victorian Lyceum creates all its own shows. Contemporary and classic theatre predominate, including Shakespeare productions. It's off Lothian Road near the West End of the city.

The Stand Comedy Club
thestand.co.uk
5 York Place, EH1 3EB
0131 558 7272
Enjoy live comedy from new and well-known Scottish comedians, seven nights a week, at this dark and intimate basement bar. Weekend shows often sell out, so advance booking is advised.

Traverse Theatre
traverse.co.uk
10 Cambridge Street, EH1 2ED
0131 228 1404
The Traverse is famous for its productions of experimental

theatre and dance, and is a good place to catch hot new work by Scottish playwrights or have dinner at The Atrium restaurant. It's located next to the Usher Hall, near the city's West End.

Usher Hall
usherhall.co.uk
Lothian Road, EH1 2EA
0131 228 1155
Edinburgh's most prestigious concert hall attracts high-quality performers such as the English Chamber Orchestra and the Moscow Philharmonic Orchestra. A distinctive circular building towards the West End, its high dome can be seen from many parts of the city.

GO TO THE MOVIES
Cameo
picturehouses.co.uk
38 Home Street, EH3 9LZ | 0131 228 2800 (24-hour recorded information)
A small, friendly independent cinema, Cameo shows low-key Hollywood, international and independent films. It's near the King's Theatre.

Dominion
dominioncinemas.net
18 Newbattle Terrace, Morningside, EH10 4RT | 0131 447 4771 (box office)
This small, family-run, independent cinema in the southern suburb of Morningside is the perfect antidote to the plethora of giant multiplex cinemas. It shows independent and mainstream movies, and has traditional leather Pullman seats. The Gold Class service even offers leather sofas along with complimentary wine or beer and nibbles. Look out for the collection of photos of famous faces that have visited the cinema over the years.

Filmhouse
filmhousecinema.com
88 Lothian Road, EH3 9BZ | 0131 228 2688 (box office) | 0131 228 2689 (recorded information)
This three-screen art-house cinema opposite the Usher Hall is popular with art-house film-lovers; it has the best range of independent and international cinema in Edinburgh and hosts a number of local film festivals.

ENJOY THE NIGHTLIFE
Bongo Club
thebongoclub.co.uk
66 Cowgate EH1 1JH | 0131 558 8844
The Bongo nightclub's club nights are diverse and cover different styles of live music, from hip hop to reggae and breakdancing. In the daytime, it's a cafe, with free internet access and exhibition space.

Cabaret Voltaire
thecabaretvoltaire.com
36–38 Blair Street, EH1 1QR
0131 247 4704
These caverns in the Old Town host club events every night, with diverse styles of dance music, big-name DJs and live music – with performances by national and international acts.

Corn Exchange

ece.uk.com

11 New Market Road, EH14 1RH

0131 477 3500

This pop and rock music venue is 2 miles southwest of the city centre and occupies the former corn exchange in Edinburgh's original agricultural quarter. Opened in 1999 by Blur, acts have included Travis, Pulp, Fun Lovin' Criminals and Coldplay.

Espionage

espionageedinburgh.co.uk

4 India Buildings, Victoria Street, Old Town, EH1 1EX | 0131 477 7007

Open Fri and Sat only except during Festival

It's late, it's free and you can dance the night away at this bar/club – small wonder it's popular with young people looking to extend their evening. Four themed bars and two dance floors spread over five floors make this an easy place to lose your friends and find new ones.

Opal Lounge

opallounge.co.uk

51a George Street, EH2 2HT

0131 226 2275

A stylish New Town basement cocktail bar and fusion restaurant where the beautiful and famous hang out. This was reputedly once a favourite haunt of Prince William.

Smash

smash.me.uk

40–42 Grindlay Street, EH3 9AP

Following the closure of the much-loved Citrus Club in 2017,

▲ Usher Hall

this small and atmospheric space has been revamped to make room for a music venue that offers something for every taste. Club nights are dedicated to everything from pop and tech/house to heavy metal and ska, and there are regular live music gigs showcasing up-and-coming bands.

GET ACTIVE

Royal Commonwealth Pool

edinburghleisure.co.uk

21 Dalkeith Road, EH16 5BB

0131 667 7211 | Open Mon–Tue, Thu–Fri 6am–9.30pm, Wed 6am–9pm, Sat 6am–7pm, Sun 10–7

This Olympic-size indoor swimming pool, below Arthur's Seat, has water slides, a diving pool and a children's pool as well as a gym, sauna and Clambers – a soft, safe play area for younger children.

WATCH A MATCH

Heart of Midlothian Football Club

heartsfc.co.uk

Tynecastle Stadium, Gorgie Road, EH11 2NL | 0333 043 1874

The Hearts ground lies one mile southwest of the city centre.

▲ Murrayfield Stadium

Hibernian Football Club
hiberianfc.co.uk
Easter Road Stadium, 12 Albion
Place, EH7 5QG | 0131 661 2159
The Hibs ground is off Easter
Road, a mile from the centre.

Murrayfield Stadium
scottishrubgy.org
Off Roseburn Terrace, Murrayfield,
EH12 5PJ | 0131 346 5000
Rugby is Edinburgh's favourite
sport, and games throughout
the year are well supported,
so advance reservations are
essential. Murrayfield can seat
67,500 and it still holds the
world record for the largest
attendance at a rugby game:
just over 104,000 packed into
the stadium to watch Scotland
play Wales in 1975. It's a mile
from the city centre.

PLAY A ROUND
Dalmahoy Hotel & Country Club
dalmahoyhotelandcountryclub.co.uk
Kirknewton, EH27 8EB | 0131 333
1845 | Open daily all year
The Championship East Course
has hosted many major events
including the Solheim Cup and
the Charles Church Seniors
PGA Championship of Scotland.
The course has long sweeping
fairways and generous greens
protected by strategic bunkers.
The shorter West Course has
tighter fairways offering more
accuracy from the tee.

Prestonfield Golf Club
prestonfieldgolf.co.uk
6 Priestfield Road North, EH16 5HS
0131 667 9665 | Contact club for
details of opening times
Parkland with beautiful views,
set under the extinct volcano of
Arthur's Seat. The course is a
gentle walk, but a challenge for
golfers of all levels.

EAT AND DRINK
Bailie Bar
thebailiebar.co.uk
2 St Stephen Street, EH3 5AL
0131 225 4673
This basement pub on the
border between New Town
and Stockbridge has an
unusual, triangular-shaped
bar, low ceilings and
sumptuous dark-red decor.

There's plenty of space, and a lounge area where you can enjoy real ales and hearty pub grub including steak-and-ale pies and fish and chips.

Bia Bistrot 🏵

biabistrot.co.uk
19 Colinton Road, EH10 5DP
0131 452 8453
This bistro merges Celtic and Mediterranean influences to create well-crafted and satisfying dishes. These include partridge breast with spelt salad and a deep-flavoured game pudding, a ballotine of roe deer with lentils, or slow braised pork cheeks, accented with apple and sage and served with celeriac. There's a good-value set lunch and early evening menu.

The Bon Vivant 🏵

bonvivantedinburgh.co.uk
51 Thistle Street, EH2 1DY
0131 225 3275
Tapas-style grazing and sharing is the drill at this trendy cocktail bar and eatery. The kitchen takes its inspiration mainly from the Med, but Scottish notes pop up here and there so get started with a

black haggis bon bon with broon sauce or crisp whitebait with a saffron emulsion. Main courses may include pork belly with fennel and cherries or lamb rump with smoked aubergine and kale; leave a corner for the calorie-laden but very special parmesan chips with truffle mayo.

Bow Bar

80 The West Bow, Victoria Street, EH1 2HH | 0131 226 7667
Halfway down Victoria Street, this blue-painted bar always has at least 140 whiskies to choose from, plus a few guest malts and blends. It also has a good selection of real ales. Inside, it's all wood panelling and old brewery mirrors.

The Cafe Royal 🏵

caferoyaledinburgh.co.uk
19 West Register Street, EH2 2AA
0131 556 1884
Edinburgh's Cafe Royal offers you the choice of gastropub eating in its grand Victorian bar, or a wider menu in even grander surroundings in the restaurant. In the bar, you'll find fishy offerings like oysters

▲ Harvey Nichols Forth Floor Restaurant

by the dozen or half-dozen in a range of styles, plus pub standards like fish and chips, steak-and-ale pie, steaks and burgers, all treated very well. In the baroque scrolled and moulded restaurant, traditional Scottish fare mingles with modern thinking on menus.

Calistoga Restaurant ◉

calistoga.co.uk
70 Rose Street, North Lane, EH2 3DX | 0131 225 1233
Calistoga's menus feature the likes of rich, creamy corn chowder, flatiron steaks, and chilli-battered pollack with aubergine and sweet potato bake in dill sauce.

Cask and Barrel

115 Broughton Street, New Town, EH1 3RZ | 0131 556 3132
An unpretentious, traditional pub with plenty of changing real ales served by staff who know their stuff. The Cask is well known as a soccer pub, and on the day of an important match

it's shoulder-to-shoulder here, with standing room only as locals pile in to watch the game on the TVs around the bar.

Castle Terrace Restaurant ◉◉◉

castleterracerestaurant.com
33–35 Castle Terrace, EH1 2EL
0131 229 1222
Castle Terrace is a soothingly contemporary place beneath Edinburgh Castle. The cooking treads a path between classical French ways and modern British thinking, delivering dishes that impress with their technical virtuosity and eyecatching delivery. A range of menus include a set lunch option, another that celebrates the seasons and a surprise tasting version that really showcases the talent in the kitchen. The à la carte menu is equally compelling.

Chop Chop

chop-chop.co.uk
248 Morrison Street, EH3 8DT
0131 221 1155

Dumplings and dim sum rule at this restaurant near Haymarket Station. The menu concentrates on *jiaozi*, the traditional savoury dumplings of northeast China. Fried pork and prawn *guo tie* (pot-stickers) are little bombs of flavour, while the boiled items include beef and chilli, lamb and leek, and chicken. Bring a hearty appetite and try the value-for-money all-you-can-eat banquet deal.

Divino Enoteca ⊛

divinoedinburgh.com
5 Merchant Street, EH1 2QD
0131 225 1770

Divino Enoteca's menu includes an excellent range of antipasti such as imported hams and salami, plus the more modern pan-fried scallops with smoked paprika polenta. Pasta options include ravioli of the day, or go for gnocchi with pancetta, clams and sautéed samphire. Pan-fried monkfish cheeks are served with salt-cod baccalà, confit lemon and braised leeks, grilled steak arrives in red wine sauce, and vegetarians can tuck into lasagne made with pumpkin and gorgonzola.

The Dogs

thedogsonline.co.uk
110 Hanover Street EH2 1DR
0131 220 1208

This centrally located eating house offers straightforward, good, honest food from David Ramsden and his team, heavily influenced by modern British gastropub cooking. The space, in a high-ceilinged New Town building, is calm and classy, the food spot-on. Expect lunchtime favourites such as fishcakes, cock a leekie soup and pickled mackerel with potatoes, or come for dinner when the choice may include crispy squid, beef short rib or roast cod.

Elliot's

apexhotels.co.uk
23–27 Waterloo Place, EH1 3BH
0131 441 0440

Elliot's Restaurant at the Apex Waterloo Place Hotel, beneath Calton Hill, serves clever contemporary food in a slick setting. The kitchen deals in modern food that makes imaginative use of high-quality ingredients to come up with starters like Lanark Blue cheese pannacotta with roast pear purée, chicory, candied walnuts and walnut dressing, and main courses such as Gressingham duck breast pointed up with satay glaze, pineapple purée, toasted cashews and hispi cabbage.

Harvey Nichols Forth Floor Restaurant ⊛

harveynichols.com/restaurants
30–34 St Andrew Square, EH2 2AD
0131 524 8350

With views of the castle and the Forth Bridge, the vista from the top floor of Harvey Nics' Edinburgh restaurant really does serve up the city on a plate. There's the usual brasserie and bar, and the more refined restaurant itself. The latter offers a slick contemporary dining room with white linen on the tables and burgundy leather seats to sink into, and on the menu is some sharp, contemporary cooking. The kitchen turns out smart seasonal dishes that don't lack for contemporary finesse and Scottish ingredients.

Hebrides Bar

17 Market Street, EH1 1DE

0131 220 4213

This is a great wee pub between Waverley Station and the Royal Mile. A fine pint of heavy awaits you alongside quality malts and there is always the chance of an impromptu live music session. A favourite with misty-eye Scottish Gaels dreaming of the islands where they were born, which you can find on the large relief map that takes pride of place on the wall.

Henry's Cellar Bar

16 Morrison Street, EH3 8BJ

0131 629 2992

This is the best place in Edinburgh for contemporary jazz, with something to suit all tastes, including Latin, free and Jamaican jazz. There's a bar, but no food is served – eat first, and then head here to see out the night. Morrison Street is a short walk from the West End.

The Honours ◉◉

thehonours.co.uk

58a North Castle Street, EH2 3LU

0131 220 2513

There's a contemporary sheen to this place and a dedication to Scottish produce that delivers some feel-good food. A starter of crab cappuccino with rouille, croutons and parmesan is a classy bowlful, or go for pressed duck and pistachio terrine with morello cherries. Next up, there's grass-fed Scottish steaks cooked on the charcoal grill (T-bone, for example, with garlic and soy marinade), or ox cheeks à la bordelaise. For dessert, rum cake competes with the soufflé du jour, and there are after-dinner cocktails if you're in for the long haul.

Jolly Judge

jollyjudge.co.uk

7 James' Court, Old Town, EH1 2PB

0131 225 2669

It's not easy to find this pub, but it's worth seeking out for its 17th-century character, complete with painted, low-beamed ceiling, and its choice of malt whiskies. At the top of the Royal Mile look out for the sign; go down East Entry into James' Court and the pub is down some steps on the left.

L'Escargot Bleu ◉

lescargotbleu.co.uk

56 Broughton Street, EH1 3SA

0131 557 1600

L'Escargot Bleu's bilingual menu deals in classic bistro dishes such as snails sourced from Barra in the Outer Hebrides. There's a Scottish flavour to a good deal of the kitchen's output, which ranges from seared Skye scallops to casserole of venison and beef cheeks with a rich red wine sauce, or pan-fried sea bass with Jerusalem artichokes and hollandaise. Desserts are as traditional as the crème brûlée that arrives without any unnecessary adornments.

La Garrigue ◎◎

lagarrigue.co.uk
31 Jeffrey Street, EH1 1DH
0131 557 3032

The regional cooking style of southern France delivers full-bore flavours, using good local produce in authentic French country dishes cooked properly. The menu is a list of things you want to eat, starting with a fish soup with croutons and rouille, tasting as if it has been flown in straight from the quayside of Marseille, cassoulet of belly pork, and duck confit.

Mother India's Cafe

motherindia.co.uk
3–5 Infirmary Sreet EH1 1LT
0131 524 5801

Come to this friendly and relaxed Indian restaurant for a new take on the cuisine of the sub-continent. It's often hard to choose from an Indian menu with its plethora of delights, but here you can sample many more than usual as all the dishes are presented tapas-style, as small tasting portions. Vegetarian dishes often outshine those with meat – try the aubergine fritters. Rice and naan bread are both authentic and properly cooked, service is speedy and it can be very busy.

Mussel Inn

mussel-inn.com
61–65 Rose Street, EH2 2NH
0843 2892 481

This friendly restaurant proudly lives up to its motto 'passionate about seafood'. You'll find the best of Scottish prawns, crab, scallops and lobster on the menu here, as well as huge and great value servings of mussels from the sea lochs. Meat eaters are also catered for and there are tables outside for good weather.

Ondine Restaurant ◎◎

ondinerestaurant.co.uk
2 George IV Bridge, EH1 1AD
0131 226 1888

Just off the Royal Mile, on George IV Bridge, Ondine has great views out over the old town, but sustainable seafood served amid an atmosphere of cheerful bustle is the main draw, and the sustainability ethos is not empty marketing speak. You could take a high seat at the central horseshoe-shaped crustacea bar, or park on a stripy banquette and get things under way with oysters – four types, no less – or something like a classic fish and shellfish soup along with the time-honoured accompaniments of rouille, gruyère and croutons.

Rabble

rabbleedinburgh.co.uk
55a Frederick Street, New Town, EH2 1LH | 0131 622 7800

This trendy basement bar in the heart of the city offers more than 20 types of vodka as well as a list of bar snacks. Rabble serves as a restaurant, cocktail bar, breakfast cafe and boutique hotel, all in one. It's just off Princes Street.

The Scran & Scallie ◉
scranandscallie.com
1 Comely Bank Road, EH4 1DT
0131 332 6281
From the local maestros behind The Kitchin and Castle Terrace, Tom Kitchin and Dominic Jack's pub is done out in fashionable shabby-chic, with exposed brick walls and heritage artworks and fabrics. First up may be a solidly stuffed raviolo parcel of ham in watercress soup, or the bracing simplicity of half-a-dozen oysters. Main-course roasted monkfish swaddled in pancetta with Puy lentils is another classy little number, as an alternative to versions of pot-au-feu or the house fish pie. The pub also serves a range of smart bar snacks and finger-food for those not up for a slap-up lunch.

21212 ◉◉◉◉
21212restaurant.co.uk
3 Royal Terrace, EH7 5AB
0131 523 1030
If you're wondering what 21212's name represents, the answer is the five-course menu format: a choice of two starters, two mains and two desserts, with one soup course and one cheese course in between. That is the offering at lunch, but at dinner an extra dish has been added to the starter/main/dessert element, so it's really 31313. This is creative and dynamic modern food, where supremely good ingredients are cleverly worked into dishes that inspire and amaze.

The Witchery by the Castle ◉
thewitchery.com
Castlehill, EH1 2NF | 0131 225 5613
This 16th-century merchant's house by the gates of the castle at the top of the Royal Mile makes a strikingly atmospheric, even Gothic-looking restaurant. The Witchery itself is lined with carved oak panelling hung with tapestries under a heraldic-painted ceiling, while the Secret Garden dining room occupies an enclosed courtyard with a painted ceiling and doors leading to a terrace with terrific views. The cooking follows a contemporary route built on Scottish traditions, with the kitchen using quality native produce. Seafood gets a strong showing, and the puddings are worth a punt.

▶ **PLACES NEARBY**

Get out of the city centre by visiting the Edinburgh suburbs of Leith (see page 280), Dalkeith and Gorebridge (see page 122), Cramond (see page 113) and South Queensferry (see page 364). Leith in particular is known for its restaurants. Fans of Dan Brown's novels will also want to visit Rosslyn Chapel (see page 342), made famous by *The Da Vinci Code*, although there's plenty more history there, too.

▲ Edzell Castle

▶ **Edzell** MAP REF 409 D5

Enter Edzell through the graceful Dalhousie Arch, built in memory of a 19th-century aristocrat, to discover a pretty village of red sandstone houses and cottage gardens along a broad main street. The village was planned in the 19th century. Its main attraction, a 15th-century castle and garden, is a short distance from the village centre.

TAKE IN SOME HISTORY
Edzell Castle
historicenvironment.scot
DD9 7UE | 01356 648631
Open Apr–Sep daily 9–5.30

The most remarkable feature of this sturdy little fortified tower house is its unusual garden, complete with bathhouse and summer house. In 1604 a walled enclosure was added onto the existing tower house and courtyard, designed to surround one of the most elegant and notable gardens of any castle in Western Europe.

The garden walls are a triumph in themselves, richly adorned with carvings and sculpted panels. The first set depicts a number of planetary deities, including Mars, Jupiter, Venus and Saturn; the second represents the liberal arts. In medieval learning, the three basic subjects were grammar, rhetoric and logic, while arithmetic, music, geometry and astronomy were the four more advanced topics. Each of these seven subjects is illustrated by seated figures busily practising their art.

The tower house was built in the 15th century as a home for the Lindsay family, and has attracted royal visitors including Mary, Queen of Scots and her son James VI and I during the 16th century, and Queen Victoria and Prince Albert in the 19th century. Other buildings, arranged around a courtyard, were added in the 16th century. Edzell saw little military action, although it was occupied by Cromwell's Parliamentarian troops in 1651, and was badly damaged during the second Jacobite uprising in 1747. Today, the tower is the most complete section, along with the quaint summer house in the southeast corner of the garden.

▶ Eigg

see **Small Isles**, page 362

▶ Eilean Donan Castle MAP REF 406 B3

eileandonancastle.com

Dornie, IV40 8DX | 01599 555202 | Open Feb–Mar and Nov–Dec daily 10–4; Apr–May and Sep daily 10–6; Jul–Aug daily 9–6

One of the most photographed and romantic castles in Scotland, Eilean Donan is perched on a rock just offshore in Loch Duich, linked to the mainland and a modern visitor centre by an arched stone bridge. There's been a fortification here since the 13th century and its 14-foot-thick walls have withstood the onslaught of both men and the elements. The castle isn't as authentic as it looks – the original castle was destroyed by government troops in 1719 and Eilean Donan owes its appearance today to restoration between 1912 and

▼ Eilean Donan Castle

1932, by Lt Col John MacRae-Gilstrap, who had a vision in a dream of how it should look.

Dwarfed by the brooding hills surrounding Loch Duich, the castle stands picturesquely at the point where three great sea lochs meet. A fortress was built here in 1220 by Alexander II to protect himself against raids by Vikings. During the Jacobite uprising the MacRaes opted to support the Old Pretender and garrisoned a small force of Spanish soldiers in the castle. In 1719 the guns of an English man-of-war pounded the castle to pieces. It remained in ruins until 1912, when MacRae-Gilstrap decided to restore his ancestral home.

Most of the rooms in the castle are open to visitors, all furnished in the style of the home of a country laird. Although mostly a 20th-century restoration, it allows the imagination to return to the time when the castle was owned by the wild MacRaes. A fearsome clan, they relished displaying the heads of their enemies on the battlements, and local legends tell how, on one occasion, they defended the castle successfully when outnumbered by their attackers 400 to 1.

▶ Eriskay
see **Western Isles**, page 392

▶ Fair Isle
see **Shetland Islands**, page 356

▶ Falkland Palace MAP REF 402 C2
nts.org.uk

Falkland, Cupar, KY15 7BUY | 01337 857397 | Open Mar–Oct Mon–Sat 11–5, Sun 12–5

The somewhat forbidding walls of Falkland Palace – likened by Scottish philosopher and satirical writer Thomas Carlyle (1795–1881) to 'a black old bit of coffin or protrusive shin-bone sticking through the soil of the dead past' – encapsulate one of the most romantic periods of Scottish history. Within these walls you will find tales of political intrigue and murder, of hunting and hawking, of art and of literature.

Stuart monarchs used this handsome Renaissance-fronted fortress in the heart of Fife as a hunting lodge and retreat. The palace dates to the 15th century, with major additions between 1501 and 1541. Mary, Queen of Scots spent part of her childhood here, but when Charles II fled to exile on the Continent in 1651, it fell into ruin. Falkland was rescued from ruin by the third Marquess of Bute, a descendant of the Royal Stuarts, who became Hereditary Keeper of the palace in 1887. He restored and rebuilt much of the palace and, although it is now in the care of the National Trust for Scotland, his descendant still lives in the building as Keeper.

Inside, the palace is furnished with huge old oak furniture, including an enormous four-poster bed said to have belonged to James VI. The old library has a remarkable trompe-l'oeil ceiling and there are 17th-century Flemish so-called Verdure tapestries along the gallery leading to the King's apartments. Falkland Palace also has a royal tennis court, which was built in 1539 for James V.

▶ Findhorn MAP REF 413 E5

At the mouth of the almost-landlocked Findhorn Bay, the village is the third on the estuary to be called Findhorn – the first was buried by wind-blown sand in the 1660s, the second washed away in 1702 when the river, dammed by a sand bank, overflowed with tremendous force. That disaster occurred in a single night, but fortunately the inhabitants had already had the foresight to start building new houses some way to the southeast. The new village has so far escaped the fate of its predecessor: trees were planted to help stabilise the sands,

▼ Forres and the River Findhorn

and new sea defences, installed after a severe storm breached the dunes in 1983, have so far proved effective.

Findhorn was once a flourishing port. The harbour is now a marina, mainly given over to pleasure craft. Recreational sailing became popular here after World War I and the first Findhorn Class boat, an affordable 18-foot sailing dinghy, was developed here in 1930, making sailing for the first time a sport that even those with a small budget could enjoy. Much of the southern area of the bay is mudflats at low tide, good for wading birds during the year and attracting migrants in spring and autumn. You may see ospreys swooping for fish in summer; seals and dolphins can be spotted in the Moray Firth.

CHECK OUT THE HERITAGE CENTRE
Findhorn Heritage Centre
findhorn-heritage.co.uk
North Shore, IV36 3YE | 01309 690659 | Open Jun–Aug daily 2–5; May, Sep Sat–Sun 2–5
Find out about Findhorn's salmon-fishing past and discover the remains of the commonly called lost village at this visitor centre. It's housed in the former ice house, and you can see the arched underground chambers where ice was stored in preparation for packing locally caught salmon that were shipped on ice as far as London.

EAT AND DRINK
The Bakehouse Cafe
bakehousecafe.co.uk
91–92 Findhorn, Forres, IV36 3YG
01309 691826
The Bakehouse Cafe, in the centre of historic Findhorn, and close to Findhorn Bay, offers a changing menu of seasonal foods, largely organic soups, snacks, sandwiches and more substantial dishes such as pasta and burgers.

▶ Forres MAP REF 413 E5

According to local legend, the ancient market town of Forres, on the River Findhorn, was once plagued by witches. This may have inspired William Shakespeare, whose murderous Macbeth encounters the so-called weird sisters in the area. Three more witches are commemorated with a stone in the town.

A huge glass box protects Sueno's Stone, on the eastern outskirts. This is a Pictish cross-slab that stands 20 feet tall and is believed to date from the ninth or tenth century (free access). The sandstone is intricately carved in five sections with vivid scenes from an unidentified and bloody battle. Some think Sueno's Stone is a Pictish cenotaph, but it's named (erroneously) after an 11th-century Danish monarch, Sweyn Forkbeard, the first Dane to become ruler of England and father of the more famous Cnut (Canute).

TOUR THE DISTILLERY
Dallas Dhu Historic Distillery
historicenvironment.scot
Mannachie Road IV36 2RR | 01309
676548 | Open Apr–Sep daily
9.30–5.30; Oct daily 10–4; Nov–Mar
Sat–Wed 10–4
Modernisation of the whisky
industry has meant that many
whisky distilleries look like any
other big factory. Dallas Dhu,
built in 1898, is somewhat more
picturesque, with its
whitewashed walls and tall
chimneys. Inside, you can see
the kilns, mash house, malt
barn, tun room and still house,
followed by a sample dram at
the end of the tour.

EAT AND DRINK
Cluny Bank ◉
clunybankhotel.co.uk
69 St Leonards Road, IV36 2DW
01309 674304
A substantial Victorian mansion
in lush, green gardens, Cluny
Bank has a lot of period charm
and an air of sophistication. The
menu is classically focused,
with the local Moray suppliers
duly name-checked.

▶ PLACES NEARBY
Pluscarden Abbey
pluscardenabbey.org
Pluscarden, Elgin, IV30 8UA
Open daily 9–5
This remarkable monastery is
the only medieval foundation in
Britain still used for its original
purpose. Lying in a green valley
6 miles southwest of Elgin, it is
the permanent home of a small
community of Benedictine
monks, and a spiritual retreat
for men and women. It was
founded in 1230 for the French
Valliscaudian order by
Alexander II, and during the
Reformation in the 16th century
was gradually abandoned. In
1943, Benedictine monks from
Prinknash Abbey in
Gloucestershire started to
restore it, and in 1974 it
received the status of abbey.
Today the white-habited monks
work in the workshops and
grounds and care for the abbey
buildings. These focus on the
massive abbey church, where
ancient stonework and frescoes
contrast with the modern
stained glass.

▶ Fort William MAP REF 406 C4
In the shadow of Ben Nevis (see page 94), Fort William's
location on road and train junctions at the head of Loch Linnhe
and the foot of the Great Glen (see page 239) makes it a
convenient touring base for the northwest. The town's heyday
as a military outpost for subduing the Highlands is long gone
– the fort, which withstood Jacobite attacks in 1715 and 1745,
was knocked down in 1864 to make space for a train station.

Fort William's greatest asset is its close proximity to Ben
Nevis, which stands sentinel over the Nevis range about
7 miles to the north. It also has its own delights, including
a museum that celebrates local life and history.

VISIT THE MUSEUM
West Highland Museum

westhighlandmuseum.org.uk
Cameron Square, PH33 6AJ | 01397
702169 | Open Jan–Apr and Oct–
Dec Mon–Sat 10–4; May–Jun and
Sep Mon–Sat 10–5; Jul–Aug
Mon–Sat 10–5, Sun 11–4
The idiosyncratic West Highland
Museum, famous for the
Jacobite collections held there,
lives up to its description as 'an
old-fashioned museum', with
an eclectic range of displays,
including natural history,
Highland clothing and crofting.

GET ON THE WATER
Crannog Cruises

crannog.net/cruises.asp
Town Pier, PH33 6BD | 01397
700714 | Mar to mid–Oct 11, 1 and 3
You'll almost certainly see seals
basking on rocky shores or
popping their heads up beside
the boat as you cruise Loch
Linnhe. The views of Ben Nevis
and other surrounding
mountains are unbeatable.

TAKE A TRAIN RIDE
Jacobite Steam Train

westcoastrailways.co.uk
Fort William Station, PH33 6TQ
01524 737751 | See website or call
for timetables
The steam train (similar to the
one featured as the Hogwarts
Express in the 2002 movie
*Harry Potter and the Chamber
of Secrets*) follows the scenic
Road to the Isles. The train
goes to Mallaig (see page 296)
via Glenfinnan (where film

▶ The Jacobite Steam Train

scenes were shot at the great
viaduct, see page 237) and
returns the same way.

WALK THE WEST
HIGHLAND WAY

west-highland-way.co.uk
01389 722600 | See official website
for guided and self-guided itineraries
and baggage transfer services
Fort William is the northern
terminus of Scotland's best
known and most popular
long-distance walking trail,
the West Highland Way. It uses
ancient cattle drovers' roads,
stretches of former railway
and parts of the network of
military roads laid out by
General Wade to help tame the
Highlands after the risings of
1715 and 1745. The northern
stretches of the 96-mile trail
are tougher, and most people
choose to walk from south to
north, but if you feel fit enough

▲ Glenfinnan Monument

to tackle the hard stretches first there's nothing to stop you starting from Fort William. You don't even have to carry all your luggage – several companies offer luggage transfers so that your bags travel ahead of you each day to your next overnight stop.

▶ PLACES NEARBY

Clan Cameron Museum
clancameronmuseum.co.uk
Achnacarry, Spean Bridge, PH34 4EJ
01397 712090 | Open Apr–Oct daily
11–4.30; Oct–Apr on request
Clan Cameron's museum tells all about the clan's turbulent past, especially during the Jacobite Rising of 1745–46, when Cameron of Lochiel was one of Bonnie Prince Charlie's most prominent supporters. It also celebrates the Queen's Own Cameron Highlanders, one of the many Highland regiments that were raised after the great defeat of the clans at Culloden. The museum also tells the story of the Royal Marines Commandos, the elite special operations force created during World War II, who trained in the harsh surroundings of Achnacarry. A statue erected in their memory in 1952 stands by the A82 road, 11 miles from Fort William.

Glenfinnan Viaduct and Glenfinnan Monument
see highlight panel on page 237

Moorings Hotel
moorings-fortwilliam.co.uk
Banavie, PH33 7LY | 01397 772797
The historic Caledonian Canal and Neptune's Staircase run right beside this modern hotel and pub. On clear days it has panoramic views towards Ben Nevis. Food features local fish and seafood, with other choices such as steak-and-ale pie, and rib-eye of Highland beef.

Snowgoose Mountain Centre
highland-mountain-guides.co.uk
The Old Smiddy, Corpach, PH33 7JH
01397 772467 | Call or see website for times and reservations
You can try outdoor activities and adventures at this centre between Fort William and Glenfinnan. Abseiling, hill-walking, kayaking and rock climbing are on offer in summer, with winter mountain sports and hill-walking Oct–Apr. Suitable for age 8 and up.

Inverlochy Castle Hotel ⊚⊚⊚
inverlochycastlehotel.com
Torlundy, PH33 6SN | 01397 702177
Inverlochy is the quintessential Victorian baronial castle, all castellated stone walls and turrets surrounded by 500 green acres overlooking its own loch. Pretty impressive then, and inside it just gets better: luxuriant furnishings and fittings, paintings, crystal chandeliers and open fires. Dining here without a jacket and tie, gentlemen, is not permitted. Given this stolidly traditional setting, the cooking is surprisingly modern, with an abundance of luxurious touches.

Treasures of the Earth
treasuresoftheearth.co.uk
Corpach, PH33 7JL | 01397 772283
Open Nov–Dec and Feb daily 10–4;
Mar–Jun and Sep–Oct daily 10–5;
Jul–Aug daily 9.30–6
Europe's largest uncut emerald is the jewel in the crown of this huge collection of rare gemstones, crystals and fossils. Collectors and craftspeople can also buy fossils and semi-precious stones from Scotland and all over the world here.

▶ **Foula**
see **Shetland Islands**, page 357

▶ Gairloch MAP REF 411 E5

This popular holiday village with its excellent Heritage Museum is spread around a sunny, sandy bay, with the heights of Flowerdale looming behind. Beside the loch of the same name, the village has a sandy beach and you can go sailing and sea-angling or take a whale or dolphin cruise. There are superb views out to the islands, and Gairloch lies at the heart of a fine scenic area that takes in Loch Maree. West from the village, the road winds around the bay and eventually turns into a track, leading to the former lighthouse at Rubha Reidh. Energetic walkers can take the long path to Diabaig on Loch Torridon.

Loch Maree, famous for its fishing, is surrounded by high mountains and scattered with darkly wooded islands. The highest peak on the northern shore is Slioch (3,219 feet/981m), while to the south Beinn Eighe, with its cap of white quartzite, lies at the heart of Britain's first National Nature Reserve. You can find out about nature trails and picnic spots at the visitor centre at Aultroy, towards the eastern end of the loch.

Isle Maree, by Letterewe, was the site of a seventh-century hermitage, and may have had older, druidical connections. Queen Victoria fell in love with the whole area when she visited in 1877, giving her name to the waterfall near Talladale.

The waters around here are among the best places in Britain to see whales, dolphins and porpoises because the Gulf Stream brings warm, plankton-rich water and the swirling currents around the islands bring nutrients to the surface.

▼ Gairloch

VISIT THE MUSEUM
Gairloch Heritage Museum
gairlochheritagemuseum.org
Gairloch, IV21 2BP | 01445 712287
Open Apr–Oct Mon–Fri 10–5,
Sat 11–3
Wooden fishing boats and a reconstructed croft house, school room and village shop are among the highlights of this lively small museum. You can also find relics of the deeper past, including a Pictish symbol stone, and learn traditions that include illicit whisky distilling.

GO WILDLIFE SPOTTING
Gairloch Marine Life Centre
porpoise-gairloch.co.uk
Pier Road, IV21 2BQ | 01445
712636 | Call or see website for
cruise departures
The Gairloch Marine Life Centre runs two-hour boat cruises, subject to weather conditions, to spot porpoises, seals and dolphins, and perhaps basking sharks. You can also watch videos of local sea creatures, seabirds, golden eagles and white-tailed sea eagles, which breed around Gairloch.

EAT AND DRINK
The Old Inn
theoldinn.net
Flowerdale Glen, IV21 2BD
01445 712006
This old coaching and drovers' inn has great views across to Skye and the outer islands. It has an on-site microbrewery, and a smokery producing smoked meats, fish and cheese. Highland game and West Coast seafood feature on the menu.

▶ Gatehouse of Fleet MAP REF 398 C5
Founded in the mid-18th century, Gatehouse of Fleet lies at the heart of the Fleet Valley National Scenic Area, an area of tidy farms and broadleaved woodland either side of the Water of Fleet. The little town was the birthplace of the once-popular (but now largely forgotten) Victorian artist John Faed, who conceived the clock tower and town hall in the centre of town. Robert Burns is alleged to have composed one of Scotland's unofficial anthems, *Scots wha hae*, one drunken night at the town's Murray Arms Hotel, and Sir Walter Scott used Gatehouse of Fleet as the basis for his fictional Kippletringan in the novel *Guy Mannering* (1815).

The Fleet Valley stretches inland to the Rig (ridge) of Drumruck and the foothills of the 2,330-foot (710m) Cairnsmore of Fleet. Seaward, it opens onto Fleet Bay, where a miniature archipelago, the Islands of Fleet, lies scattered in the shadow of the 1,500-foot (451m) massif of Cairnharrow. Two of these islets, known as the Murray Isles, belong to the National Trust for Scotland and are part of a Site of Special Scientific Interest. They're uninhabited, but home to flocks of nesting seabirds, including a substantial colony of cormorants.

TAKE IN SOME HISTORY
Cardoness Castle
historicenvironment.scot

Castle Douglas, DG7 2EH

01557 814427 | Open Apr–Oct daily 10–4

The remains of a 15th-century tower house, a 20-minute walk from Gatehouse of Fleet, cling to the cliffside above Fleet Bay. Cardoness Castle was a sturdy little fortress that was held by the McCullochs of Myreton. It was abandoned after Sir Godfrey McCulloch, the family's patriarch, was executed for the murder of William Gordon in the final act of a long-running feud between the McCullochs and their Gordon neighbours. He has the dubious distinction of being the last person executed using the Maiden, Scotland's forerunner of the guillotine.

CHECK OUT THE VISITOR CENTRES
Cream o' Galloway Visitor Centre
creamogalloway.co.uk

Rainton, DG7 2DR | 01557 814040

Open mid-Mar to Oct daily 10–5

Watch ice cream being made at this organic farm dairy, which is located in a converted 17th-century farmstead, and then choose your favourite in the shop. There are nature trails, a dry-stone dyking exhibition and playground.

Mill on the Fleet Visitor Centre
millonthefleet.co.uk

High Street, DG7 2HS | 01557 814099 | Open daily Easter–Oct 10–5

This beautifully converted 18th-century mill has two working watermills and is now a visitor centre incorporating a cafe, bookshop, craft shop, art gallery and wildlife exhibition. It is in grounds with picnic tables.

EAT AND DRINK
Cally Palace Hotel ❀
callypalace.co.uk

Cally Drive, DG7 2DL | 01557 814341

Old-school opulence is the deal in this Georgian country manor. The kitchen delivers modern country-house cooking.

▶ Glamis Castle MAP REF 408 C6
glamis-castle.co.uk

Glamis, DD8 1RJ | 01307 840393 | Open Apr–Oct daily 10–5.30

A grand, turreted pile, Glamis (pronounced Glahms) has been the seat of the Earls of Strathmore and Kinghorne since 1372. You can explore the castle on a guided tour, which lasts about an hour, and are then free to roam the beautiful landscaped park, which includes an elegant Italian garden. Glamis was the childhood home of Elizabeth Bowes-Lyon, better known as Queen Elizabeth, the Queen Mother (1900–2002).

Legends about Glamis Castle are plentiful. Shakespeare set key scenes from *Macbeth* here, Malcolm II was said to have been murdered here in the 11th century; Lady Janet Douglas, the widow of the Earl of Glamis, was burned at the stake as a witch here by James V in 1540; and there is said to be a secret room where one lord of Glamis played cards with the devil.

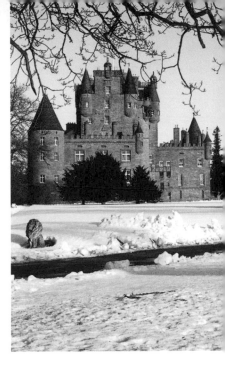

▲ Glamis Castle

There was probably a castle at Glamis in the early 14th century, but it was not until after 1376 that the L-plan tower house was built by John Lyon on land presented to him by King Robert II. The Lyon family have owned the castle ever since. It was extensively restored and developed in the 17th and 18th centuries.

Early records show that Glamis was a holy place where, in the eighth century, St Fergus came from Ireland to preach. Today, visitors can see St Fergus's Well near the kirk, and several Celtic stones found in the area date from that time. Later, Scottish royalty came to appreciate the lush Angus landscape and built a hunting lodge here. Shakespeare's witches were rather premature in naming Macbeth 'Thane of Cawdor and of Glamis', as the actual thaneage (or lordship) was not granted to Glamis until 1264, a century after his death.

The family became Bowes-Lyon when the Ninth Earl married a Durham heiress, Miss Mary Eleanor Bowes. The most famous Bowes-Lyon was, of course, the Queen Mother. When Lady Elizabeth Bowes-Lyon married Prince Albert, the Duke of York, in 1923, her mother created a suite of rooms for the exclusive use of the royal couple. The Queen Mother spent most of her childhood at Glamis, and this is where she gave birth to her second daughter, Princess Margaret. The Royal Apartments are furnished with fine antiques and porcelain and family portraits.

The gardens at Glamis include a walled garden and a delightful Dutch garden. On the east side of the castle is the Italian garden enclosed within a high yew hedge and featuring two 17th-century-style gazebos. This garden is entered through decorative wrought-iron gates, made to commemorate the 80th birthday of the Queen Mother in 1980.

▶ Glasgow MAP REF 401 F3

Scotland's biggest city is also, in many ways, its youngest. Glasgow may have been founded some 1,500 years ago, and was a flourishing place in medieval times, as surviving medieval buildings such as Glasgow Cathedral and Paisley Abbey show, but most of what you'll see when you visit in the 21st century is much more recent.

Glasgow traces its origins back to the sixth century, when St Mungo (or Kentigern, to give him his original Celtic name) established a religious community here. A bishop was appointed in 1114 and Glasgow University was founded in 1451. But the city really got into its stride with the discovery of the New World and the opening up of transatlantic trade in commodities like sugar, cotton and, above all, tobacco in the 18th century. Wealth poured in, creating a new, self-confident merchant class whose imprint can be seen on the city to this day. This commercial boom created the wealth that financed the massive industrialisation of Glasgow and Clydeside in the 19th century, when easy access to coal and iron fostered industries such as shipbuilding and textiles and made Glasgow the second city of

the British Empire. Most of the city's grand public buildings and treasuries of culture, such as the City Hall, the Hunterian Museum and Kelvingrove Gallery, and the outstanding Burrell Collection, date from this era. Various 19th- and 20th-century benefactors left their mark on the city after death, in the shape of the grandiose memorials that were built for them on the slopes of Glasgow Necropolis, high above the city.

Glasgow wasn't just dedicated to making money. It was, and is, a cultural powerhouse, too. In the late 19th century and early 20th it was home to artists and designers such as the group of painters known as the Glasgow Boys and, most famously of all, Charles Rennie Mackintosh (see page 227). In the 20th and 21st centuries it has fostered a roster of talents such as comedians Billy Connolly, Frankie Boyle and Susan Calman, rock bands like Texas, Travis, Simple Minds, Belle and Sebastian, and Franz Ferdinand, and film directors including Bill Forsyth and Danny Boyle. Glasgow's Theatre Royal is home to Scottish Opera and Scottish Ballet, while the Citizens Theatre, created in 1945, has forged a reputation for adventurous and sometimes controversial drama.

▼ Clyde Arc Bridge, River Clyde

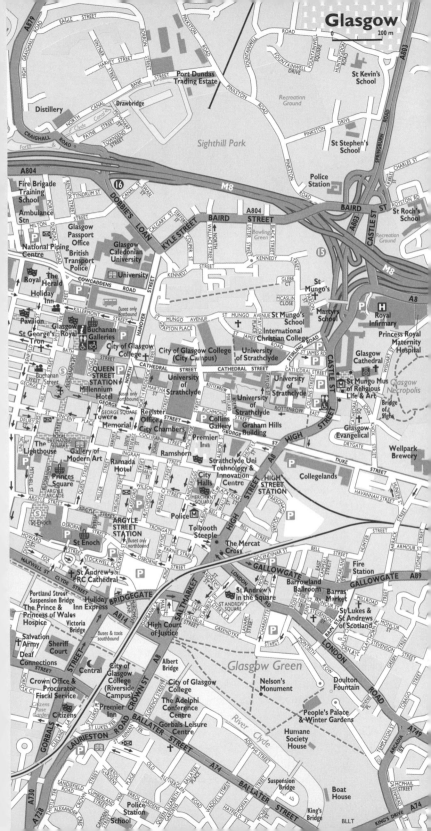

▲ George Square

Glasgow also claims to be Scotland's sporting capital, a claim that was reinforced when it was chosen to host the 2014 Commonwealth Games. Football is as much a local obsession as anywhere in Scotland, with the two clubs known as the Old Firm maintaining a keen rivalry. Glasgow nightlife is legendary, ranging from a lively clubbing scene to Scottish traditional music performed in lively bars and pubs.

Glasgow straddles the River Clyde, with most of its major sights and attractions in the grid of streets immediately north of the river and bounded by the city ring road, the M8, on its north and west sides. You can use an efficient light rail, underground train and bus network to reach attractions farther from the city centre, like the Riverside Museum, the Burrell Collection, and Kelvingrove Art Gallery and Museum.

George Square is the hub of the city centre, and much of the city's shopping, nightlife, bars and restaurants can be found within a few blocks. For a breath of fresh air you can stroll through Glasgow Green, beside the Clyde, and combine your walk with a visit to the entertaining People's Palace. To get your bearings, walk to the highest point of the Glasgow Necropolis, from where there's a panoramic view of the city.

Glasgow can claim to be one of Scotland's most ethnically diverse cities. That's been so ever since the 19th century. Glasgow's industrial boom created huge demand for labour at a time when both the Scottish Highlands and Ireland were suffering extreme poverty and even famine, so tens of thousands of people migrated to work in Glasgow's mills and shipyards. The city also had a sizeable Jewish community. In the late 19th century, large numbers of Italians migrated to the city. Many of them opened ice-cream parlours and trattorias, and their descendants are still here – they include playwright and comedian Armando Iannucci, and actor Peter Capaldi. In the second half of the 20th century, Glasgow attracted migrants from India, Pakistan and Bangladesh, and as a result you'll find some of the best Asian food in Scotland here. Since the opening up of borders within the EU, Glasgow has also welcomed new migrants from European countries, notably Poland.

5 top historic vessels

▶ Royal Yacht *Britannia*, Leith page 281

▶ RRS *Discovery*, Dundee page 139

▶ PS *Waverley*, Glasgow page 225

▶ Tall Ship *Glenlee*, Glasgow page 214

▶ *Reaper*, Scottish Fisheries Museum, Anstruther page 155

Glasgow's city centre is manageably compact, but it's surrounded by a huge conurbation that covers some 400 sq miles of west central Scotland. Including satellite towns like Cumbernauld, Greenock (see page 240), Hamilton (see page 243), Motherwell and East Kilbride (see page 153), this urban sprawl is home to in the region of 1.2 million people. But getting away from city streets is surprisingly easy. Loch Lomond and the Trossachs (see page 286) are almost on Glasgow's doorstep. Downriver from the city, the River Clyde broadens into the wide Firth of Forth, dotted with islands like Bute, Cumbrae and Arran (see page 78). South of the Clyde are the long sandy beaches, yachting harbours and world-famous golf courses of the Ayrshire coast.

▼ View north to Greenock and the River Clyde

▶ **Glasgow Necropolis** MAP REF 209

glasgownecropolis.org
Wishart Street, G4 0UZ | Open daily 7am–4pm
See website for times of tours (booking essential)

It's worth slogging up to the highest point of Glasgow's fascinating city of the dead just for the great view of the city and the Clyde, but the grandiose monuments commissioned by the city's great and good also give fascinating insight into how some of Glasgow's wealthiest and most influential figures made their fortunes and built their reputations. You can take a guided tour to hear the stories of some of these rags-to-riches titans of trade and industry.

The Necropolis is cluttered with the somewhat ostentatious and florid tombs of wealthy industrialists and tobacco merchants who developed the city in the 19th century. Their competitive spirit showed even after death, with extraordinary monuments commissioned from the finest architects of the day, including Alexander 'Greek' Thomson. The burial ground was set out in 1833 on a hilltop near the cathedral, where it was felt that it could be contained, thus avoiding the spread of infectious diseases such as cholera and typhus.

TAKE IN SOME HISTORY
City Chambers
glasgow.gov.uk
George Square, G2 1DU | 0141 287 4018 | Open Mon–Fri 9–5 | Tours at 10.30 and 2.30
This opulent, grandiose palace fills one side of George Square. From the outside, beneath the Venetian-style central tower, pediments and corner cupolas, you can glimpse the richness of the gilded ceilings and grand entrance hall; the free tours are excellent. Enjoy the murals of the vast banqueting hall, the marble staircases and the mosaic ceiling of the loggia. The design, by architect William Young, captures the confidence of Glasgow in its Victorian heyday, when it was known as the second city of the British Empire.

Glasgow Cathedral
glasgowcathedral.org.uk
Castle Street, G4 0QZ | 0141 552 6891 | Open Apr–Sep Mon–Sat 9.30–5.30, Sun 1–5.30; Oct–Mar Mon–Sat 9.30–4, Sun 1–4
With the blackness of its stonework, its modern stained glass and its setting below the Victorian necropolis, you could be forgiven for assuming that Glasgow Cathedral was also 19th century. In fact it dates from the 13th to the 15th centuries. The central tower and spire are replacements dating from about 1406. The cathedral is dedicated to St Mungo, or Kentigern, who died in AD 603. His shrine, once a major pilgrimage site, is in the crypt. The symbols of a robin, fish, bell and tree that adorn the ornamental lamp posts outside reference the miracles believed to have been performed by the saint.

Glasgow Necropolis
see highlight panel opposite

Pollok House
nts.org.uk
Pollok Country Park, 2060 Pollokshaws Road, G43 1AT
0141 616 6410 | Open daily 10–5
Pollok House, a compact grey stone mansion, built for Sir John Stirling Maxwell, second Baronet, in 1747, is set in Pollok Country Park. It stayed in the family until 1966. The 10th Baronet was a co-founder of the National Trust for Scotland, which now maintains the house. Inside it's light and airy, with comfortably small-scale rooms including a library with 7,000 volumes, in which chamber concerts are given. El Greco's portrait of *c.*1577, *Lady in a Fur Wrap*, is a highlight of a collection of Spanish paintings. Sir John also endowed the Country Park's woodland garden with many of its vividly coloured rhododendron cultivars. Shaggy Highland cattle roam in parts of the park.

Provand's Lordship
glasgowlife.org.uk
3 Castle Street, G4 0RB
0141 276 1625 | Open Tue–Thu, Sat 10–5, Fri, Sun 11–5
The oldest house in Glasgow, Provand's Lordship lies close

to the medieval cathedral and opposite the St Mungo Museum, east of the city centre. Built in about 1471 as an almshouse, until the end of World War I it was still in use as a sweet shop.

A lack of historic atmosphere is compensated for by the collection of beautiful 15th- and 16th-century wooden furniture. The story of Rab Ha', the weighty Glesca Glutton, can be seen amid the amusing 19th-century illustrations of Glasgow characters on the top floor. Rab would bet his appetite on horse races and even fox hunts, and was defeated only once, by a dish of oysters with cream and sugar. A medieval herb garden has been planted at the back.

The Tall Ship at Riverside
thetallship.com
150 Pointhouse Place, G3 8RS
0141 357 3699 | Open Feb–Oct daily 10–5; Nov–Jan daily 10–4. Guided tours Wed 10.30
Moored outside the Riverside Museum, the Tall Ship *Glenlee* is a grand survivor of the last days of sail. This three-masted, steel-hulled barque was built on the Clyde in 1898 and is one of only five surviving Clyde-built sailing ships left in the world. It last saw service as a training ship with the Spanish navy, and then rusted in harbour at Seville until it was rescued from the scrapheap, towed back to Glasgow in 1992 and lovingly restored inside and out.

You can take a guided tour or rent an audio guide to find out about the ship's history. On board, you can see the huge cargo hold, the restored crew's quarters and the galley, complete with original sounds and smells. Don't miss the tales of the ship's voyages,.

The Tenement House
nts.org.uk
145 Buccleuch Street, Garnethill G3 6QN | 0141 333 0183 | Open Apr–Jun and Sep–Oct daily 1–5; Jul–Aug Mon–Sat 11–5, Sun 1–5
In the 19th century and early 20th, most Glaswegians lived in tenement houses, or flats, with each apartment occupying rooms on one floor level, and sharing communal facilities such as a wash-house. In poorer districts these were horribly overcrowded, with families sharing one room.

This compact little house gives a clear picture of tenement life for the slightly better off. From 1911 it was the home of spinster Agnes Toward, a shorthand typist, and her mother, a seamstress. Agnes never threw anything away, and when she died in 1975, her house was found to provide a fascinating time capsule of social history. Remarkably, it was preserved, and is now in the care of the National Trust for Scotland.

VISIT THE MUSEUMS AND GALLERIES
Burrell Collection
life.org.uk

Pollok Country Park, 2062
Pollokshaws Road, G43 1AT
0141 287 2550
The collection is closed for
renovation until 2020

The superb Burrell Collection, comprising approximately 9,000 varied pieces of art from around the world, was gifted to the city of Glasgow in 1944 by Sir William Burrell (1861–1958) and his wife, Constance. After years of delay, the collection finally went on display in 1983 in a purpose-built, stream-lined museum in the leafy and airy surroundings of Pollok Country Park, south of the centre of Glasgow.

Sir William had collected rare and precious works of art since his teens, and this is a highly personal collection, strong in the areas of his interest, amassed by a collector with a brilliant eye. The overall quality of everything is superb, and it is this, as much as anything, that makes this such a fine museum. It is very strong on medieval European art, French Impressionism and Chinese and Japanese porcelain. But there's much else besides.

The refurbishment includes the upgrade of the building – which features hundreds of panels from the stained-glass collection in the windows of its South Gallery – into an energy-efficient and modern building, with two new floors of exhibition space. Previously only 20 per cent of the collection was on display, but there will now be room for far more pieces. The re-opening of the museum, scheduled for 2020, is eagerly awaited.

▼ Burrell Collection

▶ Kelvingrove Art Gallery and Museum MAP REF 401 F3

glasgowlife.org.uk

Argyle Street, G3 8AG | 0141 276 9599 | Open Mon–Thu, Sat 10–5, Fri, Sun 11–5; organ recitals 1pm 26 Apr–31 Dec

The Kelvingrove, a sprawling red sandstone pile of Edwardiana, dates from 1902 and houses outstanding art and objects. Nineteenth-century industrial money paid for the building and much of its contents, and the brash self-confidence of the age is reflected in both the exterior and interior of the building. It's one of Scotland's most popular free attractions and features 22 themed, state-of-the-art galleries displaying a mind-blowing 8,000 objects, many of them internationally significant. They include natural history, arms and armour, art from many art movements and much more. There are even daily organ recitals played on the 100-year-old Kelvingrove Organ.

Walk into the vast entrance hall and you'll be confronted by Sir Roger the Elephant, somewhat incongruously dwarfed by a Spitfire fighter plane suspended above. Around this central area, themed exhibits cover diverse subjects ranging from Scotland's Wildlife and Ancient Egypt to highly focused displays featuring Charles

Rennie Mackintosh and the Glasgow Boys. The latter were a group of Glasgow-based artists who, in the 1870s, formed a loose organisation that aimed to rid painting of its sentimental conservatism and inject an infusion of realism.

There are many more paintings on the first floor, including some superb Dutch interiors and still lives, Italian and French master pieces and wonderful works by Rembrandt, Whistler, Raeburn and the group of artists working in the 1920s and 1930s known as the Scottish Colourists. Most visitors, though, will be drawn to Salvador Dalí's Christ of St John of the Cross, an extraordinary and very powerful painting of the crucifixion seen in foreshortening from above.

If you're with children, there's plenty to keep them busy and happy, as the multi-million pound restoration during the first decade of the 21st century focused on providing an experience that would enthuse children to become life-long museum visitors. This created the Mini Museum, aimed at the under-5s, where children can have a great time trying on shoes from around the world, ogling the taxidermy or sizing up a statue of Elvis Presley. They'll also enjoy the History Discovery Centre, the Creatures of the Past gallery, with its dinosaur fossils, and Every Picture Tells a Story where there are dressing-up outfits for wannabe princesses and fairies.

Gallery of Modern Art (GoMA)

glasgowlife.org.uk

Royal Exchange Square, Queen Street, G1 3AH | 0141 287 3050

Open Mon–Wed, Sat 10–5, Thu 10–8, Fri, Sun 11–5

This exceptional contemporary art gallery at the very heart of the city never fails to provoke and inspire. GoMA occupies what was once a 1780s tobacco baron's palatial mansion. Inside, you'll find a great exhibition space, which is usually given over to some of the best contemporary works from Glasgow Museum's collection. One of the museum's aims is to foster contemporary Scottish art, and upstairs you can see recent acquisitions of works by Scottish artists.

Because this is an ever-changing exhibition, it's difficult to pin down what works are likely to still be there in six months' time. However, that is what makes the GoMA so special, and it certainly works with the public – this is the second-most-visited art gallery in Britain outside London.

Glasgow School of Art

gsa.ac.uk

167 Renfrew Street, G3 6RQ

0141 353 4500| Tours Apr–Sep daily on the hour 10–5; Oct–Mar Mon–Sat 11, 3

Glasgow's art school was founded in 1845. By 1896 it was clear that a new building was required, and a competition for a design to suit this awkward site on the side of a steep hill was announced. Charles Rennie Mackintosh was the winner, and the project launched his brilliant career.

Tragically for admirers of Mackintosh, the magnificent art nouveau library that he designed for Glasgow School of Art, with its collection of irreplaceable documents, manuscripts and paintings, was gutted by fire in May 2014. It is being painstakingly restored, using Mackintosh's original plans and drawings, at a cost of some £35 million. Restoration is expected to be complete in 2019. Until then, you can still visit and tour the elegant building, which is regarded as the famous designer's crowning masterpiece. The exterior is severe, yet the stonework is adorned with a light, confident touch of wrought iron at the windows, on railings and on the roof. Inside, he designed everything down to the light fittings, creating a practical working space with a distinctive Arts and Crafts style that still, more than 100 years later, looks fresh and modern.

House for an Art Lover

houseforanartlover.co.uk

Bellahouston Park, 10 Dumbreck Road, G41 5BW | 0141 353 4770

See website for opening times

The House for an Art Lover is a fantasy, set out on paper in 1901 without limitations of budget or client's whims, by Charles Rennie Mackintosh and his wife, Margaret Macdonald. It was for a competition set by

▶ People's Palace and Winter Gardens

glasgowlife.org.uk

Glasgow Green, G40 1AT | 0141 276 0788 | Open Tue–Thu, Sat 10–5, Fri, Sun 11–5 (gardens also open Mon). During the ongoing phased refurbishment, call ahead to check what's open

There's no better place to familiarise yourself with the wit, eccentricity and gritty character of Glasgow than at this local institution, set on Glasgow Green. The People's Palace, built in 1898, tells the history of Glasgow through familiar objects and quotes from real people.

The first floor displays shed light on everyday life in 20th-century Glasgow, with plenty of information on city life throughout both world wars plus the development of the very strong union movement and working-class struggle in the city. Probably more appealing, is the mock-up of a steamie, or communal wash-house, which you'll find opposite the Buttercup Dairy, a wonderfully evocative old-time shop. Life's little pleasures are covered by exhibits highlighting Dancing in the Barrowland, Glasgow's iconic dancehall, a night out on The Bevvy, focusing on the city's drinking culture, and Doon the Watter, telling the story of steamer trips down the Clyde.

Making it in Glasgow, in a corner of the top floor, is devoted to famous Glaswegians, including comedian Sir Billy Connolly.

▼ People's Palace

a German magazine for 'a grand house in a thoroughly modern style', but their entry was disqualified. The physical reality was achieved only in 1996, when artists and craftspeople were brought together by the City Council and the School of Art to build the dream in Bellahouston Park. And what a dream it is, with perfect proportions, light, open spaces, a harmonious balance of straight and curved lines, and every attention to detail in the elegant furnishings and fittings.

Hunterian Museum and Art Gallery

gla.ac.uk/hunterian
University of Glasgow, University Avenue, G12 8QQ | 0141 330 4221
Open Tue–Sat 10–5, Sun 11–4
The Hunterian Museum – the oldest public museum in Scotland – is a showcase for archaeological finds, coin collections and geological specimens amassed by William Hunter (1718–83), a Glasgow-trained physician and amateur scientist, who bequeathed his entire collections to his old university. If that kind of thing is too dry and dusty for your taste, cross University Avenue to the museum's art gallery annex, where you'll find a magnificent art collection. Its core is Hunter's collection of 17th-century Flemish, Dutch and Italian masterworks, which are complemented by modern

paintings. Another highlight is the Mackintosh House, a re-creation of the interior of the home that Mackintosh and his wife Margaret created together, with original furniture, as it appeared in 1906. The fittings here show clearly the influence of Japanese style on Charles' work, and its combination with Margaret's flowing, organic art nouveau patterns. You can see more Mackintosh furniture and designs in the gallery itself, along with paintings from his later travels.

Kelvingrove Art Gallery and Museum
see highlight panel on page 216

The Lighthouse

thelighthouse.co.uk
11 Mitchell Lane, G1 3NU
0141 276 5365 | Open Mon–Sat 10.30–5, Sun 12–5
Glasgow's museum of architecture and design,

▶ The Lighthouse

completed in 1895, was Charles Rennie Mackintosh's first public commission. It gets its name from the tower that dominates the structure. There's a breathtaking panorama of the city from the viewing platform.

The National Piping Centre

thepipingcentre.co.uk
30–34 McPhater Street, Cowcaddens, G4 0HW | 0141 353 0220
Open Mon–Thu 9–7, Fri 9–5, Sat 9–12

The skirl of the pipes is one of Scotland's signature sounds, and The National Piping Centre is dedicated to promoting pipe music in all its forms, from military marches played by massed bands to the mournful, evocative pibroch, or *piobaireachd*, composed for a single piper. Students from all over the world come to the museum to study. The building incorporates an auditorium for concerts, a sound archive and a small museum.

People's Palace and Winter Gardens

see highlight panel on page 219

Riverside Museum

glasgowlife.org.uk
100 Pointhouse Place, G3 8RS
0141 287 2720 | Open Mon–Thu, Sat 10–5, Fri, Sun 11–5

Glasgow's top visitor attraction for families is packed with historic vehicles, from steam locomotives and horse-drawn trams to early Scottish-built Arrol Johnson cars. The Hillman Imp car was a less enduring rival to the Mini – look for the first Imp ever to come off the production line in 1963 (blue, and driven by the Duke of Edinburgh). There are fire engines, motorbikes, model ships, the earliest pedal bicycle, prams, caravans and other transport paraphernalia. Three street scenes bring bygone Glasgow to life. A display is dedicated to the Clyde-built liner *Lusitania*, sunk by a German U-boat with the loss of almost 1,200 lives in 1915.

St Mungo Museum of Religious Life and Art

glasgowlife.org.uk
2 Castle Street, G4 0RH | 0141 276 1625 | Open Tue–Thu, Sat 10–5, Fri, Sun 11–5

This museum is set on three floors, with an international art collection, objects relating to religious life, and a section about religion in Glasgow. In the Gallery of Religious Art on the first floor, a Native American chilkat blanket rubs shoulders with an Australian Aboriginal Dreamtime painting and the popping figures of a Nigerian ancestral screen. There is also a statue of Shiva, one of the principal Hindu deities. European art is represented by exquisite stained-glass panels. The Gallery of Religious Life juxtaposes items associated with particular ceremonies from different cultures.

On the third floor, dedicated to religion in Scotland, look

for a lantern slide show used by temperance preachers to show the evils of drink. A display tells the story of the Protestant–Catholic divide in Glasgow, and there is a thought-provoking exhibit about religion, society and poverty. In a hands-on section, children can learn the basics of many other of the world's religions and faiths.

Scotland Street School Museum

glasgowlife.org.uk
225 Scotland Street, G5 8QB
0141 287 0500 | Open Tue–Thu, Sat 10–5, Fri, Sun 11–5

Another prime example of Mackintosh's architecture is the stunning Scotland Street School. Built between 1903 and 1906, it ceased to be a school in the 1970s and is now preserved as a museum of education. The front is dominated by two tall, glazed, semicircular towers that contain the main staircases – not winding round, but uncompromisingly straight and set back from the glass to create a very different sense of light and space.

Scottish Football Museum

scottishfootballmuseum.org.uk
The National Stadium, Hampden Park, G42 9BA | 0141 616 6139
Open Mon–Sat 10–5, Sun 11–5; tours hourly

Hampden Park is the home of Scotland's oldest football team, Queen's Park, and also the site of the world's first national football museum. An air of vanished glory haunts the 2,500 items on display. They include part of the original Hampden dressing room as it was known to great players of the past. You can even experience the so-called Hampden roar of the 1930s, when 140,000 people would pack in here for the big games.

Sharmanka Kinetic Gallery and Theatre

sharmanka.com
103 Trongate, G1 5HD
0141 552 7080
See website for main shows. Static display open all year Wed–Sun 1–3

Surreal scenarios created from scrap metal, plastic and other junk, carved puppets, light effects and eerie music will take you by surprise at this magical attraction.

GO ROUND THE GARDENS
Glasgow Botanic Gardens

glasgowbotanicgardens.com
730 Great Western Road, G12 0UE
0141 276 1614 | Gardens open daily 7am–dusk; glasshouses daily summer 10–6, winter 10–4.15

Whatever the time of year, a visit to Glasgow's botanic gardens makes a welcome change from city streets. In summer you can roam along the banks of the River Kelvin. In winter or on rainy days, take refuge inside the cavernous Kibble Palace, an enormous glasshouse that houses tree ferns from Australia and New Zealand and tropical and subtropical plants from Africa, the Americas and Asia. The garden grew out of a collection of plants for medical

▲ Glasgow Science Centre

use held by Glasgow University and moved to this site in the West End suburbs in 1842.

ENTERTAIN THE FAMILY
Glasgow Science Centre
glasgowsciencecentre.org
50 Pacific Quay, G51 1EA | 0141 420 5000 | Open Apr–Oct daily 10–5; Nov–Mar Wed–Fri 10–3, Sat and Sun 10–5
From the top of Glasgow Science Centre's Glasgow Tower, you can see 20 miles over the city and surrounding countryside. The tallest tower in Scotland, it's the only building in the world that can rotate a full 360 degrees into the prevailing wind. You have to hope the winds aren't too strong, as the Tower will close if they exceed 40mph. It takes two and a half minutes for the lift to get all the way up to the viewing cabin, which is 344 feet high.

The Science Centre's main attraction is the Science Mall, with four floors containing 500 interactive exhibits. The biggest laughs can be found at the distorting mirrors. Other highlights include using computer screens to design dance sequences, seeing how an artificial arm picks up signals from your body to move, the Kinex construction sector and a walk-on piano for kids. There's also an IMAX theatre housed in the gleaming, ovoid, titanium-skinned building beneath the tower.

Scottish Mask and Puppet Centre
maskandpuppet.co.uk
8–10 Balcarres Avenue, G12 0QF
0141 339 6185 | Call for show times
There's a live puppet show for children held here every Saturday and an accompanying

mask and puppet exhibition to walk around.

SEE A STYLISH CHURCH
The Mackintosh Church
mackintoshchurch.com
Queen's Cross, 870 Garscube Road, G20 7EL | 0141 946 6600 | Open Apr–Oct Mon–Fri 10–5; Jan–Mar, Nov–Dec Mon, Wed, Fri 10–4
This serene church, one of Glasgow's hidden architectural gems, and the only complete church designed by Charles Rennie Mackintosh, is a soothing space in which to relax and gather your thoughts. Completed in 1897, it follows a simple Gothic revival style. As with all of Mackintosh's buildings, attention to detail is everything here, extending to some exceptional carved woodwork depicting stylish birds and animals.

CATCH A PERFORMANCE
Barrowland Ballroom
glasgow-barrowland.com
244 Gallowgate, G4 0TS
0141 552 4601
Big-name pop and rock acts play at this venue to the southeast of the city centre.

Centre for Contemporary Arts (CCA)
cca-glasgow.com
350 Sauchiehall Street, G2 3JD
0141 352 4900 (cinema tickets)
Various contemporary art forms, including music, visual art and alternative cinema, are catered for at this cutting-edge centre. Everything from classics to foreign films.

Citizens Theatre
citz.co.uk
119 Gorbals Street, G5 9DS
0141 429 0022
The resident company at this Victorian theatre, in the Gorbals area, produces a wide range of British and European classic theatre productions.

Glasgow Film Theatre
gft.org.uk
12 Rose Street, G3 6RB
0141 332 6535
The best art-house cinema in Glasgow shows contemporary, Classic, independent and foreign films on its two screens.

Glasgow Royal Concert Hall
glasgowconcerthalls.com
2 Sauchiehall Street, G2 3NY
0141 353 8000
The most prestigious venue in the city, with a programme of Classical, pop and rock music. In January and February it hosts the international Celtic Connections music festival.

King's Theatre
atgtickets.com
297 Bath Street, G2 4JN | 0844 871 7648 (calls cost 7p per minute, plus your phone company's access charge)
Big-budget touring musicals dominate here, along with stand-up comedy and drama.

King Tut's Wah Wah Hut
kingtuts.co.uk
272a St Vincent Street, G2 5RL
0141 221 5279 | Open Mon–Sat 12–midnight, Sun 5pm–midnight
The heart of the Glasgow music scene is an unpretentious,

▲ Paddle Steamer *Waverley*

relaxed venue playing cutting-edge indie, pop and rock.

Pavilion Theatre
paviliontheatre.co.uk
121 Renfield Street, G2 3AX
0141 332 1846
Find comedy, musicals and pantomime at the last bastion of Glasgow music hall tradition.

Stand Comedy Club
thestand.co.uk
333 Woodlands Road, G3 6NG
0141 212 3389
Northwest of the city centre, this bar has live Scottish and international comedy, most nights. Over 18s only.

Theatre Royal
atgtickets.com
scottishopera.org.uk
scottishballet.co.uk
282 Hope Street, G2 3QA
0844 871 7647 (calls cost 7p per minute, plus your phone company's access charge)
You will find a rich programme of the best in opera, ballet, dance and theatre at this, the oldest theatre in Glasgow, and the home of Scottish Opera and Scottish Ballet.

Tramway
tramway.org
25 Albert Drive, G41 2PE | 0141 330 3501 | Open Tue–Fri 12–5, Sat, Sun 12–6
Art, dance and theatre, and contemporary art exhibitions, south of the River Clyde.

Tron Theatre
tron.co.uk
63 Trongate, G1 5HB | 0141 552 426
Expect contemporary Scottish and international drama, comedy, music and dance at this theatre at the eastern end of Argyle Street.

GET ON THE WATER
Paddle Steamer *Waverley*
waverleyexcursions.co.uk
36 Lancefield Quay, G3 8HA | 0845 130 4647 (local call rate) | Open May–Aug; check website for timetable
Cruise down the River Clyde or visit the islands of Arran, Bute and Cumbrae in the Firth of

Clyde aboard the *Waverley*, the only traditional sea-going paddle steamer in the world. You can join her for a day, afternoon or evening cruise.

TAKE A BUS TOUR
City Sightseeing Glasgow
citysightseeingglasgow.co.uk
153 Queen Street, G1 3BJ | 0141 204 0444 | Open all year, check website for timetable
Hop aboard a distinctive red double-deck bus for an open-top sightseeing tour of the city. Tickets are valid for two days and allow the holder to hop on and off the bus as they please. Buses leave from George Square and busier services often have a guided commentary. Buy tickets on the bus or online.

EXPLORE BY BIKE
Clyde and Loch Lomond Cycleway
sustrans.org.uk
0141 287 9171 (Glasgow City Council)
The Clyde to Loch Lomond Cycleway is a dedicated cycle route 20 miles long, taking in Clydebank, Dumbarton (see page 129), the Vale of Leven and Balloch. The path is also suitable for walkers, and follows forest trails, minor roads, old train tracks and canal towpaths.

LEARN TO SKI
Snow Factor
snowfactor.com
King's Inch Road, PA4 8XQ | 0871 222 5672 (calls cost 10p per minute, plus your phone company's access charge) | Open all year Sun–Wed 9am–10pm, Thu–Sat 9am–11pm
Inside the enormous Intu Braehead shopping and entertainment complex next to the Clyde you'll find Scotland's only indoor ski slope, where experienced skiers and snowboarders can hone their skills, beginners can take lessons and kids can hurtle downhill on toboggans.

GET KARTING
Scotkart Indoor Kart Racing and Terminator Paintball
scotkart.co.uk
33 John Knox Street Clydebank, G81 1NA | 0141 641 0222
Open Mon and Fri 12 noon–10pm; Wed and Thu 3–10; Sat and Sun 9.30–10pm
Scotland's largest indoor kart track and a laser and paintball combat zone are guaranteed to get the adrenaline flowing at this family attraction.

GO SHOPPING
The Barras
glasgow-barrowland.com
Gallowgate and London Road, between Ross Street and Bain Street
0141 552 4601 | Open Sat–Sun 10–5
The famous street market near Glasgow Green is a relic of a bygone age, a gritty, witty contrast to Glasgow's modern veneer of sleek shopping centres and debonair cafe society. It dates back to the 1920s, when enterprising street trader Margaret McIver raised a roof for stand-holders, who had previously sold their wares from

open barrows. Today it's a sprawling hotchpotch of sheds, stands and warehouses that looks forlorn during the week, but comes to life at weekends. You'll find everything from antique furniture to fortune-tellers and counterfeit designer clothing, plus a monthly farmers' market.

GO SWIMMING
Tollcross International Swimming Centre
glasgowlife.org.uk
350 Wellshot Road, G32 7QR
0141 276 8200 | Open Mon–Wed, Fri 7am–10pm, Thu 10–10, Sat 9–5, Sun 9–9
This huge leisure centre has two 50-metre Olympic pools that hosted several swimming events during the 2014 Commonwealth Games.

SPOT THE MACKINTOSH EFFECT
The Mackintosh Trail
crmsociety.com
Queens Cross Church, Garscube Road, G20 7EL | 0141 946 6600
You can hardly miss the designs of Charles Rennie Mackintosh in Glasgow today – his stylised roses and trademark lettering stare out on endless souvenirs, from mugs and tea towels to mirrors and silver jewellery. The style has become so familiar it is known affectionately as Mockintosh, and Glasgow, it seems, can't get enough of it. Yet Mackintosh's designs flourished for a relatively brief spell in the early 20th century, and it is only in the last 30 years

or so that serious attempts have been made to preserve the major works of this remarkable and original architect.

Charles Rennie Mackintosh was born in Glasgow in 1868, and was apprenticed to a firm of architects at the age of 16. While attending evening classes at the School of Art he met Herbert McNair and Margaret Macdonald (1865–1933), whom he married in 1900. McNair married Margaret's sister, Frances, and the two couples, known as the Four, came to dominate the emerging Glasgow Style.

Mackintosh's partnership with his wife extended into design, and her input became an acknowledged part of his work. Mackintosh's first project was in 1893, a workaday building for the *Glasgow Herald* newspaper, which is now the Lighthouse (see page 220). His design for his most famous structure, the Glasgow School of Art (see page 218), was commissioned in 1896; his best work was completed in the early 20th century.

By 1914, his distinctive fusion of the abstracted, flowing lines of art nouveau with the simplicity of the Arts and Crafts Movement had passed from fashion in Britain. Disillusioned, he toured Europe – delicate watercolour paintings that survive from this period can be seen at the Hunterian Museum (see page 220). He died in 1928.

You can buy a Mackintosh Trail Ticket, which includes

entry to The Hill House, the Mackintosh House, the Glasgow School of Art, House for an Art Lover, the Mackintosh Church and Scotland Street School, from the Mackintosh Society.

WATCH A MATCH
Celtic Football Club
celticfc.net
Celtic Park, G40 3RE | Tickets 0871 226 1888 (calls cost 13p per minute, plus your phone company's access charge). Tours 0141 551 4308 Open daily for tours
Celtic enjoys passionate support both at home and worldwide. Take a tour of the stadium to the east of the city, one of Europe's largest, or go to see the team in action.

Rangers Football Club
rangers.co.uk
Ibrox Stadium, 150 Edmiston Drive, G51 2XD | 0871 702 1972 (calls cost 10p per minute, plus your phone company's access charge)
Take a tour of the stadium or see a game. Tickets for an Old Firm game (the Glasgow derby between Rangers and Celtic) are very difficult to get hold of.

PLAY A ROUND
Bearsden Golf Club
bearsdengolfclub.com
Thorn Road, G61 4BP | 0141 586 5300 | Open daily
A parkland course with 16 greens and 11 teeing areas. It is easy walking and there are views of the city and the Campsie Hills. It's the home

course to Ewen Ferguson, British Boys Amateur Champion in 2013 and Scottish Boys Champion in 2014.

Glasgow Golf Club
glasgowgolfclub.com
Killermont, G61 2TW | 0141 942 2011 | Open Mon–Fri
One of the finest parkland courses in Scotland.

EAT AND DRINK
Blythswood Square ◉◉
blythswoodsquare.com
11 Blythswood Square, G2 4AD
0141 248 8888
Built in 1821 as the grand headquarters for the Royal Scottish Automobile Club on leafy Blythswood Square, this imposing building has been injected with a good dollop of boutique style. A drink in the palatial Salon Lounge among fluted columns topped with gilt capitals makes a fine first impression, before heading into the restaurant in the former ballroom. Excellent Scottish guest breed steaks sourced from local farms are among the stars of the show.

La Bonne Auberge ◉
labonneauberge.co.uk
161 West Nile Street, G1 2RL
0141 352 8310
This ever-popular venue bases its menu on the classic French brasserie repertoire, but with its own imaginative twists. Meats are cooked on the grill. The lunchtime special is terrific value for money.

▲ Cail Bruich

Cafe Gandolfi

cafegandolfi.com

64 Albion Street G1 1NY

0141 552 6813

Deagh bhiadh, deagh bheannachd; these Gaelic words meaning 'well fed, well blessed' are displayed on the wall of this stylish and popular restaurant. They sum up the philosophy behind the place, founded in 1979 and thus one of the first eateries to herald that something new was about to hit Glasgow restaurant life. Housed in an old cheese factory, the walls hung with local artwork, and furnished with purpose-crafted, sinuously comfortable fittings, the focus is on classic and classy Scots–Mediterranean cookery. Smoked salmon from the Summer Isles, haggis from Dingwall and meat from Wemyss Bay pay tribute to Scottish quality, and are transformed into dishes such as cullen skink, a delicate smoked haddock based chowder, or a classic New York pastrami on sourdough. Factor in, too, seasonal game, imaginative salads, great cocktails and a laid-back, welcoming vibe.

Cail Bruich ◉◉◉

cailbruich.co.uk

725 Great Western Road, G12 8QX

0141 334 6265

Cail Bruich is a family affair, but there's nothing remotely homespun about this slick operation. The interior looks the very image of a big-city eatery with its unclothed darkwood tables and low-slung copper lights. Artfully constructed modern European cooking is delivered via a trio of menu formats, from a well-priced market formula, trading up to the *carte* and a top-end six-course taster with an option for matching wines.

Chez Mal Brasserie ◉◉
278 West George Street, G2 4LL
0141 572 1001
This immensely popular restaurant, a favourite with locals for a special occasion, highlights modern, seasonal cooking using the best of Scottish ingredients in new takes on crowd-pleasing favourites. A mix of traditional and modern French brasserie cooking is the draw here, but it also features Asian flavours such as feather-light tempura, alongside classics such as its famous Chateaubriand and some truly decadent desserts.

Crabshakk
crabshakk.com
114 Argyle Street, Finnieston,
G3 8TD | 0141 334 6127
Buzzy Scottish fish and seafood restaurant, where piscine delights – ranging from whole lobster and oysters to a classic fish supper or sumptuous *fruits de mer* platter – are served in a wood-panelled space.

Fratelli Sarti
sarti.co.uk
133 Wellington Street, G2 2XD
0141 248 2228
The Sarti family run three authentically Italian restaurants in Glasgow and this is their flagship. Come here for breakfast, lunch or dinner and enjoy a good range of properly prepared Italian staple dishes, the recipes sourced from all over Italy and all using fresh local produce and imported Italian ingredients. They also

do great pizza and you can buy cheeses and cured meats to take away.

Gamba ◉◉
gamba.co.uk
225a West George Street, G2 2ND
0141 572 0899
This perennial favourite enjoys a well-deserved reputation as the go-to place for top-notch fish and seafood in Glasgow's West End. Warm colours, floors of dark wood and terracotta tiles, stylish fish-themed artwork and polished-wood tables create a warm feel, perfect for the Mediterranean- and Asian-influenced cooking.

The Gannet ◉◉◉
thegannetgla.com
1155 Argyle Street, G3 8TB
0141 204 2081
The Gannet is a chic 21st-century venue, with hard-lined industrial styling, all exposed brickwork, wood floors and tiny cafe tables. The kitchen aims to fill you up with plates of deceptively simple modern bistro food, full of flavours.

The Hanoi Bike Shop ◉
hanoibikeshop.co.uk
8 Ruthven Lane, G12 9BG
0141 334 7165
This vibrant venture is the brainchild of the people behind two iconic Glasgow eateries, the long-running Ubiquitous Chip and its sister restaurant, Stravaigin. It has a chilled-out, canteen-style vibe that suits the street food menu, and sharing is the way to go. The menu

gives the Vietnamese names of dishes followed by an English translation. There are classic *pho* dishes, too.

Hotel du Vin at One Devonshire Gardens ◉◉◉
hotelduvin.com
1 Devonshire Gardens, G12 0UX
0141 339 2001
The Bistro at Glasgow's Hotel Du Vin is a rather grander room than its name implies. The kitchen displays a passion for prime Scottish ingredients, which are handled with well-honed technical skills to produce sharp modern dishes.

Opium ◉
opiumrestaurant.co.uk
191 Hope Street, G2 2UL
0141 332 6668
East and West are reconciled in this contemporary-styled restaurant in the heart of Glasgow. Big picture windows allow light to flood into a slick space done out with dark wood and muted brown tones, where communal tables with high chairs share the space with conventional seating. Food is Asian fusion.

Ox and Finch ◉◉
oxandfinch.com
920 Sauchiehall Street, G3 7TF
0141 339 8627
Ox and Finch has a fashionable industrial finish with brown leather banquettes and booths. The style is modern and rustic with Modern British flavours dominating alongside some influences from Asia and North Africa. For drinks, choose from a selection of craft beers or wines by the carafe.

Rogano
roganoglasgow.com
11 Exchange Place, G1 3AN
0141 248 4055
Glasgow's longest-serving restaurant celebrated its 80th birthday in 2015. Rogano's perfectly preserved art deco interior is a delight and the place is run with old-school Gallic courtesy. An often-starry clientele returns for platters that are loaded with seafood.

Shish Mahal ◉
shishmahal.co.uk
60–68 Park Road, G4 9JF
0141 339 8256
A Glaswegian institution since the 1960s, the Shish Mahal has seen generations of curry fans pass through its doors to sample Mr Ali's classic Indian cooking. The extensive menu explores familiar variations on the traditional fare, taking in old favourites from the madras, vindaloo and bhuna stables, with plenty of other ideas to broaden your horizons, too.

Stravaigin ◉◉
stravaigin.co.uk
28–30 Gibson Street, Kelvinbridge,
G12 8NX | 0141 334 2665
The tagline of this switched-on stalwart of the Glasgow foodie scene – 'Think global, eat local' – neatly sums up its culinary ideology. Spread over two floors of cafe-bar and a

basement restaurant, the operation goes for a quirky contemporary look. Reclaimed and reinvented pieces of modern art and interesting *objets* are set against rough stone walls and beamed ceilings. This is the perfect foil to the consistently imaginative, flavour-driven cooking. The kitchen plunders Scotland's magnificent larder for its raw materials, which are allied with an eclectic approach to the world's cuisines.

Ubiquitous Chip ◉◉

ubiquitouschip.co.uk
12 Ashton Lane, G12 8SJ
0141 334 5007

The Chip has been in business since 1971, and its continuing success is down to a talent for keeping in step with the times without becoming a fickle follower of ephemeral trends. So, some dishes come and go, while others have been around since year dot. The cooking is imaginative – quirky, even – but always precise and based on superb Scottish ingredients.

Urban Bar and Brasserie ◉

urbanbrasserie.co.uk
23–25 St Vincent Place, G1 2DT
0141 248 5636

The kitchen at this sleek and modern bar-brasserie knows its stuff, producing a menu full of interesting Scotland-meets-Mediterranean ideas. There's a real sense of style about the place, and a seasonally changing menu.

Wee Lochan ◉

an-lochan.com
340 Crow Rd, Broomhill, G11 7HQ
0141 338 6606

Known to locals for the quality of its food, the contemporary Scottish cooking here delivers precise, defined flavours in thoughtfully composed dishes. There's friendly service and a relaxed atmosphere.

WEST on the Green

westonthegreen.com
Templeton Building, Glasgow Green
G40 1AW | 0141 550 0135

'Glaswegian heart, German head' is the strapline this buzzy brewpub/restaurant uses as the only UK brewery producing beers in accordance with Germany's Purity Law of 1516, which means no additives, colourings or preservatives. It occupies the old Winding House of a former carpet factory, modelled by its Victorian architect on the Doge's Palace in Venice. Look down into the brewhouse from the beer hall and watch the brewers at work. Brewery tours are conducted on selected days of the week. The all-day menu has a German flavour, too. October Fridays are beer festival days.

▶ **PLACES NEARBY**

Sprawling Glasgow's satellites include East Kilbride (see page 153), Paisley (see page 324), Coatbridge (see page 111), Dumbarton (see page 129) and Hamilton (see page 243). Greenock (see page 240) is a little farther afield.

▶ Glen Affric MAP REF 406 C3

This long, steep-sided glen runs parallel to the Great Glen
(see page 239). It's one of the best-loved beauty spots in the
Highlands, and Plodda Falls, more than 120 feet in height, is
one of its more spectacular sights. Its scenery combines forest
and moorland, river and loch with mighty mountains such as
Carn Eige. A narrow road leads up from Cannich to the River
Affric parking area, passing the Dog Falls and a beautiful picnic
area at Loch Beinn a' Mheadhoin on the way up. Footpaths are
marked, and for serious hikers a trail leads through to Kintail.
A 3,100-acre area of native woodland, incorporating fragments
of ancient Caledonian pine forest, has been established.
Crested tits and crossbills may be seen year-round in the
woods, with rarer golden eagles and capercaillie.

Glen Affric is flanked on the north side by some of the
highest mountains of the Northwest Highlands, shapely conical
peaks rising to Carn Eige at 3,881 feet (1,183m) and Mam
Sodhail at 3,875 feet (1,181m).

In the valley lie the two great lochs of Loch Affric and Loch
Beinn a' Mheadhoin. The lower slopes of the hills are clothed in
one of the most beautiful remnants of the ancient native
Caledonian pine forest, with a leavening of birches and a
sufficiently open canopy to permit the growth of purple-hued
heather and blaeberry.

▼ Glen Affric

▶ Glencoe MAP REF 406 C5

Whether your first approach to Glencoe is down from the wide, watery wasteland of Rannoch Moor (see page 340), or up from the finger of sea that is Loch Leven (see page 285), you cannot fail to be impressed by the majesty of this valley. On a clear day you can see the tops of the Aonach Eagach ridge to the north (3,169 feet/966m), with its sweeping sides of loose scree, and the peaks of the great spurs of rock known as the Three Sisters to the south, leading down from Bidean nam Bian (3,766 feet/1,148m). At the eastern end the glen is guarded by the bulk of Buachaille Etive Mor, the so-called Great Shepherd of Etive (3,343 feet/1,019m). On other days the tops are hidden in a smirr (mist) of rain clouds, the waterfalls become torrents and wind funnels up the glen at a terrific rate.

This is prime mountaineering country, and not for the unfit or unwary. In winter it becomes a snow-filled world, offering an extra challenge to climbers and regularly claiming lives.

Memories are long in the Highlands, and there is still a frisson between families MacDonald and Campbell that dates back to a February night in 1692. At a time when clan leaders were required to swear loyalty to the monarchs William and Mary, Alastair Maclain MacDonald of Glencoe missed the deadline by a few days. Campbell of Glenlyon was sent to make an example of him. Campbell's men were billeted here for two weeks before turning on their hosts in an act of cold-blooded slaughter that left 38 dead. It was a betrayal that has never been forgotten. The atrocity took place in the lower glen by Glencoe village, where the now heather-roofed Folk Museum offers displays of Highland life.

At a height of about 1,200 feet, the flat, green meadow floor of Coire Gabhail is enclosed by the walls of Gearr Aonach and Beinn Fhada, which sweep round to the great buttresses at the head of the valley and the pass of Bealach Dearg. If you are lucky, you'll be greeted by the magnificent sight of a golden eagle soaring effortlessly on fingered wings above the bealach.

VISIT THE MUSEUM
Glencoe and Folk Museum
glencoemuseum.com
Main Street, Glencoe Village,
PH49 4HS | 01885 811664
Open Apr–Oct Mon–Sat 10–4.30
Where Glencoe meets the coast, you'll find this little museum, within a group of whitewashed and thatched traditional so-called cruck cottages. There's lots to see, from tableaux depicting cottage life in the 18th century to huge shotguns used by local lairds to bring down flocks of geese.

CHECK OUT THE VISITOR CENTRE
Glencoe Visitor Centre
nts.org.uk
Glencoe, PH49 4HX
01855 811307
Open Mar–Oct daily 9.30–5.30;
Nov–Feb Thu–Sun 10–4
From the roof of the National Trust for Scotland Visitor Centre there is a fine view of the mountain scenery and glittering waterfalls. You can get details about the many exhilarating walks from the Visitor Centre; there is challenging climbing, too, for the experienced.

GO SKIING
Glencoe Mountain Resort
glencoemountain.co.uk
Kingshouse, PH49 4HZ
01855 851226

From White Corries at the top of the glen, a chairlift takes skiers (and summer visitors) high into the mountains, where there are 16 runs catering for all abilities. The Glencoe area also offers cross-country skiing, ski mountaineering, snowboarding, speed skating and paragliding.

EAT AND DRINK
Clachaig Inn
Glencoe, PH49 4HX | 01855 811252
This Highland inn has welcomed climbers, hill-walkers and skiers for more than 300 years. Real ales (sometimes as many as 15), nearly 300 malt whiskies, good food and fresh coffee are served in all three bars, each with its own distinctive and lively character.

▶ **Glenelg** MAP REF 405 E3

Glenelg has an unusual claim to fame: it's Scotland's only palindromatic place name. The village is strung out along a shallow bay, with the deserted 18th-century barracks of Bernera to the north, and looks across the narrow Sound of Sleat to Skye. Dun Telve and Dun Troddan, the well-preserved remains of two Iron-Age brochs, can be found in Glen Beag.

The old military road that leads up to Glenelg rockets off the main Kyle of Lochalsh road, climbing rapidly up the Mam Ratagain pass to a fine viewpoint offering stunning panoramas of the lovely Five Sisters of Kintail above Loch Duich.

The Glenelg road passes the gaunt remains of Bernera Barracks, built in 1722 for Hanoverian troops (the ruins are fenced off for safety reasons).

▶ **PLACES NEARBY**
Glenelg Brochs
historicenvironment.scot
Glen Beag
Open daily 24 hours

Stark, mysterious and oddly lovely, these twin, 2,000-year-old stone towers are among the best-preserved of Scotland's ancient brochs. They're also the

▶ Glenfinnan Viaduct MAP REF 406 B4

The Glenfinnan Viaduct is instantly recognisable to many; it's the viaduct over which thundered the Hogwarts Express in the *Harry Potter* films. Curving over 1,000 feet above the River Finnan, its 21 concrete arches are up to 100 feet high. You can cross it yourself on the train line that runs between Fort William (see page 198) and Mallaig (see page 296).

The viaduct was designed by Robert MacAlpine, whose nickname was Concrete Bob. It is said that buried within it are a horse and cart that fell headlong into the concrete before it set. Look down Loch Shiel as you cross and you'll catch a glimpse of the Glenfinnan Monument, built in 1815.

TAKE IN SOME HISTORY

Glenfinnan Monument

nts.org.uk

Glenfinnan, PH37 4LT

01397 722250

Monument guided tours only (via Visitor Centre). Visitor Centre: Apr–Jun and Sep–Oct daily 10–5; Jul–Aug daily 9.30–5

On 19 August 1745, Prince Charles Edward Stuart raised the Jacobite standard here at the top of Loch Shiel, a rallying cry to supporters of his father's claim to the throne of Scotland. It was the start of the Stuarts' final attempt to regain the British throne, which would end the following year in disaster at Culloden. The occasion is recalled by a large pillar monument.

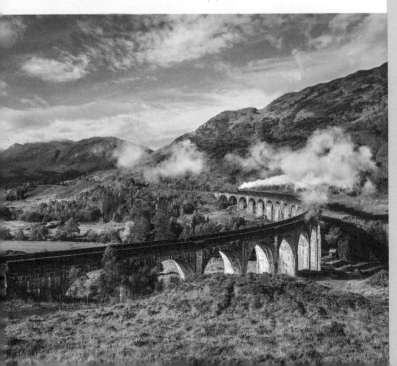

most accessible, and give a tantalising glimpse into the world of prehistoric Scotland. There's still no agreement among archaeologists and historians about what brochs like Dun Telve and Dun Troddan were actually for. But there is no denying their way with masonry. More than 30 feet in height, Dun Telve has stood the test of time remarkably well.

▶ Glenfinnan Viaduct
see highlight panel on previous page

▶ Glen Lyon MAP REF 407 D6

This long and beautiful hidden valley lies sandwiched in the mountains between Loch Tay and Loch Rannoch, and stretches for 34 miles to the Lubreoch hydroelectric dam at the eastern end of Loch Lyon. Entry is via the mountain pass at Ben Lawers (3,982 feet/1,214m) or through the dramatic, steep-sided pass at Fortingall. The road is single track and follows the route of the River Lyon, through scenery of woodland and little farms, backed by sweeping hills.

Glen Lyon is separated from Loch Rannoch by the broad summit of Carn Mairg. Said to be the longest glen in Scotland, it exhibits an enormous diversity of scenery.

Deeply entrenched between Carn Mairg and mighty Ben Lawers, the glen gradually descends from these wild, bare mountains around Cashlie, where the remains of five ancient Celtic forts have been discovered, towards Fortingall. Beyond

▼ Glen Lyon

Allt Odhar, it becomes a broad strath (valley) traversed by the leisurely loops of the River Lyon.

In Glen Lyon, the woodlands clothing the lower slopes of the mountains contrast well with the barer but colourful higher slopes, and as you descend the glen, the farmlands of the strath and the woodlands of the lower slopes become ever richer and more varied. At each turn of the road, a new scene of river, wood, mountain and meadow is revealed until, at the Pass of Glen Lyon, the river rushes through a tight, rocky gorge, closely screened by magnificent canopies of beech, to open finally on the pleasant meadows of Fortingall.

▶ Gorebridge
see **Dalkeith & Gorebridge**, page 122

▶ The Great Glen MAP REF 407 D3

Slashing for 60 miles from the head of the Moray Firth in the east to Loch Linnhe at its western end, the slanting Great Glen is a dramatic rift valley that splits northern Scotland in two. A straight, sweeping trough between bare-topped mountains, it is strung with roads, a long-distance walking trail and cycle route. Look out for the so-called Parallel Roads on the hillside at Glen Roy: they are entirely natural terracing left behind by lakes in the ice ages. Long, narrow lochs form a chain along this huge natural gutter, and are linked by one of the great engineering achievements of the 19th century. Between 1801 and 1847, the

▼ Parallel Roads, Glen Roy

Caledonian Canal's series of canals and locks connected Loch Ness (see page 294), at the northeast end of the Great Glen, with Loch Lochy, Loch Oich and Loch Linnhe. Its most impressive engineering feat is Neptune's Staircase, the group of eight locks that carried vessels to and from the highest point of the canal.

▶ **Greenock** MAP REF 401 E3

Greenock's prosperity was built on refining sugar and weaving cotton, both of which were shipped across the Atlantic from America and the West Indies to this port at the mouth of the Clyde. It was also a centre for shipbuilding, and the terminus of the world's first passenger steamship service, launched in 1812 by the paddle steamer *Comet*. All these industries have vanished, and Greenock is trying to revive its fortunes by welcoming tourists, including passengers from cruise ships that dock at its new ocean terminal.

VISIT THE MUSEUM
McLean Museum and Art Gallery
inverclyde.gov.uk
15 Kelly Street, PA16 8JX
01475 715624
The star of this museum is James Watt, the local man credited with kickstarting the Industrial Revolution. He didn't – as some believe – invent the steam engine, but his development of the steam condenser made existing engines much more powerful and compact. You can find out all about his career at this entertaining museum, which also has a collection of models of Clyde-built ships and displays featuring local history.

ENTERTAIN THE FAMILY
Funworld Leisure
funworld-leisure.co.uk
Unit 1–2, Fort Matilda Estate, Eldon Street, PA16 7QB | 01475 783003
Open daily 9.30–6.30 but times may vary so check website
This family entertainment centre is a great place to take younger children, who can play on a four-lane slide and an inflatable obstacle course and drive mini go-karts while parents relax in the cafe. There's also a laser tag area for older kids.

GET INDUSTRIAL
Greenock Cut Visitor Centre
clydemuirshiel.co.uk
Cornalees Bridge, PA16 9LX
01475 521458 | Open Apr–Oct
Sat and Sun 11–4

5 top rivers and waterways

▶ River Tay
▶ River Clyde
▶ Firth of Forth
▶ River Spey
▶ Caledonian Canal

Sloping downhill from Loch Thom to Greenock, this aqueduct was constructed in the 19th century to provide water to the town's mills and factories. You can find out about its history here, and then take one of several pretty walks to enjoy great views of the coast.

▶ **PLACES NEARBY**
Dumbarton (see page 129) is up and across the Clyde, on your way to Glasgow (see page 206).

▶ Gretna Green MAP REF 399 F5

Gretna Green's fame rests on its location on the border, and its historical association with runaway lovers from England. Several sites claim to be the original location where, under Scottish law, marriages could simply be declared in front of witnesses – and that was that.

GET HITCHED
The World Famous Old Blacksmith's Shop Centre
Gretna Green, DG16 5EA
01461 338 441 | Open daily 9–5
Tradition has it that runaway couples could be married by the smith at this early 18th-century forge and, even today, lots of people still opt for a romantic ceremony and get wed here. If you're already wed (or determinedly single) you can still watch a slightly kitsch re-enactment of an old-time wedding ceremony.

VISIT THE MUSEUM
The Devil's Porridge Museum
Annan Road, Eastriggs, DG12 6TF
01461 700021 | Open mid–Jan to mid–Dec Mon–Sat 10–5, Sun 10–4
The Devil's Porridge Museum tells the story of Gretna's role in World War I, when an important and huge munitions factory stretched for miles along the coast. The factory produced cordite, which was essential for the millions of artillery shells that were expended in the ferocious battles of the Western Front.

▼ Gretna Green

▲ St Mary's Collegiate Church, Haddington

▶ **Haddington** MAP REF 403 D3

This handsome market town is set in prime agricultural country on the River Tyne, 18 miles east of Edinburgh. It was granted the status of a royal burgh in the 12th century (the nearby port of Aberlady, now silted up, was its gateway to trade with continental Europe), and later became the county town for East Lothian. Protestant reformer John Knox was born here in *c.*1505. The original medieval town was laid out to a triangular street plan that can still be traced along High Street, Market Street and Hardgate. Painted in bright, warm colours, the 18th-century Georgian buildings of the High Street create a pleasing and harmonious facade. The graciously proportioned Town House was built by William Adam in 1748. St Mary's Church dates from the 15th century.

VISIT THE MUSEUM
John Gray Centre
johngraycentre.org
15 Lodge Street, EH41 3DX | 01620 820695 | Open Apr–Sep Mon–Fri 10–5, Sat 10–4, Sun 1–4; Oct–Mar Mon, Tue and Fri 10–5, Sat 10–4, Sun 1–4
Haddington's John Grey Centre has an eclectic collection of items and relics spanning centuries of the region's past, from an official charter sealed by Robert the Bruce in 1318 and original letters signed by Mary, Queen of Scots to Bronze Age burial goods.

▶ PLACES NEARBY
National Museum of Flight
nms.ac.uk/flight
East Fortune Airfield, EH39 5LF
0300 123 6789 | Open Apr–Oct daily 10–5; Nov–Mar Sat, Sun 10–4
This open-air museum hosts Scotland's national collection of historic aircraft, with more than 50 aircraft offering everything from a fine Glasgow-built flying machine to the majestic Concorde-G-BOAA. A number of World War II planes are on display. The museum site forms the most complete record of a World War II airbase in Britain.

▶ **Hamilton** MAP REF 402 A3

Known as Cadzow until the 17th century, Hamilton was renamed by James, Lord Hamilton, son-in-law of James VII and II. Hamilton Palace was the seat of the Dukes of Hamilton until the 1920s, when it was demolished after becoming a ruin. The Douglas-Hamiltons (who are still among the region's biggest landowners) endowed a number of other historic buildings in the area, including an 18th-century hunting lodge.

ENTERTAIN THE FAMILY
M&D's

scotlandsthemepark.com
Strathclyde Country Park, ML1 3RT
01698 333777 | Open Apr–Oct. Call or see website for times
You'll find 20 or more rides for all ages at this family attraction that bills itself as Scotland's theme park, along with a tropical rainforest encounter area where kids can meet birds, beasts and creepy-crawlies.

GET OUTDOORS
Chatelherault Country Park

slleisureandculture.co.uk
Ferniegair, Hamilton, ML3 7UE
01698 426 213 | Park open daily 9–5, Visitor Centre daily 10–5, Lodge House Sun–Thu 10–4.30
The jewel of this country park is Chatelherault, the hunting lodge designed by Robert Adam for the Duke of Hamilton in 1732. Surrounded by formal gardens, it has an elegant interior that displays some fine decorative plasterwork. In the estate that surrounds the lodge, you can walk through ancient oak woodlands and encounter long-horned white cattle.

Strathclyde Country Park

visitlanarkshire.com
366 Hamilton Road, Motherwell, ML1 3ED | 01698 402060
Open Sun–Fri 8–6, Sat 9–midnight
Surrounding Loch Strathclyde, this large country park offers lots of family activities on land and water. You can hire mountain bikes, pedalos, canoes and kayaks, sailing dinghies and windsurfers here. The park is also home to a cheesy-but-fun theme park.

▶ PLACES NEARBY
Glasgow and its suburbs are nearby, but for something a bit different head southeast to New Lanark (see page 303).

▶ **Harris**

see **Western Isles**, page 389

▶ **Helmsdale** MAP REF 413 E3

When the Duke of Sutherland turfed many of his crofter tenants off land they had farmed for centuries to make way for more profitable sheep grazing, many of them settled in this little fishing port on the site of a much earlier Viking settlement (hence its Norse-sounding name). Turning from farming to the sea, they prospered as hard-working fisherfolk. Helmsdale today is a sturdy little place of tidy stone cottages around a harbour that is still home to a working fishing flotilla.

This seems an unlikely setting for a gold rush, but in 1868 gold was discovered in the gravel of the Helmsdale River. Hundreds flocked to Helmsdale dreaming of striking it rich, and a shanty town grew up beside the river at Strath of Kildonan. It all came to nothing – there is gold in the river, but not in commercial quantities, and the Duke of Sutherland soon had the shanty-dwellers driven off his land, claiming that they were disturbing his deer and sheep. One cannot help wondering if he also wanted to keep the gold of Helmsdale for himself.

VISIT THE HERITAGE CENTRE
Timespan Heritage Centre
timespan.org.uk
Dunrobin Street, KW8 6JA | 01431
821327 | Open Mar–Oct daily 10–5;
Nov–Feb Sat and Sun 10–3, Tue 2–4

This lively village history centre opens a window or two onto Helmsdale's past, from early Viking settlers to displaced crofters, fisher-folk and the gold rush of 1868.

▶ Hermitage Castle MAP REF 399 F4

historicenviroment.scot
Newcastleton, TD9 0LU | 01387 376222 | Open daily Apr–Sep 9.30–5.30;
Oct daily 10–4

Hermitage Castle's dark sandstone walls loom menacingly above the marshy ground beside the river known as Hermitage Water, 15 miles south of Hawick. Sir Walter Scott recorded that

local people regarded this brooding fortress 'with peculiar aversion and terror'. The lack of windows indicates that this was never a homey castle, rather a grim place for fighting and foul deeds. The Douglas family took over a simple rectangular building in the 14th century and remodelled it to the massive and forbidding structure seen today. One owner was boiled alive for his crimes of murder

◀ Hermitage Castle

and witchcraft, and another, who starved a rival to death in the dungeon, was murdered in a nearby wood. Mary, Queen of Scots made a flying visit in 1566 to meet her lover Bothwell. It's a place steeped in atmosphere and history.

▶ Hoy

see **Orkney Islands**, page 321

▶ Inner Hebrides

see **Western Isles**, page 382

▶ Inveraray MAP REF 401 D1

Spread out along a bay near the head of Loch Fyne, the handsome town of Inveraray was for centuries the capital of Argyll. The ruling family, the Campbell dukes of Argyll, had a castle nearby, and when the untidy village threatened the view from his planned new mansion in 1743, the Third Duke moved the lot to its present purpose built site. This created a harmony in the buildings, many of which were designed by Robert Mylne (1734–1811). They include the parish church, which causes the main street to flow around it.

The tall brown stone tower is that of All Saints' Episcopalian Church, famous for its peal of ten bells and with panoramic views from the top. Moored in the harbour, you may be able to see one or two historic vessels, including the three-masted *Arctic Penguin*, built in 1911, and the *Vital Spark*, a last survivor of the fleet of small puffer steamships that carried freight and passengers between the Clyde and the ports of the Hebrides and the west coast until the early 20th century.

TAKE IN SOME HISTORY

Inveraray Castle

inveraray-castle.com

PA32 8XF | 01499 302203

Open daily Apr–Oct 10–5.45

Completed in the late 18th century, Inveraray Castle is a monument to the military and political skills of the Campbell chiefs, who over centuries made their clan the most powerful in the Highlands, by allying themselves with the British government against their Jacobite neighbours.

Most of what you see at Inveraray Castle today was planned by the Third Duke, including the township and the beautiful surrounding parkland. The foundation stone was laid in 1746, close to the old tower. One of the most appealing features of the estate, the watchtower high on Duniquaich, was constructed in 1748, for £46.

▲ Inveraray

There is plenty of space and light in the State Dining Room, which was created from one end of the Long Gallery when a modest entrance hall was built in the middle in 1772. Elaborate wall paintings of flower garlands and fruit are encased in gilded panels. The quality of the painting here and in the drawing room is exquisite, enhanced by the pretty French tapestry work on the furniture.

The Tapestry Drawing Room is hung with beautiful Beauvais tapestries, commissioned by the Fifth Duke, with painting on a delicate ceiling by Robert Adam. The room is dominated by a portrait by Hoppner of the Fifth Duke's daughter, Lady Charlotte Campbell, as Flora.

Inveraray Jail
inverarayjail.co.uk
Main Street, PA32 8TX | 01499

302381 | Open Apr–Oct daily 9.30–6; Nov–Mar daily 10–5 Costumed guides bring Inveraray's former courthouse and prison to life, playing the roles of severe warders from an era when the whipping table and the crank were favoured instruments of the punitive regime of the 19th century. The In Prison Today exhibit contrasts old-school incarceration with life for those in prison today.

EAT AND DRINK
George Hotel
Main Street East, PA32 8TT
01499 302111
Built in 1776 and owned by the same family since 1860, The George occupies a prime spot in the centre of town, just around the corner from the jail. More than 100 whiskies and a range of Fyne Ales are complemented

▲ Inveraray Jail

by an extensive bar menu that includes traditional haggis, neeps and tatties.

▶ PLACES NEARBY

Auchindrain Township Open Air Museum

auchindrain.org.uk
PA32 8WD | 01499 500235 | Open Apr–Oct daily 10–5, Nov–Mar call to check opening times

This unique medieval communal farming village is the only surviving example of such a settlement in Scotland. It's been kept as it was in the late 19th century, and 21st-century kids will be astonished at the primitive living conditions in thatched cottages with dirt floors and open fireplaces.

Crarae Garden

nts.org.uk
Inveraray, PA32 8YA | 01546 886614
Garden open daily 9.30–dusk. Visitor Centre open Apr–Aug daily 10–5; Sep–Oct Thu–Mon 10–5

Blazing crimson and purple are the signature colours of this hillside garden on the shores of Loch Fyne, between Inveraray and Lochgilphead. It was the creation of Captain George Campbell, who began the transformation of this narrow Highland glen into a Himalayan gorge in 1925. Today it is cared for by the National Trust for Scotland, and boasts more than 400 species of rhododendrons and azaleas, which thrive in the mild, damp climate and acid soils. This is primarily a woodland garden, with paths winding through the eucalyptuses and other trees. A 50-acre forest garden contains native, broadleaved species. Look out for the Neolithic chambered cairn (c.2500 BC) by the picnic site.

The garden was originally started by Grace, Lady Campbell, in the early years of the 20th century. She was inspired in part by her great nephew, Reginald Farrer – the plant collector and traveller who introduced into Britain a number of rhododendron species from his trips to Kansu in 1914 and to Upper Burma in 1919 – and perhaps also by Sir John Stirling-Maxwell of Pollok. Her son, Sir George Campbell, spent many years extending the original planting, eventually creating this Himalayan ravine garden in a Highland glen.

Above Crarae is Beinn Ghlas, where you can see the type of natural scrub of oak, alder, hazel, birch and rowan that had to be cleared when the garden was originally created. Sir George's son, Sir Ilay, continued to care for Crarae until the National Trust for Scotland acquired and reopened the garden to the public in 2002.

▶ Inverewe Garden MAP REF 411 F4

nts.org.uk

Poolewe, IV22 2LG | 01445 781229 | Garden and Visitor Centre open Apr and Sep daily 10.30–5; May–Aug daily 9.30–5.30; Oct daily 10.30–4: garden only Jan–Mar and Nov–mid-Dec daily 10.30–4

It's startling to see trees and shrubs from exotic, even subtropical climates flourishing as far north as this unique pocket of land with its oddly temperate micro-climate. Poolewe is, after all, as far north as Moscow or the southern end of Hudson's Bay. Polar bears, maybe – but bamboo?

Inverewe Garden is the result of the rugged determination of one man, Osgood Hanbury Mackenzie, to overcome both probability and practicality. When Osgood, at the time only 20 years old, acquired the 12,000-acre site in 1862 it was barren moorland and rocky coast. Fierce, salt-laden gales blew in from the Atlantic, burning and shrivelling any tender leafy plants in their path.

A century and a half later, Inverewe is one of the most spectacular gardens in Scotland. It hosts a national collection

of olearias, one of the most comprehensive selection of rhododendrons in the United Kingdom and a significant assortment of ourisias. The garden is dazzlingly colourful and complex all year round – even in the depths of a Scottish winter.

Osgood improved the estate's thin soil by adding a mixture of peat, seaweed, manure and clippings and, folk memory has it, loam brought by boat from Ireland. It's an ongoing project: tons of mulch are needed each year to replace soil leached away by the region's heavy rainfall.

High walls of the local pink-coloured sandstone were built to shelter Osgood's first venture, a south-facing, one-acre walled garden constructed on a former glacial raised beach. Conceived on almost cottage-garden lines, yet with plants from around the globe, this area has scarcely changed today. A further luxuriant herbaceous border runs along the front of the current Inverewe House – the original mansion having been burned down in 1914. Osgood's daughter Mairi created a courtyard garden in the ruins. Closer still to the shore there is a rock garden that experiences the full force of salty storms.

By summer, in the Walled Garden, the borders dazzle with a mingling of flowers, herbs and vegetables. Clematis and climbing roses clamber over pergolas, and roses underplanted with lavender-coloured nepeta make a beautiful central feature.

▶ Inverness MAP REF 407 E2

If you come from pretty much anywhere else in the UK, the so-called capital of the Highlands may not seem like the big city it purports to be. But with a fast-growing population of about 63,000, it's by far the biggest community in Scotland's far north. Granted city status in 2000, it's now also the hub of the University of the Highlands and Islands, created in 2011. And in many ways, Inverness is a quite modern creation. The grand-looking, imposing red sandstone Inverness Castle dominates the town, but impressive as it looks, it's actually a mundane administrative building, constructed in 1836 to house the Inverness Sheriff Court, a role it still fulfils, and so is not open to the public.

Commanding the east–west facing corridor to Moray and Aberdeen as well as the main north–south route through Scotland, its location gave Inverness strategic importance that has resulted in a much chequered history. The settlement was probably well established by the time of St Columba's visit in AD 565. Predictably, the town changed hands between Scots kings, local clan chieftains and English invaders until the final defeat in 1746 of the Jacobite cause at nearby Culloden (see page 117) brought stability to the Highlands and a degree of bourgeois prosperity to Inverness. On the shore of the Moray Firth about 11 miles northeast of Inverness, the massive walls of Fort George, built in 1769, were created as a symbol of the Crown's determination to enforce its control of the once-troublesome Highlands once and for all. It appeared to work –

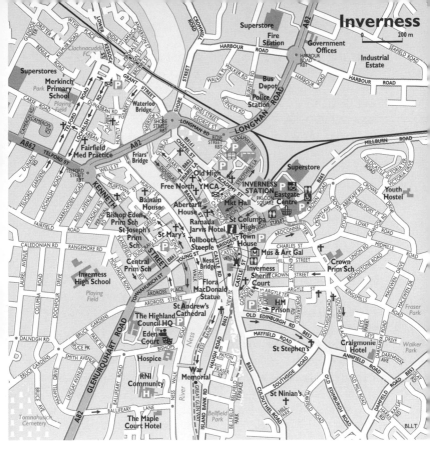

its guns were never fired in anger. Like the castle, most of the city's public buildings, including its impressive cathedral, date from the 19th century.

Inverness straddles the River Ness, which flows from the northeast end of Loch Ness into the Moray Firth, a wide arm of the North Sea. For many visitors to Inverness, a jaunt in search of the mythical Loch Ness Monster on nearby Loch Ness (see page 294) will be a high point. More realistic seekers of marine creatures have a good chance of a sighting in the Firth, which is home to hundreds of bottlenose dolphins and harbour porpoises, as well as occasional minke whales.

For drivers, the Kessock Bridge, a remarkable piece of engineering, spans the Firth to take you to the Black Isle (see page 97) and points north, while the A82 route that runs southwest through the Great Glen (see page 239) ranks as one of Britain's greatest scenic drives. If you're exploring by rail, don't miss the train trip between Inverness and Kyle of Lochalsh on the west coast – Britain's most dramatic rail journey.

◀ Opposite: Inverness Castle

VISIT THE MUSEUM AND GALLERIES

Inverness Museum and Art Gallery

highlifehighland.com
Castle Wynd, IV2 3EB
01463 237114
Open Apr–Nov Tue–Sat 10–5;
Dec–Mar Tue–Thu 12–4, Fri and Sat 11–4

This small museum in the centre of Inverness focuses on Highland Victoriana, with an eclectic collection that includes Higland dress and weaponry.

Castle Gallery

castlegallery.co.uk
43 Castle Street, IV2 3DU | 01463 729512 | Open Mon–Sat 9–5

This outstanding contemporary art gallery aims to foster new and established talents with exhibitions of paintings, prints, sculpture, ceramics, glass, wood, textiles and jewellery by British artists. It's in one of Inverness's older buildings, dating from the 18th century.

GO ROUND THE GARDENS

Inverness Botanic Gardens

invernessbotanicgardens.com
Bught Lane, IV3 5SS | 01463 713553
Open Apr–Oct daily 10–5; Nov–Mar daily 10–4

The city's botanic gardens, formerly known as the Floral Hall and Gardens, are within walking distance of the centre of Inverness. They have a surprising array of plants from every continent, including cacti and other tropical plant species that flourish within the subtropical glasshouse.

CATCH A PERFORMANCE

Eden Court

eden-court.co.uk
Eden Court, Bishop's Road, IV3 5SA
01463 234234

This is the premier arts venue in the Highlands and Islands district. It promotes film, theatre, music and dance in a variety of places that make up Scotland's biggest arts centre.

GET ON THE WATER

Loch Ness by Jacobite

jacobite.co.uk
Dochgarroch Lock, IV3 8JG | 01463 233999 | Open daily 9–5. Call or see website for schedules

Cruise the waters of Loch Ness and the Caledonian Canal aboard a Jacobite vessel, while being regaled with tales of the loch's history and the search for its most enigmatic denizen, the Loch Ness Monster.

EAT AND DRINK

Loch Ness Country House Hotel ◉◉

lochnesscountryhousehotel.co.uk
Loch Ness Road, IV3 8JN
01463 230512

This loch-side restaurant amalgamates European and East Asian influences with contemporary Scottish style.

The New Drumossie Hotel ◉◉

drumossiehotel.co.uk
Old Perth Road, IV2 5BE
01463 236451

The Grill Room, the restaurant of this stylish hotel near Culloden, serves modern Scottish dishes and there is a good choice from the grill.

Rocpool 🌀🌀

rocpoolrestaurant.com
1 Ness Walk, IV3 5NE
01463 717274

This buzzy contemporary brasserie operation capitalises on its corner site on the banks of the River Ness, with sweeping windows on two sides to open up floodlit views of the river and castle at night. The menu is an appealing mix of modern European dishes built on top-class Scottish produce.

▶ PLACES NEARBY

Ardersier, on the south shore of the Moray Firth about 11 miles northeast of Inverness, is dominated by Fort George, a fortress that was built in 1769 and was intended to deter the French from sending support to the Jacobites.

Fort George

historicenvironment.scot
Ardersier, IV2 7TD | 01667 460232
Open Apr–Sep daily 9.30–5.30;
Oct–Mar daily 10–4

It may have been obsolete almost as soon as it was completed, but Britain's largest artillery fortress, with its huge ring of walls surrounding a headland that juts into the Moray Firth, is still very impressive, and is still garrisoned by troops of the Royal Regiment of Scotland. The regimental museum highlights the history of the now defunct regiments, the Seaforth and Cameron Highlanders, and in the old barracks you can get a feel for what life would have been like for the redcoats who garrisoned the fort in the 18th and 19th centuries.

▶ Iona

see **Western Isles**, page 382

▶ Islay

see **Western Isles**, page 387

▼ Loch Ness

▶ Isle of Skye MAP REF 405 D2

The Isle of Skye, at 535 sq miles, is the largest and best known of the Inner Hebrides (see page 382). Its name is Norse, meaning isle of clouds, and the southwestern part of the island has some of the heaviest rainfall on the whole of the British coast. Despite this, it's the most visited of all the islands of the Inner Hebrides. It's dominated from every view by the high peaks of the Cuillins. The jagged gabbro (igneous rock, like basalt) of the Black Cuillins and the pink, scree-covered granite of the Red Cuillins have proved an irresistible challenge for mountaineers, and the most inaccessible peaks were only conquered towards the end of the 19th century.

Skye retains a strong Gaelic identity, with road signs in Gaelic as well as English. It's a bit of a crossroads among the Western Isles (see page 382), reached in summer by ferry from Mallaig (see page 296) or Gairloch (see page 202), or by ferry across the strong currents by Glenelg (see page 236), or at any time of the year by the convenient bridge from Kyle of Lochalsh. Ferries to the Outer Hebrides leave from Uig, and to little Raasay from Sconser.

Portree, Skye's capital, is the only real town on the island, and a centre for exploring northern Skye. It's where you'll find the fullest range of shops and other amenities. The town is the gateway to the Trotternish Peninsula. Taking the road up the

▲ Old Man of Storr rocks

eastern side, look out for the distinctive column of the Old
Man of Storr and other strange rock formations up on your
left, and for the columnar formations and dramatic waterfall
at the Kilt Rock on the coast to your right, just before Staffin.
There are marvellous views from here across to the blue hills
of the mainland. Continuing around this peninsula you pass
ruined Duntulm Castle and a memorial to Flora MacDonald.
Heading west from Portree brings you to the wilder side of the
island, with the Waternish and Duirinish peninsulas like two
long fingers reaching out towards the Outer Hebrides. At
Carbost, the Talisker Distillery produces a distinctive peaty,
smoky malt whisky. Dunvegan claims to be Scotland's oldest
inhabited castle.

Broadford is the main hub for the south, with access to the
steep, magnificently scenic road to Elgol. The road from
Broadford to Elgol winds below the mighty Red Cuillins and
beside Loch Slapin before descending an alarmingly steep road
into Elgol. Across the water lies the island of Soay, with Canna,
Rùm and Eigg to the south. These three, known as the Small
Isles (see page 362), lie off the Sleat peninsula, whose main
settlement is Armadale. After the barrenness of the mountains,
Sleat seems a veritable Garden of Eden, green and relatively
fertile, and dotted with crofts that still preserve this traditional
way of farming life.

▶ **Portree** MAP REF 405 D2

Portree is the island's capital and was named after a royal visit in 1540 by James V – Port Righ means king's harbour. It's an attractive town, its colour-washed houses ranged round the harbour, busy with fishing and pleasure vessels, and its formal square is a miniature delight. Thomas Telford designed the stone pier in the 1820s.

TAKE IN SOME HISTORY

Duntulm Castle

The dramatically sited, and extremely unsafe, ruins of this 17th-century stronghold of the MacDonalds of Sleat stand above the sea, guarding a natural harbour. Legend claims its abandonment was caused after a clumsy nurse dropped the son and heir onto the rocks below, while another tale tells of Hugh, heir to the Chiefdom. Keen to inherit sooner rather than later, he arranged for his kinsman's murder. In an act of appalling incompetence, Hugh accidentally sent the chief not the invitation to dine, but instructions to the hired killer outlining how the foul deed was to be done. Hugh was arrested and immediately incarcerated in Duntulm's vaults with salt beef and nothing to drink. It is said that many years later a skeleton was unearthed, still clutching an empty water pitcher.

VISIT THE MUSEUM

Skye Museum of Island Life

skyemuseum.co.uk
Kilmuir, IV51 9UE | 01470 552206
Open Easter–Sep Mon–Sat 9.30–5
This cluster of traditional thatched so-called blackhouses gives a vivid insight into Skye's traditional way of life. Behind here are the graves of Flora MacDonald – who smuggled Bonnie Prince Charlie 'over the sea to Skye' in 1746, a journey that inspired the 'Skye Boat Song' – and her husband.

GET OUTDOORS

Trotternish Peninsula

The Trotternish Peninsula sticks up like a long finger at the northern tip of Skye. Basalt columns have formed huge cliffs on the eastern coast, one example being the one known as the Kilt Rock, as it resembles that pleated garment. There's a dramatic waterfall here, too, and captivating views across to the blue hills of the mainland. Farther north lies the Quiraing, where bizarre rock formations formed when lava flowed over sheer cliffs. Its weight buckled the softer rocks, creating pinnacles and weird outcrops. Its most impressive formation is the Old Man of Storr, a 160-foot black obelisk.

CATCH A SHOW

Aros Centre

aros.co.uk
Viewfield Road, IV51 9EU | 01478 613750 | Open daily 9.30–5 and evening performances
The award-winning Aros Centre runs regular theatre, concerts

and film screenings. There's also an exhibition on Skye's history, a spectacular RSPB exhibit with footage of rare sea eagles and an audio-visual presentation giving a dramatic aerial view of Skye's landscapes.

EAT AND DRINK
Cuillin Hills Hotel
cuillinhills-hotel-skye.co.uk
Portree, IV51 9QU | 01478 612003

A breathtaking panorama is visible from every single table in the dining room here, which means that arrival during daylight hours is advisable. The hotel was built as a hunting lodge in the 1880s and sits in 15 acres of grounds. There's a daily menu offering modern dishes alongside some updated classics, and an excellent showing of regional seafood.

▶ Dunvegan Castle MAP REF 404 C2

dunvegancastle.com
Dunvegan, IV55 8WF | 01470 521206 | Open Apr to mid-Oct daily 10–5.30

The situation of Dunvegan, seat of the Clan MacLeod since the 13th century, is stunning, sprawled on a rocky mound above the sea and surrounded by gardens. Today's structure dates from the 1840s, all pepper-pot towers and battlements. Among its treasures are the gossamer-thin textile known as the Fairy Flag, which was allegedly brought here by the Norwegian King Harold Hardrada's Skye boatman after the Battle of Stamford Bridge in 1066. There's also a lock of Bonnie Prince Charlie's hair and, less predictably, Flora MacDonald's corsets.

EAT AND DRINK
Loch Bay Restaurant ◉
lochbay-restaurant.co.uk
Macleods Terrace, Stein, IV55 8GA
01470 592235
This tiny restaurant, in a row of old fishermen's cottages, is run with passion and enthusiasm and serves up the best of locally caught fish and seafood.

Stein Inn
stein-inn.co.uk
Waternish, IV55 8GA
01470 592362
The Stein is Skye's oldest inn, where you can choose from

among 130 single malt whiskies and enjoy local seafood, fish and meat while you gaze across the waters of Loch Bay.

▶ Dunvegan Castle

▶ Duirinish Peninsula MAP REF 404 C2

This peninsula lies along the west side of Loch Dunvegan, dominated by the flat basalt tops of MacLeod's Tables, two peaks rising above the crofting community of Glendale, making this one of Britain's most dramatic stretches of coastline.

LEARN ABOUT CROFTING
Colbost Folk Museum
Colbost, IV55 8ZT | 01470 521296
Open Apr–Oct daily 10–5.30
You can learn about 19th-century crofting at this restored 'blackhouse'.

TRY THE WHISKY
Talisker Distillery
malts.com
Carbost, IV47 8 SR | 01478 614308
Open Nov–Mar Mon–Fri 9.30–4.30;
Apr–May and Oct Mon–Sat 9.30–5;
Jun Mon–Sat 9.30–5 and Sun 11–5;
Jul–Aug 9.30–6, Sat 9.30–5, Sun 11–5
Skye's only distillery lies south of Duirinish. Take a tour of the facility, which is located on the shores of Loch Harport.

EAT AND DRINK
The Old Inn
theoldinnskye.co.uk
Carbost, IV47 8SR | 01478 640205
The Old Inn has a waterside terrace and open fires within. Daily home-cooked specials are on offer. There's live Highland music at the weekends.

The Three Chimneys ◉◉◉
threechimneys.co.uk
Colbost, IV55 8ZT | 01470 511258
Skye's premier destination restaurant has made its mark on the local economy and the island's culinary reputation. Inspired cooking is the norm, using dazzling techniques to enhance local ingredients.

▲ Elgol Beach

▶ Elgol & the Cuillin Hills MAP REF 405 D3

Elgol is the best place for non-climbers to see the Cuillins; a
boat makes the trip across Loch Scavaig to Loch Coruisk, lying
in the shadow of the Black Cuillins. Every view of the Isle of
Skye is dominated by this range of jagged mountains, which
reaches its peak in the far south with Sgùrr Alasdair (3,309
feet/1,009m). They are to be treated with respect, but Munro-
baggers can have a field day here, with 12 mountains reaching
beyond 3,000 feet. The southern mountains are the Black
Cuillins, distinct from the scree-covered granite of the lower
Red Cuillins. All are challenges for mountaineers, and the most
inaccessible peaks were conquered only at the end of the 19th
century. In geological terms, the Cuillins are comparatively
young, formed in volcanic activity at the same time as Iceland,
a mere 20 million years ago, and scoured by the ice ages.

SEE THE SEA LIFE
Aquaxplore
aquaxplore.co.uk
Elgol, IV49 9BJ | 01471 866244
Sailings run Easter–Oct; check
website for details
Join wildlife-watching tours on
rigid-hull inflatable boats, and
see the islands around Skye,
too. Trips offer the chance to
see basking sharks, dolphins,
porpoises, puffins, minke
whales, otters, seals and sea
eagles. The outings can last
from an hour and a half to a
full day.

Misty Isle Boats
mistyisleboattrips.co.uk
Elgol, IV49 1BL | 01471 866288
Boat trips Apr–Sep 5 daily,
weather permitting. Advance
booking essential

As well as breathtaking scenery
and unmatched views, a boat
trip will bring you sightings
of seals, otters and myriad
seabirds, golden and sea eagles
and the occasional dolphin or
basking shark. They also run
cruises to Canna (see page 363)
in the Small Isles.

TAKE TO THE SKIES
Skye Seaplanes
lochlomondseaplanes.com
Broadford Airfield, IV42 Z (for
satnav) | 01436 675030

Take off from the sea to soar
over Skye in a seaplane for a
top experience.

▶ Sleat & Armadale MAP REF 405 E3

The Sleat (pronounced Slate) peninsula, to the south of the
island, is so fertile it is often referred to as the Garden of Skye.
The ferry from Mallaig (see page 296) docks at Armadale,
whose main attraction is the ruined shell and lovely gardens
of Armadale Castle, seat of the Clan Donald. It stands at the
centre of a 20,000-acre estate, with woodland walks, gardens
and a fascinating museum to explore.

FIND YOUR ANCESTORS
Museum of the Isles
clandonald.com
Ardvasar, IV45 8RS | 01471 844305
Open daily Apr–Oct 9.30–5.30

Six interconnecting, themed
galleries take you through the
1,500-year history and culture
of the sea kingdom that was
centred on Skye, once known
as the Kingdom of the Isles.
This lively museum, set in a
20,000-acre estate, also holds
impressive archives and
welcomes people interested
in genealogical research.

▼ The harbour at Armadale

GO ROUND
THE GARDENS
Armadale Castle Gardens
clandonald.com
Ardvasar, IV45 8RS | 01471 844305
Open daily Apr–Oct 9.30–5.30
Explore 40 acres of sheltered and beautiful gardens and woodland, where, due to the influence of the Gulf Stream, tender plants, trees and flowers from all over the world flourish. The ruins of the neo-Gothic Armadale Castle stand at the heart of the garden.

EAT AND DRINK
Ardvasar Hotel
ardvasarhotel.com
Sleat, IV45 8RS | 01471 844223
Beside the road towards the southern tip of Skye, you can sit outside with extraordinary views, before eating in either the cosy bar or the dining room. Expect local produce, with the accent on seafood and venison.

Hotel Eilean Iarmain ◉
eileaniarmain.co.uk
Sleat, IV43 8QR | 01471 833332
The hotel is very much a part of this small community, with Gaelic spoken and regular ceilidh nights in the bar, while the owners also run a small distillery and art gallery next door. The whitewashed property is in a fabulous spot overlooking the Sound of Sleat, with spectacular views across to the Knoydart Hills on the mainland beyond. Food in the dining room is contemporary.

Kinloch Lodge ◉◉◉
kinloch-lodge.co.uk
Isleornsay, IV43 8QY
01471 833214
Kinloch Lodge is the ancestral home of the high chief of the Clan Donald and was turned into a hotel and restaurant by the current incumbents, Godfrey and Claire Macdonald. Lady Claire is a renowned cookery writer with more than a dozen books to her name. Today, the reputation of Kinloch Lodge as a dining destination is based on French-inflected modern Scottish cuisine offered via a daily-changing menu and tasting options.

▶ **Isle of Whithorn**
see **Whithorn & Isle of Whithorn**, page 395

▶ **Jedburgh** MAP REF 403 D5

The tides of war flowed back and forward over Jedburgh for centuries, finally leaving its great abbey as an evocative ruin that dominates the town centre and leaving little trace of its once formidable castle, which was demolished in 1409. Where the castle once stood is an equally formidable building that epitomises the mock-baronial architecture – but its walls were built not to keep attackers out, but to keep prisoners in.

Jedburgh Abbey was one of the greatest and richest of the medieval Border abbeys, drawing much of its wealth from the flocks that grazed on its vast lands surrounding the town. Wool from the abbey's sheep became the basis of a profitable weaving industry that made Jedburgh one of Scotland's wealthiest towns. Unfortunately for the locals, it also lay right on the line of march of any invading English army. Today, it's a peaceful country town beside the serpentine Jed Water, with only the walls of the abbey to hint at its former grandeur.

TAKE IN SOME HISTORY

Jedburgh Abbey

historicenvironment.scot
Abbey Bridge End, TD8 6JQ | 01835 863295 | Open Apr–Sep daily 9.30–5.30; Oct–Mar daily 10–4

Founded in 1138, Jedburgh Abbey was originally a priory of Augustinian canons from St Quentin, in northern France. Attracting royal patronage, it was elevated by David I to abbey status in about 1154. Ostensibly a mindful and abstemious order, the Augustinians were in fact both worldly and politically astute. Throughout the medieval era, they stuck close to centres of royal power, and benefited from grants of land and money. Jedburgh Abbey, which finally fell into ruin after the Reformation, is still a reminder of their glory days.

Jedburgh Castle Jail and Museum

Castle Gate, TD8 6AS | 01835 864750 | Open Apr–Oct Mon–Sat 10–4.30, Sun 1–4

It looks more like a castle than most real Scottish castles, but Jedburgh Castle Jail is a 19th-century architect's invention, built in the 1820s, as one of the first so-called reform prisons in Britain. The notion that convicted criminals could and should be rehabilitated, not just punished, was radical – but the regime imposed on inmates of this grim place of confinement was certainly not a soft touch, as the museum vividly shows.

Mary, Queen of Scots House

scotborders.gov.uk
Queen Street, TD8 6EN

▲ Jedburgh Abbey

01835 863331 | Open Mar–Nov
Mon–Sat 9.30–4.30, Sun 10.30–4
Mary, Queen of Scots seems to
have spent much of her life
either imprisoned or on the run
from her enemies. She stayed
in this dignified tower house in
1566 to be close to her lover
and protector, the somewhat
piratical Earl of Bothwell. The
house would have been quite
new when Mary stayed here,
and it's a very well-preserved
piece of 16th-century baronial
architecture. Inside, you can
admire some attractive period
and contemporary works of art.

▶ PLACES NEARBY
The Ancrum Cross Keys
ancrumcrosskeys.com
Ancrum, TD8 6XH | 01835 830242
A 200-year-old tavern in the
centre of Ancrum, the Cross
Keys is a country pub with an
informal restaurant. There's a

Scottish flavour to the culinary
goings on, but also some
creative and modern ideas.

Harestanes Countryside
Visitor Centre
liveborders.org.uk
Ancrum, TD8 6UQ | 01835 830306
Open Apr–Oct daily 10–5
Just three miles north of
Jedburgh, Harestanes
Countryside Visitor Centre
offers beautiful woodland
walks, an outdoor play area and
exhibitions. Adjacent craft
workshops may operate
different opening hours. There
are also various activities for
children.

Jedforest Deer and Farm Park
jedforestdeerpark.co.uk
Camptown, Jedburgh, TD8 6PL
01835 840364 | Open May–Aug
daily 10–5.30; Sep–Oct daily
11–4.30

Birds of prey and deer are to be found on this working farm, 5 miles south of Jedburgh. Eagles, owls and hawks take part in daily displays. Look for the ranger-led activities and talks on farming and the environment. For children there are indoor and outdoor play areas and special activities.

▶ John o' Groats MAP REF 415 E5

If asked to name the northernmost point on the British mainland, most people would name John o' Groats. It's 874 miles from Land's End in Cornwall – the southernmost point in England – and is said to be named after a Dutchman, Jan de Groot, who lived here in the early 16th century and operated a ferry service across the stormy Pentland Firth to Orkney.

In fact, the real northernmost point of the British mainland is Dunnet Head, whose great cliffs rise imposingly above the Pentland Firth some 2 miles farther north than John o' Groats. The northeastern, and most spectacular, point here is Duncansby Head, just one-and-a-half miles to the east of John o' Groats; a short walk over the high ground beyond the lighthouse gives dizzying views of the Geo of Sclaites, a huge cleft in the cliffs, the rock arch of Thirle Door and the spiky triangular pinnacles of rock out to sea known as the Stacks of Duncansby. There's a great view of the Pentland Firth and the cliffs of mainland Orkney (see page 312) from here, but for most visitors John o' Groats itself is a bit of an anticlimax.

▶ Jura

see **Western Isles**, page 387

▶ Kelso MAP REF 403 E4

One of the most elegant of the Border towns, Kelso has a wide cobbled square at its heart. A poignant fragment is all that remains of Kelso Abbey, once the largest of the Border abbeys, destroyed by the English in 1545. Nearby is the handsome five-arched bridge over the River Tweed built by John Rennie in 1803. From the parapet there is a fine view of Floors Castle.

TAKE IN SOME HISTORY
Floors Castle

floorscastle.com

Heiton by Kelso, TD5 7SF | 01573 22333 | Castle and grounds open May–Sep daily 11–5; Oct Mon–Fri 11–5; gardens Apr–Oct daily 10.30–5; Oct–Mar daily 10.30–4

This is the largest inhabited house in Scotland, a monument to the wealth and privilege of the dukes of Roxburghe, the Innes Ker family. It was built in 1721 for John Ker, the First Duke of Roxburghe, on the site of an older building called the House of Floris, and remodelled by William Playfair from 1837 to 1847. Fine art, tapestries and French furniture, porcelain and paintings are all on view.

The Sixth Duke, James, was responsible for changing the face of Floors, engaging the great William Playfair – noted for his work in Edinburgh New Town – to remodel and extend the house. Playfair added a delightful roofscape of lead cupolas, as well as features ranging from the Grand Ballroom to a Gothic-style chamber built to hold the Duke's collection of stuffed birds.

While the outside of Floors has barely changed since that time, extensive remodelling of the interior was undertaken during the era of the Eighth Duke, Sir Henry Innes Ker, who inherited it in 1892. In 1903 the Eighth Duke married American heiress Mary Goelet. Her greatest contribution is probably the collection of antique tapestries, many brought from her Long Island home. Duchess May, as she was known, also acquired paintings by Matisse and ornaments by Fabergé. Together they form one of the chief attractions of Floors today.

◀ Floors Castle
▶ Memorial cloister, Kelso Abbey

EAT AND DRINK

The Cobbles Freehouse & Dining ⚙

thecobbleskelso.co.uk
7 Bowmont Street, TD5 7JH
01573 223548

Tucked just off the town's main square, The Cobbles is an old inn with loads of atmosphere, especially on a Friday night when there's live music. You'll find impressive Scottish-inspired dishes in its dapper restaurant.

▶ PLACES NEARBY

Manderston House

manderston.co.uk
Duns, TD11 3PP
01361 883450
Open selected afternoons May–Sep. Call or see website for dates

Before the architect John Kinross was called upon to improve Manderston, the old house, built in the late 18th century, was solid, square and unremarkable. In 1855, the estate was bought by William Miller, who made his fortune in the trade of hemp and herrings. He went on to become Honorary British Consul at St Petersburg, and then an MP, which earned him a baronetcy in 1874.

It was Sir William's second son, Sir James Miller, who employed Kinross to transform Manderston into a house that would resemble yet surpass Kedleston Hall (his wife's ancestral home in Derbyshire) in style and grandeur.

Manderston has the largest private collection of Blue John in Scotland. This very rare, semi-precious stone is found only in Derbyshire. In the hall, the fireplace with its elaborate plasterwork is almost an exact copy of one at Kedleston.

Life below stairs can also be explored. Pity the poor servants before 1960, when the lift was installed – everything had to be carried upstairs, including coal.

Mellerstain House

mellerstain.com
Gordon, TD3 6LG
01573 410225
House open May–Sep Fri–Mon 12.30–5. Grounds open same days and dates as house 11.30–5

A superb 18th-century mansion northwest of Kelso, this great house is famous for its Adam architecture and elegant interiors, and is still the family home of the Earl of Haddington. Architect William Adam started work on the house in 1725. The large central block was completed in 1778 by his son Robert, who went on to design the interior. The delicate plasterwork throughout – but especially in the music room, library and drawing room – is outstanding.

The elegant Italian terraced gardens were designed by Sir Reginald Blomfield. They stretch out at the rear of the house, leading down to a lake from where there are wonderful views of the Cheviot Hills. The library is outstanding, its ceiling (c.1773) painted in the original soft colours reminiscent of Wedgwood china.

▶ Killiecrankie

MAP REF 408 B5

nts.org.uk

Near Pitlochry, PH16 5LG | 01796
473233 | Site open daily all year;
Visitor Centre Apr–Oct daily 10–5

This spectacular wooded
gorge is worth a visit for its
scenery alone. Woodland of
oak and beech lines the steep
sides of the valley, with the
waters of the River Garry
flowing through the rocks
below. Wild flowers are
abundant, and you may be
lucky enough to see the native
red squirrels.

Killiecrankie's fame is
twofold: as well as natural
beauty, it is celebrated for its
significance as the site of a
momentous battle in 1689,

▲ Pass of Killiecrankie

when John Graham of Claverhouse, or Bonnie Dundee (c.1649–
89), swept down here at the head of a rebel Jacobite army. The
superior government force was defeated, but Dundee was
mortally wounded in the conflict. The Soldier's Leap, below the
visitor centre, is where a fleeing soldier, Donald McBean,
jumped 18 feet across the gorge to safety.

**CHECK OUT THE
VISITOR CENTRE**

Killiecrankie Visitor Centre

nts.org.uk

PH16 5LG | 01796 473233

Open Apr–Oct 10–5

Learn about the Battle of
Killiecrankie and the wildlife
you can see here today before
walking down this beautiful
wooded gorge.

EAT AND DRINK

Killiecrankie Hotel ◉◉

killiecrankiehotel.co.uk

PH16 5LG | 01796 473220

Built for some blessed church
minister back in 1840, and
surrounded by four acres of
pretty gardens and woodland,
this family-run hotel has
charming traditional decor and
a fixed-price à la carte.

▶ Killin MAP REF 407 D6

Killin lies at the western end of Loch Tay, in the ancient district
of Breadalbane, and is a popular touring, walking and fishing
centre for the area. It has its own attractions, notably the Falls

of Dochart, a series of spectacular cascades in the middle of town. The 79-mile Rob Roy Way long-distance path between Drymen and Pitlochry passes through the town.

LEARN THE LORE
Breadalbane Folklore Centre
Killin, FK21 8XE | 01567 820254
Open Apr–Oct Mon–Sat 9–5,
Sun 11–4

The Breadalbane Folklore Centre, located in the 19th-century St Fillan's Mill, offers an intriguing insight into Scottish legends of kelpies, brownies and other mythical creatures. The mill's great waterwheel originally drove the spinning wheels and weaving looms that were at the heart of Killin's tweed industry, and it has recently been restored.

TAKE IN SOME HISTORY
Moirlanich Longhouse
nts.org.uk
FK21 8UW | 01567 820988 | Open
Easter Sun, May–Sep Wed, Sun 2–5

One of the humblest of the National Trust for Scotland's properties is Moirlanich Longhouse, a long, low 19th-century farmhouse, built with a cruck frame. At least three generations of the Robertson family lived here, until the 1960s, and the house has been preserved, complete with a 'hingin' lum' (suspended chimney) and traditional wooden box beds.

▶ Kilmartin MAP REF 400 C2

The green glen that leads to the hamlet of Kilmartin, between Oban (see page 307) and Lochgilphead, is littered with piles of boulders, the remains of burial cairns dating from approximately 3000 BC. At the centre of each was a small tomb of stone slabs, and, together with the standing stones at Ballymeanoch, the stone circle at Temple Wood and cup-and-

ring carved rocks in the surrounding hills, they form one of the most remarkable collections of early monuments in Britain. Learn more at the archaeological museum. Carved grave slabs in the churchyard date from the ninth century.

To the south, the rocky outcrop of Dunadd was the capital of the sixth-century kingdom of Dalriada: look for the footprint-shaped impression in the stone on the top of the rock.

The waters of Loch Awe once flowed southwards through the glacier-formed Kilmartin Glen, depositing sediment on the valley floor. The area was occupied by farmers from early prehistoric times, and the concentration of monuments that they left behind makes this one of the richest archaeological areas in Scotland. At Achnabreck is the largest group of cup-and-ring marked rocks in Britain, but even more impressive remains are to be found further north.

The tall, flat-faced Ballymeanoch standing stones and a line of burial cairns stretch towards Kilmartin village. Ri Cruin is a crescent of boulders in a grove, and carvings of axeheads and, possibly, a boat's keel can be seen on the stones. The three Nether Largie cairns are higher – especially the most southerly, with its large chamber topped by huge stone slabs. Central to the site is Temple Wood Circle, begun in about 3000 BC and modified several times up to 1200 BC.

TAKE IN SOME HISTORY

Carnasserie Castle
historicenvironment.scot
PA31 8RQ | Open daily all year
10–5
Carnasserie Castle is a well-preserved 16th-century fortified house, built for John Carswell, Bishop of the Isles and a close ally of the Campbell Earls of Argyll. Finely carved stonework hints at the former grandeur of this worldly prelate's lifestyle.

Dunadd Fort
historicenvironment.scot
Open daily all year
From about AD 500 the Scottish kingdom of Dalriada (Dál Riata) may have had its capital in the hill-fort at Dunadd. There are traces of buildings on the hillside and defensive terraces around the summit. Carved in the rock a little way outside is an inscription in Ogham script

◀ Temple Wood Standing Stones

– evidence of Pictish use of the hilltop – as well as a stone-cut basin and a footprint that may have been used at coronations. Some people believe that Aidan was crowned first Christian king in Britain here in AD 574 by St Columba, and that the stone used became the Stone of Scone, once in Westminster Abbey but now on display in Edinburgh Castle (see page 167). It's one of Scotland's best preserved Iron Age hill-forts, set atop a rocky hill that makes it a natural stronghold. But its design implies that it was intended as an impressive royal seat, rather than a purely functional military base – and finds from the site suggest that it was also a magnificent metal-working centre, exporting the work of its skilled smiths all over the Norse and Celtic world.

VISIT THE MUSEUM
Kilmartin House Museum of Ancient Culture
kilmartin.org

Kilmartin, PA31 8RQ | 01546 510278 | Open Mar–Oct daily 10–5.30; Nov–23 Dec daily 11–4
This museum focuses on the region's distant past, with a fascinating collection of Bronze Age finds linked to the standing stones, cairns and chamber tombs nearby. The carved ninth-century tombstones in the kirkyard nearby seem quite recent by comparison.

SADDLE UP
Lunga Riding Stables
lungaridingstables.co.uk
Lunga Estate, Craobh Haven, Lochgilphead, PA31 8UU
0185 250 0632 | Open all year
Catering to everyone from beginners to advanced riders (including children aged 4 and over), Lunga Riding Stables provides a great equestrian experience. Choose from one-hour rides to four-hour treks. The stables also offer longer breaks and tuition, and benefit from a natural setting near Craobh Haven Marina.

▶ Kingussie MAP REF 407 E3

The little town of Kingussie lies in the heart of beautiful Strathspey. Once the capital of the ancient area of Badenoch, its history dates back to pre-Pictish times. It grew up around Ruthven Castle, the home of the Stewart lords of Badenoch (one of whom, Alexander, the notorious Wolf of Badenoch, went down in history for burning the town of Elgin and its cathedral). However, most of the town you see today is a 19th-century creation that grew up when the advent of the railway line between Perth (see page 327) and Inverness (see page 250) turned it into a popular resort. Today it is best known as home to the Highland Folk Museum, a place with fascinating indoor and outdoor exhibits, and it's also a good base for exploring the distilleries and other attractions of Speyside (see page 366).

Kingussie is known as a stronghold of the Gaelic sport of shinty. It's a team game similar to hockey, and the highlight of the shinty players' year is the Camanachd Cup Final, held in September in different venues across the country.

Kingussie is about 12 miles from Aviemore (see page 109), Scotland's main ski resort, and offers an alternative place to stay if accommodation isn't available in Aviemore itself.

TAKE IN SOME HISTORY
Ruthven Barracks
historicenvironment.scot
Ruthven, Kingussie, PH21 1NR
Open daily, dawn until dusk
Ruthven Barracks stand just outside Kingussie, on a grassy mound where the castle of the Stewart lords once stood. Built in the early 13th century, the original castle was severely damaged during Oliver Cromwell's invasion of Scotland and the Jacobite rising of 1715. The barracks were built on the site in 1718, to house a garrison of government troops guarding General Wade's new military road through Strathspey. Their presence failed to deter the second Jacobite rising, in 1745, when Bonnie Prince Charlie's Highlanders torched the barracks. They have remained in ruins ever since.

EAT AND DRINK
The Cross ⊚⊚⊚
thecross.co.uk
Tweed Mill Brae, Ardbroilach Road, PH21 1LB | 01540 661166
The Cross is tucked away in a peaceful spot with four acres to call its own. The Gynack Burn once powered the former tweed mill, but today the old stone building is the setting for a restaurant that makes use of a good deal of produce from around these parts, with fixed-price and tasting menus.

▼ Ruthven Barracks

▶ **PLACES NEARBY**

Highland Folk Museum

highlifehighland.com

PH20 1AY | 01540 67355

Open Apr–Aug daily 10.30–5.30;
Sep, Oct daily 11–4.30

The Highland Folk Museum offers an unsanitised picture of rural life in the Highlands over the centuries, through reconstructed buildings, a working croft and collections of everyday objects. You can see crops and livestock, a cottage, garage and even a little post office. Living history actors bring the place to life.

Highland Wildlife Park

highlandwildlifepark.org.uk

Kingussie, PH21 1NL | 01540
651270 | Open Jul–Aug daily 10–6;
Apr–Jun, Sep, Oct daily 10–5;
Nov–Mar daily 10–4

Just to the north of Kingussie is the noted Highland Wildlife Park, part of the Royal Zoological Society of Scotland. A driving tour takes in herds of red deer, as well as ancient breeds of bison and horse, before you explore the rest on foot. Look out for otters, owls, boars, Arctic foxes, wildcats and eagles. You can also take a guided tour. The centre is perhaps best known for its collection of wolves, and a raised walkway takes visitors safely into the heart of their enclosure. The last wild wolf in Scotland was killed in 1743.

Insh Marshes Nature Reserve

The adjacent Insh Marshes Reserve (RSPB), an important site for breeding waders and wintering waterfowl, has hides and nature trails, plus a guided tour. You can walk from here to Glen Tromie. A church on the loch shore reputedly stands on a site where worship has been continuous since the sixth century.

Kincraig

The nearby village of Kincraig is the access point for Loch Insh, popular for water sports, and its ski school has a dry ski slope (200 feet).

Kingussie Golf Club

kingussie-golf.co.uk

Gynack Road, PH21 1LR | 01540
661600 | Open daily all year

Golf has been played on this upland course with its natural hazards and magnificent views for more than 100 years. It stands about 1,000 feet above sea level at its highest point, and the River Gynack, which runs through the course, comes into play on five holes.

Newtonmore
Sometimes referred to as the Walking Centre of Scotland because of its location just a few miles from the geographical centre of the country, and ideally positioned for all sorts of walking opportunities, Newtonmore is a small village, much quieter these days since it was bypassed by the A9 in 1979.

▷ Kintail NSA MAP REF 406 B3

The 60-sq-mile Kintail National Scenic Area (NSA) adjoins the Glen Affric NSA (see page 233) and covers the mountainous head of Loch Duich, including the famous ridge of the Five Sisters of Kintail and the Saddle across Glen Shiel.

The great glory of the Kintail NSA is the splendid hills that crowd together around the head of Loch Duich on either side of Glen Shiel. Three mountain ranges terminate here: Beinn Fhada (the Long Mountain) at 3,386 feet (1,032m); the Five Sisters of Kintail (culminating in Sgurr Fhuaran) at 3,504 feet (1,068m); and the South Cluanie Ridge, which extends for 9 miles and includes seven Munros (Scottish mountains more than 3,000 feet) leading up to Aonach air Chrith (3,350 feet/1,021m) and the Saddle (3,314 feet/1,010m), via the formidable Forcan Ridge.

Much of the northern side of Glen Shiel, including the Five Sisters ridge and remote Beinn Fhada between Glen Lichd and Glen Choinneachan, is now in the safe hands of the National Trust for Scotland (NTS). Its Kintail estate extends north to the difficult-to-reach but spectacular Falls of Glomach, one of the highest waterfalls in Britain and a Site of Special Scientific Interest (SSSI), where the Glomach Burn tumbles for 367 feet, contained within the walls of a narrow ravine. There is an NTS visitor centre at Morvich at the end of the eastern arm of Loch Duich. The glens radiating from Loch Duich are uniformly steep-sided and narrow, with rushing burns that cascade through waterfalls and pools lined with birch, rowan and alder, to eventually reach the sea loch.

▷ Kintyre MAP REF 400 C5

Ex-Beatle Paul McCartney put the Mull of Kintyre on the map when he wrote a lyrical song about it, recorded in 1977 with the local pipe band backing his group Wings.

Kintyre is a long, thin peninsula that points south from the mainland, sheltering the mouth of the Firth of Clyde from the open sea. It's very nearly an island, with just a narrow isthmus connecting it with Knapdale, to the north. The Norse King Magnus Barelegs famously had one of his longships

▲ Dunaverty, Mull of Kintyre

manhandled across this narrow neck of land in 1090, claiming that this meant Kintyre was indeed an island, and therefore, like the other Scottish isles, the property of Norway. At the north end of Kintyre and 38 miles from Campbeltown, the pretty fishing port of Tarbert has rows of colour-washed houses and the remains of a 15th-century tower house built on the site of a former royal castle. The road follows the windswept west fringe of Kintyre, with wide views over to Jura and Islay (see page 387), and the handsome harbour of Campbeltown. By the waterfront is the 15th-century Campbeltown Cross, and nearby is an unexpected delight – the 1913 art deco front of the 256-seat Picture House. Davaar Island, reached on foot at low tide, shelters the harbour, and on its south side is a restored cave painting of the crucifixion, originally created by Archibald MacKinnon in 1887. Many townsfolk saw the appearance of the painting as a sign from God, and it is said that the artist was ostracised when he finally admitted to the work.

St Columba landed near Southend at the foot of the peninsula – a ruined chapel and two footprints carved in a nearby rock mark the spot. A winding road eastwards goes to the Mull of Kintyre, with its lighthouse – a stark, windswept place, only 12 miles from Ireland. A single-track, hairpin road with breathtaking views over Arran follows the western coast back to Campbeltown.

▲ Campbeltown Harbour

To the north of Campbeltown, the east-coast route has tree-lined glens and fertile valleys. Further up the valley from the battlemented castle by the shore at Saddell (now let by the Landmark Trust) are the remains of Saddell Abbey, with its impressive collection of carved gravestones. Carradale, further up the coast, is a small village beside a beautiful sandy bay. You can catch the summer ferry from Claonaig to Lochranza on Arran, and at Skipness you can explore the fine castle ruins or wander around the 13th-century Kilbrannan Chapel.

VISIT THE HERITAGE CENTRE
Campbeltown Heritage Centre
campbeltownheritagecentre.co.uk
Big Kiln Street, PA28 6JF
01586 551400 | Open May–Sep
Mon–Thu 10.30–5
In a disused church, sometimes referred to as the Tartan Kirk because of its banded stripes of stonework, the Campbeltown Heritage Centre has exhibits on the history of south Kintyre, along with local archaeological finds. There is also information about Kintyre residents such as landscape painter William McTaggart and shipping magnate Sir William Mackinnon, the founder of the British India Steam Navigation Company and the Imperial British East Africa Company.

TOUR THE DISTILLERY
Springbank Distillery Tour
springbankwhisky.com
9 Bolgam Street, PA28 6HZ | 01586 552009 | Tours Mon–Sat 10 and 2

Kintyre was once home to more than 30 distilleries (some of them illicit). This is one of the survivors. Whisky has been made here since 1828, and the tour shows you how, from the process of malting barley through to the finished product, which you'll be invited to sample at the end of your tour.

▶ Kirkcudbright MAP REF 398 C5

This pretty harbour town (the name is pronounced Kirkoobree) lies southwest of Castle Douglas on the road to nowhere, which is perhaps why it has retained so much character. The street plan is medieval and the gap-toothed castle ruin at its heart dates from the 16th-century. Its fame as a centre for painters dates from 1901, when artist and 'Glasgow Boy' E A Hornel (1864–1933) settled here, among others.

It is said that local residents approached Hornel and his friends for advice whenever their house fronts needed repainting – and this is the explanation for the harmonious shades seen in the High Street today.

TAKE IN SOME HISTORY
Broughton House
nts.org.uk
12 High Street, DG6 4JX | 01557 330437 | House and garden open Apr–Oct daily 12–5; garden only Feb–Mar Mon–Fri 11–4
A E Hornel's former home is an attractive pink-harled building. It's filled with paintings by the artist and his contemporaries; fans of Robert Burns will find one of the world's biggest collections of the poet's works here, too. Behind the house is a beautiful Japanese garden, lovingly tended by the National Trust for Scotland.

VISIT THE ARTS CENTRE AND MUSEUM

Tolbooth Art Centre

dumgal.gov.uk
High Street, DG6 4JL
01557 331556
Open Apr–Sep Mon–Sat 11–5;
Oct–Mar Mon–Sat 11–4
In the town's 17th-century Tolbooth you can learn the story of the Kirkcudbright artists with a video presentation and paintings by artists including Jessie M King, S J Peploe and Charles Oppenheimer. The gallery upstairs exhibits contemporary art and crafts.

Stewartry Museum

dumgal.gov.uk
St Mary Street, D6 4AQ
01557 331643
Open Apr–Sep Mon–Sat 11–5;
Oct–Mar Mon–Sat 11–4
The eastern Galloway region is known as the Stewartry, and this museum's collection focuses on its social history and traditions, with displays of book illustrations and locally made pottery. There's a section on the notorious privateer and father of the US Navy John Paul Jones – born in Kirkcudbrightshire, he emigrated to America, joined the rebel cause during the American War of Independence, crossing the Atlantic to harry British shipping and raid the coasts of Scotland and England. In 1778, he sailed into Kirkcudbright Bay and attacked St Mary's Isle, the home of the Earl of Selkirk. Jones hoped to kidnap the earl, and then exchange him for United States seamen held prisoner by the British. Unfortunately for him, Selkirk wasn't home when Jones's men landed, so they contented themselves with plundering his estate.

EAT AND DRINK

Selkirk Arms Hotel

selkirkarmshotel.co.uk
Old High Street, DG6 4JG
01557 330402
In 1794, when dining here, Robert Burns reputedly penned and delivered *The Selkirk Grace*. In the bar, Sulwath Brewery's eponymous ale celebrates the occasion. A good choice of dishes is offered in both the homely lounge and bistro and the more intimate Artistas Restaurant.

▶ PLACES NEARBY

Galloway Wildlife Conservation Centre

gallowaywildlife.co.uk
Lochfergus Plantation, DG6 4XX
01557 331645
Call for opening times
Founded as a private zoo, this much-loved family-run educational and conservation enterprise has now been handed over to a new charity. It will continue to care for the animals and carry out research and conservation.

▶ **Kirkwall**
see **Orkney Islands**, page 318

▶ **Kirriemuir** MAP REF 408 C5

Kirriemuir is a proud little town built of red sandstone. The playwright and novelist J M Barrie, creator of *Peter Pan*, was born here in 1860. Although he lived for most of his life in London, Barrie wrote with great affection about the small-town life of Kirriemuir, disguised as Thrums in his tales. In 1930 the now-wealthy and famous Barrie was granted the freedom of the town, and in return presented Kirriemuir with an unusual gift: a camera obscura (now closed) on nearby Kirrie Hill, with far-reaching views over the surrounding countryside.

TAKE IN SOME HISTORY
J M Barrie's Birthplace
nts.org.uk
9 Brechin Road, DD8 4BX | 01575 572646 | Open Jul–Aug Thu–Mon 12–5; Apr–Jun, Sep Sat–Mon 12–5

J M Barrie, son of a weaver and one of ten children, was born in this cottage. The wash-house at the back of the property served as Barrie's first theatre, and probably inspired the Wendy House in *Peter Pan*. The house is furnished as it would have been during his childhood.

▶ **PLACES NEARBY**
The Angus Glens

Kirriemuir is the gateway to the little Angus Glens, valleys that stretch from the low farmlands of Strathtay into the moorland of the Grampians and the fringes of the Cairngorms. All five glens (Glen Clova, Glen Prosen, Glen Esk, Glenisla and Glen Lethnot) offer great hill walking, with a choice of gentle strolls or more challenging longer traverses. A less demanding walk can start at Clova village and take you round the horseshoe-shaped ridge of Green Hill, above little Loch Brandy. From the high ground, you have soaring views of Lochnagar and the moors surrounding it, and on a clear day you can see right across Strathtay and Fife to Edinburgh. The glens are home to red and black grouse, golden eagles, ptarmigan, capercaillie and red and roe deer. Antarctic explorer Robert Falcon Scott – whose

◀ Statue of Peter Pan

research vessel *Discovery* was built in nearby Dundee (see page 135) – and his fellow-explorer Edward Wilson came to Glen Prosen to walk and toughen up before their fatal expedition to the South Pole, and are commemorated by a memorial cairn there.

Meigle Sculptured Stone Museum

historicenvironment.scot

Dundee Road, Meigle, Blairgowrie, PH12 8SB | 01828 640612 | Open daily Apr–Sep 9.30–5.30; Oct Mon–Fri 10–4

Knowledge about the Picts, who lived in Scotland in the Middle Ages, is limited. Much of what we do know has been gleaned from their remarkable legacy of stone carvings, and this museum, located in a former schoolhouse at Meigle, is a good place to see the best of the best.

The area was probably an ecclesiastical centre during the Dark Ages, with most of the 26-or-so carved stones and cross slabs on display dating from about AD 800 or later. The stones are carved with Pictish symbols and beasts, as well as some Christian subjects. You'll be able to pick out salmon, dogs and horsemen fairly easily, although it can be hard to make sense of the strange elephant-like creatures, camels or birds with bulbous eyes.

Glen Clova Hotel

clova.com

Glenclova, DD8 4QS | 01575 550350

The Glen Clova Hotel is the only eating place for miles around, and its hearty menu will set you up for an afternoon's walking or satisfy an appetite whetted by a day on the hills. Ingredients are locally sourced.

▶ Knoydart MAP REF 405 E3

Adjoining the Kintail NSA (see page 273) at Glen Sheil Forest, and northwest of the busy ferry port of Mallaig (see page 296), the Rough Bounds of Knoydart are among the best places in Scotland to see the magnificent golden eagle soaring on its massive 6.5-foot wingspan above the glens and lochs.

The Knoydart Peninsula between Loch Nevis and Loch Hourn contains some of the wildest scenery in Scotland, protected in this 153-sq-mile NSA. No roads cross this uninhabited wilderness. For many visitors, Knoydart's lack of human habitation is part of its charm, but this emptiness is the result of an unhappy episode in Scotland's past, when during the notorious Highland Clearances the local landowner, Josephine McDonnell of Glengarry, evicted her crofter tenants to make way for sheep. The crofters emigrated to Nova Scotia, where many of their descendants still live.

The Sound of Sleat coastline contributes much to the beauty of the NSA, and the western sea lochs of Nevis and Hourn both

have wide outer stretches that give way to narrow, fjord-like inner lochs as they penetrate deep into the mountains.

The deep, finger-like glens of Knoydart, such as Gleann na Guiserein and Gleann an Dubh Lochain, have long, stepped profiles, where broad marshy flats and lochans alternate with steep, wooded gorges. Most of the mountain slopes consist entirely of rocky scree and crags, while the lower slopes are enriched by bracken, sedges and rough grasses. Remnants of former oak, ash and birch woodlands still survive in the rocky ravines, where the burns rush down to meet the main glens.

....

▶ Leith MAP REF 402 C3

Leith is probably best known for The Proclaimers' song 'Sunshine on Leith' and as the down-and-dirty setting for Irvine Welsh's gritty tale of 1980s lowlife, *Trainspotting*. There's a bit of irony there: the movie adaptation of Welsh's novel had to be filmed in Glasgow (see page 206) because Edinburgh's city council, fearing it would cast the city in a bad light, refused to issue the permits required to shoot it there.

Leith was an important seaport and a centre of industries such as shipbuilding and weaving from early times until the 20th century. It was a separate community until 1920, when it was merged with the city of Edinburgh (see page 161). Leith has witnessed its share of history – Mary, Queen of Scots

◀ Loch Quoich and the mountains of Knoydart ▲ Royal Yacht *Britannia*

landed here from France in 1561 and is said to have stayed at Andro Lamb House, in Water Street. Where Tower Street meets The Shore, look for the Signal Tower, built in 1686 as a windmill.

Leith's docklands went into steep decline in the 1960s and 1970s. Over the last 20 years, however, the waterfront has been comprehensively gentrified, and smart restaurants and bars have sprung up along The Shore, where the Water of Leith flows into the harbour. A shiny retail and entertainment complex, Ocean Terminal, occupies a swathe of former industrial wasteland beside the broad Albert Dock. Moored next to it, The Royal Yacht *Britannia* is Leith's iconic attraction.

TAKE IN SOME HISTORY
Royal Yacht Britannia
royalyachtbritannia.co.uk
Ocean Terminal, Leith, EH6 6JJ
0131 555 5566 | Open Apr–Sep daily 9.30–4.30; Oct daily 9.30–4; Jan–Mar, Nov, Dec daily 10–3.30
It is said that many a royal tear was shed when *Britannia* was decommissioned in 1997. Since its launch at Clydebank in 1953, it had carried the Queen and her family on official voyages to all parts of the world. Now it's a floating museum, where you can visit the royal apartments and bedrooms, the gleaming engine room and the royal limo, a Rolls Royce Phantom V, in its on-board garage.

EAT AND DRINK

Restaurant Martin Wishart ⊚⊚⊚⊚

restaurantmartinwishart.co.uk
54 The Shore, Leith, EH6 6RA
0131 553 3557

Martin Wishart has been at the forefront of Scotland's culinary renaissance since 1999. There are three tasting menus to choose from – seafood and veggie versions alongside the regular one – and a concise fixed-price carte. The balance of flavours and textures in each dish is stunning.

The Kitchin ⊚⊚⊚⊚⊚

thekitchin.com
78 Commercial Quay, Leith, EH6 6LX | 0131 555 1755

A former whisky warehouse in Leith's regenerated docklands is home to a stylish space that combines the cast-iron girders of the building's industrial heritage with textures of slate and oak echoing the natural environment. Tom Kitchin's cooking is a good fit with the 21st-century zeitgeist – smart but not starchy, serious but not pretentious.

▶ Lerwick
see **Shetland Islands**, page 353

▶ Lewis
see **Western Isles**, page 389

▶ Linlithgow Palace   MAP REF 402 B3

historicenvironment.scot
Kirkgate, EH49 7AL | 01506 842896 | Open Apr–Sep daily 9.30–5.30;
Oct–Mar daily 10–4

Rising dramatically from the shores of Linlithgow Loch is a great square palace-fortress, dating from the 15th century. There was a fortified residence here as early as the mid-12th century, and Edward I built a manor here in 1302, but it was not until 1425 that work began on the castle that you see today.

King James I of Scotland gave orders that a royal residence should be constructed on the site of the earlier buildings, and although Linlithgow was primarily a palace, the architect incorporated a number of defensive features including a drawbridge and a barbican. The windows in the lower floors were protected by iron bars, holes for which can still be seen.

Linlithgow has played its part in Scotland's history. Mary, Queen of Scots was born here in 1542, Charles I slept here in 1633 and Oliver Cromwell stayed in the palace in the winter of 1650–51. When the Duke of Cumberland's army bivouacked in Linlithgow in 1746 en route to their encounter with Prince

Charles Edward Stuart's army at Culloden Moor, fires were left burning that gutted this handsome building.

▶ **PLACES NEARBY**

Champany Inn 🏅🏅
champany.com
Champany Corner, EH49 7LU
01506 834532
The Champany Inn deals in properly hung, chargrilled slabs of Class-A meat. The rambling cluster of buildings dates from the 16th century, and focuses on the main circular restaurant in a former horse-powered flour mill, with candlelit wooden tables and bare-stone walls beneath a vaulted roof.

Linlithgow Canal Centre
lucs.org.uk
Manse Road Basin, EH49 6AJ
01506 671215 | Call or see website for timetables

The Linlithgow Union Canal Society operates regular canal cruises and hires out boats with crews for larger groups. It also has a small museum – Scotland's only canal museum – in a former stables that once housed the heavy Clydesdale horses that towed narrowboats along the canal. The centre is entirely run by volunteers.

Union Canal
The Union Canal, linking Edinburgh and Falkirk, passes through Linlithgow. You can take a boat trip through town, or go all the way to the Falkirk Wheel (see page 373) where the Union Canal and Forth Clyde Canal meet.

▼ Linlithgow Palace

▶ Loch Awe MAP REF 401 D1

A narrow loch, 23 miles long, Loch Awe lies amid the dark green forested hills of Argyll, surrounded by scattered small villages, castles and hotels. There are little islands and the remains of crannogs, and the clear waters teem with trout and pike. The Duncan Ban McIntyre Monument, signposted from Dalmally, is an excellent viewpoint.

At the northern end, tantalisingly surrounded by marsh, sits the picturesque ruin of Kilchurn Castle. It dates from 1440 and was built by Colin Campbell of Breadalbane, with additions into the 17th century. Where the northwest corner of the loch narrows into the awesome Pass of Brander, a hydroelectric power station lies on the shore below the bulk of Ben Cruachan (3,688 feet/1,124m). A minibus takes you half a mile into the mountain to see the mighty turbines (reserve in advance).

▶ Lochleven Castle MAP REF 402 C2

historicenvironment.scot
Kinross, KY13 8UF | 01577 862670 | Open Apr–Sep daily 10–4.15; Oct daily 10–3.15

The stark grey, roofless tower of Lochleven Castle beckons from its little island in Loch Leven. Just getting here is a mini-adventure, as you have to take a small boat from Kinross, on the west side of the loch. This 15th-century fortress gained notoriety as the prison of Mary, Queen of Scots after her defeat in 1567. After her forced abdication she escaped and sought refuge with Elizabeth I of England, who promptly imprisoned her again. The castle was abandoned in the mid-18th century.

The waters of the loch today are lower than they were in the 14th century when the castle was built. This is because the course of the River Leven was altered in the 19th century, and the level of the loch was lowered as a result. The castle itself is a simple square tower of five storeys, surrounded by a towered wall that was a later addition. The third floor of the tower was possibly where Mary, Queen of Scots was imprisoned between June 1567 and May 1568.

Queen Mary was unwell for much of the time she was imprisoned at Loch Leven, and she suffered a miscarriage. She escaped from the castle by befriending the boat keeper, but after the Battle of Langside, during which Mary and her supporters were soundly defeated, she fled the country.

GET OUTDOORS
Vane Farm Nature Centre
rspb.org.uk

Kinross, KY13 9LX | 01577 862355

Open Apr–Oct daily 9–5; Nov–Mar daily 9–4. Trails and hides daily 24 hours

Loch Leven is a nature reserve noted for its huge over-wintering flocks of pink-footed geese. You can watch these, and other waterfowl, from the RSPB's visitor centre on the south shore of the loch. There are also hides dotted along a network of waymarked trails, including one that stretches all the way round Loch Leven.

▶ PLACES NEARBY
Rumbling Bridge
KY13 0PX

It's not the bridge that rumbles at this beauty spot along the River Devon, rather the waters that thunder through the rocky gorge beneath when the river is in spate. And there's not one bridge, but two, with one built above the other. The lower bridge dates from 1713, the upper one, 120 feet above the water, from 1816. Visitors used to flock here in such numbers that it once had its own train station. Now it's a peaceful backwater, with pleasant walks to the waterfalls of the Devil's Mill and the Cauldron Linn.

10 top castles and stately homes

▶ Loch Lomond & The Trossachs National Park MAP REF 401 F2

The romantic beauty of the Highland landscape, epitomised by this accessible and scenic area, was first discovered in the late 18th century. Novelist and poet Sir Walter Scott did much to bring it to the popular eye, with his thrilling poem *The Lady of the Lake* (1810) set in identifiable locations across the Trossachs, ending at Loch Katrine. Today, the 720-sq-mile national park, Scotland's first, stretches from the Argyll Forest Park in the west across to Callander, and from Killin in the north to Balloch in the south, just 18 miles from Glasgow.

This is popular hiking country, with plenty of waymarked trails and a lovely stretch of the West Highland Way long-distance path, which runs down the eastern shore of Loch Lomond. Some 24 miles long, the loch is a water-sports playground littered with 38 islands. It narrows to the north, where the mountains become bigger and bleaker. Ben Lomond, on the eastern shore, is a popular so-called Munro hill climb at 3,192 feet (973m). On the western side, Luss, off the A82, is the prettiest village to explore and was the setting for the popular TV series *Take the High Road*.

Loch Lomond has two very distinct characters – the narrow upper loch is hemmed in by mountains, and stretches up into

▲ Loch Lomond

the heart of the Highlands, while the broad, island-speckled southern end is bordered by fertile farmland. Some of the loch's most popular attractions are here. Balloch, with its modern castle, country park and opportunities for boat cruises, sits astride the only natural outlet from the loch, and is a popular centre. The Loch Lomond Shores Visitor Centre includes an information centre and shopping outlets.

Lomond's east side is much quieter, offering walking and outdoor pursuits. From Balmaha there are some good views over several of the loch's 38 named islands – especially Inchcailloch, once the site of a nunnery, and now part of the Loch Lomond National Nature Reserve. Much of the eastern shore is within the 50,000-acre Queen Elizabeth Forest Park. The narrow road ends at Rowardennan, from where there is a stiff climb up Ben Lomond. To visit the beautiful Inversnaid, approach from Aberfoyle or by ferry from Inveruglas – unless you are energetic enough for the walk along the West Highland Way from Rowardennan.

Seventy per cent of Scotland's population now live within an hour of the national park, and visitor numbers are up to more than four million per annum. What attracts visitors is the subtle mixture of the beauty of loch and mountain and the vital, softening aspect of the extensive areas of semi-natural deciduous woodland, much of which was regularly coppiced to supply the needs of the newly emerging industrial city of Glasgow (see page 206). But the popularity of the traditional song *Loch Lomond* indicates that the area has held a special place in the affections of local people for many years prior to the writings of Scott and the arrival of the railway.

At its northern end, Loch Lomond narrows into deep defile between the rugged hills of Arrochar, sometimes known as the Arrochar Alps, and Breadalbane to the west, with the reigning peak of Ben Lomond and its outliers looming to the east. The northern end of the loch has more of the feel of a Highland glen, with steep walls of rock rearing straight up from the water. The loch is dotted with islands. Some are no more than rocky dots, but it's worth taking a boat trip to the wooded island of Inchcailloch (Innis na Cailleach), the largest in the Loch Lomond National Nature Reserve, which is usually reached from Balmaha. There is an ancient church settlement here, and the remains of a convent dedicated to St Kentigern (also known as St Mungo, and the patron saint of Glasgow), and the evocative graveyard is the burial place for many MacGregors and MacFarlanes. Wildlife on Inchcailloch includes a large population of garden warblers, unmatched elsewhere in northern Britain.

The reigning peaks of Ben Lui at 3,708 feet (1,130m) and Ben Ime at 3,318 feet (1,011m) dominate Breadalbane and the Arrochar Alps, but perhaps the most charismatic mountain on the western side of the loch is Ben Arthur. Familiarly known in the climbing world as the Cobbler, this craggy, triple-summit peak is not even a Munro (a summit of more than 3,000 feet) because it rises to only 2,900 feet (884m). Nevertheless, it is a true mountain summit that can only be fully traversed by the use of hands, so many people prefer to stop at the Central Peak between the precipitous South and overhanging North Peaks, which are known as the Cobbler's Wife and the Cobbler's Last respectively.

The mountain scene that makes up the western frame of the loch has been materially altered by the construction of the Loch Sloy dam and its accompanying reservoir, between Ben Vorlich and Ben Vane. The water conduit pipes and power lines feed down to the monolithic Inveruglas hydroelectric plant on the A82. On the opposite side of the loch and beneath the northern slopes of Ben Lomond, Loch Arklet has been similarly artificially enlarged by a dam and provides fresh Highland water to Glasgow and other towns in the Central Belt. The wild pass between Ben Venue and Ben An gives access to the Trossachs, whose name is said to mean 'the rough or bristly country'. It's well named. This pocket wilderness was for a long time the haunt of cattle rustlers and thieves, like Rob Roy MacGregor. The name of the pass at the eastern end of Loch

▼ West Highland Way

Katrine and below the slopes of Ben Venue gives a clue to its turbulent past. Bealach nam Bo literally means 'the pass of the cattle', and this was where the bandit MacGregors and others drove their stolen booty into the secret heart of the mountains.

The name Trossachs is now more generally applied to the triangle of mountains and woodland between Loch Katrine, Aberfoyle and Callander, all of which now falls within the national park. Loch Katrine, at the heart of the Trossachs, is a loch of clear, sparkling water studded with pretty islands and surrounded by woodland and mountains. In fact, its water level is artificially controlled to serve central Glasgow with fresh water, and part of its peaceful aspect comes from the fact that only three motorised boats have access to its waters. They include the elegant old steamship, SS *Sir Walter Scott*.

Purists, however, prefer the intimacy of the smaller, tree-lined Loch Achray or the crooked loch, Loch Lubnaig, which lies over the Pass of Leny, with its spectacular Falls of Leny, to the northeast. One of the most intriguing names in the Trossachs is the Wood of Lamentation, which lies on the northern side of Loch Venachar. In days gone by, children were warned to stay away from the waterside in case the *each uishge*, a mystical water horse similar to Loch Ness's fabled monster, should lure them into the water to their deaths.

Ben Ledi, simply known as The Ben in these parts, in days gone by was known as a Beltane hill, or *La Buidhe Bealltuinn*, which translates as the yellow day of the fires of Bel. On the Celtic New Year, the first of May, young people of the locality would meet on the 2,875-foot (876m) summit to commemorate the ancient rite of the lighting of the Beltane fires in honour of the Celtic sun god. Down below, all fires were extinguished before midnight and then relit from the purifying flames from the top of the mountain. Sometimes cattle were driven between the fires in the belief that this would protect them from disease during the coming year.

The romantic ruins of Inchmahome Priory on the island of Inchmahome are reached by a short ferry trip from Port of Menteith. Walter Comyn, Earl of Menteith, brought the monks to Inchmahome in 1238, and it was known to Robert the Bruce and Mary, Queen of Scots who was sent there for her safety when she was a child, after Henry VIII had made it known that he wanted her to marry his son, Edward.

The village of Aberfoyle is the key to this region, giving easy access to the wooded hills of the Queen Elizabeth Forest Park and the peak of Ben Venue (2,391 feet/729m), and Loch Katrine to the north. There are great opportunities for walking and cycling, including a pretty cycle route that runs through the

Forest Park and continues along the shores of Loch Venachar and Loch Lubnaig to Balquhidder, Lochearnhead and Killin. The Trossachs Discovery visitor centre in Aberfoyle is a mine of information about activities in the area. The Scottish Wool Centre behind it offers an entertaining Sheepdog Show, as well as a chance to see lambs and sheep shearing in season.

GET OUTDOORS

Balloch Castle Country Park

Balloch, G83 8LX | 01389 722600
Open all year

The park is quintessentially a 19th-century private estate, developed as a park at the beginning of the 20th century. Its design and layout has remained largely unaltered since 1800, at the time the current castle was built. In the park you can explore the Fairy Glen, Chinese Garden, Pleasure Grounds, Quarry Pond, Kitchen Garden, Secret Garden, Woodlands and Parklands.

MEET THE SEA LIFE

Loch Lomond Sea Life Aquarium

visitsealife.com/loch-lomond
Loch Lomond Shores, G83 8QL
01389 721500 | Open all year 10–5

Loch Lomond Shores is primarily a vast shopping centre, but its biggest visitor attraction is this cavernous modern aquarium where sharks and rays swim in vast tanks and kids can handle creatures like starfish and crabs in the touch pool. You can also encounter a charming family of otters, and find out about some of the unique aquatic life of the loch, including rare and endangered species such as sea lampreys and whitefish.

GET ON THE WATER

Maid of the Loch

maidoftheloch.org
The Pier, Pier Road, Balloch, G83 8QX | 01389 711865 | Open Apr–Oct daily 11–4; winter weekends only

Loch Lomond's paddle steamer, Maid of the Loch, is docked at Balloch. Volunteers are on hand to answer questions about the craft, built in 1953.

Loch Katrine

lochkatrine.com
Trossachs Pier Complex, FK17 8HZ
01877 376316 | Open daily all year. Call or check website for details

Take a steamship cruise around beautiful Loch Katrine, at the heart of the Trossachs, aboard the 100-year-old SS Sir Walter Scott and the SS Lady of the Lake. Combine with a bike ride by contacting Katrinewheelz on the same number.

TOUR THE DISTILLERY

Glengoyne Distillery

glengoyne.com
Dumgoyne, near Killearn, G63 9LB
01360 550254 | Open Mar–Nov Mon–Sat 10–4, Sun 12–4,; Dec–Feb Mon–Sat 11–3, Sun 12–3. All tours start on the hour

Glengoyne is picturesquely located between the loch and a pretty waterfall, but it's the whisky that's the main attraction. You can take a guided tour, and then sip a dram in the reception room overlooking the loch and waterfall, and visit the heritage room and shop.

WALK THE WEST HIGHLAND WAY

west-highland-way.co.uk
Carrochan Road, Balloch, G83 8EG
01389 722600

Scotland's first long-distance walking trail is 96 miles long. It begins just south of Loch Lomond, and as it skirts the loch, it makes the transition from easy lowland walking to the more rugged terrain of the Highlands. Starting from Milngavie on the outskirts of Glasgow, the route makes its way north to Fort William (see page 198), often using ancient and historic routes – drove roads by which cattle dealers reached market; military roads instituted by General Wade to aid in suppressing the clans; and old coaching roads and discarded railway lines.

Walk all the way if you wish – experts recommend going south to north, to build up stamina for the hills – or take a short walk along the route; there is no shortage of breathtaking sections, and you may see red deer and, possibly, golden eagles. The Way now connects at Milngavie with the John Muir Way (see page 134), Scotland's newest long-distance footpath, which stretches to Dunbar on the east coast (see page 132).

EAT AND DRINK

The Coach House Coffee Shop
Church Road, Luss, G83 8NN
01436 860341

Gaelic music, log fires and a kilted proprietor set the scene at this friendly coffee and gift shop on Loch Lomond's western shore. The perfect spot

▼ The West Highland Way

for a light meal or tea stop, it offers homemade rolls and soup, and speciality fruit cake.

The Inn on Loch Lomond

innonlochlomond.co.uk
G83 8PD | 01436 860678
Today a good road skirts Loch Lomond's western shore, but it wouldn't have been so good in 1814, when this wayside inn opened its doors. Today it incorporates Mr C's Fish & Whisky Bar. More than 200 whiskies are available, but if you prefer ale, there's Deuchars IPA, Fyne Highlander and Houston Killellan. Live folk music is played nightly throughout the summer.

The Lodge on Loch Lomond ◉◉

loch-lomond.co.uk
Luss, G83 8PA | 01436 860201
Perched on the edge of the loch, The Lodge turns out great steaks and imaginative dishes such as pork cheeks with a burned apple puree and black pudding, fish stew with confit lentils and pepper meringue with a blackberry parfait. Scottish cheeses are served with chutney, apple and grapes.

Macdonald Forest Hills Hotel & Resort ◉

macdonald-hotels.co.uk/foresthills
Kinlochard FK8 3TL | 01877 389500
Twenty-five acres of mature gardens run down to the shore of Loch Ard at this white-painted mansion. In the restaurant, a curved wall of floor-to-ceiling windows gives magnificent views over the gardens and loch, and staff are friendly.

Village Inn

classicinns.co.uk/villageinnarrochar
Shore Road, G83 7AX | 01301 702279
On the east shore of Loch Long, just a few minutes from Loch Lomond, the Village Inn was originally built in 1872 as a church manse. There's a large beer garden and superb views of the so-called Arrochar Alps. Ideally located for the hills and trails of the national park, it has a friendly atmosphere, quality Scottish food and Scottish cask ales in the cosy bar.

▶ **PLACES NEARBY**

Inchmahome Priory

historicenvironment.scot
Port of Menteith, FK8 3RA | 01877 385294 | Open Apr–Sep daily 9.30–4.30; Oct daily 9.30–3.30
You can take a boat trip over to this charming 13th-century Augustinian monastery located on a small island in the Lake of Menteith.

Lake of Menteith Fisheries

menteith-fisheries.co.uk
Ryeyards, Port of Menteith, FK8 3RA | 01877 385664
Lake Menteith has excellent fly-fishing for rainbow trout. Hire a boat through the booking office; a qualified instructor can also be arranged.

▸ Loch Ness & Drumnadrochit

MAP REF 407 D3

It would be difficult for anyone but the most hardened sceptic to
gaze out over the waters of Loch Ness without just the small
hope of seeing something that may be interpreted as a sighting.
Monster or no, Loch Ness is beautiful and it contains more water
than all the lakes and reservoirs in England and in Wales put
together. The loch is 24 miles long, one mile wide and 750 feet
deep, making it one of the largest bodies of fresh water in Europe.
Mentioned in writing as long ago as the seventh century, when
St Adamnan's *Life of St Columba* tells of the saint saving a
swimmer from being attacked by a creature, the Loch Ness
Monster – or, familiarly, Nessie – has become the focus of the
tourist industry here.

Until the building of the A82 road along the north shore of Loch
Ness, and the wave of supposed monster sightings that followed
from the 1930s onwards, Drumnadrochit was a sleepy, tiny village
well off the beaten track. Today, tourism and monstermania are its
main sources of prosperity, with an array of rival Nessie-related
attractions and activities, including the Original Loch Ness Visitor
Centre with a large-screen cinema, exhibition and sonar scanning
cruises, and the Official Loch Ness Monster Exhibition.

You can hire a cabin cruiser, or visit the ruined Urquhart Castle
on the shores of the loch, from where most sightings have been
made. The loch forms a major part of the Caledonian Canal, which
links the west coast with the Moray Firth, and follows the line of
the dramatic Great Glen (see page 239), cutting Scotland in two
halves. This spectacular geological fault has provided a way
through the mountains for centuries of travellers and is tracked
today by the A82 between Fort William (see page 198) and
Inverness (see page 250).

TAKE IN SOME HISTORY
Urquhart Castle

historicenvironment.scot
Drumnadrochit, IV63 6XJ | 01456
450551 | Open Apr–Sep daily
9.30–6; Oct daily 9.30–5; Nov–Mar
daily 9.30–4.30

The broken battlements of
this castle, 2 miles south of
Drumnadrochit, are testimony
to its place in the history of
the 13th to the 17th centuries.
It was built on a rocky
promontory sticking out into
Loch Ness, offering strategic
command of the Great Glen
to whoever could hold it. It
changed hands many times
between Durwards,
MacDonalds and Grants, with
an early spell in English hands,
and in the 14th century a brief
period of ownership by Robert
the Bruce. It was finally blown
up in 1691 to prevent its use by
Jacobite rebels. The modern
visitor centre exhibits medieval
fragments discovered here,
including an ancient harp.

In view of its turbulent
history, it is not surprising
that Urquhart's defences are
formidable. A walled causeway,
with a drawbridge halfway
along, led to the castle
gatehouse. Great walls that
followed the contours of the
rock protected it from attack,
strengthened by a ditch at the
front and the loch at the back.
Inside the walls were a variety
of buildings, including living
quarters, a chapel, kitchens
and a dovecote.

Although much of the
building is dilapidated, apart
from the 16th-century tower
house, which is still largely
intact, this romantic ruin
huddled on the loch shore is
well worth a visit. It is also
the site from where many
people claim to have spotted
the Loch Ness Monster, and
webcams are set up above
the castle just in case Nessie
should make an appearance
in the loch.

GO MONSTER CRAZY
Loch Ness Exhibition Centre

lochness.com
Drumnadrochit, IV63 6TU | 01456
450573 | Open Apr–Jun and Sep–
Oct daily 9–5; Jul–Aug daily 9.30–6;
Nov–Mar daily 10–3.30

Drumnadrochit's longest-
established monster attraction
uses a hi-tech audio-visual
presentation to tell the story of
the monster legend from the
earliest times right up to
the latest attempts to locate
Nessie using state-of-the-art
techniques. There's also plenty
of information about Loch
Ness's history and ecology.

Nessieland Castle Monster Centre

nessieland.co.uk
Drumnadrochit, IV63 6TU | 01456
450342 | Open mid-Apr–Sep daily
9–7; Oct–mid-Apr daily 11–3

Nessieland makes monster
hunting fun with its collection
of monster caves, blow-up
dinosaurs, and displays of
images purporting to be
Nessie herself. There are also
slides, climbing frames and
woodland paths.

▶ **Mainland**
see **Orkney Islands**, page 312

▶ **Mallaig** MAP REF 405 E4

This bustling little fishing port, facing the Isle of Skye across the Sound of Sleat, truly is the end of the road, where the romantically named Road to the Isles hits the coast and comes to a full stop. Today, the road's more prosaic nomenclature is the A830, but it still holds promise for travellers as one of the gateways to Skye (see page 254) and the Small Isles (see page 362). It's the last stop on one of the world's great railway routes, the famous West Highland Line. Mallaig's lively Heritage Centre, bang next to the station, will fill you in on this and lots more besides.

The West Highland Line was built when the line from Glasgow, which had struggled across Rannoch Moor (see page 340) to Fort William by 1894, was extended to Mallaig in 1902. Its construction was no easy task – Rannoch Moor's peat bogs were ingeniously traversed with a floating bed of brushwood, beneath tons of ash and earth, while the heights of Glenfinnan and the deeply indented coastline had to be crossed. Contractor Robert MacAlpine pioneered the structural use of concrete, building the high viaducts that give such magnificent views.

VISIT THE HERITAGE CENTRE
Mallaig Heritage Centre
mallaigheritage.org.uk
Station Road, PH41 4PY | 01687 462 085 | See website for opening times

Mallaig's Heritage Centre tells the story of West Lochaber, an area known as the 'Rough Bounds' due to its remote location, and a Jacobite stronghold. You can learn about the history of the town and its fishing industry and trace the development of the ferry system serving the islands.

TAKE A TRAIN RIDE
Jacobite Steam Train
westcoastrailways.co.uk
Mallaig Station, PH41 4PY

0844 850 4685 (calls cost 7p per minute plus your phone company's access charge) | Open mid-May to mid-Oct, see website for details. See also page 199

Most passengers take this iconic journey from Fort William to Mallaig, but, if you're based in the west, there's no reason not to do the trip in reverse. It's an 84-mile round trip that takes you from the coast through stunning scenery to Fort William, which lies in the shadow of Britain's highest mountain, Ben Nevis. En route you'll pass the village of Arisaig and its white sands, Loch Morar, Scotland's deepest freshwater loch, and the tiny River Morar, the shortest river

▲ Lochaber Harbour, Mallaig

in Britain. Sit on the right to catch the best views, and book in advance.

GO SWIMMING
Mallaig Swimming Pool
mallaigleisure.org.uk
Fank Brae, PH41 4RG | 01687 462229 | Open daily, see website for details
The community runs this pool and leisure centre, where you can take a swim, work out in the gym or head for the spa and sauna. There are daily exercise classes and kids activity sessions in the holidays, both of which warmly welcome visitors.

▶ **PLACES NEARBY**
A couple of miles outside Mallaig, at Morar, the waters of Scotland's deepest freshwater loch tumble and cascade down a spectacular waterfall and into a beautiful sandy bay. The drive southwards along the coast is enchanting, passing through woodland and past a string of lovely beaches, with fine views to the islands. One of the long, white-sand beaches along here provided the setting for the film *Local Hero*, although the iconic telephone box lies on the other side of Scotland at Pennan in Aberdeenshire.

▶ **Melrose** MAP REF 403 D4
Melrose, clustering round the ruins of its ancient abbey, is a typically Borders town, couthy, genteel and quietly prosperous. The Romans built a massive fort here, which they called Trimontium after the three peaks of the neighbouring Eildon Hills. The Eildons, formed by volcanic action about 350 million years ago, stand out as heather- and rough grass-covered islands in a sea of rich lowland farming country.

Eildon Hill North is topped by a monument to Scott and ringed by the embankments of a massive 40-acre Iron Age hillfort built by the native tribe of the Selgovae. Legend has it that the three peaks were once one hill, split into three by a wizard – a fitting backstory for the tale that tells of King Arthur and his knights slumbering beneath their grassy slopes. The Three Hills Roman Heritage Centre, in the town centre, will fill you in on the more concrete aspects of the distant past.

Melrose's more visible history dates from 1136, when David I founded the pink sandstone abbey, whose ruins lie just below the town. The great Cistercian abbey of St Mary served the church and the state of Scotland for four centuries, from its foundation in 1136 to its dissolution in about 1556. Today's ruins are those of the second abbey on this spot – the first was destroyed by Richard II in 1385.

Like most of the towns and villages around here, Melrose developed later on the back of the tweed and knitwear industry, which brought wealth to the Scottish Borders, utilising the distinctive, Roman-nosed Cheviot Hill sheep and the availability of water power for the looms. The weaving and bleaching industries gave the name Bleachfield to an area to the west of the town, and the impressive remains of a large, water-powered textile mill still exist at Leaderfast.

Just 2 miles to the west of the town lies Abbotsford, built by the novelist Sir Walter Scott (1771–1832) for himself in 1812. The painter J M W Turner (1775–1851) visited Abbotsford in 1831 and the paintings he did during his visit perfectly catch the Tweed valley landscape and the countryside around Melrose.

TAKE IN SOME HISTORY

Abbotsford
see page 56

Melrose Abbey
historicenvironment.scot
TD6 9LG | 01896 822562 | Open Apr–Sep daily 9.30–5.30; Oct–Mar daily 10–4

Once one of Scotland's richest monasteries, Melrose Abbey is a romantic mix of soaring pinkish sandstone, predominantly Gothic in style. Like other Border abbeys, Melrose was devastated in 1544 by the Earl of Hertford, and the ruins were later plundered for stone by the Douglases, who used them to build a house. Repairs in the 19th century were at the instigation of novelist Sir Walter Scott; the ruins are majestic, and the exterior stone carving outstanding – take time to look upwards to identify saints, dragons, flowers and a pig playing the bagpipes.

The burial spot of Robert the Bruce's embalmed heart in the abbey is marked by an engraved inscription. No one knew for sure where it was

▲ Melrose

until an excavation in 1921
when the casket, still sealed,
was found by schoolchildren
taking part in the search. It
was not opened, but was
further sealed and reburied
in its present location.

GO ROUND THE GARDEN
Priorwood Garden
nts.org.uk
TD6 9PX | 01896 209504 | Garden
open Apr–Oct Mon–Sat 10–5,
Sun 1–5; shop open same hours
as garden
Lying within the abbey
precincts, this tranquil walled

garden grows a wonderful
variety of flower species for
drying, which you can buy at
the on-site shop. There's an
orchard full of historic apple
varieties and a woodland area
as well.

GO BACK IN TIME
**Three Hills Roman
Heritage Centre**
trimontium.org.uk
The Ormiston, Market Square, TD6
9PN | 01896 822651 | Open Apr–
Oct daily 10.30–4.30
This well laid-out centre
tells the story of the Roman

settlement through artefacts, information panels, models and maps. There's the Newstead charger for children to ride and mock-ups of a Roman kitchen and blacksmith's workshop, while videos fill you in on the Roman Empire's northern frontier.

GET ACTIVE
Active Sports
activitiesinscotland.com
Chain Bridge Cottage, Annay Road, TD6 9LP | 01896 822452
Choose from a half-day or full-day activity at this outdoor centre, the only one of its kind in the Borders. Hire a mountain bicycle, go quad biking or enjoy water sports. Most activities take place just outside Selkirk; reservations are recommended.

CATCH A PERFORMANCE
The Wynd Theatre
The Wynd, TD6 9LD
01896 820028
A small theatre just off the High Street with films, concerts including blues, big band and folk music, plays and pantomime. A bar is open on performance evenings.

PLAY A ROUND
Melrose Golf Course
melrosegolfcourse.co.uk
Dingle Road, TD6 9HS | 01896 822855 | Open daily all year
There are splendid views from the fairways of this nine-hole course, laid out in 1880. There are plenty of bunkers and ponds and streams to negotiate on four of the holes.

EAT AND DRINK
Burts Hotel ◎◎
burtshotel.co.uk
Market Square, TD6 9PL
01896 822285
Built in 1722 and owned and run by the Henderson family for four decades, the interior of this hotel, all modern comfort and charm, belies its historic exterior. The restaurant serves modern and innovative food using local ingredients, or you can enjoy something simpler in the Bistro Bar while debating which of the 90 single malts on offer you may enjoy.

▶ PLACES NEARBY
A drive through the lovely Border countryside and down the beautiful Tweed valley will bring you to the ruins of another great abbey at Dryburgh. Pause on your way at **Scott's View**, the famous viewpoint over the river at Bemersyde.

Dryburgh Abbey
historicenvironment.scot
TD6 0RQ | 01835 822381
Open Apr–Sep daily 9.30–5.30; Oct–Mar daily 10–4
Both Sir Walter Scott and Earl Haig, founder of the British legion and Commander-in-Chief during World War I, are buried among the ruins of this Augustinian abbey. It flourished until the late 14th century, but never recovered after Richard II burned it in 1385.

Dryburgh Abbey Hotel
dryburgh.co.uk

St Boswells, Melrose, TD6 0RQ
01835 822261
Overlooking the abbey ruins, this country-house hotel sits in wooded grounds. Produce from the garden is used in the cooking, local ingredients star, and imaginative combinations sit happily on the menu alongside traditional favourites.

▶ Montrose MAP REF 409 E5

The town of Montrose lies at the mouth of the River South Esk on Scotland's eastern seaboard, much of it built on a sandy spit that almost cuts off the tidal wildlife reserve of Montrose Basin from the North Sea. Its comfortable prosperity was built up in the 18th century, largely on the back of trade with continental Europe, and some of its architecture echoes the elegance of Edinburgh's New Town. A particular feature are the houses built with their gable ends to the street, influenced by the European style that local merchants would have seen on their travels. They're so distinctive that even now Montrose locals – and their football club – are nicknamed The Gable-Endies. The fine Montrose Museum and Art Gallery is one of Scotland's oldest, dating from 1842, its classical building intended to look like a temple of learning.

East of the town, Montrose beach has fabulous golden sands exposed at low tide. To the north is the Montrose Air Station Heritage Centre, on the site of Britain's first military airfield. Behind the harbour, the Montrose Basin, a shallow inland sea, is emptied twice a day by the tide: its mudflats are noted for migrant birds, with thousands of pink footed geese returning every winter. The Basin was important for salmon, mussel and eel fishing, which made it a focus for early settlement.

TAKE IN SOME HISTORY
House of Dun
nts.org.uk
DD10 9LQ | 01674 810264 | House open Apr–Sep Sat–Wed 10.30–4.30; Oct–Nov Sat & Sun 11–2.30; garden open all year 9am to dusk
The House of Dun, a fine Georgian mansion on the northern shore of the Montrose Basin, was designed in 1730 by architect William Adam for David Erskine, a judge at the Court of Session. It's home to some of the finest furniture and paintings in the National Trust for Scotland's collections.

VISIT THE MUSEUM AND HERITAGE CENTRE
Montrose Museum and Art Gallery
visitangus.com
Panmure Place, DD10 8HE | 01674 662660 | Open Tue–Sat 10–5
There's local history galore here, with lots on the region's archaeology and the elusive Picts, as well as displays on the

history of the town and its role as a whaling base.

Montrose Air Station Heritage Centre

rafmontrose.org.uk
Waldron Road, DD10 9BD | 01674 678222 | Open Apr–Oct Wed–Sat 10–4; Nov–Mar Sat 10–4, Sun 12–4
Britain's first operational military airfield was set up in Montrose by the Royal Flying Corps in 1913. A collection of photographs and artefacts tells the story of Royal Flying Corps (RFC)/Royal Air Force (RAF) Montrose through the words and deeds of the men and women who served here through two world wars.

GO BIRDING
Montrose Basin

montrosebasin.org.uk
01674 676336 | Visitor Centre open Mar–Oct daily 10.30–5; Nov–Feb Fri–Sun 10.30–4
This local nature reserve combines a recreational stretch of water with a wonderfully varied habitat of mud, water, marsh and reedbeds that supports a huge variety of resident and migratory birdlife.

PLAY A ROUND
Montrose Golf Links

montroselinks.co.uk

Traill Drive, DD10 8SW | 01674 672932 | Open daily all year
The links at Montrose, like many others in Scotland, are on common land. The Medal Course is the fifth oldest in the world – the earliest record of the game here dates from 1562.

▸ PLACES NEARBY

West of Montrose, in the valley of the Lunan Water, lies the little village of Guthrie, whose fairytale castle was once the seat of the head of the Clan Guthrie – nowadays it hosts weddings rather than clansmen. Nearby are the tranquil gardens of Pitmuies.

House of Pitmuies

pitmuies.com
Guthrie, DD8 2SN | 01241 828245 Open Apr–Oct daily 10–5
Pitmuies House is 18th century, but the origins of the garden pre-date this. What you see today are three gardens of great beauty and variety, with fountains, roses rambling everywhere, long beds of massed perennials and walkways lined with clematis, more roses and stately beech and lime trees. The woodland walk runs through woods of rhododendrons and azaleas to the Black Loch.

▸ Muck
see **Small Isles**, page 363

▸ Mull
see **Western Isles**, page 382

▶ **New Lanark** MAP REF 402 B4

newlanark.org
New Lanark Mills, Lanark, ML11 9DB | 01555 661345 | Visitor centre open
Apr–Oct daily 10–5; Nov–Mar daily 10–4

Glasgow philanthropist David Dale (1739–1806) first developed a
cotton manufacturing plant and settlement in this steep sided
valley in 1786, harnessing the power of the River Clyde as it roars
over spectacular waterfalls. However, it is his son-in-law, the
Welshman Robert Owen (1771–1858), who is most clearly identified
with the village, which he purchased in 1799. A pioneer of social
reform, over the next two decades he established a utopian society
here – a model community with improved conditions for the
workers and their families, complete with a school (with the first
day nursery and playground in the world, it's claimed), institute for
adult education and co operative village store. As modern industry
developed New Lanark lost its starring role, until in 1973 the New
Lanark Conservation Trust started to restore the site, with the
stunning results seen today. Restoration work was carried out so
well that in 2001 New Lanark was included on the United Nations
Educational, Scientific and Cultural Organizarion's (UNESCO's) list
of World Heritage Sites. It is one of only six in Scotland.

The workers' houses are lived in once more, although the mill
no longer manufactures cotton. Understand it through the Annie
MacLeod Experience Ride, a weird and fascinating journey of

discovery led by the ghostly figure of a mill girl who worked here in the 1820s. You can also explore a millworker's cottage, Owen's house, an interactive village store – try to outwit the unscrupulous shop owner – and the school. Here you'll find a 21st-century playroom for kids that reflects Owen's ideas of infant education through the themes of music and art.

Then head up to the Roof Garden, the best place for a bird's-eye view over the entire site. If this isn't enough there's always something showing at the film theatre to deepen your experience, or the year-round programme of temporary exhibitions.

You should certainly muster your remaining energy for the walk upstream to the three waterfalls, particularly after rainfall when they are at their best. It was the existence of these waterfalls, known as the Falls of Clyde, and of the fast-flowing River Clyde, that brought David Dale here in the first place. The deep gorge was inaccessible before he saw the potential of the area, and the natural power that the water could provide. It's a testimony to his vision and energy that New Lanark existed at all, let alone that it has survived and helped to preserve the landscape in which it is set for more than 200 years.

5 top industrial heritage locations

▶ **Forth Rail Bridge**, page 364

▶ **Verdant Works**, page 141

▶ **Riverside Museum**, Glasgow, page 221

▶ **New Lanark**, see above

▶ **National Mining Museum Scotland**, page 124

▶ **North Berwick** MAP REF 403 D2

Tucked in beside a rocky headland, North Berwick Harbour is now a yachting and lobster fishing centre backed by smartly converted old warehouses. For 500 years it also provided a ferry on the pilgrimage route to St Andrews, which dramatically shortened the journey from the south. North was added to its name to distinguish the town from Berwick-upon-Tweed, which the Scots knew as South Berwick. The town developed as a resort for the population of Edinburgh in the late 19th century around the sandy bays each side of the harbour. Impressive Victorian villas were later constructed along the two seafronts.

Above the town is North Berwick Law, an outcrop of volcanic rock 613 feet high, topped with the remains of a Napoleonic-era signal station, and by the replica of a whalebone arch that once stood here. Panoramic views from here take in the sights of Edinburgh Castle and the Forth Bridge to the west, the Fife coastline to the north and the ancient curtain walls of Tantallon Castle and the Lammermuir Hills to the east.

Offshore is the slanting bulk of the Bass Rock, once the plug of a volcano and now an island inhabited by more than 150,000 gannets; their guano gives the rock a white-capped, almost snowy appearance. Boat trips from North Berwick go round the rock in fair weather, or you can get a taste of the avian delights at the Scottish Seabird Centre, overlooking the harbour.

▲ North Berwick's harbour

TAKE IN SOME HISTORY
Tantallon Castle

historicenvironment.scot
Near North Berwick, EH39 5PN
01620 892727 | Open Apr–Sep daily
9.30–5.30; Oct–Mar daily 10–4

Twenty days of blasting from King James V's cannons in 1528 could not destroy this mighty fortress, three miles east of North Berwick. Its great red walls form one of the strongest and most daunting castles in Scotland. Perched on a spur of rock, with sheer cliffs plummeting into frothing seas on three of its sides, the fourth side is protected by a formidable array of ditches and walls. Rising from one of the three great gaping ditches, and sweeping clear across the neck of the promontory, is a vast curtain of red sandstone. This wall is 12 feet thick, and a staggering 50 feet tall. It remains one of the most impressive defensive features of any castle in Britain.

From the 14th century, grim Tantallon was the stronghold of one of Scotland's most famous families – the Red Douglases, Earls of Angus. It came into their hands at the end of the 14th century, and became their base as they plotted and fought against their enemies. It was finally wiped out during the Civil War in 1651 after a long and bloody siege, by General Monk.

GO BIRDING
Scottish Seabird Centre

seabird.org
The Harbour, EH39 4SS | 01620 890202 | Open Apr–Aug daily 10–6; Feb–Mar, Sep–Oct Mon–Fri 10–5, Sat–Sun 10–5.30; Nov–Jan Mon–Fri 10–4, Sat–Sun 10–5.30

Perched on the edge of the sea, the Seabird Centre is the key to the birdlife of the Firth of Forth, in particular the gannet colony that inhabits the Bass Rock. Panoramic views to the islands are excellent. In winter, fluffy white seal pups can be observed on the Isle of May (see page 157), home to Britain's largest grey seal colony.

PLAY A ROUND
North Berwick Golf Club

northberwickgolfclub.com
Beach Road, EH39 4BB | 01620 892135 | Open Mon–Fri, Sun

This is a challenging and traditional links course, with nine holes out and nine in, winding along the shores of the Firth of Forth. Founded in 1832, the club is used as a qualifying course for the Open Championship.

◄ Tantallon Castle

Glen Golf Club

glengolfclub.co.uk
Tantallon Terrace, EH39 4LE
01620 829726 | Open all week,
booking required

This historic course wends its way over the town's East Links. Golf has been played here since the 17th century but the modern course dates from 1906.

EAT AND DRINK

Macdonald Marine Hotel & Spa ⚅⚅

macdonaldhotels.co.uk/marine
Cromwell Road, EH39 4LZ
01620 897300

The wide bay windows of the Craigleith Restaurant overlook the sweep of the East Links. The friendly service keeps things relaxed in this oak-panelled dining room. The food shows some contemporary touches, and is well done. For something less formal, try the Links Bar.

▶ PLACES NEARBY

Dirleton Castle

historicenvironment.scot
EH39 5ER | 01620 850330
Open daily all year

This sturdy castle, now an imposing ruin, was raised in the 13th century, probably on the remains of an earlier fortress. The principal building was the impressive three-storeyed round keep or so-called drum tower, supported by a complex arrangement of other towers and walls.

Dorothea, wife of the rebellious Earl of Gowrie, was probably one of the saddest residents of Dirleton Castle. Her husband was executed in 1585 after a plot to seize Stirling Castle was discovered, and all his lands and castles were taken by King James VI, leaving Dorothea and her 15 children poverty-stricken. The castle and its lands were restored to Dorothea almost two years later. Then, in 1600, two of her sons were involved in the mysterious so-called Gowrie Conspiracy, when it was alleged that they tried to kill the King. Although the maiming of the corpses of Dorothea's sons was very public, details of the entire affair remained secret.

▶ North Uist

see **Western Isles**, page 392

▶ Oban MAP REF 406 B6

There can be few more beautiful settings for a town than that of Oban, a busy rail-head and ferry port for the Western Isles (see page 382), which stands on a curving bay sheltered by the low island of Kerrera.

Its homogenous string of solid Victorian waterfront buildings went up after the railway reached here in 1880. Above the seafront hotels and the bulk of St Columba's Cathedral looms the bizarre granite amphitheatre of McCaig's Tower, erected in 1897 by banker and philanthropist John Stuart McCaig as a family memorial and to relieve local unemployment. It was to have held a museum, with statues in each of the windows, but McCaig died before it could be completed. Today its sheltered interior garden provides a superb viewpoint, and you should climb up here at dusk to watch the glorious sunset over the Firth of Lorne and the mountains of Morvern and Mull.

Oban is definitely the tourist honeypot for this stretch of the western Highlands, with bus tours stopping here all season and day excursions running to Mull and the islands as well as the regular ferry services. The ferries share the harbour with the fishing boats.

SAMPLE THE WHISKY
The Oban Distillery
malts.com
Stafford, Street, PA34 9NH | 01631 572004 | Jul–Sep Mon–Fri 9.30–7.30, Sat–Sun 9.30–5; Mar–Jun, Oct–Nov daily 9.30–5; Dec daily 12–4.30; Jan–Feb daily 9.30–4
There's been a distillery in the centre of Oban since 1794. Take a tour and see how the coastal location affects the taste of the whisky – it's rich and sweet, with a subtle hint of sea salt.

VISIT THE MUSEUM
Oban War and Peace Museum
obanmuseum.org.uk
Old Oban Times Building, Corran Esplanade, PA34 5PX
01631 570007 Open May–Oct Mon–Thu 10–6, Fri–Sun 10–4;

▼ Oban

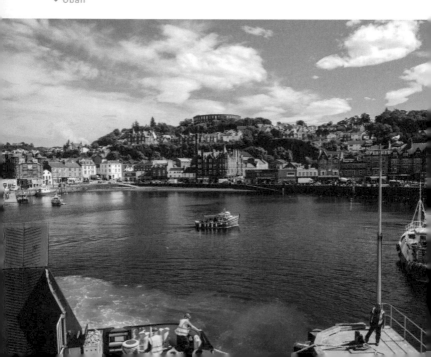

Mar–Apr and Nov daily 10–4

The War and Peace Museum, in the old newspaper offices of the Oban Times, offers an insight into the town during the war years, when flying boats operated from here.

EXPLORE THE DEPTHS
Puffin Dive Centre

puffin.org.uk

Port Gallanach, PA34 4QH | 01631 566088 | Shop open May–Oct Mon 10.30–4.30, Tue–Thu 9–5, Fri 8–5, Sat 8–6, Sun 9–4; Nov–Apr Mon 10.30–4.30, Tue–Sat 9–4.30, Sun 9–4

For an underwater view of Scotland's marine life try a shallow dive with an instructor at this dive centre, one-and-a-half miles south of Oban. All equipment, including dry suits, is included. Advance reservations essential. Not suitable for under-eights.

CATCH A PERFORMANCE
Skipinnish Ceilidh House

34–38 George Street, PA34 5NL 01631 569599 | Open Easter–Oct from 8pm

It may be touristy, but this venue overlooking Oban Bay is still a good option for those wanting to sample the culture. The Scottish Music Show brings Highland dancing, fiddlers, bagpipes and Gaelic singing to the stage. There are ceilidhs and live music throughout the year.

PLAY A ROUND
Glencruitten Golf Club

obangolf.com

Glencruitten Road, PA34 4PU 01631 562868 | Open daily all year

Popular with holidaymakers, the beautiful, isolated course is hilly and testing.

EAT AND DRINK
Coast ❀

coastoban.co.uk

104 George Street, PA34 5NT

01631 569900

Next door to the art gallery, Coast is the very image of a modern brasserie, its granite frontage and expansive windows looking distinctly stately (it used to be a bank). The interior is clean-lined and sharp, the unclothed tables simply laid, with a seasonally changing menu of vivacious brasserie dishes offering something for everyone.

Cuan Mor

cuanmor.co.uk

60 George Street, PA34 5SD

01631 565078

Cuan Mor means big ocean, clearly a reference to the Atlantic. This restaurant and bar makes effective use of reclaimed Ballachulish slate and timbers from the old lighthouse pier in its decor; food is locally sourced with plenty of fish and other seafood. The on-site Oban Bay Brewery produces the real ales, and there are a hundred or so single malts and special blends.

The Lorne

thelornebaroban.co.uk

Stevenson Street, PA34 5NA

01631 570020

Perfectly placed for travellers between the station and the

Mull ferry terminal, this is a family-friendly haven that serves food all day, with the emphasis, during the season, on locally caught seafood. Evenings often offer live music or DJ nights.

Manor House Hotel ⊚⊚
manorhouseoban.com
Gallanach Road, PA34 4LS
01631 562087
If you're looking for something a bit special, head for the wood-panelled dining room hung with oil paintings at the Manor House. Built for the Duke of Argyll in 1780, this hotel sits in a suitably commanding position overlooking the harbour. Cooking is Scottish country house at its best, with local produce well to the fore.

▶ **PLACES NEARBY**

Oban makes a splendid centre for local exploring, and you should certainly head north to take in the stunning coast road.

Dunstaffnage Castle is the first stop, and then pause at Connel, where a fine cantilevered bridge, built in 1903, crosses the mouth of Loch Etive, famous for the tidal waterfall known as the Falls of Lora. North from here you'll find the Sea Life Sanctuary, before heading on and taking a side road that leads down to lovely little Port Appin with Castle Stalker in its bay, just across the water from the long island of Lismore.

Airds Hotel and Restaurant ⊚⊚⊚
airds-hotel.com
Port Appin, PA38 4DF
01631 730236
Beautifully set not far from the ferry landing on Loch Linnhe, the dining room at Airds is a long, tastefully furnished space with large picture windows opening up views over the narrow road towards the loch – naturally enough, the tables closest to the windows are the ones to go for. Expect fine dining using imagination and flair to make the best of local and seasonal ingredients.

Argyll Pottery
Barcaldine, by Oban, PA37 1SQ
01631 720503
Simple, high-quality stoneware pottery is hand-thrown on the wheel at this pottery workshop and shop on the southern shore of Loch Creran, eight miles north of Oban.

◀ A ray, Scottish Sea Life Sanctuary

Dunstaffnage Castle

historicenvironment.scot

PA37 1PZ | 01631 562465

Open Apr–Sep daily 9.30–5.30; Oct daily 10–4; Nov–Mar Sat–Wed 10–4

Built by the MacDougalls as their stronghold in about 1220 – making it one of the oldest stone castles in Scotland – Dunstaffnage Castle guarded the seaward approach to the Firth of Lorne and, by extension, the heart of Scotland.

Today, the castle is a mostly ruined mass of stone, but the gatehouse, two round towers and 10-foot-thick walls survive, standing on a rocky outcrop above the sea. It oversaw the constant struggle to subdue the west by the Crown and Clan Campbell, and was briefly the prison of Flora MacDonald, the gentlewoman who helped Bonnie Prince Charlie escape his pursuers following the Battle of Culloden in 1746.

The Oyster Inn

oysterinn.co.uk

Connel, PA37 1PJ

01631 710666

This 18th-century inn once served ferry passengers, the cannier among them knowing they could be effectively stuck here between ferries and thus evade Oban's Sunday licensing laws. Overlooking the tidal whirlpools and white water of the Falls of Lora, the ferry is long gone, superseded by a modern road bridge, but seafood lovers will find plenty to enjoy on the menu.

The Pierhouse Hotel ❀

pierhousehotel.co.uk

Port Appin, PA38 4DE

01631 730302

Right next to the pier for the Lismore ferry, this waterside restaurant specialises in fish and other seafood. Oysters are hand-picked from the Lismore oyster beds, mussels and langoustines come from Loch Linnhe, and lobsters are kept in creels at the end of the pier, where day boats drop off fish practically at the door.

Scottish Sea Life Sanctuary

sealsanctuary.co.uk

Barcaldine, by Oban, PA37 1SE

01631 720386 | Open daily from 10; call to check closing times

This is Scotland's leading marine animal rescue centre, caring for unwell and injured seals, fish and otters. There are feeding displays, talks, an outdoor play area and an underwater observatory.

Seafari

seafari.co.uk

Easdale Harbour, Seil Island, PA34 4RF | 01852 300003 | Trips run all year, mainly Easter–Oct, and are weather dependent. Book in advance

Enjoy an exhilarating trip on a rigid inflatable boat to see wildlife such as deer, wild goats, seals, seabirds, porpoises, dolphins and the occasional minke whale. Waterproof clothing is provided. There's a minimum age of four. Easdale (Ellanbeich) village is on the bridge-linked island of Seil.

▶ Orkney Islands MAP REF 415 D2

This cluster of more than 70 islands and skerries lies off the northern coast of Scotland and is separated from it by the churning waters of the Pentland Firth. Approaching on the ferry from Scrabster or Aberdeen, the first view of Hoy, with its tall rock stacks and slabby red sandstone cliffs, is misleading. Only when the boat swings towards the harbour at Stromness on Mainland is a more typical view of Orkney revealed – low, green and fertile, with cattle grazing and crops growing. On a warm summer day, the scent of wild flowers in the clean air of these islands is invigorating. Kirkwall, on the eastern side of Mainland – the largest island in the archipelago – is the capital. There is much to explore among the islands, which are linked by causeway, ferry or air, including the shortest scheduled air route in the world – just under two minutes for the one-and-a-half-mile flight between Westray and Papa Westray.

Orkney, like Shetland (see page 352), shares a close history with Scandinavia and tends to regard itself as separate from Scotland, having little in common with, say, the deeply religious and Gaelic culture of the Western Isles (see page 382). Orkney was totally ruled by Norse earls until 1231, and only became part of Scotland in the 15th century, part of a dowry when Margaret of Denmark married Scottish king James III. Today, these islands ring with the Norse place names of the Scandinavians who lived here – although Picts and Celts pre-dated the Vikings by at least 3,500 years, leaving incredible signs of their presence at Maes Howe and Skara Brae. Reminders of a more recent history are also all around, in the remains of gun emplacements and the giant concrete blocks of the Churchill Barriers, recalling a time when the sheltered bay of Scapa Flow was a vital naval base through two world wars.

▶ Mainland MAP REF 415 D3

Mainland is the main island of Orkney. Both of Orkney's burghs, Kirkwall and Stromness, lie on the island, which is also the heart of Orkney's ferry and air connections. There is fertile farmland and an abundance of wildlife, seabirds in particular.

Seventy-five per cent of Orkney's population live on Mainland, which is more densely populated than the other islands of the archipelago. The lengthy history of the island's occupation has provided numerous important archaeological sites and the sandstone bedrock provides a platform for fertile farmland. There is an abundance of wildlife, especially seabirds.

▲ Harray Loch, Orkney

EXPLORE THE TOWNS
Kirkwall
see page 318

Stromness
see page 320

TAKE IN SOME HISTORY
Earl's Palace
historicenvironment.scot
Birsay, KW15 1PD
Open access
Until the construction of
Kirkwall Cathedral, the heart
of Norse power lay in Birsay,
in the northwest corner of
Mainland, and it was here that
their successors, the Scottish
earls, built their vast Earl's
Palace, whose gaunt sandstone
ruins still survive. The
courtyarded castle you see
today, now ruined, went up in
the early 1570s, and was built
for Earl Robert Stewart,
half-brother to Mary, Queen of
Scots – he was the illegitimate
son of King James V by his
mistress Euphemia Elphinstone
– and a much-hated tyrannical
outsider to the Orcadians. He
died in 1593.

Brough of Birsay

historicenvironment.scot
Birsay, KW17 2LX | Open mid-Jun to
Sep daily, 2 hours each side of low tide

On a small islet accessible only
during two hours each side of
low tide, is the Brough of Birsay,
originally a substantial Pictish
settlement and later a monastic
complex. Its focus is the
12th-century sandstone church
of St Peter's, and there are
Viking remains to explore,
including a sauna and some
remarkably sophisticated drains.

GO BACK IN TIME

Maes Howe, Stenness and the Ring of Brodgar

historicenvironment.scot
KW16 3HH | 01861 761606
Open Apr–Sep daily 9.30–5; Oct–
Mar daily 10–4; guided tours only,
departing from Maeshowe Visitor
Centre, advance booking essential

Near the Bridge of Waith, at
the end of the Loch of Harray,
stands a group of some of the
most impressive Neolithic
monuments in Europe, a World
Heritage Site since 1999. A
grassy mound 23 feet high in
a field, Maes Howe looks
unpromising at first sight.
Under the turf, however, lies a
chambered grave dating from
about 2800 BC, the finest
passage grave in Britain and
one of the wonders of the
prehistoric world.

You must take your turn
and bend double to walk
through the 47-foot entrance
passageway, before you
emerge into the beautifully
formed inner chamber, which is
almost 12.5 feet high and 15
feet square. The walls are lined
with neatly fitting stone slabs,
the roof is corbelled and there

◀ Whalebone, Birsay

are three small side chambers. A large monolith stands at each corner of the chamber, while, on both sides, regular rectangular openings give access to the small side cells, which may have been used to inter the bones of the tomb's occupants.

It has been estimated that the construction of Maes Howe, incorporating 30 tons of Orcadian sandstone, would have taken 100,000 man hours – an incredible feat of Neolithic organisation and engineering. This is manifest in the incredible fact that the tomb is aligned so that the rays of the sun on the winter solstice reach straight down the passage and illuminate one of the interior ledges. While the contents were looted centuries ago and can only be guessed at, the structure itself has survived more or less undamaged, barring some runic graffiti left by passing Vikings.

Nearby, standing between the lochs of Stenness and Harray, are the Ring of Brodgar and the Stenness stone circles, also dating from the New Stone Age. The 340-foot-wide Ring of Brodgar is the third largest stone circle in the British Isles. Covering an area of 90,793 sq feet, it stands on an eastward-sloping plateau on the Ness o' Brodgar – the thin strip of land separating the Harray and Stenness lochs. It's enclosed within a massive 345-foot diameter rock-cut ditch, with two entrance causeways. It originally consisted of about 60 standing stones, of which only 27 remain today. They are thought to have been erected some time between 2500 and 2000 BC.

The sheer scale of the four elegant, blade-like standing stones of Stenness, which reach a height of almost 20 feet, makes it one of the most striking of Orkney's prehistoric monuments. Located on the southeastern shore of the Loch of Stenness, about a mile from the Ring of Brodgar, the Stones of Stenness were originally laid out in about 3100 BC in the form of an ellipse, and, like Brodgar, the Stenness circle has been classed as a henge, as it was originally surrounded by a 144-foot-diameter rock-cut ditch. The henge had a single entrance causeway on the north side, outside which was a substantial earth bank, although little remains of this today.

Skara Brae
see highlight panel overleaf

▶ **PLACES NEARBY**

North of Mainland are other islands to explore, all linked by ferry and air to Kirkwall. Many have prehistoric remains, ruined castles and other attractions, and all have a strong sense of community. If you have time, Westray and North Ronaldsay are particularly worth a visit.

▶ Skara Brae MAP REF 415 D3

historicenvironment.scot
KW16 3LR | 01861 841815 | Open Apr–Sep daily 9.30–5.30; Oct–Mar
daily 10–4

The remains of a stone-built Neolithic village, concealed for
centuries under the sand, are Orkney's must see sight, offering
a unique window into a domestic world long gone.

It's sometimes tempting to believe that our prehistoric
ancestors, who left so little record of their daily existence, were not
very clever and lived wretchedly in dark hovels. A visit to Skara
Brae suggests otherwise, and can be an eye-opening experience.
Here you can get an unparalleled taste of what life was like more
than 4,000 years ago as you step into one of the eight surviving
dwellings. Lying 19 miles northwest of Kirkwall, the village was
inhabited between 3100 and 2500 BC, probably originally some
distance from the sea. At some point the sands encroached and
covered the houses, which lay undiscovered until a great storm in
1850 revealed the presence of stone structures. Subsequent

excavation showed eight houses linked by winding passageways, their dry-stone walls buried to the eaves by the surrounding midden pits, which probably provided some degree of insulation.

As you walk around the site today, you are looking down into the houses from above, through what would have been roofs of skin and turf laid over timber spars or whalebone. Slabs of the local flagstone were used to create central hearths, cupboards in the walls, bed surrounds, clay-lined troughs in the floor and even a dresser, suggesting a level of sophistication that is as delightful as it is unexpected.

A reconstructed house by the visitor centre shows how animal skins and bracken would have helped to make the dwellings cosy, and fragments of jewellery, tools and pottery give further insights into the lives of these mysterious people. And although very little is known about them, it's easy to relate to the kind of people they must have been – fixing their fishing hooks, eating seafood (myriad mussel shells were found in the middens), protecting themselves against the elements, and occasionally putting on their finery, just as people still do today.

▶ Kirkwall MAP REF 415 E4

There's been a settlement here since the 11th century, and today Kirkwall – the name means church bay – is the main town of Orkney. Many of the compact buildings in the narrow, paved streets of the old harbour town date from the 16th to the 18th centuries, and the long main street is lined with little shops, including high-quality crafts and jewellers. Dominating all is the red sandstone bulk of St Magnus Cathedral on Broad Street.

TAKE IN SOME HISTORY

St Magnus Cathedral

stmagnus.org

Broad Street, KW15 1NX | 01856 874894 | Open Apr–Sep Mon–Sat 9–6, Sun 1–6; Oct–Mar Mon–Sat 9–1, 2–4

St Magnus Cathedral was begun by Earl Rognvald in 1137 and completed in the 15th century; he was the great-nephew of St Magnus, murdered 20 years previously, and both he and the saint are buried here. Inside, the huge Romanesque pillars and decorative stonework create a sense of space and peace.

Bishop's and Earl's Palaces

historicenvironment.scot

Watergate, KW15 1PD | 01856 871918 | Open Apr–Sep daily 9.30–5.30; Oct daily 10–4

Nearby are the ruins of the Bishop's Palace, residence of the Bishops of Orkney from the 12th century. Its tower is still intact and there's a great view from the top. It's just a few steps from here to the far better-preserved Renaissance

▼ Kirkwall Harbour

Earl's Palace, built using forced labour in about 1600, complete with a splendid central hall, dungeons and a very civilised set of 17th-century toilets.

TRY THE WHISKY
Highland Park
highlandparkwhisky.com
Holm Road, Kirkwall, KW15 1SU
01856 874619 | Open May–Sep
Mon–Sat 10–5, Sun 12–5; Sep–Apr
Mon–Fri 10–5; Tours Apr–Sep hourly
until 4pm, Oct–Mar 2 and 3pm
Explore the most northerly malt whisky distillery in the world, founded in 1798. Watch the audio-visual presentation 'The Spirit of Orkney' and then take a guided tour.

CATCH A PERFORMANCE
Orkney Arts Theatre
orkneytheatre.co.uk
The Meadows, Kirkwall, KW15 1QN
07562 355111
This small theatre in the town centre hosts a variety of amateur theatre, opera and touring productions through the year. Check locally for show information.

GO TO THE MOVIES
New Phoenix Cinema
pickaquoy.com
Muddisdale Road, Kirkwall,
KW15 1LR | 01856 879900
Britain's most northerly cinema is in the Pickaquoy leisure centre. The centre also has a gym, sports arena and athletics track.

PLAY A ROUND
Orkney Golf Club
orkneygolfclub.co.uk
Grainbank, Kirkwall, KW15 1RD
01856 872457
This open parkland course has few hazards and superb views over Kirkwall and islands. It's very exposed to the elements, which can make play tough.

▶ Stromness MAP REF 415 D4

Orkney's second town, Stromness, with its narrow, paved
streets and quaint closes, climbs steeply from its harbour on
Orkney Mainland across the impressive tidal race of Hoy Sound.
Its history has always been closely tied to the sea; its
foundation dates back at least to Viking times, and its natural
harbour and relatively calm waters have provided a haven for
generations of seafarers using the surrounding storm-tossed
waters of the Atlantic Ocean and the North Sea.

Orkney and its seaways have always been a strategic
point for navigation, and in times of war, such as during the
Napoleonic Wars and World Wars I and II, they have been used
as an alternative route to the potentially dangerous English
Channel. Stromness boomed in the early 19th century as a
centre for Arctic whaling, and a key stopping point for vessels
of the Hudson's Bay Company who took on crew and supplies
here, and fresh water from nearby Login's Well. The houses
and stores on the waterfront date from the 18th and 19th
centuries and each has its own slipway, while the town's
winding main street is paved with the local huge sandstone
slabs and cobbles.

VISIT THE MUSEUM AND ARTS CENTRE

Pier Arts Centre
pierartscentre.com
Victoria Street, KW16 3AA | 01861
850209 | Open Mon–Sat 10.30–5
For some cutting-edge culture,
take in the impressive Pier
Arts Centre, beacon of
contemporary art in the
shape of both permanent and
temporary exhibitions.

Stromness Museum
orkneycommunities.co.uk/
stromnessmuseum
52 Alfred Street, KW16 3DH
01861 850025 | Open Apr–Oct daily
10–5; Nov–Mar Mon–Sat 11–3.30
At the southern end of the
town's main street, various
maritime delights are
displayed in the excellent
Stromness Museum.

EXPLORE THE DEPTHS

Scapa Scuba
scapascuba.co.uk
Lifeboat House, Stromness,
KW16 3DA | 01856 851218
Scapa Flow is rated as one of
the world's greatest dive sites,
and those with suitable
scuba-diving qualifications and
experience can take a guided
dive among the Scapa Flow
shipwrecks. Scapa Scuba also
operates guided dives from the
beautiful shoreline at the
Churchill Barriers.

EAT AND DRINK

The Ferry Inn
ferryinn.com
Stromness, KW16 3AD
01856 850280
With its prominent harbour-
front location, the Ferry Inn
has long enjoyed a reputation

for local ales – although the beers change regularly, look out for the island's own Dark Island and Skull Splitter. If beer isn't your thing, there are plenty of wines and malt whiskies to choose from, as well as an appealing menu.

▶ Hoy MAP REF 415 D4

The second largest of the Orkney islands, Hoy derives its name from the Old Norse term Haey, meaning high island, and its soaring west-coast cliffs and isolated sea stacks, known as geos, are a huge contrast with the pastoral landscape of Mainland. Its best-known feature is the columnar stack of red sandstone just off the western cliffs, known as the Old Man of Hoy. Standing 450 feet high, it was first climbed in 1966, and remains a challenge for climbers.

All the cliffs of Hoy provide a home to numerous seabirds, and for this reason the west coast of Hoy is an RSPB reserve, providing an airy home for about 120,000 birds. These include nationally important populations of fulmar, great black-backed gull and guillemot. Among the big attractions at the reserve are the ever-popular puffins, great skuas and raptors such as hen harriers. These are best seen in the spring, while in summer the cliffs are alive with the squabbling, nesting seabirds. You can also see whales and dolphins in the waters here during the warmer summer months.

The heather-covered hills of Cuilags (1,420 feet) and Ward Hill (1,570 feet) offer excellent walking country, or you could track down the Dwarfie Stane, a unique Neolithic rock-cut chambered tomb carved out of a huge block of sandstone. There is a poignant monument on Hoy to a girl named Betty Corrigall, who was left, unmarried and pregnant, when her boyfriend departed on a whaling ship. She killed herself, and

▼ Mountains of Hoy

▲ Churchill Barriers

as a suicide she could not be buried in consecrated ground. For years she lay in an unmarked grave until her body was moved in 1940 to its present location and she was given a decent reburial.

GO TO THE VISITOR CENTRE
Scapa Flow Visitor Centre
scapaflow.co.uk
Lyness, KW16 3NT | 01856 790300
Closed until 2019 for redevelopment; temporary centre during 2018 at Lyness
This fascinating centre will fill you in on the wartime history of Scapa Flow.

▶ **Scapa Flow, Churchill Barriers & South Ronaldsay** MAP REF 415 E4

Scapa Flow is the vast, sheltered bay enclosed by the islands of Mainland, Hoy and South Ronaldsay, which was once a main base for the Royal Navy. It was its home during two world wars, and famously the site of the scuttling of the German fleet after the end of World War I, in 1919. The remains now prove popular with wreck divers.

Mainland and South Ronaldsay are linked by a causeway, via the small island of Burray, known as the Churchill Barriers. These were built in 1940 as anti-submarine defences after a

German sub slipped into the Flow and sunk the battleship HMS *Royal Oak* in 1939. They were largely built by Italian prisoners-of-war, who, far from home and in a strange culture, converted two Nissen huts to make a chapel. The inside is beautifully painted with frescoes and trompe-l'oeil on plasterboard and concrete mouldings, with even a rood screen. The extraordinary result is a moving tribute to the ingenuity, skill and imagination of the prisoners, which the islanders have carefully preserved.

South Ronaldsay's main settlement is the little village of St Margaret's Hope, named after Margaret, daughter of the King of Norway, who is thought to have died here in 1290 on her way to her wedding with the English Prince Edward (later Edward II).

GO BACK IN TIME
Tomb of the Eagles
tomboftheeagles.co.uk
Liddle, KW17 2RW | 01856 831339
Open Mar daily 10–12; Apr–Sep daily 9.30–5.30; Oct daily 9.30–12.30
The Tomb of the Eagles is a chambered prehistoric cairn on a cliff's edge, with a visitor centre.

5 top ancient sites

▶ **Skara Brae**, page 316

▶ **Calanais Standing Stones**, page 390

▶ **Maes Howe**, page 314

▶ **Dun Telve and Dun Troddan brochs**, page 236

▶ **Jarlshof**, page 359

▶ **Oronsay**
see **Western Isles**, page 386

▶ **Outer Hebrides**
see **Western Isles**, page 389

▶ **Paisley** MAP REF 401 F3

Paisley, on Glasgow's western outskirts and just south of the
airport, is a historic town that in the Middle Ages was as
important, or arguably more important, than Glasgow itself.
It was an important weaving town, lending its name to the
colourful woollen shawls that were manufactured here during
the 19th century. It's also home to one of Scotland's best
preserved medieval churches. It's claimed that the Scots hero
William Wallace was born at Elderslie, south of the town
centre, where you'll find a monument to him – one of many
scattered all over Scotland.

TAKE IN SOME HISTORY
Paisley Abbey
paisleyabbey.org.uk
Abbey Close, PA1 1JG | 0141 889
7654 | Open Mon–Sat 10–3.30; Sun
services at 11, 12.15 and 6.30pm

Paisley Abbey, founded in 1163,
escaped the devastation visited
on the abbeys of Border towns
like Melrose (see page 297) and
Jedburgh (see page 262) by
English invaders, only to fall
victim to Presbyterian
iconoclasts during the
Reformation. It was restored
during the 19th century, and is
now graced by colourful
stained-glass windows and fine
stonework. King Robert III is
buried here, and you can also
see the ancient Barochan
Cross, one of the oldest Celtic
Christian relics in Britain.

VISIT THE MUSEUM
Paisley Museum
museumsgalleriesscotland.org.uk
High Street, PA1 2BA | 0300 3001210
Open Tue–Sat 11–4, Sun 2–5

◀ St Mirin, patron saint
of Paisley

▲ Neidpath Castle

The swirling patterns associated with Paisley's weaving mills didn't, in fact, originate here – they were borrowed from north Indian traditions. Vintage Paisley shawls are sought-after collectors' items, commanding high prices. You can see some gorgeous examples in this museum, which also has a collection of portraits and landscapes by Scottish painters.

▶ **PLACES NEARBY**

Glasgow (see page 206) is just 25 minutes by car, or 10 by rail.

▶ **Peebles** MAP REF 402 C4

The broad main street of this bustling Borders town, 35 miles south of Edinburgh, always seems busy, its small shops and family businesses – there are few high-street multiples here – doing a brisk trade. Visitors come here to shop for locally made knitwear and enjoy the peace and fresh air of this pleasant country town. There's a fine five-arched bridge over the Tweed, first erected in 1476, a venerable Mercat Cross and the remains of a couple of early churches.

Walks, trails and cycleways lead into the wooded countryside, starting with the walk upstream from the park along the River Tweed to Neidpath Castle, a 14th-century tower set high above the river, now used for weddings and events.

TAKE IN SOME HISTORY
Neidpath Castle
neidpathcastle.co.uk
EH45 8NW | 01721 720333
This historic and interesting tower house is mainly used for events, and it's an intriguing building, its four main floors intersected with mural passages and entresols, or mezzanine floors, giving the impression that the castle is full of small chambers and passages, all at different heights. Its L-plan tower was built in the second half of the 14th century, when local landowners had the task of establishing law and order in their domains.

The upper two floors were remodelled in the 17th century, while the lower floor contained a pit prison and a well. On the second floor is a room with some fine 17th-century panelling. You can arrange a private visit for small groups by telephoning.

Traquair House
see page 377

PLAY A ROUND
Macdonald Cardrona Golf
macdonaldhotels.co.uk/cardrona
EH45 8NE | 0344 879 9024 | Open daily all year
Designed and opened in 2001, these two championship courses were laid out with the American market in mind and feature wide fairways and undulating greens set in park and woodland.

Peebles Golf Club
peeblesgolfclub.com
Kirkland Street, EH45 8EU
01721 720197 | Open daily all year
This parkland course is one of the most picturesque in Scotland, shadowed by the border hills and Tweed Valley and set high above the town. The tough opening holes are balanced by a more generous stretch through to the 14th hole but from here the closing five prove a challenging test.

EAT AND DRINK
Macdonald Cardrona Hotel, Golf & Spa
macdonaldhotels.co.uk/cardrona
EH45 8NE | 0844 879 9024
Renwicks Restaurant is housed in this swish modern hotel on the banks of the River Tweed, and a wall of glass is all that separates diners from the championship golf course. You can expect straightforward and gently modern cooking, with the accent on regional produce.

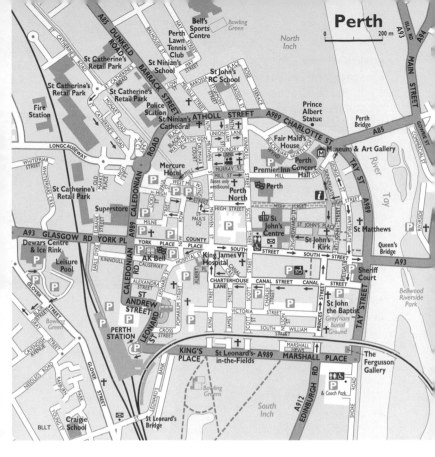

▶ Perth MAP REF 402 B1

The Roman settlement of Perth was founded along the banks of the Tay, Scotland's longest river, in the first century AD; by the Middle Ages it was the capital of Scotland. It's been a Royal Burgh since 1210, when William I granted its charter, and it regained city status in 2012, when Elizabeth II restored this in honour of her Diamond Jubilee. Today, it's a lively city at the centre of a prosperous farming community, whose February and October bull sales are the biggest of their kind in Europe, with buyers jetting in from all over the world. The city's compact and attractive core offers great shopping and bohemian cafes that spill onto the pavements, while its riverside setting, with Kinnoull Hill rising on the opposite bank, adds to its appeal.

With its theatre, City Hall, up-to-the-minute concert hall and other venues, not to mention galleries and cinemas, Perth is an active centre for music and the arts, culminating in a lively festival in May. The centre is enclosed by two historic parks, the North and South Inches, and there are several gardens to explore nearby.

Historic Scone Palace (see page 350) lies virtually on the outskirts of the city. It's still the family seat of the Earls of Mansfield, and was the ancient crowning place of Scottish kings from the time of Robert the Bruce. Forty-two kings were crowned on the Stone of Scone. After its theft from Westminster Abbey in 1950, the Stone was left at Arbroath Abbey before being returned to London. Since 1996 the rugged block has been kept in Edinburgh Castle.

▲ Kinnoull Hill

TAKE IN SOME HISTORY
St John's Kirk

st-johns-kirk.co.uk
31 St John's Place, PH1 5SZ | 01738 633192 | Open Apr daily 11–3; May–Sep daily 10–4, Oct–Mar service times only

Perth was once called St John's Toun, and this is the church that gave the city its name – still held by Perth's football club. It's the city's oldest surviving building and dates from the 13th century. John Knox preached fire and brimstone here and thus launched the Reformation in Scotland, Bonnie Prince Charlie worshipped here, and it's been a prison and a courthouse. Today, it's a tranquil and welcoming church in the heart of the city.

VISIT THE MUSEUMS AND GALLERY
Black Watch Regimental Museum

theblackwatch.co.uk
Balhousie Castle, Hay Street,
PH1 5HR | 01738 638152 | Open Apr–Oct daily 9.30–4.30; Nov–Mar daily 10–4

There's been a castle here since the 12th century; today's structure dates from the 1860s, and is now home to one of Scotland's most iconic regimental museums, the famous Black Watch, founded in Perthshire in 1739. There are films to watch and stories to listen to, as well as uniforms, paintings, medals, diaries, weapons and photographs, all telling the story of the Regiment right up to the recent conflicts in Iraq and Afghanistan.

Perth Museum and Art Gallery

pkc.gov.uk
78 George Street, PH1 5LB | 01738 632488 | Open Apr–Oct Tue–Sun 10–5; Nov–Mar Tue–Sat 10–5

Perth Museum is a fine provincial collection, which, as well as wide and eclectic

▲ Branklyn Garden

applied arts and archaeological
sections, also has some good
paintings, mainly donated and
reflecting the tastes of the
Perthshire gentry. Among the
works by Scottish masters like
Raeburn and MacTaggart, look
out for a charming clutch of
mushrooms by Beatrix Potter
and a series of Perthshire
landscapes – fun to compare
with what we see today.

GO ROUND THE GARDEN
Branklyn Garden
nts.org.uk
Dundee Road, PH2 7BB | 01738
625535 | Open Apr–Oct daily 10–5
Branklyn covers just 2 acres
and has plants predominantly
from China, Tibet and Bhutan,
with an outstanding collection
of Himalayan poppies, which
flourish in its micro-climate.
It's a plantsman's garden,
where keen gardeners will
find rare treasures and a lot
of inspiration.

ENTERTAIN THE FAMILY
**Noah's Ark Family
Entertainment Centre**
noahs-perth.co.uk
Western Edge, PH1 1QE | 01738
445568 | Open daily 10–6
Family fun, with a soft play
area for very young children,
an indoor karting track and
10-pin bowling alley. There's
also a ceramic-painting studio
and a cafe.

GO SWIMMING
Perth Leisure Pool
Glasgow Road, PH2 0HZ | 01738
454654 | Open Mon–Sat 10–8.30,
Sun 10–5
The pool complex at this
leisure centre is great for rainy
days. A range of water slides,
flumes, shallow areas and
interactive water play areas for
smaller children will help keep
all the family entertained. The
slides and flumes are often
closed during school hours
so call ahead.

▲ Perth Concert Hall

CATCH A PERFORMANCE
Perth Concert Hall
horsecross.co.uk
Mill Street, PH1 5HZ
01738 621031
Perth Concert Hall, opened in 2005, is home to an exciting programme of music, new media arts, community events and conferences. The concert hall has a year-round music programme of world-class classics, world and Scottish traditions, living legends, breaking artists and more. Look out too for a mix of comedy, dance, film and children's events.

Perth Theatre
horsecross.co.uk
185 High Street, PH1 5UW
01738 621031
Behind an art deco frontage on the High Street lies Perth's only theatre, home to a resident company of actors, and visiting shows. Film star Ewan McGregor learned his craft here. There's music and comedy as well as drama.

PLAY A ROUND
Craigie Hill Golf Club
craigiehill.com
Cherrybank, PH2 0NE | 01738 622644 | Open daily all year
This slightly hilly, heathland course, with panoramic views of Perth and the surrounding hills, was founded in 1911. It has one of the generally acknowledged most challenging holes in Britain, the famous Spion Kop, a tough par four.

King James VI Golf Club
kingjamesvi.com
Moncreiffe Island, PH2 8NR | 01738 632460 | Open daily all year
You'll have to cross a footbridge to get to this parkland course, set on Moncreiffe Island in the River Tay. It's gentler than some, with easy walking and a lovely position.

Murrayshall House Hotel & Golf Course
murrayshall.co.uk
Murrayshall, PH2 7PH | 01738 658217 | Open daily all year

Set within 350 acres of undulating parkland, Murrayshall offers 36 holes of outstanding golf. The original championship course is set out within the parkland estate and the Lynedoch is a woodland-style course, full of natural features. Many of the fairways are lined by majestic trees, while white-sand bunkers and water hazards with natural stone bridges protect the generous greens.

EAT AND DRINK

63 Tay Street Restaurant ◉◉

63taystreet.com
63 Tay Street, PH2 8NN
01738 441451

This popular local restaurant occupies part of the ground floor of an imposing stone building on the Tay riverside. A shipboard feel is created by porthole mirrors, and the decor is all about stripped-back elegance, with a bare floor and claret-hued seating. 'Local, honest, simple' is the stated motto.

Deans Restaurant ◉◉

letseatperth.co.uk
77 79 Kinnoull Street, PH1 5EZ
01738 643377

Deans really is a family-run joint, right in the centre of town, in the heart of the action, and it delivers modern Scottish flavours in a vibrant and easy-going atmosphere. The red room provides a soothing respite if the weather is grim, with colourful prints adorning the walls and the darkwood

tables left free of formal white linen. The kitchen turns out some skilfully executed dishes.

Pig'Halle ◉

pighalle.co.uk
38 South Street, PH2 8PG
01738 248784

On a busy street in the centre of Perth, Pig'Halle has been given a Parisian look, with a map of the Métro embossed on a large mirror, wine memorabilia, some banquette seating and red-upholstered round-backed chairs at darkwood tables. It's an atmospheric, buzzy sort of place, with people drawn by the bistro-style cooking and the French-inspired menu.

Tabla ◉

tablarestaurant.co.uk
173 South Street, PH2 8NY
01738 444630

Don't miss out on the richly satisfying, traditional Indian home-cooking of this central Perth eatery. The ambience has more personality than many a formula Indian restaurant, with exposed stone walls, full-drop windows and a glass panel looking into the kitchen. Indian music featuring the eponymous tabla drums plays softly.

▶ PLACES NEARBY

Scone Palace (see page 350) is the obvious attraction, but you can also head west to Crieff (see page 114), east to Dundee (see page 135), or north to Dunkeld (see page 149). Lochleven Castle (see page 284) is to the south.

▶ Peterhead MAP REF 409 F2

Built of the local red granite, Peterhead is Scotland's most easterly town. It owed its early development to the Keith family, the Earls Marischal. Their castle at Inverugie, outside Peterhead, is now a melancholy ruin. In the 18th century the town became for a time a smart spa for upper-crust patrons of its warm springs. The harbour proved a more durable asset, however; in the 1880s a prison was built on the bay, and felons were put to work on harbour improvements.

By the 19th century Peterhead had become a leading whaling port, later turning to herring fishing, and later still to white fish. In 1990, it was the premier white-fish port in Europe, with approximately £70 million worth of catches landed in the capacious harbour of Peterhead Bay. Overfishing of cod and haddock, however, and quotas to protect stocks, have made the future uncertain, although the fishing trade remains important. The town has developed a second string to its bow as a supply base for the North Sea oil and gas rigs.

VISIT THE MUSEUM
Arbuthnot Museum
aberdeenshire.gov.uk
St Peter Street, AB42 1QD | 01779 477778 | Open Mon–Tue, Thu–Fri 10–12.30, 1.30–4, Sat 10–12.30, 1.30–3.30
The focus is on the maritime history of Peterhead, with lots on the whaling and fishing industries and some fascinating photographs of the time when sailors from here spread across the world, bringing back the Inuit artefacts still displayed.

PLAY A ROUND
Peterhead Golf Club
peterheadgolfclub.co.uk
Riverside Drive, AB42 1LT | 01779 472149 | Open daily all year
There's both an 18- and a 9-hole course here; equally challenging, these are classic dune links, set beside the sea, with all that that implies.

EAT AND DRINK
Buchan Braes Hotel ❀
buchanbraes.co.uk
Boddam, AB42 3AR | 01779 871471
About five minutes' drive from Peterhead, Buchan Braes won't win any architectural prizes, but it's a spiffy contemporary hotel with lovely views to Stirling Hill. There's also the Grill Room restaurant, serving award-winning food, and a lounge for quick meals and snacks.

5 top views

- Edinburgh from **Arthur's Seat**, page 178
- Glasgow from **Glasgow Necropolis**, page 212
- Firth of Tay and the Sidlaws from **Dundee Law**, page 143
- Scott's View, Melrose, page 300
- Queen's View, Perthshire, page 336

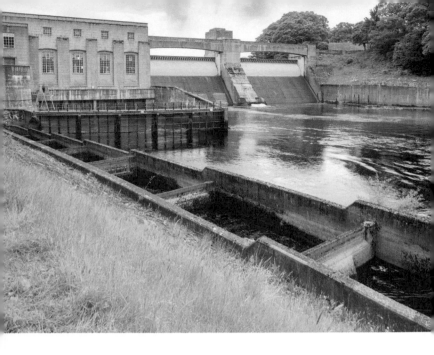

▲ Hydroelectric power station, River Tummel

▶ Pitlochry MAP REF 408 B5

This bustling town in the wooded valley of the River Tummel
is based around one long main street. The geographical heart
of Scotland, it's surrounded by some wonderful scenery, and
boasts two distilleries. It first appeared on the map when
General Wade built a military road through here, and it's been
a popular holiday resort since the 19th century.

From the town centre a footbridge leads across the river to
the Festival Theatre, with its Explorers' Garden, opened in 2003
to celebrate 300 years of botanical exploration. The theatre
hosts an ever-changing programme of drama and concerts.
There's a view from the footbridge to the hydroelectric dam,
which features a salmon ladder, a series of rising artificial
pools to enable wild migrating salmon to get upriver to their
spawning grounds. The building of the dam, part of a system
along the river and through the surrounding hills, also created
Loch Faskally, a local beauty spot above the dam. Pitlochry's
two distilleries both welcome visitors: the Blair Athol Distillery
in the town centre, and tiny Edradour on the outskirts.

VISIT A DAM
Pitlochry Dam Visitor Centre
and Salmon Ladder
pitlochrydam.com
Armoury Road, PH16 5AP

01796 484111
Open daily 9.30–5.30
The story of the construction of
the dam and how the intricate
inter-linked system of pipes

and tunnels generates power throughout the whole of Highland Perthshire is here, but the main draw is the salmon ladder observation chamber. Peer through the window into the peaty water and you may be lucky enough to spy a salmon making its way through the chambers to Loch Faskally, at the top of the dam.

TRY THE WHISKY
Bell's Blair Athol Distillery
bells.co.uk/the-distillery
Perth Road, PH16 5LY | 01796 482003 | Open Easter–Sep Mon–Sat 9.30–5, Sun 12–5; Oct Mon–Fri 10–5; Nov–Easter Mon–Fri 10–4, Founded in 1798 this is one of the oldest working distilleries in Scotland.

Edradour Distillery
edradour.co.uk

Moulin, PH16 5JP | 01796 472095
Open 3 Apr–Oct Mon–Sat 10–5, Sun 12–5; Nov–Mar Mon–Fri 10–4.30
Scotland's smallest distillery produces a mere 12 casks of malt whisky a week, and is set in a picturesque hillside location east of Pitlochry.

EXPLORE BY BIKE
Escape Route
escape-route.co.uk
3 Atholl Road, PH16 5BX | 01796 473859 | Open Mon–Sat 9–5.30, Sun 10–5
Staff at this bicycle hire shop are real outdoor enthusiasts and can provide maps and advice about the best local routes. Mountain and hybrid bicycles, tandems, trailers and child seats are available. Walking gear is also available to buy or hire.

▼ Loch Tummel from Queen's View, Pitlochry

CATCH A PERFORMANCE
Pitlochry Festival Theatre
pitlochryfestivaltheatre.com
Port Na Craig, PH16 5DR | 01796
484626 | Open May–Oct;
performances daily during main
season, see website for rest of year

A modern venue with lovely
views across the River Tummel
to the town, the Festival Theatre
is open in summer and autumn,
with different concerts and
touring shows every night.

EAT AND DRINK
Fonab Castle Hotel
fonabcastlehotel.com
Foss Road, PH16 5ND
01796 470140

Fonab is a castellated pile of
reddish stone with glassed-in
views over Loch Faskally from
both the Brasserie and the
upmarket Sandeman
restaurant, the latter so-named
in honour of the port-shipping
family who once owned the
house. A display of pedigree
single malts and gins adds
distinction. The cooking, based
on local produce, goes for a
bold contemporary approach,
producing dishes that are full of
striking combinations without
too much showing off.

Green Park Hotel
thegreenpark.co.uk
Clunie Bridge Road, PH16 5JY
01796 473248

There are lovely views over
Loch Faskally from the dining
room here, where you can enjoy
country-house cooking for the
21st century, with traditional
and friendly service.

Knockendarroch 🏵🏵
knockendarroch.co.uk
Higher Oakfield, PH16 5HT
01796 473473

This is a country-house hotel
with a country-house
restaurant, where traditional

hospitality goes hand-in-hand with food that emphasises seasonality and local produce.

▶ **PLACES NEARBY**

Some three miles north of Pitlochry is the narrow, wooded gorge of Killiecrankie (see page 267), on the River Garry. This was the site of a battle in 1689.

On the way there you'll pass the conservation village of Moulin, with its 17th-century church and ruined castle in the shadow of Ben Vrackie. The writer Robert Louis Stevenson stayed here in 1881, and described it as a 'sweet spot'.

A short drive to the west along the River Tummel, meanwhile, is the **Queen's View**. This vantage point overlooks Loch Tummel, and is one of Scotland's iconic panoramas.

▶ **Plockton** MAP REF 405 E2

Palm trees grow in Plockton, encouraged by the mild Gulf Stream air. Also encouraged are small-boat sailors, artists, holidaymakers and retired people, who come to this sheltered bay on Loch Carron, with its tidy cottages commanding marvellous views seawards, or inland to the mountains and forests.

Plockton is a planned fishing village established in the early 19th century, and is now within the National Trust for Scotland's magnificent Balmacara Estate. It faces across the narrow neck of the inner loch to the ruins of Strome Castle, once a formidable stronghold of the MacDonalds.

At one time the harbour, protected by a promontory running out into the loch like a natural pier, was busy with cargo schooners plying to and from Baltic ports, and with the local fishing boats. Herring was taken by sea down to Glasgow (see page 206), Greenock (see page 240) and the Clyde, and salt and other necessities were brought back. All that changed with a decline in the herring stocks and the potato famine of the 1840s: the village became depopulated, with many of those unable to make a living by the sea deciding to emigrate abroad.

LEARN ABOUT CROFTING

Balmacara Estate

nts.org.uk

Kyle, IV40 8DN | 01559 566325

Plockton Visitor Centre open Apr–Oct daily 11–7; woodland walks daily all year 9–dusk

This crofting estate of more than 6,000 acres (2,500 hectares) on the Lochalsh peninsula has a huge range of superb and diverse scenery and some fascinating archaeological and historical features. There are two crofting townships, Drumbuie and Duirinish, on the NTS land. You can learn more at the Plockton Visitor Centre before striding out on the Lochalsh Woodland Walk.

MEET THE ANIMALS
Craig Highland Farm and
Conservation Centre
craighighlandfarm.co.uk
Plockton, IV52 8UB | 01599 544205

This croft with ancient and rare breeds of Scottish farm animals and fowl is in a beautiful setting on the shores of Loch Carron.

▶ Portpatrick MAP REF 398 A5

What Gretna Green (see page 241) was to runaway English couples, so was Portpatrick to eloping lovers from Ireland – a place where they could be married with no inconvenient questions asked. Until 1826 the Church of Scotland ran a profitable trade in quick and easy weddings here: 'Landed on Saturday, called on Sunday, married on Monday', as the saying went.

Scotland's southwest corner is the closest point to Ireland, and Portpatrick was the Scottish end of the 21-mile crossing to Donaghadee in Ulster. A military road was constructed in the early 17th century, linking the town to Dumfries: Portpatrick was the main embarkation point for thousands of British troops and settlers. The mail coaches to Ireland took this route, while Irish cattle in their bellowing thousands came the other way.

The snag was that Portpatrick's harbour lay at the mercy of the savage southwesterly gales. A pier was built in the 1770s, but it was not adequate and new harbour works on a massive scale began in 1820. The sea swept them all away, and in 1849

♥ Portpatrick lighthouse

the packet boats carrying mail, cargo and passengers to Ireland were transferred to nearby and more sheltered Stranraer. Portpatrick was left to become a pleasant small resort for sailing, sea fishing and nowadays water sports.

Today the harbour, ringed with low hills and old waterside buildings, is the starting point for the 212-mile Southern Upland Way long-distance path. The 17th-century church has an unusual Irish-style round tower and the graveyard is the final resting place of many sailors. Just to the south is the ruin of Dunskey Castle, the remains of a fortified tower house of the early 16th century, standing proudly on a cliff top above the sea.

TAKE IN SOME HISTORY
Dunskey Castle
visitscotland.com
6 miles southwest of Stranraer.
Exterior viewing only. Keep to the path

Little is known of this ruined tower house standing on a rocky peninsula that juts out into the sea. A castle is mentioned in records dating to 1330, but was burned down early in the 15th century. A new tower was raised by William Adair of Kinhilt, but this was deserted in the middle of the 17th century and was little more than a ruin by 1684.

Dunskey is a simple L-plan tower house, with cellars and two floors. Walls were built around the small peninsula, so that the castle would have been protected by two lines of defence: first the sea and ditches hewn from the rock, and second the castle walls. Virtually nothing remains of these walls, although there are still some traces of other buildings in what would have been the courtyard.

It is likely that Dunskey Castle would once have been a fine, proud fortified dwelling. The windows and doors were once decorated with dressed stones, but these, being expensive and much in demand for building, have been stripped away over the centuries by local looters. It is their absence that gives the roofless walls of Dunskey Castle their forlorn, rugged appearance.

When viewing the castle you are advised to stay on the coastal path, as the surrounding cliffs are steep and dangerous.

◄ Dunskey Castle

GO ROUND THE GARDENS
Dunskey Estate Gardens
dunskey.com
DG9 8TJ | 01776 810211
Open Apr–Oct daily 10–5
Particularly lovely in spring, the woodland gardens here surround a walled garden, complete with a range of 19th-century glasshouses, still used for growing peaches, grapes and exotic flowering plants. Outside there's a maze where the kids can let off steam.

WALK THE SOUTHERN UPLAND WAY
southernuplandway.gov.uk
01387 260000
Portpatrick is the starting point for the Southern Upland Way, a long-distance 212-mile route that runs across Scotland to Cockburnspath on the east coast. It's a tough route, usually taking anything between 10 and 20 days traversing some very testing countryside, but you can walk, cycle or even ride parts of it and the accommodation providers along the way will often offer to transport luggage or rescue exhausted walkers.

EAT AND DRINK
Knockinaam Lodge ⊛⊛⊛
knockinaamlodge.com
Portpatrick, DG9 9AD
01776 810471
A single-track lane leads through beautiful countryside to an old hunting lodge, where log fires and an oak-panelled bar stocked with more than 120 single malt whiskies await. The smart, traditional dining room is the setting for the classically inspired cooking.

▶ **PLACES NEARBY**
Logan Botanic Garden
rbge.org.uk
Port Logan, Stranraer, DG9 9ND
01776 860231 | Open Mar–Oct daily 10–5; Feb Sun 11–3 (for snowdrops)
This frost-free corner of the Rhinns of Galloway, in the far southwest, serves as an annexe for tender plants from the Royal Botanic Garden in Edinburgh (see page 176), and is a plant-lover's delight. Exotic species from the southern hemisphere thrive on the acid soil. Feature plants include Himalayan poppies and South African proteas, and there are bright floral displays throughout summer in the walled garden.

▶ Logan Botanic Garden

▶ **Rannoch Moor**

MAP REF 407 D5

The rolling plateau of Rannoch
Moor is one of Britain's
greatest pocket wildernesses.
It's a wild, windswept expanse
of moorland, pocked with
lochs and tarns and criss-
crossed by fast-flowing,
peat-tinted burns.

Not many places in Britain
let you get so far from
civilisation: just one road, the
A82, crosses this bleak but
beautiful landscape, plunging
into the upper end of Glencoe
(see page 234) on the western
fringe of the moor. Get your
walking boots on, and you may
be rewarded by sightings of
golden eagles, buzzards and
red deer on the moors and in
the patches of oak, rowan, ash and birch dotted across it – the
oldest deciduous woodland in Scotland. Overlooking it all is the
lonely peak of Schiehallion, a conical mount that rises to 3,553
feet (1,083m) above sea level. Its name means holy place of the
Sidhe (pronounced Shee) – the mythical fairy-folk venerated by
the pagan Picts and Scots – and the so-called Maiden's Well on
its eastern slope is associated with ancient fertility rites.

On the moor's southern boundary, Loch Rannoch is an open,
spacious loch, running east to west from the Bridge of Gaur to
Kinloch Rannoch, famous for the varied and beautiful
woodlands that surround it. On its southern slopes, the Black
Wood of Rannoch is one of the best surviving examples of
Scotland's once-extensive native Caledonian pine forest.

Ben Lawers, at 3,983 feet (1,214m) the highest mountain in
the region, is famous for its arctic/alpine flora. Among the rare
survivors from the last Ice Age are purple saxifrage, alpine
gentian, alpine lady's mantle and alpine cinquefoil. This unique
flora was once seriously threatened by over-grazing, but Ben
Lawers is now in the hands of the National Trust for Scotland
(NTS). This rich collection of plants, normally found only in the
high Arctic or in the European Alps, is due to a series of
coincidences – a small stratum of ideal rock on a mountain that
is so high that the habitat has existed unchanged since the
departure of the Ice Age glaciers about 10,000 years ago.

▲ River Ba, Rannoch Moor

Rannoch Moor may seem gloriously remote, but in reality you can get there quite easily on the west Highland railway line that passes through. Rannoch Station, in the heart of this seeming wilderness, has several trains a day from Glasgow (see page 206) and Inverness (see page 250), plus an overnight sleeper from London, making it the ideal jumping-off point if you're planning to yomp across the moor to Glencoe.

EAT AND DRINK
Rannoch Station Tea Room
rannochstationtearoom.co.uk
Rannoch Station, PH17 2QA
01882 633247 | Open Mar–Oct
Sat–Thu 8.30–4.30

The Rannoch Station Tea Room serves hearty breakfasts, lunches and evening meals and also provides picnic meals for walkers and train travellers.

▸ **Rosslyn Chapel**
see highlight panel overleaf

▸ **Rùm**
see **Small Isles**, page 362

▶ Rosslyn Chapel MAP REF 402 C3

rosslynchapel.com
EH25 9PU | 0131 440 2159 | Open Apr–Sep Mon–Sat 9.30–6, Sun 12–4.45;
Oct–Mar Mon–Sat 9.30–5, Sun 12–4.45

In a mining village six miles south of Edinburgh (see page 161) you'll find one of Scotland's most mysterious buildings. Rosslyn Chapel was founded here in 1446 by William St Clair, Third Earl of Orkney. It is linked with the Knights Templar and other secretive societies, and believed by some to be the hiding place of the Holy Grail, a role publicised in Dan Brown's novel *The Da Vinci Code*. Inside is a riot of medieval stone carving. Every part of the roof rib, arch, corbel and pillar is encrusted with mouldings, foliage and figures, including representations of Green Men, the Seven Deadly Sins and other religious themes.

It is from the chapel's crypt that the Holy Grail legend arose. The crypt has been sealed and inaccessible for many years, and this has naturally led to many stories and suppositions as to what it may contain. Some say it's sealed to prevent people discovering that it leads to an even larger underground

vault, and this is where Rosslyn's secret really lies. It may be the Holy Grail, the Ark of the Covenant, a piece of the True Cross or even the mummified head of Jesus Christ. It could hide the treasures of the Knights Templar, or Scotland's original crown jewels, preceding those that are now on show in Edinburgh Castle.

It seems more likely, though, that it contains the remains of some of the Barons of Rosslyn, buried in their full armour. Before the second Earl of Rosslyn died in 1837, he asked to be buried in the vault where his ancestors lay, but no one could find any signs of an entrance to the vault. Instead the Earl was buried in the Lady Chapel.

Look for the famous Prentice Pillar with its spiralling strands of foliage and winged serpents, necks intertwined, biting their own tails. It was carved by a young apprentice and, the story goes, when his master saw how beautiful it was he struck the lad in a jealous rage. The master is said to have hit the apprentice with a mallet, cutting his head and killing him. In the northwest corner of the chapel and set into the ceiling is the figure of a man with a cut forehead. This is said to be the apprentice, secretly commemorated, while on the opposite side of the chapel is another head – that of the murderer.

Regular services are still held and the chapel is part of the Episcopal Diocese of Edinburgh.

EAT AND DRINK
The Original Rosslyn Inn
theoriginalhotel.co.uk
Rosslyn, EH25 9LE | 0131 440 2384
Just a short walk from Rosslyn Chapel, this family-run village inn has been in the same family for 40 years. Robert Burns stayed here in 1787 and wrote a two-verse poem for the landlady about his visit. Today you have the chance to catch up with the locals in the village bar, or relax by the fire in the lounge while choosing from the menu.

▶ St Abb's Head National Nature Reserve

MAP REF 403 E3

nts.org.uk

St Abbs, Eyemouth, TD14 5QF | 01890 771443 | Open access all year. Visitor centre open Easter–Oct daily 10–5

St Abb's Head is a wild and beautiful landscape at any time of year, with the spectacular cliffs of soft red sandstone, sculpted by wind and waves, reaching 300 feet above sea level. Fulmars, kittiwakes, guillemots, puffins and razorbills are the most prominent breeding species, and when they are in residence in late spring, the cliffs become an astonishing vertical city. While the steep cliffs are home to most of the seabirds, the low, flat rocks below are the favoured nesting site of shags. These large black birds are almost indistinguishable from cormorants, except for the distinctive crest on their heads that gives them a quizzical appearance. They tend to fly low over the water, in contrast to the graceful fulmars that frequently soar along the cliff tops, riding on convenient currents of air. Guillemots and razorbills are difficult to differentiate, as they are both black and white, and both resemble small, perky penguins. Both birds belong to the auk family, the most famous member of which is probably the great auk, which became extinct in 1844 – a victim of the contemporary passion for egg collecting.

A pleasant circular walk to the lighthouse brings you past Mire Loch, where little grebes and tufted ducks may be seen, or you could walk some of the Smugglers' Trail, which follows the Berwickshire coastline from Burnmouth to Cove.

Just along the coast from St Abb's is the little village of Eyemouth. It has been a fishing port since the 13th century and the industry still flourishes here today.

▼ Nesting puffins

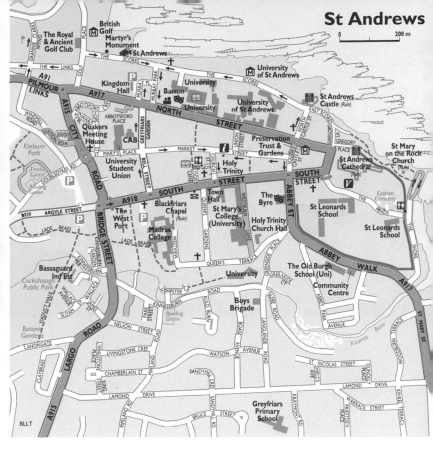

▶ St Andrews MAP REF 403 D1

St Andrews is a small town on the east coast of Fife, with a
sandy bay to the north and a narrow harbour to the south.
Before the Reformation it was the ecclesiastical and scholarly
centre of Scotland, a great place of pilgrimage. It is also the
home of the Royal and Ancient Golf Club, founded in 1754 and
still the ruling authority on the game worldwide.

The town received its royal charter in 1140, and construction
of the cathedral started 20 years later. It was dedicated to St
Andrew by a Greek monk, who was shipwrecked here while
carrying holy relics of the saint in AD 347. Climb the spiral stairs
of the tower (108 feet) for great views over the town, revealing
the medieval grid of its streets. The two main roads are North
Street, which leads to the famous St Andrews Links, and South
Street, with the restored city gateway of 1589, the West Port, at
its far end.

Northwards along the shore lie the ruins of the castle,
rebuilt in about 1390. It was the site of a battle and siege in
1546–47. Look for the mine and counter-mine tunnels under
the walls, which date from this time. The chilling bottle-shaped

▲ St Andrews Cathedral

dungeon in the northwest corner of the castle was cut from solid rock, 24 feet deep, offering prisoners no chance of escape.

The undulating turf between the golden sand beaches and the more fertile farmland is known in Scotland as the links, a term that has become almost synonymous with golf courses. St Andrews is where the game is said to have originated; the town has seven courses, of which the Old Course is the most famous.

Today, what may have become simply an elegant and sleepy resort town is kept wide awake by its thriving university – Scotland's most venerable – that dates from 1413. It is the oldest in Scotland, and third oldest in Britain, after Oxford and Cambridge. The first faculties were theology, canon law, civil law, medicine and arts, with theology being of particular importance. Proud university traditions include a Sunday walk along the pier after church, and a mass dawn swim in the sea on May morning (1 May). Given the icy nature of the waters, this is not an activity to be attempted by the faint-hearted.

TAKE IN SOME HISTORY
St Andrews Castle
historicenvironment.scot
East Scores, KY16 9AR | 01334 477196 | Open Apr–Sep daily 9.30–5.30; Oct–Mar daily 10–4 Built by the bishops and archbishops of St Andrews, the castle in its present form dates from about 1390. It comprises a five-sided enclosure, with buildings dating from the 12th to the 16th centuries that served as palace, fortress and prison. A mine and counter-mine are legacies of an attempt

to break a siege of 1546–47 by the Duke of Argyll. His men tunnelled towards the castle but were thwarted when the defenders dug out a counter-mine and headed them off.

St Andrews Cathedral and St Rule's Tower

historicenvironment.scot
The Pends, KY16 9QL | 01334 472563 | Open Apr–Sep daily 9.30–5.30; Oct–Mar daily 10–4
Founded in 1160 and consecrated in 1318, this was once Scotland's largest cathedral; today the central aisle is a stretch of turf around which the remaining walls soar, with the great east window dominating the ruins. It's an impressive sight, which you can view by climbing the 157 steps to the top of the Romanesque St Rule's Tower next to it. The cathedral was plundered by John Knox's supporters in 1559, and its stones were used for buildings throughout the town.

VISIT THE MUSEUM
British Golf Museum

britishgolfmuseum.co.uk
Bruce Embankment, KY16 9AB
01334 460046 | Open daily 10–4
The museum tells the story of British golf, with more than 16,000 items dating from the 17th century to the present day.

MEET THE SEA LIFE
Aquarium

standrewsaquarium.co.uk
The Scores, KY16 9AS
01334 474786
Open daily 10–6

There's a wide variety of marine life here, with observation pools and daily seal and penguin feeding sessions. Staff give talks throughout the day.

CATCH A PERFORMANCE
The Byre Theatre

byretheatre.com
Abbey Street, KY16 9LA
01334 475000
The Byre Theatre hosts productions and touring shows, including dance, music, comedy and poetry.

TAKE A SPOOKY TOUR
Original St Andrews Witches Tour

st-andrewswitchestour.co.uk
Balgarvie Road, Cupar, KY15 4AJ
07580 221481
Enjoy a thrilling night-time guided walk through the centre of St Andrews, with spooky tales of local witches. Advance reservations recommended.

PLAY A ROUND
St Andrews Links

standrews.org.uk
West Sands, KY16 9XL
01334 466718 | Open daily all year
For many golfers, it's a life's ambition to play a round at St Andrews, with the venerable Old Course clearly taking prize place. There are seven courses, and, with some forward planning, it's possible to play on all of them. If you want to play the Old Course, you'll need to enter the ballot for a tee time and produce your handicap certificate; it's advisable to do this some months in advance.

EAT AND DRINK

The Adamson ◉◉

theadamson.com
127 South Street, KY16 9UH
01334 479191
Justifiably proud of its multiple
awards, this town-centre
restaurant, housed in a
handsome old building, has a
cool, rustic-chic finish, with
exposed bricks, darkwood
tables and a bar that serves up
a nifty cocktail. The menu has
contemporary style and
high-quality ingredients.

Hams Hame Pub & Grill

oldcoursehotel.co.uk
The Old Course Hotel, Golf Resort &
Spa, KY16 9SP | 01334 474371
This pub, with low ceilings,
beams and wooden floors, is
over the road from the famous
Old Course's 18th green. This
being the 19th hole, your fellow
diner or drinker may well be a
golfing legend, sharing your
enjoyment of some of Scotland's
best brews and menus
showcasing its finest produce.

Hotel du Vin St Andrews ◉

hotelduvin.com
40 The Scores, KY16 9AS
01334 845313
The usual high standard of this
upmarket chain prevails here,
with stylish and laid-back
informal decor, French and
British classic cooking and a
fabulous wine list.

The Jigger Inn

oldcoursehotel.co.uk
The Old Course Hotel, Golf Resort &
Spa, KY16 9SP | 01334 474371
Golfing history is an all-
embracing experience at this
former stationmaster's lodge on
the now long-disused railway
line to Leuchars. Seafood
landed in nearby fishing villages
is available all day.

Road Hole Restaurant ◉◉◉

oldcoursehotel.co.uk
The Old Course Hotel, Golf Resort
& Spa, KY16 9SP | 01334 474371
Right next to the 17th hole on
the famous Old Course, this
is a superbly elegant hotel
restaurant, with impeccable
service and modern Scottish
cuisine that matches up to the
surroundings.

Seafood Restaurant

theseafoodrestaurant.com
Bruce Embankment, KY16 9AB
01334 479475
Less than 200 yards from the
Old Course at St Andrews, the
restaurant sits precariously
balanced over the edge of the
sea wall, with breathtaking
views of the distant North Sea
rollers. The restaurant has an
open kitchen, where the kitchen
team produce fish and seafood
dishes that are as fresh and
enlivening as the sea spray.

▶ **PLACES NEARBY**

A string of fishing villages and
sandy beaches encircles the
Fife coast east and south from
St Andrews. This is the East
Neuk (see page 154), where
you'll find coastal walks and
golf courses and tucked away
fishing harbours such as Crail,
Anstruther and Pittenweem.

Inland lies fertile farmland, scattered with solid houses, the odd castle and the fascinating Secret Bunker near St Monans.

The Inn at Lathones

innatlathones.com

Lathones, KY9 1JE | 01334 840494

The footprint of this late 17th-century coaching inn takes up most of the hamlet of Lathones in the East Neuk of Fife. In 1718 a minister blessed a young couple's marriage here, and their wedding stone has served as the lintel over a fireplace ever since. The oldest part, the stone-walled Stables, is home to the Grey Lady, a friendly ghost with her equally spectral horse. More practically, it's also the bar, with its own menu and real ales from Belhaven and Eden.

Kellie Castle

nts.org.uk

Pittenweem, KY10 2RF | 01333 720721 | Gardens open daily 9–dusk; Castle open Jun–Aug daily 11–5; Apr–May, Sep–Oct Thu–Mon 11–5

This much-restored, but beautiful and atmospheric castle dates from the 16th–17th centuries and was restored by the Lorimer family in the 1880s. Robert Lorimer and his son Hew were among Scotland's leading architects and sculptors, and it was Robert who designed the stunning garden that surrounds the castle.

Scotland's Secret Bunker

secretbunker.co.uk

Crown Buildings, Troywood, KY16 8QH | 01333 310301 | Open mid-Mar to Oct daily 10–5

Scotland's Nuclear Command Centre, buried in a hole 131 feet deep, between St Andrews and Anstruther, is a secret no longer. The hole was originally dug out after World War II to house a radar installation; in the 1950s it was secretly lined with ten feet of reinforced concrete, and a bomb-proof warren was built inside, with an innocuous-looking farmhouse on the top to deter the curious. Explore the eerie chambers, complete with original communications equipment, and see the cramped dorms where up to 300 personnel would have slept in rotation.

▷ St Ninian's Isle

see **Shetland Islands**, page 357

▷ Scalloway

see **Shetland Islands**, page 358

▷ Scapa Flow

see **Orkney Islands**, page 322

▶ Scone Palace MAP REF 402 B1

scone-palace.co.uk

Scone, PH2 6BD | 01738 552300 | Open May–Sep daily 9.30–5; Mar, Apr, Oct
daily 9.30–4; grounds only Nov, Dec, Feb, Mar 10–4

Centuries ago, the site of Scone Palace was where the
coronations of Scottish kings took place. Early records tell of a
monastery here and then an Abbey of Augustinian Canons, but
the Abbey and the Bishop's House were burned down in 1559 by
a mob incited by the sermons of John Knox. Fortunately, the
Palace of Scone, residence of the Abbot, survived.

It was around this early structure that the present palace
grew, enlarged in 1802, in a Gothic style in keeping with its
monastic past. The 19th-century Gothic influence in design is
most enchanting in the pretty Anteroom, painted in white with
architectural details highlighted in gold and silver. The same
style continues in the majestic Long Gallery, with an unusual
floor of Scottish oak inset with bog oak. Family portraits line
the walls, and the gallery also contains a unique collection of
Vernis Martin ware – papier mâché made by the Martin family
in 18th-century France. The library is home to a fabulous
collection of 18th- and 19th-century porcelain.

Allow time to explore the lovely grounds, where you'll find
Moot Hill, the original place of coronation for the Scottish
kings, complete with a replica of the Stone of Scone used in the
ceremony. There's a must-see pinetum for tree lovers, but
children will want to head for Perthshire's only maze. It's
planted with 2,000 green and copper beech trees in the shape
of the five-pointed star that's part of the Murray family crest.

◀ Scone Palace

▶ Scourie MAP REF 412 A2

On a desolate stretch of the coast the village of Scourie is a welcome base for birdwatchers, walkers and anglers. It is a country of deep sea lochs and inlets, sandy bays, scattered small islands and very few roads.

Grey seals are a familiar sight offshore, while further north, Kinlochbervie on Loch Inchard developed as a fishing port after World War II. The coast running up to Cape Wrath is made mainly of Lewisian gneiss of astounding antiquity: rocks at Scourie have been dated at nearly 3,000 million years old. Scotland's first Geopark, a community and cultural enterprise based on the region's geological heritage, covers the area.

Scourie was the main settlement for the MacKay clan. In 1829 the Scourie estate was sold to the Duke of Sutherland, one of the landowners most active in the notorious Highland clearances; many local people were compelled to emigrate to Canada, Nova Scotia or Australia.

▶ PLACES NEARBY

Handa Island Nature Reserve

scottishwildlifetrust.org.uk
3 miles off shore from Tarbet, PA29 6UB | 07920 468572 | Ferry runs Apr–Aug Mon–Sat 9–5 (last sailing out at 2pm)

Handa Island, reached by boat from Tarbet, is an important nature reserve managed by the Scottish Wildlife Trust. Seabird eggs, fish and potatoes used to be the diet of the island's hardy seven-family population, who had their own queen – the oldest widow. They used fulmar oil for lighting and traded feathers for supplies. The 1848 potato famine drove the population away and Handa's birds have had the island to themselves ever since: 150 species are found here, some 100,000 guillemots included.

Northwest Highland Geopark

nwhgeopark.com
The Rock Stop Visitor Centre, Unapool, IV27 4HW | 01971 488765 | Open daily 11–4.30

This vast area of the northwest Highlands has been designated by UNESCO as being of international geological importance. It runs from Ullapool in Wester Ross up the coast to Durness in Sutherland, which lies east of Cape Wrath, and takes in about 770 sq miles of mountain, moorland, peat bogs, beach, forest and coastline. Besides its great beauty, it's a mecca for geologists, with rocks as old as 3,000 million years. You can learn more, and find out about activities on offer, at the visitor centre at Unapool.

▶ Shetland Islands MAP REF 414 a1

Shetland, with a population of about 24,000, is the most northerly part of Britain, lying as close to the Faroes and Bergen in Norway as it does to Aberdeen. Its place on northern trade routes has given it an unusually cosmopolitan air, and a culture that is more Viking than Scottish, with a broad dialect and a Viking festival in January in the shape of Up Helly Aa. There's a rich heritage of skilled knitting, and a vibrant tradition of fiddle music that has been exported around the world.

The landscape of these islands is wild and rugged, with low hills, exposed rock and peaty, waterlogged moorland. The cliffs are impressive; according to Scottish Natural Heritage, Shetland has nearly 250 miles of cliffs, a fifth of Scotland's total. Winters are stormy and few trees survive the wind, but the wild flowers in summer are spectacular, and nowhere is farther than 5 miles from the sea. Seals and porpoises are common sights around the coastline, and thousands of seabirds nest here, including puffins, black guillemots and gannets. The capital is the harbour town of Lerwick, halfway up the east side of the main island, Mainland. Scalloway, west of Lerwick, was the medieval heart of the island, and is dominated by its ruined castle, built in 1600.

Shetland's prosperity rose sharply at the end of the 20th century with the exploitation of oil and gas fields in the North Sea. The money has funded new roads, new inter-island ferries and modern community centres on many of the islands, as well as other public facilities. Sullom Voe, one of the largest oil and gas terminals in Europe, lies at the north of the main island.

The other Shetland islands are also worth exploring if you have time; all are linked by ferry. Bressay and Noss lie just east of Mainland, whose wild northern end is worth seeing if only for the sheer scale and incongruity in this remote setting of the Sullom Voe Oil Terminal. You can walk on the rocky island of Papa Stour, off the west coast of Mainland, or take a boat or plane to the tiny islands of the Out Skerries, to the northeast of Lerwick. North from Mainland lie Yell and Fetlar, which you'll pass through if you're heading to Unst (see page 360).

▶ **Lerwick** MAP REF 414 b3
It was Dutch herring fishermen who made Lerwick the capital of the islands, when they started using its sheltered harbour in the 17th century. Today the compact grey town stretches out to

either side, with the bustling, stone-flagged main thoroughfare, Commercial Street, one row back. The old harbour is active with local ferries, fishing boats and pleasure craft, while bigger ferries, cruise ships and support vessels for the oil industry tend to use the less vibrant modern harbour located one mile to the north. In the shops, knitwear produced using traditional, intricate patterns is a local speciality, and if you can't see what you want, nimble-fingered workers will soon make you an original garment to your own choice of pattern or colour.

Fort Charlotte, a five-sided artillery fort dating from 1665, is one of the oldest buildings in Shetland, and is worth seeing (keys available locally; call 01856 841815). There are good views to the island of Bressay. The Shetland Museum overlooks the harbour and has more than 3,000 artefacts on local heritage and culture, displayed over two floors.

TAKE IN SOME HISTORY
Fort Charlotte
historicenvironment.scot
Harbour Street, Lerwick, ZE1 0JL
Open daily 7–8, keys available on site
Five-sided Fort Charlotte looms at the west end of Commercial Street and was begun for Charles II in 1665. It's been a prison and a Royal Navy training centre, and saw action in the 17th century.

VISIT THE MUSEUM
Shetland Museum
shetlandmuseumandarchives.org.uk

Hay's Dock, Lerwick, ZE1 0WP
01595 695057 | Open Mon–Sat 10–4, Sun 12–5
The museum covers all aspects of the islands' history, from archaeology to textiles and fishing to folklore. Everything you see is relevant to the islands, and many items on display were made on Shetland. Exhibits include a block of butter, found preserved in a peat bog, that was a tax payment to the King of Norway before Shetland became part of Scotland.

◄ Lerwick ▲ Croft on Fair Isle

GO BACK IN TIME
Clickimin Broch
historicenvironment.scot
Telephone for keys: 01856 841815
Open access all year
This ancient, and much-reduced, broch stands at the centre of what was an Iron Age settlement, enclosed by a wall.

GET ACTIVE
Clickimin Leisure Complex
srt.org.uk
Lochside, Lerwick, ZE1 0PJ | 01595 741000 | Open Mon–Fri 7.30am–11pm
One of eight well-equipped leisure complexes scattered throughout Shetland, Clickimin provides great facilities, including a 25m (82-foot) pool, river ride and flumes and a toddlers' pool, as well as health and fitness suites.

TAKE IN A SHOW
Garrison Theatre
shetlandarts.org
Market Street, Lerwick, ZE1 0JN
01595 743843

The main performing arts venue in Shetland, with everything from touring theatre productions to dance, music and a wide variety of lively community events. Films are also shown here.

SEE THE SEALIFE
Shetland Seabird Tours
shetlandseabirdtours.com
Victoria Pier, Lerwick, ZE1 0LL
07767 872260 | Cruises May–Oct daily 9.45 and 2.15; call or book online
Take to the waters in a purpose-built rigid-inflatable boat (RIB) to explore the incredibly rich and diverse sea bird life around Shetland. The enthusiastic owners of this company are ornithologists and conservationists, who will give you a truly memorable birding experience.

PLAY A ROUND
Shetland Golf Club
shetlandgolfclub.co.uk
Dale, Gott, ZE2 9SB | 01595 840369

This is a challenging moorland course with some hard walking. A burn runs the full length of the course and provides a natural hazard. Every hole provides a new and varied challenge with no two holes similar in layout or appearance.

▶ Fair Isle MAP REF 414 b4

Said to be the most isolated inhabited island in Britain, Fair Isle lies midway between Orkney (see page 312) and the Mainland of Shetland. Only three miles long and one and a half miles wide, it's famous for its highly patterned knitwear, made by a women's co-operative and now sold to passing cruise ships. Fair Isle has a great diversity of cliffs, geos, sea stacks, skerries, natural arches, isthmuses and small bay-head beaches, and about 10 acres of pasture on its sloping summit. This was so valuable to the islanders that they used to climb it with chains, using ropes to raise and lower the sheep.

For such a small island, the seabird population of Fair Isle is unequalled in Europe, and it is a prime location for spotting rare and unusual species of birds. The tiny island's total species list stands at more than 360, but it's primarily noted for the seabirds, such as puffins, gannets, guillemots and skuas. It became a haven for ornithologists in the 1930s, and one of the first to flock there was George Waterston of Edinburgh, who immediately fell in love with the island and began to make plans to open a bird observatory there.

In 1947, Waterston, later to become director of the RSPB in Scotland, purchased the island, and in the following year, the Fair Isle Bird Observatory was established in the old naval huts near North Haven.

▼ Sheep on Fair Isle ▶ St Ninian's Chapel

▶ Foula MAP REF 414 A3

The island of Foula rises to 1,371 feet at its highest point of Da Sneug, which overlooks the towering 1,200-foot red sandstone cliffs of Kame on its northwestern coast. This dramatic island, one of the most isolated inhabited islands in Britain, lies 18 miles to the west of the Mainland of Shetland. Other notable geological features include sea stacks, skerries, caves and towering headlands, such as those at Waster Hoevda and Logat Head. It is accessible by ferry or plane.

▶ St Ninian's Isle MAP REF 414 b3

St Ninian's Isle is a green jewel, a tiny grass-covered island off the western side of southern Shetland. It is joined to the land by a curved tombolo of silvery shell sand, which permits access except during the highest tides of the year, and makes for lovely walking.

St Ninian came from the monastery at Whithorn (see page 395) in Dumfries, the first Christian missionary to reach Shetland, and the ruins of a church from the 12th century are on the island. In 1958 a hoard of beautifully worked Pictish silver was discovered, buried under the nave. The treasure is now in the National Museum of Scotland in Edinburgh (see page 174), but replicas can be seen in the Shetland Museum in Lerwick.

▶ PLACES NEARBY

Mousa Broch
historicenvironment.scot
historic-scotland.gov.uk
Sandwick, ZE1 9HP | 07901
872339 | Sailings Apr to mid-Sep
Mon–Fri, Sun

Wonderfully set on a small island off the coast of southern Mainland, the double-skinned circular tower of Mousa Broch dates from 100 BC to AD 300, and is the best-preserved example of its kind in Scotland. The

▲ Sumburgh Head

walls stand up to 43 feet high, and the small gaps between the neatly placed stones now provide nesting sites for tiny storm petrels. The fact that the broch was built on this small island suggests it had a defensive role at some time – but nobody quite understands how people lived in and used these structures. The island has no human inhabitants today, and is a designated Site of Special Scientific Interest.

GO WALKING
Island Trails
island-trails.co.uk
Hillview, Ireland, Bigton, ZE2 9JA
07880 950228
Several guided walking tours are offered, including an exploration of historic Lerwick, a visit to the smugglers cave, a trek around St Ninian's Isle and wildlife walks. Advance reservations are essential, via the tourist office in Lerwick.

▶ Scalloway MAP REF 414 b3
The little town of Scalloway, once Shetland's capital, runs down a hill to its harbour, which is dominated by the ruins of Scalloway Castle, built in 1600 by the Earl of Orkney. The key is available from the museum.

VISIT THE MUSEUM
Scalloway Museum
scallowaymuseum.org
Castle Street, ZE1 0TP | 01595
880734 | Open Apr–Sep Mon–Sat
11–4, Sun 2–4
The Scalloway Museum features a fishing boat that took part in the secret Shetland Bus sea link to resistance fighters in Norway during World War II.

EAT AND DRINK
Scalloway Hotel ◉◉
scallowayhotel.com
Main Street, ZE1 0TR | 01595 880444

The bounty of the Atlantic is landed practically on the doorstep of this family-run hotel on the waterfront of Shetland's former capital. It's an unpretentious place with a genuine community feel that opens its arms to all-comers, from oil rig workers to passing ships' crews, making the bar a convivial haunt for casual and traditional, unpretentious pub food. The restaurant presents itself very nicely with linen tablecloths and quality glasses and there are some bright ideas on a seasonal menu that showcases the islands' abundant produce.

▶ **PLACES NEARBY**

Houlls Horses and Hounds
houllshorsesandhounds.co.uk
Houlls, Burra, ZE2 9LE
01595 859287
You can canter along a sandy beach and trek through stunning coastal scenery at this friendly centre, which uses Icelandic ponies.

▶ Sumburgh Head MAP REF 414 b3

There's a huge Iron Age settlement next to the airport, where you can see what life was like in Norse and Pictish times in a reconstructed wheelhouse. The cliffs of Sumburgh Head are one of the easiest places to visit to experience some of Shetland's remarkable bird life, including shags, gannets, kittiwakes, fulmars and razorbills. Stars of the show are the puffins, which nest in burrows below the western wall of the lighthouse complex.

GO BACK IN TIME

Jarlshof Prehistoric and Norse Settlement
historicenvironment.scot
Sumburgh, ZE3 9JN | 01950 460112 | Open Apr–Sep daily 9.30–5.30; Oct–Mar phone 08156 841815 for information
Complex layers of history were first uncovered at this fascinating site, near the southern tip of Shetland, when a mighty storm dislodged the covering turf. The most obvious survivor is the shell of the 16th-century Laird's House, which is the only structure that shows above ground. The land around overlies a prehistoric broch that, it would seem, was converted during the Iron Age into a roundhouse. All around the site are the remains of a Viking farm dating from the ninth century, complete with the outline of a communal longhouse that was almost 68 feet long. Further layers have revealed a settlement from the second century BC, a medieval farm dating from the 14th century and the laird's house itself, making an intriguing record of life here over the years. Signboards clarify what you see. Hooper swans can be seen in autumn on the nearby reserve of Loch of Spiggie.

▲ Neolithic stone, Unst

▶ Unst MAP REF 414 c1

Much of Unst's fame rests on its status as the most northerly of the Shetland Islands. In this way, it can claim the most northerly house in Britain, at Skaw.

The first lighthouse on Muckle Flugga was built in 1854, and the Scottish author Robert Louis Stevenson (1850–94) visited the present building (completed in 1858) in 1869, with his father Thomas Stevenson, who was then the construction engineer to the Board of Trade. Some people believe that the island of Unst influenced Robert in the writing of his classic adventure tale of pirates and buried gold, *Treasure Island*, published in 1883 – allegedly, the map of Treasure Island itself bears a certain resemblance to Unst.

The nature reserve at Herma Ness is home in summer to more than 100,000 screaming seabirds that nest on and around the 558-foot cliffs. Look out for puffins and guillemots, fulmars and large, creamy gannets. Beware the great brown Arctic skuas, which are inclined to dive-bomb visitors if they feel their moorland nest sites are threatened (local people know them as bonxies). There are great views to the lighthouse, which was automated in 1995, on the exposed rock of Muckle Flugga.

GO BIRDING

Hermaness National Nature Reserve Visitor Centre
nature-shetland.co.uk
Unst, KW15 1XA | 01595 693345
Open Apr–Sep daily 10–4

You can plan your four-mile walk over the moor to the seabirds' cliffs and learn about what you'll see en route at this informative centre, set inside the former lighthouse-keeper's lodgings.

▶ Shieldaig & Torridon MAP REF 411 F5

Shieldaig, with its white-harled and slate-roofed cottages, lies close to the head of Loch Shieldaig in some of Scotland's most breathtaking scenery. It was established in 1800, with grants for families who wished to move there and take up fishing for a living. The project was intended to build a supply of trained seamen for the Royal Navy to call on during the Napoleonic Wars. Official sponsorship came to an end in 1815, but the village survived by fishing the herring that were once plentiful in the loch.

The loch opens into Loch Torridon, by common consent one of the most magical of all Scotland's beautiful lochs. To the south lie the mountains, moors and deer forest of the Applecross Peninsula (see page 72), and a coast road, opened in 1976 to link the scattered crofting settlements together, commands views over the Inner Sound to Raasay and Skye (see page 254). East from Shieldaig, the road along Upper Loch Torridon yields prospects of the red sandstone crags of Beinn Alligin and Liathach, a row of seven peaks rising above 3,000 feet. The Torridon Forest Estate was Britain's first National Nature Reserve, founded in 1951 to protect the native Caledonian pine forest. It has a countryside centre and museum.

SEE THE RED DEER
Torridon Countryside Centre and Deer Museum
nts.org.uk
Achnasheen, IV22 2EZ | 01445 791368 | Open Apr–Sep Sun–Fri 10–5; Deer enclosure open daily all year round
You can walk, explore or learn more about the life of the red deer and how the deer population is managed.

EAT AND DRINK
The Torridon ◉◉
thetorridon.com
Torridon, IV22 2EY | 01445 791242
There's a cosy atmosphere and good home-cooked food at this remote but bustling inn. The beers are from the Highlands and islands, and they source as much food as they can locally, as well as fine local produce from the estate and their own kitchen garden.

Shieldaig Bar & Coastal Kitchen
tighaneilean.co.uk
Shieldaig, IV54 8XN | 01520 755251
The beer comes from the brewery at Loch Broom and the fish and seafood is landed daily at this remote hotel near Upper Loch Torridon, from where you can view a spectacular sunset as you eat.

▶ Skye
see **Isle of Skye**, page 254

▶ Small Isles MAP REF 405 D4

Rùm, Eigg, Muck and Canna make up this island group due west of Mallaig (see page 296). Each has its own distinct identity, but they share a reputation as remote islands where you can truly 'get away from it all'. They are reached by ferry from Mallaig.

▶ Rùm MAP REF 405 D4

Rùm is much the biggest, and the wettest, of the Small Isles, with the high mountains of Askival and Sgùrr nan Gillean to the southeast, and a reputation for vicious midges. Once cleared as a private sporting island, it is now a nature reserve owned by Scottish Natural Heritage, home to red deer, feral goats and some 100,000 Manx shearwaters. Most of the island consists of large tracts of moorland and mountains, and the Scottish National Heritage (SNH) reintroduced white-tailed sea eagles from Norway in 1975. These magnificent birds share the Rùm skies with a good population of native golden eagles.

About 30 people live in the small settlement around the Edwardian castle at Kinloch, a huge and incongruous pile that is preserved in its Edwardian splendour. In 2010 the Rùm Community Trust purchased the area and buildings around Kinloch Castle, and crofting was revived.

TAKE IN SOME HISTORY
Kinloch Castle
isleofrum.com
PH43 4RR | 01687 462037 | Tours daily (to coincide with ferry) Apr–Oct
The crenellated red sandstone Kinloch Castle was built with Lancashire cotton profits by Rùm's then-owner George Bullough in 1897; its interior is an eyepopping example of Edwardian decadence, complete with an electric organ and bathrooms whose showers run with both fresh and salt water.

▶ Eigg MAP REF 405 D4

The Sound of Rùm separates Rùm from Eigg, which is formed mainly from volcanic basalts and is, therefore, much more fertile than its larger neighbour. A steep-sided ridge forms impressive cliffs in the north of the island, while the southern end is dominated by the imposing Sgurr of Eigg, a block of volcanic pitchstone lava that forms a long, undulating ridge of bare grey rock. Viewed end-on from the sea, it forms a tremendous vertically walled, flat-topped tower, while a series of large caves punctuates the rest of the coastline.

▲ Canna

This is an island of small crofts with rich grazing pastures and meadows, deciduous woodlands, conifer plantations and some exotic garden plantings, although there are large areas of rough moorland to the southwest and north. The Isle of Eigg Heritage Trust, set up in 1997, owns the island. This has provided its small population with a real sense of community, making it by far the most buoyant and welcoming of this island group. There's accommodation for visitors, a couple of places to eat out, and you can take boat trips, cycle, walk or go fishing.

▶ Muck MAP REF 405 D4

Muck, the smallest island, low-lying, treeless and fertile, has just one farm, a craft shop, tea room and limited visitor accommodation. Most of the 30-strong population live in Port Mor on the southeast coast. The areas around the summit of Beinn Airein, at 453 feet, and the islet of Eilean nan Each remain uninhabited. The island is formed of basalt, which gives it that familiar stepped profile, and the rock has been worn into a series of cliffs and caves around the coast. Inland, fertile green pastures rise to the summit of Beinn Airein in the west.

▶ Canna MAP REF 404 C3

At the northern end of the Small Isles archipelago is Canna, another basaltic island but with inland cliffs above its grassy slopes and a spectacular northern coastline of caves, arches and sea stacks. Compass Hill contains large deposits of iron that can sometimes affect sailors' compasses. It's owned and run as a single farm by the National Trust for Scotland.

▶ **South Queensferry** MAP REF 402 B3

The Edinburgh suburb of South Queensferry sits beside its harbour on the Forth shore, literally in the shadow of two great bridges. From the early 12th century until the late 19th century, the ferry that crossed the firth to North Queensferry, on the Fife shore, was the only alternative to making the long detour inland to Stirling (see page 369), the lowest point at which the Forth could be bridged. In 1890 the first Forth Bridge was completed, carrying a new railway across the river, but the ferry continued to carry passengers and cars until 1964, when the Forth Road Bridge finally made it obsolete.

These two marvels of 19th-century and 20th-century engineering now stand next to a 21st-century technological achievement, the Queensferry Crossing – the world's longest three-tower, cable-stayed span – which opened in 2017. If you're in an energetic mood, you can walk across the road bridge to Fife. On your way, you'll be rewarded with views of the bridges to either side, and on a clear day you can see all the way west to the Trossachs and east to the North Sea. In 2015, the first bridge received UNESCO World Heritage status. There are ambitious plans to create a viewpoint and visitor centre at the bridge's highest point.

TAKE IN SOME HISTORY
Hopetoun House
hopetoun.co.uk
EH30 9RW | 0131 331 2451
Open Apr–Sep daily 10.30–5
Hopetoun House, one of Scotland's finest mansions, is a splendid early 18th-century architectural masterpiece, completed in about 1767 by William Bruce and William Adam. Its 150 acres of parkland give great views to the bridges, and it's home to the Marquess

◀ Forth Rail and Road bridges

▶ **PLACES NEARBY**

Deep Sea World
deepseaworld.com
North Queensferry, KY11 1JR
01383 411880 | Open Mon–Fri
10–5, Sat–Sun 10–6
It's worth crossing the Forth
Road Bridge by car or bus to get
to this mega-aquarium and seal
sanctuary just outside North
Queensferry, at the north end of
the bridge. This underwater
wonder-world claims the
world's longest underwater
walkway (360 feet), where a
transparent tunnel lets you view
the sharks without getting wet.
Or bitten.

You can see tanks full
of piranhas, sharks and
stingrays, and get your hands
wet in the rock pools with safer
creatures such as starfish.
There's also a tropical
rainforest section full of fish
and amphibians such as
electric eels and tiny, brilliantly
coloured poison-dart frogs from
the Amazon. If you're more
than 16, and a certified diver,
try joining a shark dive by night.

Inchcolm Island
maidoftheforth.co.uk
Hawes Pier, South Queensferry, EH30
9TB | 0131 331 5000 | Call for
sailing times
Hop aboard *Maid of the Forth*
for a cruise to Inchcolm Island,
the most interesting of the
mini-archipelago of
uninhabited islands in the
Firth of Forth. You can see
the ruins of a medieval abbey

of Linlithgow. Hopetoun
contains fine paintings, original
furniture, tapestries and rococo
details. The state rooms, with
their silk damask walls, fine
furniture, and paintings by
artists such as Gainsborough
and Sir Henry Raeburn, were
designed by William Adam and
decorated under the
supervision of his son, John.

VISIT THE MUSEUM
Queensferry Museum
edinburghmuseums.org.uk
53 High Street, EH30 9HP | 01313
315545 | Open Mon, Thu–Sat 10–1,
2.15–5, Sun 12–5
This lively small museum is
dedicated to local events and
traditions like the annual Ferry
Fair and the Burry Man who
parades through the streets on
the first weekend in August
every year. There are also
exhibitions dedicated to the
building of the Forth Bridges
and the history of the ferries
that carried folk across the river
before the bridges were built.

here, but perhaps more interesting are the flocks of puffins, cormorants and other seabirds that nest on this rocky islet. You're almost certain to see seals, and with luck you'll see porpoises and dolphins, too. If you're very fortunate, you may even encounter a whale – several have wandered into the Firth in recent years.

Look out for the silhouette of Inchmickery, a tiny island that served as a gun battery in World War I and World War II. According to a local yarn, its concrete buildings were deliberately designed to make it look, from a distance, like a mighty battleship. It's now an RSPB reserve where rare roseate terns nest.

▶ South Ronaldsay
see **Orkney Islands**, page 322

▶ South Uist
see **Western Isles**, page 392

▶ Speyside Distilleries
MAP REF 408 C2

maltwhiskytrail.com

The River Spey flows from the Cairngorms near Aviemore and winds northeast through a green landscape of gentle hills and woodland to pour into the sea between Lossiemouth and Buckie. Along its course, it is fed by streams from high in the Cairngorms, including the Feshie and the Nethy. It flows under Thomas Telford's magnificent iron bridge at Craigellachie, lends its name to the historic Strathspey Railway at Aviemore and the town of Grantown-on-Spey, and picks up a long-distance trail, the Speyside Way, which runs north from Tomintoul to

◀ Glenfiddich Distillery

▲ Speyside Cooperage

Spey Bay. It's also one of the foremost salmon rivers in Scotland, attracting fishermen from all over the world and earning hefty revenues for the local economy.

Speyside is a name associated with the area between Elgin, Keith and Grantown, and more particularly with the production of some of Scotland's most famous single malt whiskies; place names here can read like a well-stocked bar. There are more than 30 distilleries along the river and its tributaries and eight of these, mostly founded in the early 19th century, are linked by the signposted Malt Whisky Trail: Glen Grant, Cardhu, Strathisla, Glenlivet, Benromach, Dallas Dhu (both in Forres, see page 197), Glen Moray and Glenfiddich. Each offers guided tours and whisky tastings, but opening times and admissions vary so check ahead – you can go online or pick up a leaflet from local tourist information offices.

You can also visit the Speyside Cooperage, where the thousands of oak barrels essential to the whisky industry are produced and maintained. None of the distilleries of Strathspey could thrive without the wooden barrels or casks in which the spirit is left to mature. Oak for the barrel staves is largely imported from the US, and the cooperage produces in the region of 100,000 casks a year for shipping around the world.

Solidly built, tidy stone houses line the streets of Dufftown right in the centre of Speyside, with no fewer than nine distilleries, not all of them working. It's a good place for starting a tour of whisky country, or you could take a ride on the Keith and Dufftown Railway to Keith, home to the Strathisla distillery.

Craigellachie, site of Telford's famous bridge, and Aberlour are attractive stopping points. Aberlour, with its flower-filled central square and long main street running down to the river, is the home of Walker's Shortbread, whose tartan-bedecked tins make their way all over the world.

Grantown-on-Spey is one of the largest settlements along the riverbank. The township was planned out in 1765, and has a spacious, genteel feel to it today. Its creator was James Grant, and the arrival of the railway here in 1863 heralded the town's popularity as a health resort. The railway folded in the 1960s, and the town is now better known as a centre for anglers, and walkers keen to explore the Cairngorms. Its story is told in the local museum.

TAKE IN SOME HISTORY
Ballindalloch Castle
ballindallochcastle.co.uk
Lagmore, AB37 9AX | 01807 500205
Open Sun–Fri Easter–Sep 10–5
You can tour both the warm and welcoming castle and beautiful gardens, or play a round on the golf course here. Still very much a family home, Ballindalloch has been in the hands of the Grant family and their descendants since 1532.

TRY THE WHISKY
The Macallan Distillery
themacallan.com
Easter Elchies, Craigellachie, Aberlour, AB38 9RX | 01340 872280 | Open Easter–Aug Mon–Sat 9.30–4.30; Sep–Oct Mon–Fri 9.30–4; Nov–Easter Mon–Fri 11–3
Although not on the official whisky trail, you can enjoy a guided tour and tasting here, home to one of Scotland's favourite single malts.

SEE THE WILDLIFE
WDC Scottish Dolphin Centre
dolphincentre.whales.org
Tugnet, Spey Bay, IV32 7PJ | 0134 382 0339 | Open Apr–Oct daily 10.30–5; call for out-of-season hours

Spey Bay and the nearby nature reserve are home to many birds, animals and plants including otters, ospreys, seals and bottlenose dolphins. Explore the dolphin exhibition with videos of the Moray Firth and farther afield.

WALK THE SPEYSIDE WAY
morayways.org.uk
The Speyside Way long-distance footpath follows the route of the River Spey for 84 miles from the police station at Aviemore to the coast, passing Grantown-on-Spey, Cromdale and the Craigellachie Forest, with spur paths joining from Tomintoul and Dufftown. It's easy to walk just part of this well-signed route, where dogs, cyclists and riders are welcome.

TAKE A TRAIN RIDE
Keith and Dufftown Railway
keith-dufftown-railway.co.uk
Dufftown, AB55 4BA | 01340 821181 | Open Apr–Sep Sat–Sun
This 11-mile heritage railway uses old diesel engines to cover the route between Dufftown and Keith.

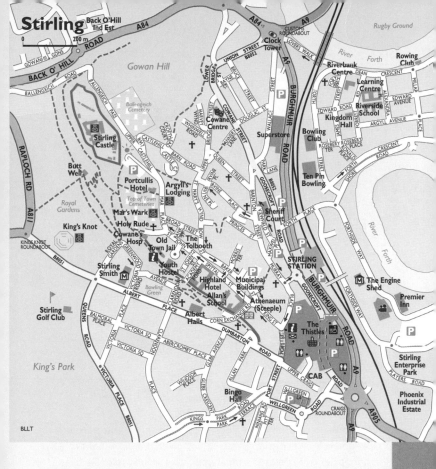

Stirling MAP REF 402 A2

The ancient royal burgh of Stirling grew up around a strategic crossing point of the River Forth before it widens and becomes impassable on its journey to the east. At the northern end of the town, the Old Bridge carried the only route north on the east of Scotland, and the city remained the key to the north and Highlands. Stirling is most famous for its castle, yet it has many other fascinating buildings and sites of national importance.

The city was of particular importance in the wars of independence, and fought against England in the 13th and 14th centuries. Notable Scottish victories included the Battle of Stirling Bridge (1297), fought at the Old Bridge just north of the town centre, when William Wallace split the opposing army in two, and the famous Battle of Bannockburn (1314), when Robert the Bruce took charge and defeated the English yet again. Within the town you'll find information plaques marking notable historic buildings and features – considering this is the smallest city in Scotland, there are a surprising number.

▶ Stirling Castle MAP REF 402 A2

stirlingcastle.gov.uk

Castle Wynd, FK8 1EJ | 01786 450000 | Open Apr–Sep daily 9.30–6;
Oct–Mar daily 9.30–5

Stirling Castle's commanding position, perched on its towering cliffs above the once-marshy plain, has given it a prominent role in history as one of Scotland's most important strongholds.

The castle's history began in the late 11th century, when a wooden structure was raised here. Edward I seized Stirling in 1296, only to see it recaptured by William Wallace in 1297. After a siege, the English retrieved the castle in 1304, and this time held it until Edward II's defeat at Bannockburn in 1314.

The current castle dates mainly from the 16th century. It was favoured by the Stuart kings, becoming birthplace to James II and James IV, temporary home to Mary, Queen of Scots, and the site for the coronation of James V and the baptism of James VI.

Today, it's still dominated by the Great Hall, probably the finest early Renaissance secular building in Scotland. Outside here, James V's Palace dates from 1540. Nearby is the Chapel Royal, built by James VI in 1594 to replace an earlier building. The highlight for many visitors is the spectacular view from the esplanade, which extends to the Campsie Fells in the west and the start of the Highlands to the north.

The Castle Exhibition will help you make sense of it all, and you can explore the hidden corners, battlements, cannon ports and staircases that meander throughout the site, all interspersed with tiny gardens and patches of lawn.

TAKE IN SOME HISTORY
Church of the Holy Rude
holyrude.org
St John's Street, FK8 1ED | No phone
Open daily May–Sep 11–4
The medieval Church of the
Holy Rude has beautiful stained
glass and a timber roof. It was
rebuilt in the early 1400s
after the original church
was destroyed in a fire that
devastated the town in 1405.

Argyll's Lodging
historicenvironment.scot
Castle Court, FK8 1EG | 01786
450000 | Check website for opening
times
This 17th-century town house
was built by Sir William
Alexander, the first Earl of
Stirling. Its highlights are the
dining and drawing rooms, but
more than that, the attraction
lies in the sense of history.
Don't miss the Great Kitchen
with its massive fireplace, or
My Lady's Closet, where the
Earl's wife would have spent
much of her time.

National Wallace Monument
nationalwallacemonument.com
Abbey Craig, FK9 5LF | 01786
472140 | Open Mar daily 10–5;
Apr–Jun and Sep–Oct daily 9.30–5;
Jul–Aug daily 9.30–6; Nov–Feb
daily 10–4
This five-storey tower was built
in 1869 in a surge of nationalist
sentiment to commemorate
the Battle of Stirling Bridge in
1297, when William Wallace
won a famous victory against
Edward I's English forces,
killing thousands and hounding
the wounded into the marshes
to die.

If you can manage the 246
steps to the top after the
lengthy walk up, then the
reward is a breathtaking view.
Wallace's steel sword is on
display, and a Hall of Heroes
depicts other Scots of note.

TAKE A TOUR
Old Town Jail
oldtownjail.co.uk
St John Street, FK8 1EA | 01786
464640 | Tours Apr–Sep daily
10.15–4.15
Stirling's Victorian prison
comes to life on guided tours,
with costumed guides
explaining the jail's history,
helped by audio-visual
presentations. Be sure to
ascend to the Observation
Tower for some fantastic views
of the city and surroundings.

CATCH A PERFORMANCE
The Tolbooth
culturestirling.org
Jail Wynd, FK8 1DE | 01786 274000
Open daily 10–6 and for
performances
The Tolbooth dates from 1705
and used to be a jail and
courthouse. It's now a lively
venue and hosts jazz, world
music, ceilidhs, comedy and
storytelling events. Look for the
hidden stairway outside the
toilets, opposite the old jail.

GET ACTIVE
The Peak
the-peak-stirling.org.uk
Forthside Way, FK8 1QZ | 01768
273555 | Open Mon–Fri 6am–

◀ Giraffe, Blair Drummond

▶ **PLACES NEARBY**

Around Stirling there's family fun in the shape of Scotland's best-known safari park, castles to visit and the emotive site of the country's proudest victory over the English. Just to the south of Stirling, Bannockburn was the site of a major Scottish victory in their wars against English oppression in 1314. Robert the Bruce took on the superior forces of Edward II and won decisively. Stirling was the last English stronghold north of the River Forth, and while its fall was only a stage in the fight for independence (which would continue for another 14 years), this victory consolidated the power of Robert I, effectively silencing any rival claimants to the Scottish throne.

10pm, Sat 7am–8pm, Sun 8–8
There's a swimming pool, ice rink, climbing wall and lots more besides at this state-of-the-art leisure centre on the outskirts of the city – perfect for wet days.

PLAY A ROUND
Stirling Golf Club
stirlinggolfclub.com
Queen's Road, FK8 2QY | 01786 464098 | Open Mon–Fri and Sun
Undulating parkland with magnificent views of Stirling Castle and the Grampian Mountains. The fifteenth, Cotton's Fancy, is testing.

EAT AND DRINK
The Stirling Highland Hotel ◉
stirlinghighlandhotel.co.uk
Spittal Street, FK8 1DU | 01786 272727
Once a school, this hotel, set just down the hill from the castle, has three dining rooms, all with high ceilings and large windows. Cooking is assured and modern, with beautifully presented dishes featuring seasonal local ingredients.

Blair Drummond Safari and Adventure Park
blairdrummond.com
Blair Drummond, FK9 4UR | 01786 841456 | Open Mar–Oct daily 10–5.30
This is a drive-through safari park to the west of Stirling, where you'll find animals that roam free, including elephants, giraffes, lions and camels. The pets' farm has llamas, pigs and goats, and there are birds of prey flying demonstrations, a boat safari and a playground. There's an adventure and climbing area for children of all ages, plus pedal boats and an 'astraglide' funfair ride and picnic and barbecue areas.

▶ Falkirk Wheel

Castle Campbell

historicenvironment.scot
Dollar Glen, FK14 7PP | 01259
742408 | Open Apr–Sep daily
9.30–5.30; Oct–Mar daily 10–4
The original name of this
dramatic stronghold was the
Castle of Gloume, but the First
Earl of Argyll disliked the name
and changed it by an Act of
Parliament in 1489 to the less
dismal Castle Campbell. The
castle stands on a rocky spur of
land between two streams,
rather mournfully named the
Burn of Care and the Burn of
Sorrow. It is not known exactly
when the first castle was raised
here, but the earliest surviving
building dates from the end of
the 15th century and is in an
excellent state of preservation.

Bannockburn Heritage Centre

nts.org.uk
Bannockburn, FK7 0LJ
01786 812664 | Open Mar–Oct
daily 10–5.30; Nov–Feb daily 10–5
There is some dispute as to
whether the Heritage Centre
is actually on the place where
the battle took place, but it's
still a stirring story. It fills you
in on the story of the battle,
including the 3D Battle of
Bannockburn Experience.

Doune Castle

historicenvironment.scot
Castle Hill, Doune, FK16 6EA
01786 841742 | Open Apr–Sep daily
9.30–5.30; Oct–Mar daily 10–4
This impressive half-ruined
castle, set round an inner
courtyard, dates from the 14th
century, and stands on a small
hill above the River Teith. Its
modern claim to fame is as the
setting for the 1970s movie
Monty Python and the Holy Grail.

Falkirk Wheel

scottishcanals.co.uk
35 Lime Road, Tamfourhill, FK1 4RS
0870 050 0208 (calls cost max 24p
per minute, plus your phone
company's access charge)
Open Mar–Oct Mon–Fri 10–5.30,
Sat–Sun 10–6.30; Feb daily 10.30–4;
Nov–Dec Wed–Sun 10.30–4;
Jan Wed–Sun 11–3. Book boat
trips online or call for times
and reservations
You can watch this unique,
state-of-the-art boat lift in
action from the glass-sided
visitor centre or take a one-
hour boat ride between the
Forth and Clyde and Union
canals. The Falkirk Wheel was
opened in 2002, linking the two
canals and replacing the stair
of 11 locks that originally
transported boats between
them. Claimed to be the world's
only boat lift, it's 115 feet high.

▶ Strathpeffer MAP REF 412 C5

Once hailed as the Harrogate of the North, Strathpeffer is a curious phenomenon to find above the Highland line – an attractive little spa town, complete with Victorian architectural twirls such as verandas and ornamental barge-boards.

Locals had known about the curative properties of the mineral springs here for centuries, but thanks to a serious scientific analysis of the water in 1819, Strathpeffer became a boom town. The first pump room opened the following year, and visitors flocked to fill the new hotels and villas. While never perhaps in the same league as Bath in Somerset, the town did attract some royal visitors from overseas, and the railway had to be specially extended from Dingwall to cater for the number of people drawn here. At the height of its fame there were even through-trains from London.

Inevitably, tastes change, and Strathpeffer's popularity declined after World War II. Many of the spa buildings have disappeared, and the old wooden railway station now houses a museum of childhood. The Pump Room has been restored with interpretative displays covering the history of the spa. The town offers excellent golfing and other recreational facilities to its visitors. Don't miss the Pictish stone slab, set in a field near the station. Deeply carved with an inverted, patterned horseshoe shape above a standing eagle, its original purpose is unknown.

There are several good places to walk here, including the ridge of Knock Farril to the south, and through the woods to the Falls of Rogie to the west.

WATCH FOR WILDLIFE
RSPB Tollie Red Kites
rspb.org.uk
Dingwall, IV7 8HQ | 01463 715000
Visitor centre open daily 9–5; kite feeding times 2.30 (summer) and 1.30 (winter)
Red kites, extinct in Scotland for almost 100 years, were first reintroduced in 1989, when about 90 birds from Sweden were released into the wild on the Black Isle.

There are now about 50 breeding pairs of these spectacular birds in the region, and you can see them up close at this nature reserve, near Dornoch, where kites come to be fed by RSPB volunteers.

PLAY A ROUND
Strathpeffer Spa Golf Club
strathpeffergolf.co.uk
Golf Course Road, IV14 9AS | 01997 421219 | Open daily all year. Booking required for Sat
A wonderfully scenic 18-hole course, laid out in the 1890s by the famous golfer Tom Morris of St Andrews. More difficult than it first would appear, the course's fast sloping greens and four ponds make up for the relatively few bunkers.

▲ Strathpeffer

▶ Stromness
see **Orkney Islands**, page 320

▶ Sumburgh Head
see **Shetland Islands**, page 359

▶ Thirlestane Castle MAP REF 403 D4

thirlestanecastle.co.uk

Lauder, TD2 6RU | 01578 722430 | Open May–Sep Tue–Thu, Sun 10–3

This fairytale castle, one of the most sumptuously decorated great houses in Scotland, has been home to the Maitland family since the 13th century. A simple pink sandstone tower house just east of Lauder was transformed between 1670 and 1676 for the Duke of Lauderdale, Secretary of State, by architect William Bruce and master craftsman Robert Mylne. They succeeded in creating a splendid palace without destroying the character of the original castle. Bruce also supervised the interior work, which included some magnificent plasterwork in the state rooms. The Duke died in 1682 and, with no male heir, his title died with him. His brother, Charles, became the Third Earl of Lauderdale.

Visitors may well complete a tour of the castle with a crick in their neck from gazing up at all the wonderful ceilings – the richest of all is in the Large Drawing Room – but in every room it is worth looking upwards. Fine 19th-century French Empire-style furniture, vast gilded mirrors and one of the most comprehensive collections of family portraits in Scotland adorn the state rooms. The charming nurseries house a delightful collection of historic toys, with some modern replicas, too, for visiting children to play with, as well as a dressing-up chest.

▶ Thurso MAP REF 415 D5

Thurso was the Vikings' gateway to mainland Scotland, and its neighbouring port of Scrabster is still the departure point for Orkney (see page 312). Much of the town dates from the 1790s, the heyday of its life as a fishing port, and its grid of tidy streets are lined with fine Victorian buildings. Most visitors are in transit, with the exception of surfers from all over the world who head east to Dunnet Bay to catch the reef breaks, considered to be among the world's finest.

VISIT THE MUSEUM
Caithness Horizons
caithnesshorizons.co.uk
High Street, KW14 8AJ
01847 816508 | Open Apr–Oct
Mon–Fri 10–6, Sat 10–5, Sun 12–5;
Nov–Mar Mon–Sat 10–5
This excellent museum and exhibition gallery tells the story of Caithness from earliest times to the present day. You'll find Bronze and Iron Age artefacts, Pictish stones, Viking exhibits, as well as information on the nuclear reactors along the coast at Dounreay, which once provided many local jobs.

PLAY A ROUND
Thurso Golf Club
thursogolfclub.co.uk
Newlands of Geise, KW14 7XF
01847 893807 | Open daily all year
This parkland course has fine views of Dunnet Head and the Orkney Islands. Trees line the fairways; the fourth and sixteenth holes are testing.

EAT AND DRINK
Forss House Hotel ◉◉
forsshousehotel.co.uk
Forss, KW14 7XY | 01847 861201
The dining room of this elegant Georgian country-house hotel serves proper Scottish country cooking with a modern twist, using produce from around Caithness.

◀ Dunnet Beach

▶ **PLACES NEARBY**
West of Thurso, the coast gets wilder and more remote, and there are settlements to explore such as Durness and Tongue, and scenic grandeur in the shape of Loch Eriboll and the wild beauty of lonely Cape Wrath, where the north coast turns south towards Scourie and Kylesku. To the east is John o'Groats (see page 264), with the Castle of Mey en route.

Castle of Mey
castleofmey.org.uk
KW14 8XH | 01847 851473 | Open daily mid-May to Sep 10.30–4

Queen Elizabeth, the Queen Mother, purchased and then restored this 16th-century castle – formerly known as Barrogill – as her Scottish hideaway after the death of her husband, King George VI, in 1952, and spent her Augusts at this surprisingly homely place.

Inside, the rooms are modest and comfortable, with things left very much as they were during her lifetime. There are wonderful views north to Orkney. The Gardens of Mey, sheltered from the ceaseless winds by 12-foot-high walls, are a delight.

▶ Tiree
see **Western Isles**, page 386

▶ Torridon
see **Shieldaig & Torridon**, page 361

▶ Traquair House MAP REF 402 C4

traquair.co.uk
Innerleithen, EH44 6PW | 01896 830323 | Open Apr–Sep daily 11–5;
Oct daily 11–4; Nov Sat–Sun 11–3

An air of romance and ancient secrecy surrounds Traquair, a beautiful old house hidden in the trees 6 miles southeast of Peebles (see page 325). It started out as a royal hunting lodge at the time of Alexander I of Scotland – its modern extensions were made way back in the 17th century, and today it presents a serene, grey-harled face to visitors. Once the River Tweed ran so close that the laird could fish from his windows. That changed when the river was re-routed by Sir William Stuart, who also built most of what we see now, in 1566.

Part of Traquair's sense of mystery comes from its connections with the doomed Stuart cause: Mary, Queen of Scots stayed here in 1566 (her bed is now in the King's Room), and the famous wrought-iron Bear Gates have not been opened since 1745, when Bonnie Prince Charlie last rode through. The

Fifth Earl vowed they would remain closed until another Stuart king was on the British throne. There are secret stairs to the hidden Priest's Room, and touching relics of a time when Catholics were persecuted in Scotland.

Traquair's exterior is remarkably plain, its high walls regularly punctuated with unornamented windows that break into the line of the high, steeply pitched roof. A hint of a turret in the centre marks one corner of the oldest section, but otherwise Traquair is refreshingly free of crenellations, castellations, machicolations, Gothic windows and all the other architectural paraphernalia without which no 18th-century stately home was considered complete. Inside, it is a quiet, living, breathing home, continuing much as it has done for hundreds of years.

Traquair was first recognised as a royal hunting lodge in 1107 by King Alexander I of Scotland, who stayed here and granted its charter. It remained a royal property until the 15th century, when the First Earl of Buchan passed it to his illegitimate son Sir James Stuart; it remains in Stuart ownership today.

Outside, features include attractive gardens with a maze. It's a sizeable puzzle and even if you were to go straight to the centre, it would involve a walk of about a quarter of a mile. There is also the 1745 Cottage Restaurant, which serves excellent food and is well worth a visit. Take in the brewery underneath the chapel, too; re-established in 1965, it has proved highly successful, and now produces three rich, dark ales that you can sample in the brewery shop.

▶ The Trossachs

see **Loch Lomond & The Trossachs National Park**, page 286

....

▶ Ullapool MAP REF 412 A4

Ullapool is the gateway to the remote northwestern tip of Scotland, as well as the main ferry port for Stornoway in the Outer Hebrides. As you drive down the north side of Loch Broom, this little whitewashed town lies ahead, neatly laid out on a spit of land curving into the loch. It's a popular holiday destination for those planning to explore the Highlands.

The tidy gridplan of the streets reveals that this is a model town, laid out to a plan developed by the British Fishery Society in 1788. The site was chosen to provide a good fishing harbour, and to squeeze out the Dutch herring vessels that had taken advantage of the lack of local boats. The herring did not last, however, and, without the lifeline of the railway, the settlement declined.

The Fishery Society had chosen their site well, however, and in the first half of the 20th century boats came over from the east coast and fortunes revived. Until the mid-1990s, the local economy was given a boost by the Klondyker factory ships from Eastern Europe, processing the catches made by the east-coast trawlermen in the loch's sheltered waters. They disappeared after the collapse of the Russian economy and now tourism is the main industry.

▲ Corrieshalloch Gorge, Ullapool

VISIT THE MUSEUM
Ullapool Museum
ullapoolmuseum.co.uk
7–8 Argyle Street, IV26 2TY
01854 612987 | Open Easter–Oct
Mon–Sat 10–5
Learn more about crofting, fishing and emigration at Ullapool's small museum, in a former church. There's an audio-visual presentation and touch-screen displays, and the museum puts on temporary exhibitions with local themes.

GET ACTIVE
Loch Broom Leisure Centre
lochbroomleisure.co.uk
Quat Street, IV26 2UE
01854 612884
There's plenty of wet-weather family entertainment here, with a pool, sports centre and gym, a climbing wall and tennis. Lots of activities are on offer and holidaymakers are made welcome.

GET ON THE WATER
Shearwater Cruises
summerqueen.co.uk
1 Royal Park, IV26 2XT | 01854 612472 or 07713 257219
Two sailings Apr–Sep daily; weather dependent, advance booking essential
The MV *Summer Queen* cruises to the green bumps of the Summer Isles, 12 miles northwest at the mouth of the loch, twice daily in summer. En route you should see a great range of seabirds, seals and cetaceans. The morning cruise offers time ashore on Tanera, the largest of the isles.

EAT AND DRINK
The Ceilidh Place
theceilidhplace.co.uk
14 West Argyle Street, IV26 2TY
01854 612103
An Ullapool institution since it opened in 1970, this unique complex combines an all-day coffee shop, a bar and a restaurant with a bookshop, art gallery and welcoming performance venue.

▶ PLACES NEARBY
South of Ullapool lies some of Scotland's most beautiful coastal scenery, a string of sea lochs and white-sand beaches with spectacular views; hit the coast road to take in the best of this and visit the celebrated gardens at Inverewe (see page 248). Heading north, you'll enter one of Scotland's most remote regions, with the landscape growing increasingly wild and less fertile. Tiny crofting settlements and ports, such as Lochinver, Kylesku and Kinlochbervie, are all there is in the way of habitation, but there's scenic grandeur on an epic scale, wildlife galore and a wonderful sense of finding yourself on the edge of Britain.

Corrieshalloch Gorge
nts.org.uk
Braemore, IV23 2JP | 01445 781229
Open daily 24 hours
At the head of Loch Broom, the River Droma drops over the mighty Falls of Measach into a gorge, the walls constantly wet with spray and spangled with a huge range of plants. You can view the falls either from the vertiginous viewing platform or from the suspension bridge just below.

Achiltibuie Hydroponicum
thehydroponicum.com
Achiltibuie, IV26 2YG | 01854 622202 | Open Apr–Sep Mon–Fri 11–1, 2–4
This is a working garden, where plants are grown in water supplied with their exact nutritional requirements. This means each plant receives exactly what it needs for maximum growth and the vegetables grown in these polytunnels are truly impressive, as well as some being surprising to find in northern Scotland – banana, anyone?

Summer Isles Hotel and Bar
summerisleshotel.com
Achiltibuie, IV26 2YG
01854 622282
There are wonderful views to the Summer Isles from this open-all-day hotel and bar. Seafood and fish are landed nearby, meat is local and the beer comes from a croft house brewery a few miles away – what's not to like?

▶ Unst
see **Shetland Islands**, page 360

▶ Western Isles

The offshore islands lying to the west of Scotland's north coast
fall into two groups, the Inner and Outer Hebrides.

   Those nearer the mainland are by far the most visited,
particularly Mull, a mere 40-minute ferry crossing from Oban
(see page 307). The Outer Hebrides lie beyond Skye (see page
254), far across the storm-tossed waters of the Minch, and, like
Orkney and Shetland, are really a destination in their own right.

▶ The Inner Hebrides MAP REF 400 A1

The islands of the Inner Hebrides, each with its own character
and community life, fall into distinct groups. Largest by far
– discounting Skye, to the north – is Mull, characterised by
mountains and moorland with pockets of more pastoral
landscape, small towns, settlements and castles to visit, and
giving access to holy Iona and the drama of Staffa and Fingal's
Cave. The low-lying islands of Coll, Tiree, Colonsay and
Oronsay lie west of Mull, windswept and remote. To the south
lie Islay and Jura, one producing some of Scotland's finest
whiskies, the other home to many more red deer than people.

▶ Mull & Iona MAP REF 405 D6/400 A1

The second-largest of the Inner Hebrides, lying across the Firth
of Lorne from Oban, Mull is traditionally a crofting, fishing and

distilling island. From a 19th-century high of 10,000, the population has dwindled to about 3,000, but in Highland terms Mull is a success story, with a growing population of settlers drawn by the prospect of a peaceful way of life in unspoiled countryside. The island covers some 350 sq miles, with scenery that ranges from undulating tracts of moor and bog, to its highest point, Ben More, an extinct volcano. The coastline, particularly to the west, is one of Mull's greatest assets; white-sand beaches around Calgary contrast with soaring cliffs at Loch na Keal. North of here is the capital, Tobermory, with its jolly coloured houses – a familiar sight to fans of the children's TV series *Balamory*. The road south leads via pastoral Salen to Craignure, the main ferry port, and the castles of Torosay and Duart. From Craignure, a lonely road crosses the Ross of Mull to Fionnphort, the jumping-off point for Iona and the magical island of Staffa, with its black basalt columns that inspired Felix Mendelssohn's overture *The Hebrides* (1830).

Iona's story is inextricably linked with St Columba, who founded his monastery in AD 563. From this remote spot, the teachings of Christianity, told through beautifully illuminated manuscripts such as the *Book of Kells*, radiated throughout Europe. Columba's foundation ended in AD 806 with the Vikings, but in the 12th century Benedictine monks built a church and abbey, a beacon of learning and burial place of Scottish kings, until the Reformation left this foundation, too, in ruins. In 1910 restoration started, and today the Iona Community welcomes pilgrims from around the world.

▼ Tobermory

TAKE IN SOME HISTORY
Duart Castle
duartcastle.com

PA64 6AP | 01680 812309 | Open Apr to mid-Oct daily 10.30–5.30

Records date Duart's foundation as some time in the 13th century, when it first became the seat of the clan chiefs of the Macleans. Burned by the Campbells, it was confiscated after the 1745 Jacobite rebellion. In 1911, the 26th clan chief, Fitzroy Maclean, vowed to restore it. What you see today is the result. Its position is superb, a craggy point overlooking the Sound of Mull, and the interior is full of memorabilia, with magnificent views of the sea and mountains.

Iona Abbey
historicenvironment.scot

PA76 6SQ | 01681 700512 | Open Apr–Sep daily 9.30–5.30; Oct–Mar Mon–Sat 10–4

Take the ferry from Fionnphort for the short crossing to Iona, where you can explore the priory ruins, the abbey itself and perhaps walk to the far side of this beautiful island.

VISIT THE MUSEUM
Mull Museum
mullmuseum.org.uk

Colomba Buildings, Main Street, Tobermory, PA75 6NY

01688 301100 | Open Mon–Fri 10–4, Sun 2–4

Learn about Mull's history through the centuries via displays, photographs and artefacts – good for a day when the midges drive you mad.

TOUR A DISTILLERY
Tobermory Distillery
tobermorydistillery.com

Ledaig, Tobermory, PA75 6NR

01688 302647 | Open Mon–Fri 10–5, Sat, Sun 10–4

Two single malt whiskies are produced here, the unpeated Tobermory and the smoky Ledaig. Tours explain the distilling process, and there's a wee dram to taste at the end.

CATCH A PERFORMANCE
Comar
comar.co.uk

An Tobar: Argyll Terrace, Tobermory, PA75 6PB | 01688 302211

Comar was formed by the merger of An Tobar arts centre and Mull Theatre. An Tobar showcases visual and performing arts. It has a busy music calendar, a shop and a cafe. Mull Theatre puts on original and established plays in summer, and may also tour productions around the Highlands. Advance reservations essential.

SAIL TO STAFFA
Staffa Tours
staffatours.com

07831 885 985 or 07732 912 370

This company runs regular tours to Staffa and the Treshnish Isles from both Fionnphort and Tobermory; see the website for more details.

Turus Mara
turusmara.com

Penmore Mill, Dervaig, PA75 6QS

0800 085 8786 | Open Easter–Oct, weather permitting

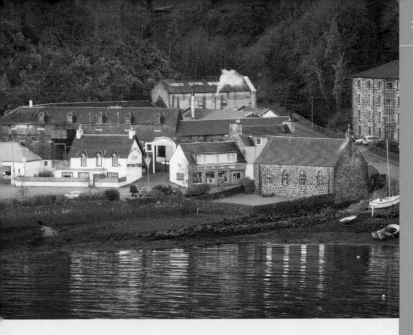

▲ Tobermory Distillery

Summer wildlife cruises to Staffa, Iona and the Treshnish Isles leave from Ulva Ferry. Potential sightings include seabirds, sea eagles, common and grey seals, basking sharks, dolphins and porpoises. Advance booking essential.

MEET THE SEA LIFE
Wildlife and Birdwatch Safaris
mullwildlife.co.uk
Torr na Craoibhe, Bunessan, PA72 6DH | 01681 700090
Join a full-day wildlife tour of the island, with a chance to see peregrine falcons, golden eagles, owls, otters, seals and porpoises. Lunch, snack and binoculars provided. Advance reservations essential. Not suitable for very young children.

PLAY A ROUND
Tobermory Golf Club
tobermorygolfclub.com
PA75 6PS | 01688 302783
Open daily all year
This nine-hole course, hilly, tough and windy, has superb views over the Sound of Mull.

EAT AND DRINK
Ninth Wave Restaurant ◉
ninthwaverestaurant.co.uk
near Fionnphort, PA66 6BL
01681 700757
Dinner only is on offer at this tiny and remote restaurant, stylish and contemporary, where fish and seafood come off the owner's boat and the vegetables are from the garden of the restaurant's own croft.

Highland Cottage ◉◉
highlandcottage.co.uk
24 Breadalbane Street, Tobermory, PA75 6PD | 01688 302030
The dining room of this charming small restaurant with rooms, whose lounges are all

▲ Coll

squashy sofas and interesting books, serves as much as it can from Mull, with fish from the coast and Scottish meat.

The Bellachroy Inn
thebellachroy.co.uk
Dervaig, PA75 6QW | 01688 400314

Mull's oldest inn dates back to 1608, and the hospitality tradition continues with local crab, mackerel and haddock to eat and some good beer from Loch Fyne – drink it on the terrace and you may catch a glimpse of a sea eagle.

▶ Coll, Tiree, Colonsay & Oronsay

COLL MAP REF 404 C5; TIREE 404 B6; COLONSAY 400 A2; ORONSAY 400 A2

To the west of Mull, the low-lying islands of Coll and Tiree are noted for their sandy beaches, their flower-studded machair (sea meadow) and rare birds, including corncrakes and little terns. You can reach them via a three-and-a-half-hour ferry journey from Oban. Tiree has more hours of sunshine a year than anywhere else in Scotland, making it wonderful for walking, and cycling too, if you're prepared to battle with the virtually incessant wind – on the plus side, the wind keeps the midges away. The less-visited islands of Colonsay and Oronsay, to the south, also have fine sands and birdlife.

EAT AND DRINK
Coll Hotel
collhotel.com
Arinagour, PA78 6SZ
01879 230334

The Coll Hotel has some stunning views over the sea to Jura and Mull, and being the Isle of Coll's only inn, it is, naturally, the hub of the island

community. Come here to mingle with the locals, soak in the atmosphere, and enjoy pints of Fyne Ale and malt whiskies.

In the summer months the fabulous garden acts as an extension to the bar or the Gannet Restaurant.

▶ Islay & Jura MAP REF 400 B4/B3

Islay is a working island with an atmosphere very different from that of those reliant on visitors for most of their income. Some of the world's finest connoisseur single malt whiskies are produced at its eight distilleries, all of which offer guided tours and tastings. The peaty, smoky quality of Islay whisky is unmistakable, even if you have had little tasting experience.

The distilleries are scattered around the island, one sited at Bowmore, Islay's capital. It's a planned village, laid out in 1768 on a grid of streets lined with whitewashed houses. You'll have to head out of town to enjoy Islay's other main attraction, the incredible resident and overwintering birdlife. The island is a major winter habitat for thousands of Greenland barnacle and white-fronted geese. You'll find information on seeing them at the Wildlife Information Centre at the island's prettiest village, Port Charlotte, which is also home to the island's museum.

Ferries run hourly across the Sound of Islay to Jura, a long island that stretches northeast for 28 miles and is only eight miles wide. Wild and mountainous, Jura is dominated by the swelling mounds of the Paps of Jura, visible from all over this part of Scotland. There's one village at Craighouse, where Jura Malt is distilled, and the red deer population on the island outnumbers that of the humans by 33:1. George Orwell's *1984* was written on Jura when he lived here in 1946.

VISIT THE MUSEUM
Museum of Island Life
islaymuseum.org
Port Charlotte, PA48 7UA | 01496
850358 | Open Apr–Oct Mon–Fri
10.30–4.30
The story of Islay and its people
is told here through a collection
of exhibits, photographs and
papers. There's a children's
corner and quizzes to do.

GO BIRDING
Islay Natural History Centre
islaynaturalhistory.org
Port Charlotte, PA48 7TX | 01496
850288 | Open May–Sep Mon–Fri
10.30–4.30
Displays fill you in on the
island's wildlife, there's a library
to track down what you've seen,
and the centre organises walks,
talks and activities.

TOUR A WHISKY DISTILLERY
ardbeg.com
bowmore.com
bruichladdich.com
bunnahabhain.com
discovering-distilleries.com (for
Caol Ila and Lagavoulin)

kilchomandistillery.com
laphroaig.com
The eight distilleries on Islay all
welcome visitors, and all
explain the process of the
distillation of the so-called
water of life. See individual
websites for opening times.

PLAY A ROUND
The Machrie Golf Links
machrie.net
Port Ellen, PA42 7AN
01496 302310
This championship links
course opened in 1891, and it
was where golf's first £100
Open Championship was played
in 1901. Fine turf and many
blind holes.

EAT AND DRINK
The Port Charlotte Hotel
portcharlottehotel.co.uk
PA48 7TU | 01496 850360
The conservatory of this solid
Victorian hotel opens onto the
beach and garden. The cooking
showcases as much local
produce as possible. The bar
serves great seafood lunches.

▶ The Outer Hebrides MAP REF 410 A4

Like the inner isles across the Minch, the Outer Hebrides fall
into natural island groups. Ferries link them to Oban, Ullapool
and Uig on Skye (see page 254), and there are mainland flights
to three islands, Lewis, Benbecula and Barra.

To the north lie Lewis and Harris, geographically one island,
with Lewis, the most densely populated region of the Outer
Hebrides, forming the northern part of this area, and Harris,
far more mountainous, occupying the southern part. From its
southern tip, ferries cross to a chain of four islands, North Uist,
Benbecula, South Uist and Eriskay, all linked by causeways.
South again, tiny Barra marks the end of the inhabited islands.

All the Outer Hebrides share a strong Gaelic culture, and
you'll hear Gaelic widely spoken. The northern islands of Lewis,
Harris and North Uist follow the Protestant faith and keep strict,
traditional observance of the Sabbath, so plan ahead if you're
visiting on a Sunday, as restaurants, shops and petrol stations
will be closed. The southern islands retained the Roman Catholic
religion and you'll see wayside shrines to the Virgin which
wouldn't look out of place in the Catholic countries of Europe.

▶ Lewis & Harris MAP REF 411 D2/410 C4

Lewis and Harris, although joined by a narrow neck of land,
have their own distinct and individual identities and
atmosphere. Lewis, the northern part, has great undulating
blanket peat moors scattered with lochs, and a surprising
density of population for such an isolated place. The main
town is Stornoway (Steornabhagh), the administrative centre,
a busy fishing port on the east coast and the only real town
on the island.

West of Stornoway, overlooking Loch Ròg, loom the islands'
most important prehistoric ruins, the Callanish standing
stones. You can reach these and the northern part of Lewis,
Ness, on good roads leading through the crofting communities
that hug the shore, or head to the mountainous southwest
corner, where the white sands of Uig and Reef compete with
lush green islands to steal the view. On a clear day, you can see
the pointed peaks of St Kilda, 41 miles away on the horizon.

Harris, the southern sector, is the most beautiful of the
Outer Hebrides, with high mountains and deep-cut bays. The
west coast is fringed with white-sand beaches, backed by

◀ Calanais Standing Stones

machair pastures, carpeted with wild flowers. The subtle browns, greens and smoky greys of the landscape are reflected in the island's most famous export, Harris Tweed, a handwoven wool cloth of high quality made here since the 1840s.

TAKE IN SOME HISTORY
St Clement's Church
historicenvironment.scot
Roghadal, HS5 3TW
Open Mon–Sat 10–5
This pre-Reformation church, dating from about 1500, is the burial place of the MacLeods of Harris, and was saved from ruin and restored in the 19th century. Its serene interior has remarkable wall tombs with sculpted figures, including a stag hunt and St Michael and the Devil weighing the souls of the dead. There are great views to Taransay island from the luminous sands and turquoise waters of Tràigh Luskentyre.

VISIT THE MUSEUM
Museum nan Eilean
cne-siar.gov.uk/museum
Lews Castle, Stornoway, HS1 2BW
01851 600 501 | Open Apr–Sep Mon–Wed, Fri and Sat 10–5; Oct–Mar Mon–Wed, Sat and Sun 1–4
In a modern extension, contrasting with the Gothic revival grandeur of Lews Castle, this museum displays local treasures alongside important loans from the National Museum of Scotland and the British Museum. Together, these explore the distinct identity of the islands and how this has been shaped by the unique combination of people, land and sea. You'll be able to learn how people have lived and worked in the islands throughout history and see how their culture has been expressed, through community life, religion and the Gaelic language.

GO BACK IN TIME
Calanais Standing Stones
historicenvironment.scot
calanaisvisitorcentre.co.uk
Callanish, HS2 9DY | 01851 621422
Open Apr–Sep daily 10–6; Oct–Mar Wed–Sat 10–4
Lewis has many prehistoric monuments and monoliths, of which the avenue and circle of stones at Calanais (Callanish), dating to about 3000 BC, is outstanding. The fantastically patterned stones are of the underlying rock of the island, Lewisian gneiss, some 2,900 million years old; their history is explained in the Calanais Visitor Centre.

Baile Tughaidh
Carloway, HS2 9Al
01851 643416
Open May–Sep Mon–Sat 9.30–5.30
This cluster of traditional thatched crofters' houses will take you back in time and fill you in on the old way of life.

Dun Carloway Broch
calanaisvisitorcentre.co.uk
Carloway, HS2 9AZ
Dun Carloway Broch is an excellent example of a stone-built circular Iron-Age dwelling,

its walls standing 30 feet high. Learn more at the visitors' centre, which features a reconstructed broch.

TOUR THE DISTILLERY
Isle of Harris Distillery
harrisdistillery.com
Tarbert, HS3 3DJ | 01859 502212
The first whisky distillery in Harris only opened in autumn 2015, so you'll need to wait a few years for its product to be ready to sample. Meanwhile, they welcome visitors: telephone for information.

GET ACTIVE
Ionad Spors Leodhais
cne-siar.gov.uk
Springfield Road, Stornoway, HS1 2PZ | 01851 822800 | Open Mon–Fri 8am–10pm, Sat 9–8
There's a swimming pool, sports hall, climbing wall and gym at the Outer Hebrides' main leisure centre.

CATCH A PERFORMANCE
An Lanntair
anlanntair.com
Kenneth Street, Stornoway, HS1 2DS
01851 708480
There's live music, films and exhibitions here, the main arts centre for the Outer Hebrides.

LEARN TO SURF
Hebridean Surf Holidays
hebrideansurf.co.uk
Lower Barvas, Na h-Eileanan an Iar, HS2 0RA | 01851 840343
Offering surfing lessons for everyone, they also hire out wetsuits, body boards and surfboards.

PLAY A ROUND
Stornoway Golf Club
stornowaygolfclub.co.uk
Lady Lever Park, Stornoway, HS2 0XP | 01851 702240 | Open Mon–Sat
This is a short but tricky undulating, 18-hole parkland course set in the grounds of Lews Castle with fine views over the Minch to the mainland. The terrain is peat based and there has been substantial investment in drainage works.

Isle of Harris Golf Club
harrisgolf.com
Scarista, HS5 3HX | 01859 550226
This stunningly located links course is bordered on three sides by the Sound of Taransay and looks out towards the Atlantic Ocean; beautiful white sands stretch down the western side of the course.

Many of the course's nine holes are very demanding, with natural hazards to negotiate. Professional golfers who have tested their skills here include Nick Faldo and Ronan Rafferty.

EAT AND DRINK
Hotel Hebrides ⊛
hotel-hebrides.com
Pier Road, Tarbert, HS3 3DG
01859 502364
This modern boutique hotel is the focal point of a village of some 500 souls on the Isle of Harris. You roll in on the ferry from Skye, overseen by diners in the Pierhouse seafood restaurant, where everything piscine on offer is locally sourced and caught. There are light meals served in the bar.

▶ North Uist, Benbecula, South Uist & Eriskay

NORTH UIST MAP REF 410 B5; BENBECULA 404 B2; SOUTH UIST 404 B2;
ERISKAY 404 B3

South of the bulk of Lewis and Harris, this chain of four islands is linked by a series of causeways. The islands are characterised by low, peaty ground glittering with a thousand trout-stocked lochans (small lakes), with big bare hills and beaches of sparkling white shell sand to the west. Benbecula (Beinn na Faoghla) is their main administrative centre, and boasts a small airport.

North Uist (Uibhist a Tuath) is rich in standing stones and other prehistoric remains, signs that these islands have been inhabited for more than 4,000 years. Today, its main settlement is Lochmaddy (Loch nam Madadh), the ferry port. Communities are widely scattered and surprisingly numerous, for crofting on the fertile machair (sea meadow) is still viable. This machair is the outstanding characteristic of South Uist (Uibhist a Deas), a riot of colour in early summer with a dazzling profusion of up to 45 wildflower species per sq metre, producing a flora unmatched in Britain. The islands also provide vital wetland habitat for birds such as corncrakes, red-necked phalaropes, geese and mute swans.

The Sound of Eriskay, which links South Uist and Eriskay (Eirisgeigh) – now crossed by a stone causeway – is where the whisky-laden SS *Politician* foundered in 1941, giving novelist Compton Mackenzie the idea for his comic tale *Whisky Galore* (1947); the classic film was shot on neighbouring Barra the following year.

VISIT THE MUSEUMS
Kildonan Museum
kildonanmuseum.co.uk
South Uist, HS8 5RZ | 01878 710343 | Open Apr–Oct daily 10–5
The Kildonan Museum reveals the history and cultural heritage of the people here. Chief draw is the Clanranald Stone, carved with the arms of the clan that ruled South Uist from 1370 to 1839. Down the road you'll find the ruined croft that was the birthplace of Flora MacDonald (1722–90); it's signed from the main road near the turning to Gearraidh Bhailteas.

Taigh Chearsabhagh
taigh-chearsabhagh.org
Lochmaddy, North Uist, HS6 5AA
01870 603970 | Open Mon–Sat 10–5, Sun 10–3
This museum and arts centre is housed in a converted 18th-century merchant's house and serves both the local community and visitors with a great range of cultural activities. There's an excellent museum, which stages exhibitions, shows films and sponsored the seven sculptures that are dotted about the Uists.

GO BIRDING
Balranald RSPB Reserve
rspb.org.uk
Houghharry, North Uist, HS6 5Dl
01876 560287
This visitor centre is a great place to learn not only about birds but the other wildlife of North Uist. From the centre, trails lead out through the machair, beautiful walking with the chance to see – and you'll certainly hear from May to July – the elusive corncrake, one of Britain's rarest birds.

GET ACTIVE
Uist Outdoor Centre
uistoutdoorcentre.co.uk
Cearn Dusgaidh, Lochmaddy, HS6 5AE | 01876 500480
This outdoor activities centre offers diving, canoeing, rowing, sea kayaking, rock climbing and abseiling, which you can do as a day visitor. Lochmaddy is noted for the richness of its birdlife. Advance reservations essential.

EAT AND DRINK
Polochar Inn
polocharinn.com
Lochboisdale, South Uist, HS8 5TT
01878 700215
Standing virtually alone overlooking the Sound of Eriskay and a prehistoric standing stone, this white-painted inn is the former change-house, where travellers waited for the ferry to Barra. It serves Hebridean real ales and specialises in local meats and seafood. Beautiful sunsets and live Saturday night music add to its appeal.

▼ North Uist

▲ Barra

▶ Barra MAP REF 404 A3

This island at the foot of the Outer Hebridean chain has an interest out of all proportion to its size, just five miles across and eight miles long. Arriving is part of the fun – especially if you choose to come by air and land on the tidal shell beach of Traigh Mhor.

A road runs around the island but is only 12 miles long, making this a haven for bicycling and walking. In spring and summer the island is rich in wild flowers, with the machair (sea meadow) on the western side at its best. Barra, whose main settlement is Castlebay (Bagh a Chaisteil), survives on crofting and tourism, and the Gaelic culture flourishes.

TAKE IN SOME HISTORY
Kisimul Castle
historicenvironment.scot
Castlebay, Barra, HS9 5UZ
01871 810313 | Open Apr–Sep daily 9.30–5.30
The historic seat of the Clan MacNeil sits on a tiny island in the middle of Castlebay. This medieval castle, the only one surviving in the Outer Hebrides, was restored by the 45th Chief, an American architect. Get the ferry across and enjoy exploring it.

EXPLORE BARRA'S HERITAGE
Dualchas
Castlebay, Barra, HS9 5XD
01871 810413
Open Apr–Oct daily 10.30–4.30
There are two galleries of local history displays to help you understand the history of the island. The centre is run by volunteers who live and work on Barra, and it plays host to temporary exhibitions and cultural events.

▶ **Whithorn & Isle of Whithorn** MAP REF 398 B6/C6

The name's confusing. Scotland has no shortage of islands, but this isn't one of them. One of the most southerly villages in Scotland, Isle of Whithorn was the port serving pilgrims heading for the town of Whithorn. The harbour at Isle of Whithorn was once on an island, but a causeway constructed in the late 18th century linked it to the mainland.

It is disputed whether St Ninian made his first landing here, or at the bay near St Ninian's Cave, three miles to the west, but the harbour is the location of St Ninian's Chapel. This substantial, although roofless, building dates to about 1300, and would have been where pilgrims landing by sea stopped to give thanks for a safe journey. On the walk here from the harbour you pass a seat in Galloway granite, a memorial to seven local fishermen who died when their boat, the *Solway Harvester*, sank in a storm off the Isle of Man in 2000.

Overlooking the harbour is the castellated white wall of the so-called Captain's Garden, a 19th-century whimsy with mock gun ports. Behind the harbourside buildings, Isle of Whithorn Castle, a 17th-century tower house, can be seen but not visited, as it is a private home. It features in the 1973 cult horror film *The Wicker Man*, in which the then-owners appeared as extras.

Little Whithorn is Scotland's oldest Christian settlement, where St Ninian is said to have founded his early church, Candida Casa (the White House), towards the end of the fourth century. Royalty and commoners flocked to the shrine and priory that grew up here right up to the Reformation in 1581. In 1986 the Whithorn Trust was set up to explore the archaeology and history of the area. Excavations have unearthed a 12th-century religious building, stone carvings and smaller, more personal treasures left by the pilgrims; ongoing archaeological work is uncovering the remains of a fifth-century village.

TAKE IN SOME HISTORY
Whithorn Priory and Museum
historicenvironment.scot
6 Bruce Street, Isle of Whithorn, DG8 8PY | Open Apr–Oct daily 10.30–5
Whithorn Priory and Museum embraces the roofless ruin of St Ninian's Chapel (not the original dwelling, but a 14th-century construction), the remains of the medieval Whithorn Priory, and several early stone crosses.

GO BACK IN TIME
The Whithorn Story
whithorn.com
45–47 George Street, Whithorn, DG8 8NS | 01988 500508 | Open Apr–Oct daily 10.30–5
The Whithorn Story reveals what became of this very early Christian foundation, from disastrous Viking raids to royal pilgrimages and its downfall during the Reformation of the 16th century. The new variant of

the Christian faith abhorred the veneration of relics such as those kept in Whithorn's churches and chapels, and the lucrative pilgrim business was banned on pain of death.

▶ PLACES NEARBY

North of Whithorn lies Wigtown, dominated by a vast triangular medieval square. Today, it sells itself as Scotland's Book Town, with more than 25 specialist and antiquarian bookshops and an annual festival.

Bladnoch Distillery and Visitor Centre

bladnoch.com
Bladnoch, DG8 9AB
01988 402605

Scotland's most southerly distillery, lying two miles south of Wigtown, dates from 1817. Enjoy a guided tour of the distillery, see a film of how the whisky is produced and then taste a dram yourself. There's a picnic area, and nearby Cotland Wood has rare orchids and is a pleasant place for a walk.

▶ Wick MAP REF 413 F2

Like Ullapool (see page 379) in the west, Wick, in the northeast corner of Scotland, was built up as a fishery town in the 19th century to take advantage of the herring boom.

The new development, known as Pultneytown, was designed by Thomas Telford for the British Fisheries Society, and stands to the south of the river, complementing the older settlement on the north bank. By the 1850s Wick was Europe's busiest herring port, with a fleet of over 1,100 boats. Today, the harbour plays host to yachtsmen, and the old fishermen's cottages are being transformed.

VISIT THE HERITAGE CENTRE
Wick Heritage Centre

wickheritage.org
18–27 Bank Row, KW1 5EY
01955 605393 | Open Easter–Oct Mon–Sat 10–5

The Heritage Centre is a local attraction, run by volunteers. It tells of the town's heyday as one of the busiest herring ports in the world, when the harbour bristled with boats and the population was swelled by migrant workers from the west coast and Ireland. Some of the boats and whole rooms are preserved here, and you can see the old smokehouse, complete with its original soot.

EAT AND DRINK
Mackay's Hotel ◉

mackayshotel.co.uk
Union Street, KW1 5ED
01955 602323

Situated on the shortest street in the world – and that's official – Mackay's Hotel is a local institution that has been run by the same family for 40 or so years. The kitchen makes good use of quality local ingredients, and there's a definite modernity to the output.

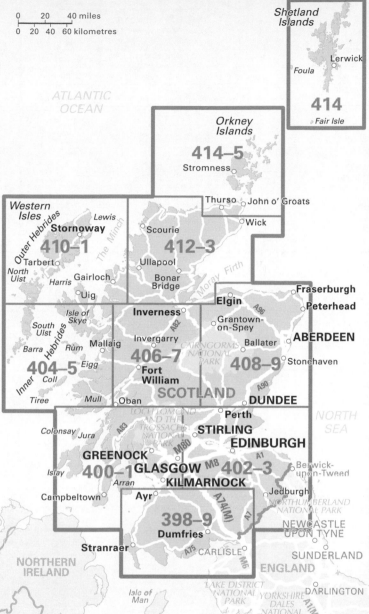

0   20   40 miles
0   20   40   60 kilometres

ATLANTIC OCEAN

Shetland Islands
Lerwick
Foula
414
Fair Isle

Orkney Islands
414–5
Stromness

Thurso   John o' Groats

Wick

Western Isles
Lewis
Stornoway
Outer Hebrides
410–1
Tarbert
North Uist
Harris   Gairloch
Uig

Scourie
412–3
Ullapool
Bonar Bridge

Moray Firth

The Minch

Elgin   **Fraserburgh**
A96   **Peterhead**
Inverness
Grantown-on-Spey
Invergarry   **ABERDEEN**
CAIRNGORMS NATIONAL PARK   Ballater
406–7   **408–9**   Stonehaven
Fort William
Isle of Skye
South Uist
Inner Hebrides
Barra   *Rùm*   Mallaig
404–5   Eigg
Coll
Tiree   *Mull*   Oban

A82

A90
SCOTLAND
DUNDEE
LOCH LOMOND AND THE TROSSACHS NATIONAL PARK
Perth
Colonsay   *Jura*   **STIRLING**
A83   M80   **EDINBURGH**
GREENOCK   M8   A1   Berwick-upon-Tweed
Islay   **400–1**   **GLASGOW**   **402–3**
Arran   **KILMARNOCK**   Jedburgh
Campbeltown   **Ayr**   *NORTHUMBERLAND NATIONAL PARK*
398–9   A7
Dumfries   **NEWCASTLE UPON TYNE**
A74(M)
NORTHERN IRELAND   **CARLISLE**   **ENGLAND**
A75   M6   **SUNDERLAND**
Isle of Man   *LAKE DISTRICT NATIONAL PARK*   DARLINGTON
A1(M)
YORKSHIRE DALES NATIONAL PARK
Lancaster
Stranraer

NORTH SEA

BRADFORD   LEEDS
MANCHESTER
LIVERPOOL   SHEFFIELD
STOKE-ON-TRENT
WALES   DERBY   LEICESTER
WOLVERHAMPTON
BIRMINGHAM
COVENTRY

ATLAS

★ A–Z places listed

• Places Nearby

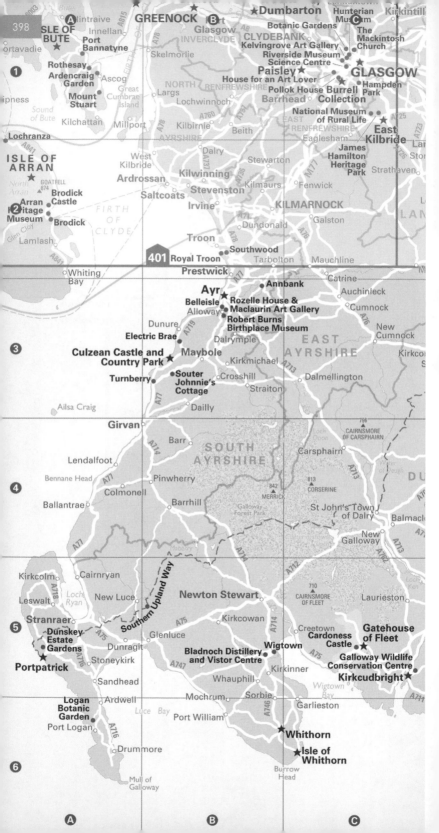

402

840 BROAD LAW

569 CRIFFEL

931 SKIDDAW

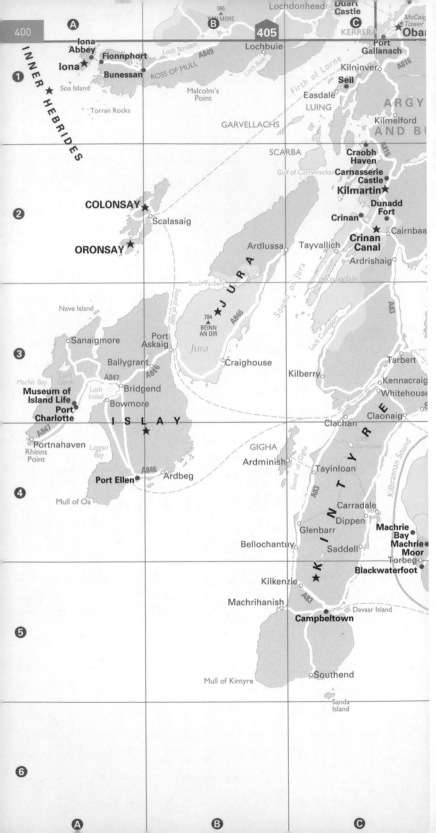

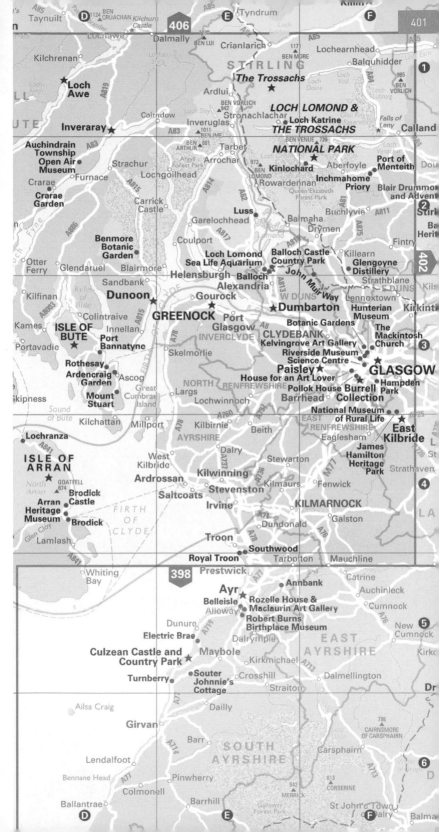

Museum of Transport
Brougty Ferry
DUNDEE
Newport-
on-Tay

Leuchars *St Andrews*
Guardbridge *Bay*
St Andrews Links
★ **St Andrews**
FIFE
Kingsbarns
Fife Ness

Ceres **Scotland's**
Secret
Lathones **Bunker**
Kellie
Castle Crail
East Neuk Cellardyke
Scottish Fisheries Museum
Upper **Anstruther**
Largo **Pittenweem**
Elie Elie **St Monans** Isle of May
Harbour

FIRTH OF FORTH

Bass Rock
North
Berwick **Tantallon Castle**
Dirleton **John Muir**
Castle **Country Park**
Gullane NORTH BERWICK **Belhaven Bay**
LAW ★ **Dunbar**
National **East**
John Museum **Linton**
Muir of Flight
elburgh **Way** ★ **Haddington** Cove
EAST **St Abb's Head**
Cockburnspath **National Nature**
LOTHIAN **Reserve**
Glenkinchie ★St Abbs
Distillery Coldingham
LAMMERMUIR HILLS **Eyemouth**
Cranshaws Burnmouth
Longformacus Ayton
Carfraemill **Southern Upland Way** Preston Chirnside
Thirlestane Westruther Duns **Manderston**
Castle **House** **Berwick-**
Lauder Swinton Norham **upon-Tweed**
Stow Greenlaw Ancroft Beal Holy Island
Mellerstain Gordon Eccles
House Hume Ednam **Coldstream** Etal Lowick
Galashiels Smailholm Wark Ford Belford
Melrose Milfield Doddington
Floors ★ **Kelso**
Abbotsford **Castle** Kirknewton Chatton
Dryburgh **Harestanes** Town ROS
Selkirk **Abbey** **Countryside** Wooler CASTLE
Lilliesleaf **Visitor Centre** Yetholm
Ancrum Crailing Morebattle Eglingham
TISH A698 816
DERS Denholm ★ **Jedburgh** THE CHEVIOT HILLS
berton Powburn
Hawick CHEVIOT **Alnwick**
Bonchester **Jedforest**
Bridge **Deer and** CARTER
Farm Park BAR NORTHUMBERLAND
Teviothead NATIONAL
Rothbury
Thropton Longframlington
Hermitage Rochester PARK
Castle Longhorsley
Otterburn Elsdon
castleton **NORTHUMBERLAND**
holm West Cambo Hartburn
Woodburn Ridsdale Kirkwhelpington
Bollingham

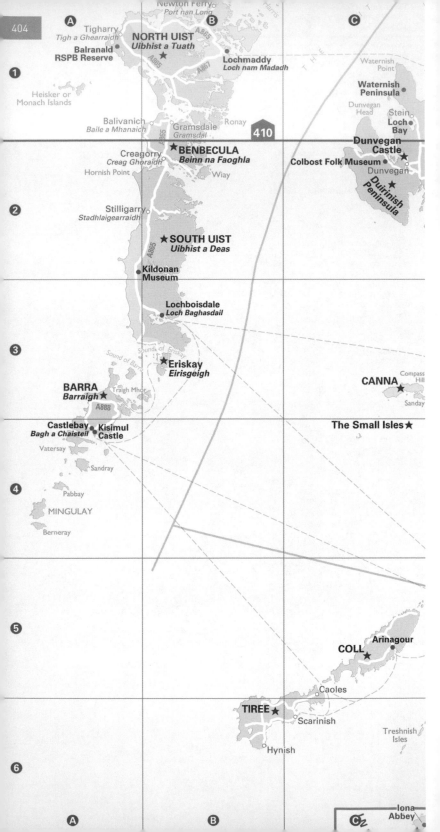

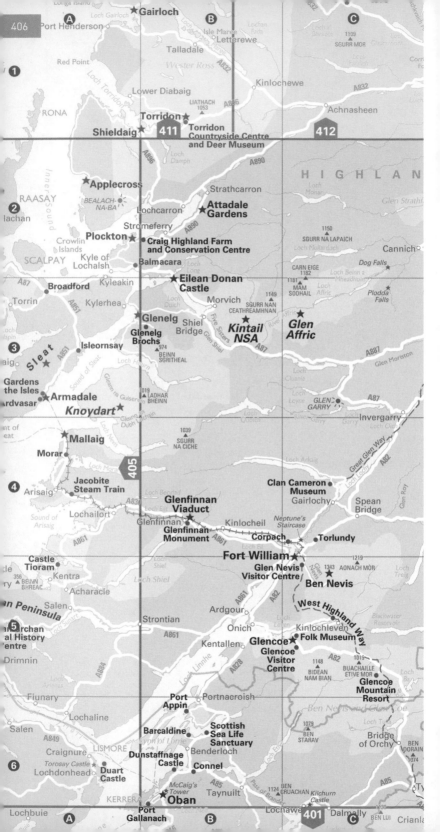

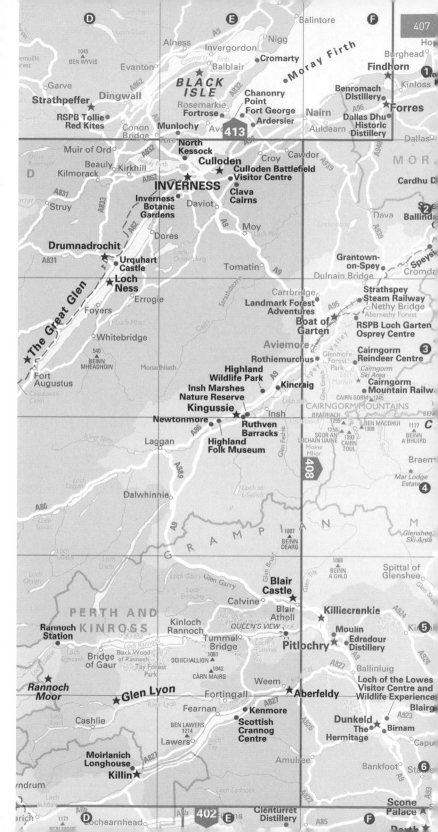

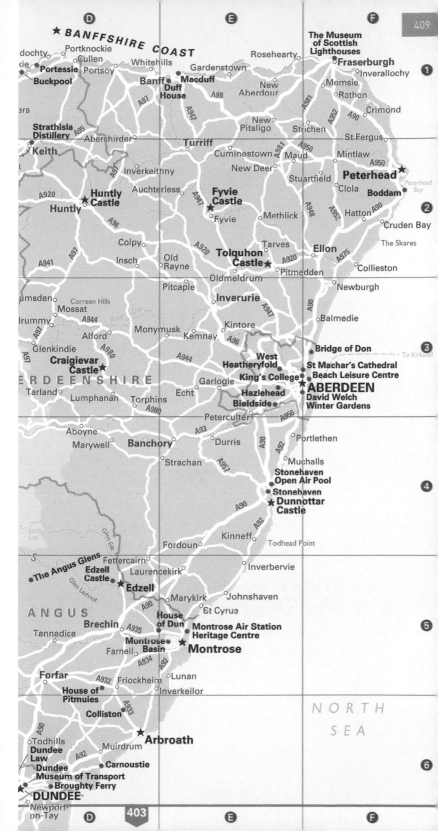

★ BANFFSHIRE COAST

D **E** **F**

...dochty Portknockie Cullen
...kie **Portessie** Whitehills Gardenstown Rosehearty
Buckpool Portsoy
...ers **Banff** **Macduff** New The Museum
Duff Aberdour of Scottish
House A98 Lighthouses
Fraserburgh Inverallochy
Strathisla A947 Memsie
Distillery Aberchirder New Rathan
Keith Pitsligo Strichen Crimond
Turriff St Fergus A90
Inverkeithny Cuminestown Maud Mintlaw A950
New Deer Stuartfield **Peterhead**
...msden **Huntly** Auchterless **Fyvie** Methlick Clola **Boddam**
Castle **Castle** Hatton Peterhead
Huntly Fyvie Tarves **Ellon** Cruden Bay
A96 Colpy A920 Pitmedden The Skares
Insch Old **Tolquhon** Collieston
Rayne **Castle** Oldmeldrum
Pitcaple Newburgh
...umsden Correen Hills **Inverurie** Balmedie
Mossat River Don
...rummy A944 Alford Monymusk Kemnay A96
Glenkindie Kintore **Bridge of Don** To Kirkwall
Craigievar West St Machar's Cathedral
Castle A944 **Heatheryfold** Beach Leisure Centre
ERDEENSHIRE Garlogie **King's College** **ABERDEEN**
Tarland Echt **Hazlehead** David Welch
Lumphanan Torphins **Bieldside** Winter Gardens
Peterculter A966
Aboyne A93 **Durris** Portlethen
Marywell **Banchory** Muchalls
Strachan A957 **Stonehaven**
Loch **Open Air Pool**
Lee **Stonehaven**
Glen Esk **Dunnottar**
Castle
Kinneff Todhead Point
Fordoun
The Angus Glens Fettercairn Inverbervie
Edzell Laurencekirk
Castle Glen Lethnot **Edzell** Johnshaven
ANGUS Marykirk St Cyrus
Brechin A935 **House** Montrose Air Station
Tannadice **of Dun** Heritage Centre
Montrose **Montrose**
Farnell **Basin**
Forfar A934 A92
House of A932 Friockheim Lunan
Pitmuies Inverkeilor
Colliston A933 NORTH
SEA
A90 **Arbroath**
Todhills Muirdrum
Dundee
Law A92 **Carnoustie**
Dundee
Museum of Transport **Broughty Ferry**
DUNDEE
Newport- **D** 403 **E** **F**
on-Tay

A **B** **C**

1

2

Baile
Tughaidh
Dun Carloway ● ○Carloway
Broch● Carlabhagh
Gallan
Head GREAT
BERNERA Breasclet
Miavaig Breascleit
Miabhig ○Callanis
Calanais Calanais
Standing
Stones

NA H-EILEANAN

3 SCARP AN IAR

S 799
▲
CLISHAM Seaforth
Island

TARANSAY Isle of Harris
Distillery

Tarbert●
Tairbeart

Scarista● HARRIS Scalpay
4 Pabbay Scarasta ★
Leverburgh
Berneray ○An t-Ob

Boreray ● St Clement's
Church

Newton Ferry○
Port nan Long

Tigharry A865 Waternish
Tigh a Ghearraidh Point

5 Balranald ● NORTH UIST ● Lochmaddy
RSPB Reserve Uibhist a Tuath Loch nam Madadh Waternish
A865 ★ A867 Peninsula

Heiser or Dunvegan
Monach Islands Head Stein○
Loch●
Balivanich Ronay Bay
Baile a Mhanaich
Gramsdale Dunvegan
Creagorry Gramsdal ★BENBECULA Castle
404 Creag Ghoraidh Beinn na Faoghla Colbost Folk Museum ●
Hornish Point Wiay Dunvegan
Duirinish
Peninsula

6 Stilligarry○
Stadhlaigearraidh

★SOUTH UIST
Uibhist a Deas
● Kildonan

A **B** **C**

★ OUTER HEBRIDES

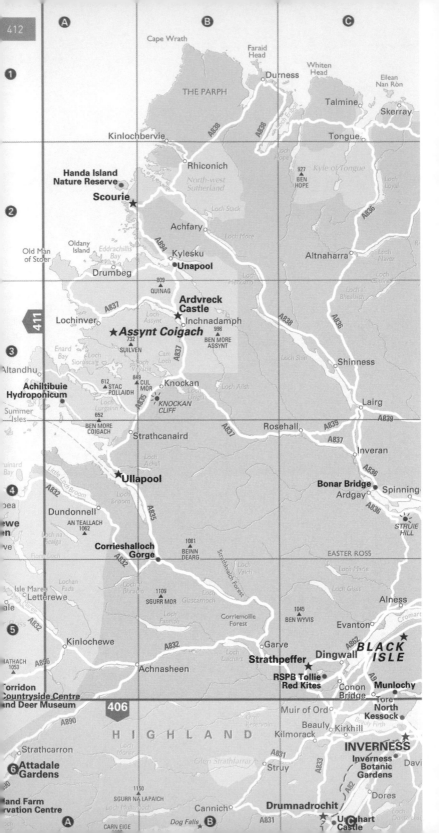

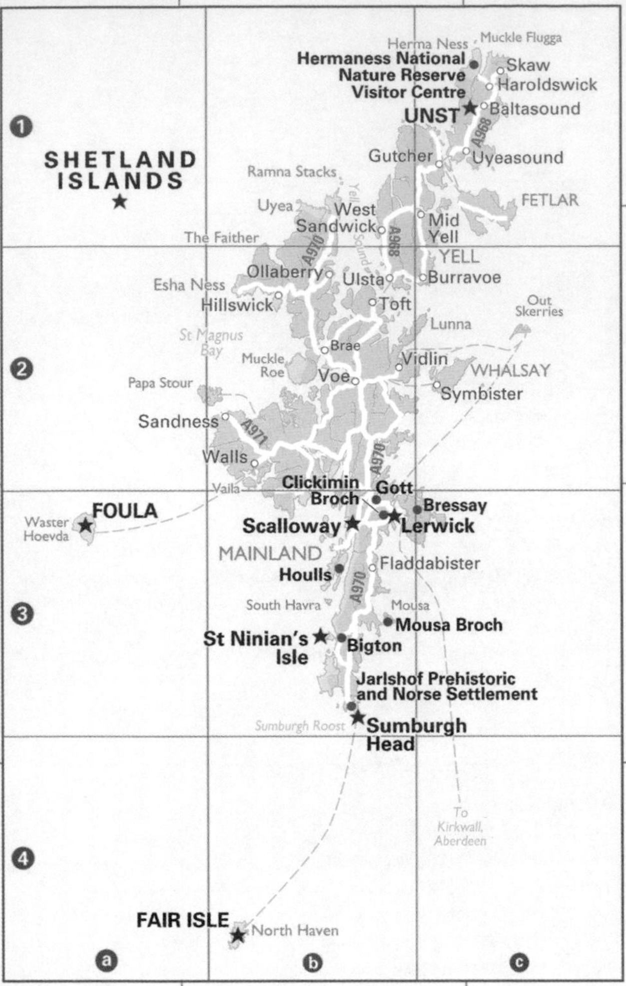

SHETLAND ISLANDS ★

Herma Ness
Muckle Flugga
Hermaness National Nature Reserve Visitor Centre
Skaw
Haroldswick
UNST ★ Baltasound

Gutcher
Uyeasound
FETLAR

Ramna Stacks
Uyea
West Sandwick
Mid Yell
YELL

The Faither
Ollaberry
Ulsta
Burravoe

Esha Ness
Hillswick
Toft
Lunna
Out Skerries

St Magnus Bay
Brae
Muckle Roe
Voe
Vidlin
WHALSAY

Papa Stour
Symbister

Sandness
A971
Walls
Valla

Clickimin Broch
Gott
Bressay
Scalloway ★
Lerwick

Waster Hoevda
FOULA ★

MAINLAND
Houlls
Fladdabister

South Havra
Mousa
Mousa Broch

St Ninian's Isle ★
Bigton

Jarlshof Prehistoric and Norse Settlement

Sumburgh Roost
Sumburgh Head

To Kirkwall, Aberdeen

FAIR ISLE ★
North Haven

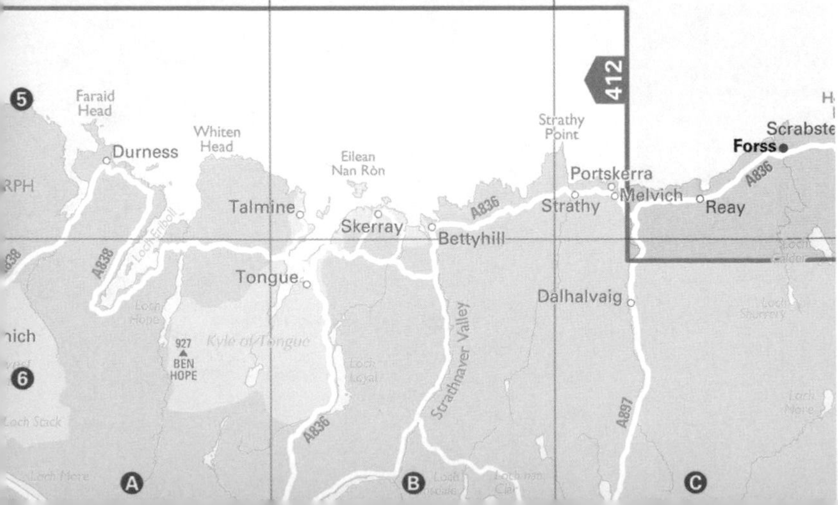

ⓐ ⓑ ⓒ

412

Faraid Head
Whiten Head
Strathy Point
Scrabste
Forss

Durness
Eilean Nan Ròn
Portskerra
Melvich
Reay

Talmine
Skerray
Strathy
A836

Bettyhill
Tongue

927 ▲ BEN HOPE
Kyle of Tongue

Dalhalvaig

Loch Stack
Loch More

Ⓐ Ⓑ Ⓒ

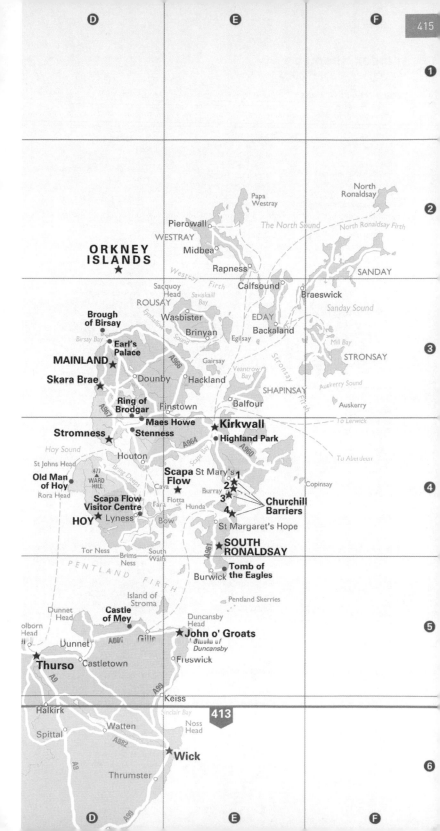

D　　**E**　　**F**

1

2

North
Ronaldsay

Papa
Westray

Pierowall○　*The North Sound*　*North Ronaldsay Firth*

WESTRAY

Midbea○

Rapness○

SANDAY

Westray Firth

Calfsound○

Sacquoy
Head

Braeswick●

*Saviskaill
Bay*

Sanday Sound

**ORKNEY
ISLANDS**
★

ROUSAY

Wasbister○

EDAY

Brinyan○

Backaland●

**Brough
of Birsay** ●

*Eynhallow
Sound*

Egilsay

Mill Bay

3

Birsay Bay

**Earl's
Palace** ★

Gairsay

STRONSAY

MAINLAND

Dounby○

Hackland○

*Veantrow
Bay*

Auskerry

Stronsay Firth

Skara Brae ★

SHAPINSAY

Auskerry Sound

**Ring of
Brodgar** ★

Finstown○

Balfour●

To Lerwick

Maes Howe ★

Kirkwall ★

Stromness ★

Stenness

Highland Park ●

A965

A964

Scapa Flow

A960

To Aberdeen

Hoy Sound

Houton○

St Johns Head

477
WARD
HILL

**Scapa
Flow**

St Mary's

1 ★

Copinsay

**Old Man
of Hoy** ●

Cava

2 ★

Burray

Rora Head

Flotta

3 ★

**Churchill
Barriers**

**Scapa Flow
Visitor Centre** ●

Fara

Hunda

4 ★

HOY ★ Lyness○

Bow

St Margaret's Hope ●

A961

**SOUTH
RONALDSAY** ★

Tor Ness

Brims
Ness

South
Walls

PENTLAND

FIRTH

**Tomb of
the Eagles** ●

Burwick ●

Pentland Skerries

Island of
Stroma

**Castle
of Mey** ●

Duncansby
Head

Dunnet
Head

Olborn
Head

Gills○

John o' Groats ★

*Muckle of
Duncansby*

5

Dunnet○

Castletown○

Freswick○

Thurso ★

A9

A99

Halkirk○

Keiss○

A882

Spittal○

Watten○

Sinclair Bay

Noss
Head

A9

Wick ★

6

Thrumster○

D　　**E**　　**F**

413

Index, themed
Page numbers in **bold** refer to main entries

Index, places

Page numbers in **bold** refer to main entries; page numbers in *italics* refer to town plans

The Automobile Association wishes to thank the following photographers and organisations for their assistance in the preparation of this book.

Abbreviations for the picture credits are as follows – (t) top; (m) middle; (b) bottom; (l) left; (r) right; (c) centre; (AA) AA World Travel Library.

4tl AA/J Smith; 4b AA/M Hamblin; 4–5 AA/R Weir; 5bl AA/S Whitehorne; 5r AA/K Blackwell; 8–9 Brian Jannsen/Alamy; 11 AA/DW Robertson; 12t Tony Smith/Alamy; 12b AA/J Smith; 13t AA/K Paterson; 13c AA/R Elliott; 13b AA/S Gibson; 14t craige bevil/Alamy; 14c AA/DW Robertson; 14b AA/K Blackwell; 15t AA/S Gibson; 15b AA/J Smith; 16t AA/J Carney; 16c AA/J Henderson; 16b AA/S Day; 17t AA/S Whitehorne; 17c AA/M Alexander; 17b Iain Sarjeant/Alamy; 18 AA/Jo Hunt; 23 John Carroll Photography/Alamy; 24–5 AA/M Hamblin; 25t AA/M Hamblin; 25bl AA/ Campbell; 25br AA/R Coulam; 27 AA/M Hamblin; 28 John Carroll Photography/Alamy; 30 AA/S Anderson; 31 AA/S Whitehorne; 32 Guillem Lopez/Alamy; 33 AA/K Blackwell; 34 AA/S Whitehorne; 35 Courtesy of New Lanark Trust; 37 S Spraggon/Alamy; 38–9 Jan Holm/Alamy; 40 AA/I Little; 41 AA/K Blackwell; 43 AA/J Tims; 47 AA/J Tims; 49 AA/J Smith; 52 AA/J Tims; 54–5 Benny Marty/Alamy; 56 AA/K Blackwell; 57 S Finn/Alamy; 60 AA/S Whitehorne; 63 Simon Price/Alamy; 65 Mic Walker/Alamy; 67 AA/J Henderson; 68 JOHN BRACEGIRDLE/Alamy; 70–1 AA/S Day; 72 ScotImage/Alamy; 73 allan wright/Alamy; 75 GC Stock/Alamy; 77 AA/Eric Ellington; 78 Scott Hortop Travel/Alamy; 79 AA/K Paterson; 80–1 Phil Seale/Alamy; 83 Simon Wilkinson/Alamy; 87 AA/P Sharpe; 88 Courtesy of

Royal Troon/Mr Ken Ferguson; 90 Globuss Images/Alamy; 92 Courtesy of Aberdeenshire Council; 94–5 AA/S Whitehorne; 97 Andrew Ray/Alamy; 100 AA/S Whitehorne; 102 A.P.S. (UK)/Alamy; 104 AA/M Alexander; 105 AA/M Hamblin; 106 AA/M Hamblin; 107 AA/M Hamblin; 108 AA/J Smith; 110l AA/M Hamblin; 110r AA/J Smith; 112 JOHN BRACEGIRDLE/Alamy; 113 Loop Images Ltd/Alamy; 117 AA/S Anderson; 118 Doug Houghton SCO/Alamy; 119 Jan Holm/Alamy; 120 david pearson/Alamy; 121 D.G.Farquhar /Alamy; 123 Courtesy of Arniston House; 125 Benny Marty/Alamy; 126 Grant Glendinning/Alamy; 127 Courtesy of Drumlanrig Castle/Euan Myles; 128–9 John McKenna/Alamy; 131 AA/M Alexander; 132 D.G.Farquhar/Alamy Stock Photo; 133 Michelle Bailey/Alamy Stock Photo; 135 John Peter Photography/Alamy; 138–9 S Finn/Alamy; 140 allan wright/Alamy; 141 AA/J Smith; 142 AA/M Taylor; 146 Frame Focus Capture Photography/Alamy; 148 Courtesy of the Andrew Carnegie Birthplace Museum; 150 AA/J Smith; 152 AA/S Anderson; 155 AA/J Smith; 156 MSP Travel Images/Alamy; 159 South West Images Scotland/Alamy; 160 MIKEL BILBAO GOROSTIAGA–TRAVELS/Alamy; 164 AA/K Blackwell; 165l AA/K Blackwell; 165r AA/K Blackwell; 167 David Robertson/Alamy; 168 AA/K Blackwell; 169 AA/K Blackwell; 171 AA/K Blackwell; 172 AA/K Blackwell; 173 Ivan Vdovin/Alamy; 174 tony french/Alamy; 177 AA/K Blackwell; 178 AA/J Smith; 179 AA/K Blackwell; 180 AA/K Blackwell; 185 John Peter Photography/Alamy Stock Photo, 186–7 AA/K Blackwell; 188 AA/K Blackwell; 193 Scotland/Alamy; 194 Ian Thraves/Alamy; 196 AA/S Anderson; 199 AA/S Day; 200–1 AA/S Whitehorne; 202 mauritius images GmbH/Alamy; 205 AA/R Weir; 206–7 Kenny Williamson/Alamy; 210 travellinglight/Alamy; 211 Douglas Carr/Alamy; 212 Alan Wilson/Alamy; 215 Stephen Dorey/Alamy Stock Photo; 216-7 Findlay/Alamy; 219 travellinglight/Alamy Stock Photo; 220 Courtesy of The Lighthouse/Simon Tsang; 223 AA/S Whitehorne; 225 Courtesy of Paddle Steamer Waverley; 229 Courtesy of Cail Bruich; 233 John Potter/Alamy; 235 Gordon McManus/Alamy; 237 RooM the Agency/Alamy; 238 S Smith/Alamy; 239 AA/S Day; 241 Stocksolutions/Alamy; 242 Bill Miller/Alamy; 244 AA/Roger Coulam; 246 Matthew Bruce/Alamy; 247 Courtesy of Inveraray Jail; 248–9 AA/S Whitehorne; 250 AA/J Smith; 253 AA/J Smith; 254–5 John Michaels/Alamy; 257 Petr Svarc/Alamy; 258–9 robertharding/Alamy; 260-1 David Lichtneker/Alamy; 263 AA/K Blackwell; 264 AA/K Blackwell; 265 Angus McComiskey/Alamy; 267 AA/J Smith; 268–9 AA/S Anderson; 271 AA/ J Smith; 274 Grant Glendinning/Alamy; 275 Phil Seale/Alamy; 276 Mike Rex/Alamy; 278 AA/S Anderson; 280 Vincent Lowe/Alamy; 281 AA/K Blackwell; 283 Hemis/Alamy; 284 Alistair Petrie/Alamy; 286 AA/S Day; 288 AA/David W Robertson; 291 craige bevil/Alamy; 293 AA/David W Robertson; 294 AA/J Smith; 297 AA/Dennis Hardley; 299 AA/K Blackwell; 303 Courtesy of New Lanark Trust; 304 Courtesy of New Lanark Trust; 305 AA/K Blackwell; 306 AA/K Blackwell; 308 Angus Alexander Chisholm/Alamy; 310 Premium Stock Photography GmbH/Alamy; 313 mark ferguson/Alamy; 314 Les Gibbon/Alamy; 316-7 funkyfood London – Paul Williams/Alamy; 318 9 imageBROKER/Alamy; 321 mark ferguson/Alamy; 322–3 David Gowans/Alamy; 324 myfocus/Alamy; 325 Rolf Richardson/Alamy; 328 AA/S Day; 329 Scottish Viewpoint/Alamy; 330 Heritage Image Partnership Ltd/Alamy; 333 PearlBucknall/Alamy; 334–5 AA/J Smith; 337 InfotronTof/Alamy; 338 John Potter/Alamy; 339 Courtesy of Logan Botanic Gardens; 340–1 AA/S Day; 342–3 AA/K Blackwell; 344 AA/Roger Coulam; 346 AA/Ronny Weir; 350 AA/J Smith; 352–3 Nicholas Dawson/Alamy; 354 imageBROKER/Alamy; 355 Robert Harding World Imagery/Alamy; 356 Robert Harding World Imagery/Alamy; 356–7 ATStockFoto/Alamy; 358 Scottish Viewpoint/Alamy; 360 imageBROKER/Alamy; 363 Canna Mouse Photography/Alamy; 364–5 Richard Newton/Alamy; 366 AA/S Anderson; 367 AA/S Anderson; 370 David Robertson/Alamy; 372 AA/Photodisc; 373 AA/J Smith; 375 Douglas Carr/Alamy; 376 mark ferguson/Alamy; 378 AA/K Blackwell; 379 FreespiritCoast/Alamy; 380 Ian Francis/Alamy; 382–3 Realimage/Alamy; 385 Courtesy of Tobermory Distillery; 386–7 Robert Harding World Imagery/Alamy; 388 AA/S Whitehorne; 393 Zoonar GmbH/Alamy; 394 Cultura RM/Alamy; 432 AA

Series editor: Rebecca Needes
Authors: Robin Gauldie and Sally Roy
Updater: Sally Roy
Project editor: Cambridge Publishing Management

Proofreader: Laura Booth
Designer: Tom Whitlock
Digital imaging and repro: Ian Little
Cover Picture Research: Daniel Little
Art director: James Tims

Additional writing by other AA contributors. *Lore of the Land* feature by Ruth Binney. Some content may appear in other AA books and publications.

Has something changed? Email us at travelguides@theaa.com.

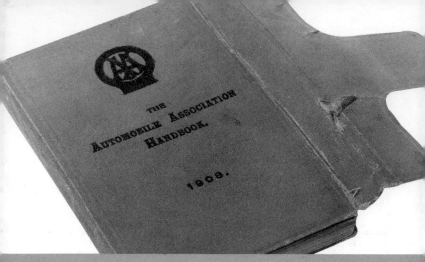

YOUR TRUSTED GUIDE

The AA was founded in 1905 as a body initially intended to help motorists avoid police speed traps. As motoring became more popular, so did we, and our activities have continued to expand into a great variety of areas.

The first edition of the *AA Members' Handbook* appeared in 1908. Due to the difficulty many motorists were having finding reasonable meals and accommodation while on the road, the AA introduced a new scheme to include listings for 'about one thousand of the leading hotels' in the second edition in 1909. As a result the AA has been recommending and assessing establishments for more than a century, and each year our professional inspectors anonymously visit and rate thousands of hotels, restaurants, guest accommodations and campsites. We are relied upon for our trustworthy and objective Star, Rosette and Pennant ratings systems, which you will see used in this guide to denote AA-inspected restaurants and campsites.

In 1912 we published our first handwritten routes and our atlas of town plans, and in 1925 our classic touring guide, *The AA Road Book of England and Wales,* appeared. Together, our accurate mapping and in-depth knowledge of places to visit were to set the benchmark for British travel publishing.

Since the 1990s we have dramatically expanded our publishing activities, producing high-quality atlases, maps, walking and travel guides for the UK and the rest of the world. In this new series of regional travel guides we are drawing on more than a hundred years of experience to bring you the very best of Britain.